HUMAN ECOLOGY OF SPIRITUAL TRADITIONS

ENCYCLOPEDIA
of
HUMAN ECOLOGY

HUMAN ECOLOGY OF SPIRITUAL TRADITIONS

(In 5 Volumes)

(Volume-1)

Editor

K.S. Gulia

ISHA BOOKS

New Delhi - 1100 09

Human Ecology of Spiritual Traditions

ISBN: 81-8205-400-1 (Set)
ISBN: 81-8205-400-X

Publised in 2007 in India by
Isha Books, B-63, 1st Floor, New Gupta Colony,
Near DDA Market, Delhi-110 009

Lasertype Setting by: Best Computers, Delhi
Printed at: Salasar Imaging Sysem, Delhi

Contents

Introduction

The volume aims to establish the fact that the religious outlook of people can help determine the extent to which they will modify the environment. While it is easy to take credit for successes we meet as we journey into the world but the harder and nobler habit is accepting the responsibility for the world around us.

Most of the ideas and themes in this volume are as old and universal as human nature, it would be difficult to put together such a collection without the contribution of specialists in the field of ecology, psychology, theology, indology and environment.

Chapter One on 'Religion and Environment Interrelationship' attributes the influence of environment on various religions while the physical environment's influence on the major religions is less pronounced than in animistic faiths, it is still evident. Environmentally auspicious sites are chosen for houses, villages, temples and graves. The veneration of rivers, mountains, rocks and forests comes in this category. River Ganges for Hindus, Jordan River for Christians, Mount Fujiyama is sacred for Japanese Shintoism and holy volcanoes in Mexico. The famous Black Stone in Mecca has a special significance.

The Judeo Christian tradition teaches that humans have dominion over nature and they are not lacking in their concern for the environment. Religion can also influence peoples perception of their physical environment—the perception of floods, storms and droughts. Whereas Hinduism and Buddhism consider natural disaster as natural and unavoidable, Christians view them as unusual and preventable. They view them as divine punishment which can be prevented by repenting.

Chapter Two 'The Geography of Religion' addresses the theme of interrelationship of Religion with the Physical Environment. A major function of many religious systems is to appease and placate the forces of nature and to achieve harmony between the people and the physical environment. Religions differ in their outlook on environmental modification by humans. Some religious groups view such alterations as an affront to the gods. Religion is firmly interwoven in the fabric of culture, a bright hue in the human mosaic, for religious and individual religious elements vary greatly from one area to another. Several major religions and many minor ones form variety of culture religions.

Chapter Three 'Interpretation of Buddhist Teachings' is grounded on the teachings of Buddha where he offers us a Middle Path which enables us to go on being effective without feeling defeated. The path relies neither upon an external nor an internal all powerful God. It is not the means to eliminate suffering but is the outcome of facing the reality of affliction and working through what then comes up for us in a courageous and authentic way. The Middle Path emerges directly from the practice of the 'Four Noble Truths.' The path is described through eight perspectives known as 'The Eightfold Path of Buddha'.

Chapter Four 'Spiritual Perspectives of Natural Environment' gives us an overview of the many ways that nautre—centred spiritual traditions, Asian religions and philosophies and monotheist religions have influenced socio-natural relationships. First way is through spiritual environment activism which includes a wide variety of change initiatives including grass-roots protest and resistance activities, the reinterpretation and rewriting of religious texts and edicts, the creation of environmentally symbolic rituals and ceremonies, the development of environmental demonstrations and educational projects and environmental advocacy for collaboration to influence government policy at national and international levels.

Next, the ways that spirituality has been integrated into contemporary eco-philosophies as well as informed environmental activism is explored. And finally the implications of organizing for environmental change are presented.

Chapter Five focuses on 'The Assertion of Power of Women and Goddess Symbol'. Our lives are shaped to a great extent not by the differences between the sexes, but by the cultural response to those differences. In our patriarchal cultures the male is considered the norm and the female is considered 'the other'. The symbol of Goddess has much to offer women who are struggling to be rid of the powerful pervasive structure of devaluation of female power. The Goddess symbol brings with it the symbol of new found beauty, strength and power of women.

Chapter Six is based on 'The Hindu Perspective of Environmental Ethics'. The Hindu Philosophy believes in the equality of human beings and looks at them as soul-parts of the same God. Vedic scriptures maintain that the earth does not belong to any individual or set of people or races. It belongs to everyone, to all races regardless of their language, colour, religion and place of birth. It belongs to humans and non-humans alike. Human beings and all other creatures inherit the qualities of the mother earth in the same way they inherit the qualities of their own mother. As children of the mother earth, human beings have to have an attitude of love, peace, harmony and mutual coexistence towards all that belongs to earth namely Vanaspati, wild life, plants, birds, insects, rivers, mountains, springs, lakes and waterfalls. Man's survival and well being depend upon the survival of the eco system of which he is an integral part.

Chapter Seven is 'Interpreting Rgveda in Todays Environmental Context.' Both Ecologists and Indologists have used ancient texts to describe Indian ideas about the cosmological workings of nature and to bring an understanding of balance and harmony with the world. Both appeal to a kind of Romantic ideal of 'nature in the abstract'. Although the texts interpreted are sacrificial texts which do involve a level of violence to nature, they are taken in the non-violent way and not otherwise by talking about ecological balance and harmony.

Chapter Eight investigates into the 'Cultural Dimension of Religious Analysis'. The notion that religion turns human action to an envisaged cosmic order and projects images of cosmic order onto the plane of human experiences is hardly novel but it has hardly been investigated. The definition of 'religion as a system of symbols....' is being analysed in parts in this chapter.

Chapter Nine is on 'Understanding God and Humanity Through Process Theology'. In practice powerless human beings and societies are being treated as resources for exploration by those who have the power to establish goals and pursue them. In response to this situation the task cannot be simply to improve practice in light of existing theories. It must be to change the theory. Process thought has been protecting against such theories which are damaging and has offered an alternative to the dominant dualism of soul and body, spirit and nature, mind and matter, self and other. The theology which has appropriated these contributions of process thought is 'Process Theology.' We humans exercise a unique power over all the other creatures. Hence we are responsible for the welfare of the whole created order on our planet as no other creature could be. That we are exercising that power so extensively for the degradation of the biosphere as well as the oppression of our powerless brethren expresses the depth of our betrayal of God's trust.

Chapter Ten describes the 'Forests in the Epics'. The epic forest is an imagined landscape—more a state of mind than a tangible environment. Mythology and the classical Indian epics in particular offer a rich terrain for imaginative journeying and introspective discovery that can proceed quite independent of circumstances in the physical environment. The two epics *Mahabharata* and *Ramayana* so different in character both contains a vast section which is spent in the forests. The Epics consist of description of Hunting Forays, of Forest Exiles, to its Voluptous Women, Rampaging *Rakhshas* (Devils) and Serene Sages.

Chapter Eleven on 'Evolution of Eco Karma brings about the realization that we have lost our way in the technological jungle enmeshed by our scientific inventions. In the process we have lost the sacred and alienated ourselves from nature and from ourselves. The socalled civilized man has been immature as while he was rushing from one action to another, exploring and conquering, he was not quite clearly seeing what he was doing. We also see the immaturity of organized religions as they pitted people against people and allowed human to savage nature and other beings. This has produced bad karma for the whole living family. We are now trying to rectify the situation. The healing of the earth is part of our new Dharma to overcome the past bad karma through the path of 'Eco Karma.'

Chapter Twelve on 'Islamic Perspective of Environmental Ethics' addresses the view on the role of environmental education in the protection of our environment. Biocentrism is the Islamic approach to environmental ethics. This chapter discusses the concepts of biocentrism, supported by examples from the Holy Qur'an and Hadith.

Chapter Thirteen 'Living in Harmony with Nature' is a write up on nature, Prakrti and its 'Five Elements' and their significance and role. The wealth of this world is based on these elements which must be shared equally by the people among themselves and with other creatures.

Chapter Fourteen on 'The Self in Defence of the Earth' lets us into the moral goal of self realization or the awakening of our true self breaking out of the prison-self of separate ego. The one who perceives this is the Bodhisattva. We are all Bodhisattvas as we are all capable of experiencing that—it is our true nature. That true nature of ours is present in our pain for the world. The ecological self that is arising in our time is making moral exhortations irrelevant.

Chapter Fifteen on 'Hindu Strategy for Dharma Ecology' enlightens us on the contribution of Hindu Religion in environmental preservation. Undoubtedly environmental ethics propounded by ancient Hindu scriptures and seers was practised by not only the common persons, but by rulers and kings. The Hindu belief that so long as the Mother Earth is able to sustain magnificient mountains, lush forests, streams and rivers and related endowments, she will be able to mourish all, particularly the human race and its progeny. Dharmic Ecology in action has been seen among the Bishnoi community of Rajasthan who practice environmental conservation as part of their daily religious duties and the Chipko Movement in Chamoli district where villagers formed a human chain and encircled earmarked trees to keep them from being felled.

Chapter Sixteen on 'Honouring Our Planet' reinforces the fact that our planet the earth is highly reverential but for the fact that it is being plundered by vested interests. As the earth moves ahead growing and learning even closer to the sacred moment of her realization, his turmoil, intensity, agony and conflict increases.

Lastly, Chapter Seventeen 'The Dharma of Ecological Philosophy' helps us understand the importance of Ecological Dharma not only for the preservation of the earth but for the preservation of the conditions which enable us to become human enabling us to follow the path of Buddha, Shiva, Krishna. If you are a spiritual person, you must care for ecology for it is your spiritual cradle. A form of meditation and action which helps to heal the planet and other living beings in the new form of Dharma—the Ecological Dharma.

1

Religion and Environment Interrelationships

Environment and Religion

One of the main functions of many religions is the maintenance of a harmonious relationship between a people and their physical environment. That is, religion is at least perceived by its adherents to be part of the adaptive strategy, and for that reason physical environmental factors, particularly natural hazards and disasters, have exerted a particularly powerful influence on the development of various religions. Environmental influence is most readily apparent in the tribal animistic faiths. In fact, an animistic religion's principal goal is to mediate between the people and the spirit-infested forces of nature. Animistic ceremonies and even the rites of great religions often are intended to bring rain, quiet earthquakes, end plagues, or in some other way manipulate environmental forces by placating the spirits believed responsible for these events (see box, "How to Intercede with the Cloud People").

Sometimes the link between religion and natural hazard is even visual. The great pre-Columbian temple pyramid at Cholula, near Puebla in central Mexico, strikingly mimics the shape of the awesome nearby volcano Popocatepetl, towering to the menacing height of nearly 18,000 feet (5,500 meters). Catholic missionaries retained the sacred status of the Cholula pyramid, though not its imagined volcano-appeasing attribute, by erecting a church atop it.

Environment and Animistic Faith

While the physical environment's influence on the major religions is less pronounced than in animistic faiths, it is still evident. Animistic nature-spirits lie behind certain practices found in the great religions, such as the previously described of Chinese and Korean Buddhism, by which environmentally auspicious sites are chosen for houses, villages, temples, and graves. In the same category is the veneration of rivers, mountains, rocks, and forests. For instance, the River Ganges is holy to the Hindus. Hindus bathe in the River Ganges in Varanasi (Benares), India. Hindus regard this as a holy river. Many travel to Varanasi to cremate relatives along the banks of the river, and millions come for religious festivals. The Jordan River has a special meaning to Christians. In the same category is the veneration of high places—for example, Mount Fujiyama, sacred in Japanese Shintoism, and holy volcanoes in Mexico. Rocks and stones sometimes retain holy status. The famous Black Stone at Mecca has a special significance for Muslims who believe that this stone was sent down from heaven by Allah. In fact, it is probably a meteorite. Trees and forests have an honored position in certain major religions. In some areas, Christians use evergreen trees in Christmas celebrations and plant evergreens in cemeteries as symbols of everlasting life — both are relics of the pre-Christian tree worship that covered much of heavily forested northern Europe.

We can also see the survival of animistic worship of the heavenly bodies in the placement of the Christian day of worship on Sunday and the celebration of Christmas near the winter solstice. Perhaps the widespread sacred or semisacred status of cattle is related to the former worship of the moon, This phenomenon, most notable in Hinduism, also appears elsewhere in the Old World. Scholars have suggested that the crescent shape of cattle horns led early humans to associate these animals with the crescent moon, Indeed, humans may have originally domesticated cattle because of this animal's sacred quality.

Even today, environmental stress can evoke a religious response not so different from that of animistic cults. Local ministers and priests often attempt to alter unfavorable weather conditions with special services, and there are few churchgoing people in the Great Plains of the United States who have not prayed for rain in dry years. In northeastern China, repeated plagues of crop-destroying locusts gave rise over the centuries to a number of "locust cults," complete with temples. Almost 900 such temples were built, providing a place of worship for the locust and locust-gods. Suitable sacrifices and rituals were developed in an effort to avert the periodic infestations.

Environment and Monotheism

On a much broader scale, some geographers have sought to explain the origins of monotheism by environmental factors. The three major monotheistic faiths—Christianity, Islam, and Judaism—all have their roots among the desert dwellers of the Middle East. Lamaism, the most nearly monotheistic form of Buddhism, flourishes in the deserts of Tibet and Mongolia. In all of these cases, the people involved (Hebrews, Arabs, Tibetans, Mongolians) were once nomadic herders, wandering from place to place in the desert with flocks and herds of livestock. The geographer Ellen Churchill Semple argued in the early twentieth century that such desert-dwelling peoples "receive from the immense monotony of their environment the impression of unity". Semple believed that the unobstructed view of the stars and planets provided by the clear desert skies allowed the herders to see that the heavenly bodies moved across the sky in an orderly, repeated progression. This revelation supposedly suggested to the desert stargazers that a single guiding hand was responsible for the orderly system. Semple, in the classic style of environmental determinism, concluded that desert dwellers "gravitate inevitably into monotheism."

Other possibilistic rather than deterministic explanations have been proposed for the origins of monotheism. Some cultural geographers feel that we should look at the social structure of nomadic herding people for answers. Desert nomads are organized into tribes and clans ruled by a male chieftain who has dictatorial powers over the members of the group, It is possible that the all-powerful male deity of Middle Eastern monotheism is simply a theological reflection of the all-powerful, secular, male chieftain. Significantly, female deities are usually associated with farming societies, probably because women represent fertility and are the original domesticators of plants, while male deities are linked with herding or hunting peoples.

Other geographers have noted that these nomadic peoples lived on the edges of larger, more established culture regions. New ideas, these scholars feel, have a tendency to develop at the borders, not at the core or the regions where older structures and ideas are firmly entrenched. The fact is, however, that we do not know enough about early monotheism to say with certainty why or even where it arose. We are not even certain that the first monotheists were desert nomads, and we do know that some desert dwellers were polytheistic.

Religion and Environmental Modification

The religious outlook of a people can help determine the extent to which they will modify their environment. Just as the physical environment can influence religious belief and practice. In the words of Professor Lynn White, Human geology is deeply conditioned by beliefs about our nature and destiny—that is by religion." In some faiths, human power over natural forces is assumed. The Maori people of New Zealand, for example, believe that humans represent one of six aspects of creation, the others being forest/animals, crops, wild food, sea/fish, and wind/storms. People rule over all of these except the latter, in the Maori world view. The Judeo-Christian religious tradition also teaches that humans have dominion over nature, but goes further to promote a teleological view. Teleology is the doctrine that the Earth was created especially for human beings, who are separate from and superior to the natural world. This view is implicit in God's message to Noah after the Flood, promising that "every moving thing that lives shall be food for you, and as I gave you the green plants, I give you everything."

The same theme is repeated in the Psalms, where Jews and Christians are told that "the heavens are the Lord's heavens, but the earth he has given to the sons of men." Within the teleological view is the belief that humans are not part of nature, but are separate, forming one member of a God-nature-human trinity. Believing that the Earth was given to humans for their use, Christian thinkers in medieval Europe adopted the view that humans were God's helpers in finishing the task of creation. These theologians believed that human modifications of the environment were God's work. Small wonder that the medieval period in Europe witnessed an unprecedented expansion of agricultural acreage, involving the large-scale destruction of woodlands and drainage of marshes.

It is not surprising that Christian monastic orders, such as the Cistercian and Benedictine Fathers, supervised many of these projects, directing the clearing of forests and the establishment of new agricultural colonies. Christianity, according to Professor White's view, destroyed classical antiquity's feeling for the holiness of natural things. Subsequently, he argues, scientific advances permitted the Judeo-Christian West to modify the environment at an unprecedented rate and on a massive scale. This marriage of technology and teleology is, White proposes, the root of our modern ecological crisis.

By contrast, the great religions of the Orient and many animistic tribal faiths contain teachings and beliefs that are protective of nature (see box, "The Yanoama World View"). In Hinduism, for example, geographer Deryck O. Lodrick found that the doctrine of ahimsa had resulted in the establishment of numerous animal homes, refuges, and hospitals, particularly in the northwestern part of India. The hospitals, or *pinjrapoles,* were closely linked to the Hindu Jain sect. People are part of and at harmony with nature. Such religions do not threaten the ecological balance, says Professor White. Geographer Yi-Fu Tuan disagrees. He points to a discrepancy between the stated ideals of religions and reality. Even though China enjoys an "old tradition of forest care" based in its composite religion, the Chinese woodlands have been systematically destroyed through the millennia. Nor are the Oriental and tribal religions consistently protective of the environment. Buddhism, for example protects temple trees but demands huge quantities of wood for cremations.

Animistic shifting cultivators sometimes make offering to appease the woodland spirits before destroying huge acreages of forest with machete and fire. Civilization itself, argues Tuan, is the exercise of human power over nature. Religion can resist but not overcome that exercise. Also, if people are assumed to be part of nature, then one might conclude that no stewardship of the land by, humankind seems logical, since we and all our works are "natural." Other ecologists point out, too, that the Judeo-Christian tradition is not lacking in concern for environmental protection. In the Book of Leviticus, for example, farmers are instructed by God to let the land lie fallow one year in seven and not to gather food from wild plants in that "sabbath of the land." Robin W. Doughty, a cultural geographer, suggests that "Western Christian thought is too rich and complex to be characterized as hostile toward nature," though he feels that Protestantism, "in which worldly success symbolizes individual predestination," may be more conducive to "ecological intemperance."

Religion and Environmental Perception

Religion can also influence the way people perceive their physical environment. Nowhere is this more evident than in the perception of environmental hazards such as floods, storms, and droughts. Hinduism and Buddhism teach followers to accept such hazards without struggle, to regard them as natural and unavoidable. Christians are more likely to view storm, flood, or drought as unusual and preventable. As a result, they will generally take steps to overcome the hazard. Sometimes, however, Christians see natural disasters as divine punishment for their sins, in which case worshipers feel they can prevent future disasters by repenting.

Within a single major religion, people's relationship with the land can vary from one sect to another. We have already discussed the overall Judeo-Christian view of the God-nature-human trinity. A study conducted in several small southwestern settlements in the United States by Florence Kluckhohn suggests that individual religious groups see this trinity differently. The large majority (72 percent) of Spanish-American Catholics interviewed felt that humans are subject to nature. Most Mormons (55 percent) saw humans in harmony with nature, a relationship preserved by proper living and hard work. The most common response from Protestant Anglo-Texans (48 percent) held that humans control nature and can overcome environmental hazards. Two-thirds of the Zuni and Navaho Indians, most of whom cling to animism, favored the view of humans in harmony with natural forces. Similarly, a study by John Sims and Duane Baumann revealed that residents of Alabama, where intense, conservative Protestantism prevails, were more likely to react to a tornado threat fatalistically, relying on God to see them through, while Illinoisans, as adherents of a liberal, low-intensity Protestantism, felt in control of their own destinies and took more measures to protect themselves. Perhaps partly as a result, the mortality rate in tornadoes is markedly lower in the Midwest than in the South.

The world view of the Yanoama, an animistic Indian tribe of the Brazilian-Venezuelan borderland, is instructive.

> Religion impinges on all aspects of life, without the conceptual distinction between *man, nature,* and the *divine* that characterizes Judeo-Christianity. No omnipotent God exists. There is no material world surrounding the Yanoama and existing independently of them, no world that they view as capable of being dominated and turned to satisfy their own needs. . . . Mysteriously, man can share a common life with an animal, or even with some natural phenomenon, such as the wind or thunder.

Reducing the Disparity between Religion and Ecology

Religion that sets itself in opposition to nature and vehemently resists the resacralizing of the natural world on the grounds that it would be "pagan" to do so is not sustainable over time. In 1967 Lynn

White, a professor of history at UCLA, published in *Science* "The Historical Roots of our Ecological Crisis," a critical analysis of the attitudes Western religion has encouraged toward our environment. Since then ecologists often point to the injunctions in Genesis that humans should attempt to "subdue" the earth and have "dominion" over all the creatures of the earth as being bad advice with disastrous results. (Many of those critiques, however, have lacked a full sense of the Hebrew words.) Bill Devall, coauthor of *Deep Ecology,* spoke for many activists when he declared in August 1984, "Unless major changes occur in churches, ecologists and all those working in ecology movements will feel very uncomfortable sitting in the pews of most American churches."

The disparity between Judeo-Christian religion and ecological wisdom is illustrated by the experience of a friend of mine who once lived in a seminary overlooking Lake Erie and says he spent two years contemplating the sufferings of Christ without ever noticing that Lake Erie was dying.[1] Even when Catholic clergy speak today of St. Francis of Assisi, whom Lynn White nominated as the patron saint of ecologists, they often take pains to insist that he was not some "nature mystic,"[2] which, of course, would taint him with "paganism."[3]

Religious Interpretation of Ecology

The cultural historian Thomas Berry has declared that we are entering a new era of human history, the Ecological Age.[4] How could our religion reflect ecological wisdom and aid the desperately needed transformation of culture? First, suggestion is that Judaism and Christianity should stop being ashamed of their "pagan" inheritance, which is substantial, and should proudly proclaim their many inherent ties to nature. How many of us realize that the church sets Easter on the first Sunday after the first *full moon* after the *vernal equinox* and that most of the Jewish holy days are determined by a lunar calendar.[5] Numerous symbols, rituals, and names in Jewish and Christian holy days have roots directly in the nature-revering Old Religion. Second, I hope the stewardship movement, which is gaining momentum in Christian and Jewish circles, should continue to deepen its analyses and its field of action. Those people are performing a valuable service by reinterpreting the overall biblical teachings about the natural world and finding ecological wisdom that balances or outweighs the "dominance" message.

Creation Spirituality

Virtually all spokespersons for the stewardship movement emphasize that 'nature is to be honored as God's creation.[6] Infact, that position is firmly rooted in the work of several noted theologians whose orientation is known as "creation spirituality." They emphasize the interrelatedness of all creation, the understanding that humans do not occupy the central position in the cosmic creation but have a responsible role to play, and the transformation of society in directions that will further the continuation of life. Hence peace is a central issue for creation theologians, as is justice. Nearly all of them give greater importance to the female dimension of creation than do other theologians. Among the Catholic, Protestant, and Jewish theologians of creation spirituality are Bernhard W. Anderson, Thomas Berry, Walter Bruggemann, Martin Buber, Marie-Dominique Chenu, Matthew Fox, Abraham Heschel, Jurgen Moltmann, Paul Santmire, Edward Schillebeeckx, Odil Hannes Steck, Pierre Teilhard de Chardin, and Samuel Terrien.[7]

The experience of knowing the Divine through communication with nature has been a recurrent theme in art. Recently Alice Walker described a theologically sophisticated, elementally spiritual experience in her Pulitzer Prize-winning novel *The Color Purple* when one black woman in rural Georgia explains to another that God "ain't a he or a she, but a It":

> It ain't a picture show. It ain't something you can look at apart from anything else, including yourself. I believe God is everything, say Shug. Everything that is or ever was or ever will be. And when you can feel that, and be happy to feel that, you've found it. ... My first step away from the old white man was trees. Then air. Then birds. Then other people. But one day when I was sitting quiet and feeling like a motherless child, which I was, it come to me: that feeling of being part of everything, not separate at all. I knew that if I cut a tree, my arm would bleed. And I laughed and I cried and I run all around the house. I knew just what it was. In fact, when it happen, you can't miss it. It sort of like you know what, she say, grinning and rubbing high up on my thigh.[8]

Religion based Respect for Nature

It is encouraging to see that a religion-based respect for nature is showing up in numerous articles and books, especially books like The Spirit *of the Earth* (1984), in which John Hart urges study of and respect for Native American religious perspectives on nature because that is the indigenous tradition of our land and suggests compatibility between their religion and the Judeo-Christian tradition. Yet why is it that attention to loving and caring for nature rarely makes it into the liturgy today?.. . Harold Gilliam in the San Francisco Chronicle describ[ed] a magnificent ecological service that spanned twenty-four hours, beginning at sunrise on the autumnal equinox, and took place in the gothic cathedral on Nob Hill in San Francisco, Grace Cathedral.

Poets, spiritual teachers, musicians, and ecologists all participated in the service, which included whale and wolf calls emanating from various corners of the cathedral's sound system, as well as the projection of nature photography onto the walls and pillars. Gary Snyder and his family read his "Prayer for the Great Family," which is based on a Mohawk prayer.[9] The celebrants poured water from all the rivers of California into the baptismal font. They committed themselves to changing our society and our environment into "a truly Great Family," and they assigned to each U.S. senator a totemic animal or plant from his or her region in order to accentuate the rights of our nonhuman family members.

At the sound of a bell and a conch shell, the Episcopal Bishop of California opened the service:

> We are gathered here at sunrise to express our love and concern for the living waters of the Central Valley of California and for the burrowing owls, white-tailed kites, great blue herons, migratory waterfowl, willow trees, cord grass, water lilies, beaver, possum, striped bass, anchovies, and women, children, and men of the Great Family who derive their life and spiritual sustenance from these waters. Today we offer our concerns and prayers for the ascending health and spirit of these phenomena of life and their interwoven habitats and rights....

This service ook place on 17 October 1971. (No subsequent ecological services took place in that church because a few influential members of the congregation pronounced it paganism.) How many species have been lost since then, how many tons of topsoil washed away, how many aquifers polluted—while we have failed to include nature in our religion?

Knowledge of nature must precede respect and love for it. We could urge that ecological wisdom regarding God's creation be incorporated in Sunday school as well as in sermons and prayer. We could suggest practices such as the planting of trees on certain holy days. We could mention in the church bulletin ecological issues that are crucial to our community.[10] There is no end to what we could do to focus spiritually based awareness and action on saving the great web of life.

Status of Women in different Cultures

Our lives are shaped to a great extent not by the differences between the sexes, but by the cultural response to those differences. There is no need to focus on the point that in patriarchal cultures the male is considered the norm and the female is considered "the Other." It is however, relevant to note that Judeo-Christian religion has played a central role in constructing the subordinate role for women in Western culture. Suffice it to say that the eminent mythologist Joseph Campbell once remarked that in all his decades of studying religious texts worldwide he had never encountered a more relentlessly misogynist book than the Old Testament. Numerous Christian saints and theologians have continued the tradition.

The results for traditional society of denying women education and opportunity have been an inestimable loss of talent, intelligence, and creativity. For women it has meant both structural and direct violence. Of the former, Virginia Woolf observed that women under patriarchy are uncomfortable with themselves because they know society holds them in low esteem. The structural violence of forced dependency sometimes provides the conditions for physical violence, that is, battering. Finally, patriarchal culture usurps control over a woman's body from the woman herself, often inflicting torturous pain.

Attitude Towards Abortion

It has been reported that in China today women are forced to undergo abortions even in the third trimester under the government's one-child-only policy. (The women who must undergo forced abortion are those who have incurred shame and the wrath of their husbands and in-laws by previously giving birth to a girl and later try desperately to carry a boy baby to term unnoticed by the government. Sometimes the women in that patriarchal culture simply drown themselves immediately after giving birth to a daughter.)

Pro Abortion Stance: Some people accuse the greens of being hypocritical in calling themselves a "party of life" and adopting a "pro-choice" stance on abortion. In spring 1984, the European Greens, a coalition of green parties throughout Western Europe endorsed, after much debate, a position against social and political sanctions that force birthing and for free choice. The quality of the debate in green parties over abortion has more integrity than that currently being waged in American politics precisely because all aspects of the issue are considered. In our country half of the debate often seems to be missing: women's suffering. The issue is obviously complex, and there are people of good conscience on both sides.

Anti Abortion Stance: Church leaders of many varieties are demanding an end to all legal (that is, medically safe) abortion. They can maintain a position demanding the criminalization of abortion only because they have never witnessed a woman going through pregnancy, labor, and delivery—or else they believe the biblical injunction that woman is *supposed* to suffer. Sometimes birth is textbook simple, but usually it is not. Some men say they remember their wife's screams for months. Many men say the birth experience made them "pro-choice" on the abortion issue because they would never want to force any woman to go through such an ordeal against her will.

As one of the most popular right-wing Christian preachers, Pat Robertson, likes to tell his TV audience (16.3 million households per month), "We are offering up 1½ million babies per year upon the altar of sensuality and selfishness."[11] Is that what it's all about—millions of sex-crazed, hedonistic women? Where is the compassion for the lonely teenager from an unnurturing family situation who tried to find affection and love where she could? Where is the compassion for the innocent victims of rape, including incestual rape and the increasing frequency of the "date rape" and "acquaintance rape"? Where is the compassion for *any* woman who discovers that she is "in trouble"?

Solutions to Issue of Abortion: The number of abortions needed in this country would plummet if the problematic conditions were addressed effectively: disintegrated families, widespread pornography depicting violence against women, culturally approved hyper-macho behavior on dates, what has been called "patriarchy's dirty little secret" (the shocking statistics on sexual abuse by male relatives), selfishness and lack of spiritual grounding on the part of men who emotionally coerce their girlfriends, and lack of self-confidence and spiritual grounding in their own being among young women.

There comes a time at the end of many lives when life is not viable without machinery, and most people say they would like the machinery turned off if it came to that. Similarly, there is a time at the beginning of life when a fertilized egg and then a foetus is not viable life *unless* the woman is willing to give over her body and accept the suffering.

To force a woman either to give birth or to abort is violence against the person. Most men and women know this in their hearts. They also know that countless women do not have the financial and other resources for the twenty-year task of raising a child. That is why a Gallup poll in June 1983 found that only 19 percent of American Catholics and 16 percent of the total American population want abortion to be illegal in all circumstances.[12] That is to say most of them are pro abortion. The Gallup organization released a poll on 20 February 1986 showing that the American public is evenly divided (45 percent to 45 percent) on the 1973 U.S. Supreme Court ruling that a woman may go to a doctor to have an abortion during the first three months of pregnancy.

Attitude of Males Pro-abortion: Interestingly, women's views were found to be statistically the same as in 1983, but men's support for the court ruling had fallen by 11 percent. Male fears of women's controlling their own sexuality are deeply rooted in patriarchal culture; during the Renaissance, for example, peasant healers were burned as "witches" for providing women with contraception and abortion. So the debate we are embroiled in is a very old one, and the campaign to "save the embryo; damn the woman has been mounted many times before. Men, too, suffer under patriarchal culture. Because woman is regarded as the denigrated Other, men are pressured to react and continually prove themselves very unlike the female. This dynamic result in what some men have called "the male machine." It has also skewed much of our behavioral and cognitive science since thousands of careers and volumes of commentary on "sex differences" have been funded but no recognized field of "sex similarities" exists.[13] That would be too unnerving. The most serious effect of men under patriarchy needing to prove themselves very different from women is the function of military combat as an initiation into true manhood and full citizenship. This deeply rooted belief surfaced as an unexpected element in the struggle to pass the Equal Rights Amendment, for instance. Feminist lobbyists in state legislatures throughout the 1970s were repeatedly informed, "When you ladies are ready to fight in a war, we'll be ready to discuss equal rights!"[14] Such an orientation is not sustainable in the nuclear age.

Role of Religion

What role could religion play in removing the cultural insistence on women as Other and men as godlike and hence inherently superior? How could religion further the green principle of postpatriarchal consciousness? We know the answers because they are already being tried: women must have equal participation in ritual (as ministers, rabbis, and priests), language in sermons and translations must be inclusive, and the godhead must be considered female as well as male. These solutions are not new, but neither are they very effective, because so many people do not take either the need or the means seriously. Instead, they resent these efforts and feel silly and somewhat embarrassed with the notion of a female God. Being forced to say "God the Mother" once in a while is pointless if people have in mind Yahweh-with-a-skirt, We must first understand who She is: She is not in the sky; She is earth. Here is Her manifestation in the oldest creation story in Western culture:

> Having addressed the self, nature, and gender, we now come to the last half of the last basic question, *How shall we relate to groups and other individuals?* There are, of course, a multiplicity of groups in society at the levels of family, community, region, state, nation, and planet. The following are merely some general considerations.

Creating a Spirit of Inquiry

We must first analyze how our own mode of living affects others in the great family: Does the nature of our existence impose suffering on others— or does it support and assist those who are less privileged than we? Here we can enjoy the convergence of spiritual growth and political responsibility in the spiritual practice of cultivating moment-to-moment awareness, being fully "awake" and focused on our actions— a simple-sounding yet demanding task.

There is a story in Zen of a student who studied very hard to master certain religious texts and then went before his spiritual teacher to be questioned. The *roshi* asked simply, "On which side of the umbrella did you place your shoes?" The student was defeated; he had lost awareness (or "spaced out," as we might say). We can begin our day by focusing mindfulness on our every act.

Turning on the water in the bathroom. Where does it come from?

Is our town recklessly pumping water from the receding water table instead of calling for conservation measures? Where does our wastewater go when it leaves the sink? What happens after it is treated? Later we are in the kitchen, making breakfast. Where does our coffee come from? A worker-owned cooperative in the Third World or an exploitative multinational corporation? Obviously, it is exhausting to continue this practice very long unless one is adept. (It is difficult—so much so that a friend of mine has added an amendment to a popular spiritual saying: "Be here now—or now and then.")

But everyone can practice *some* mindfulness. If we analyze our own situation, we may discover that we are benefiting from the suffering of others—and that we ourselves are uncomfortable with the structural systems in which we work. When one thinks of religious people working for economic or social change, the "liberation theology" movement probably comes to mind because of its size in Latin America and its coverage in the press lately. In that movement, grass-roots Catholic groups (base communities) meet frequently to discuss the teachings in the Gospels and applications of Marxist analysis.

Principles of Private Ownership and Cooperative Economics and Religious Activism

But there is another way: a religion-based movement for social change is beginning to flourish that is completely in keeping with green principles of private ownership and cooperative economics, decentralization, grass-roots democracy, nonviolence, social responsibility, global awareness—and the spiritual truth of oneness. This type of call for economic and social change is gaining momentum in Catholic, Protestant, and Jewish communities. We see it, for example, in the statement issued by the Catholic Bishops of Appalachia, *This Land Is My Home: A Pastoral Letter on Powerlessness in Appalachia,* which calls for worker-owned businesses and community-based economics. We see it in *Strangers and Guests: Toward Community in the Heartland* by the Catholic bishops of the heartland (Midwest) and in *The Land: God's Giving, Our Caring* by the American Lutheran Church, a statement which was then echoed by the Presbyterian Church. Both of these statements address ecological use of the land, and Strangers *and* Guests calls for small-is-beautiful *land reform* as the only sustainable course for rural America. Developing the applications of such principles as "the land should be distributed equitably" and "the land's workers should be able to become the land's owners," the heartland bishops discuss elimination of capital-gains tax laws which favor "wealthy investors and speculators" and disfavor "small and low-income farm families," taxation of agricultural land "according to its productive value rather than its speculative value," "taxing land progressively at a higher rate according to increases in size and quality of holdings" (a proposal in the Jeffersonian tradition), and low-interest loans to aspiring farmers as well as tax incentives for farmers with large holdings to sell land to them.

Justice and Ecological Wisdom

We see green-oriented economic and social change now promoted in the Jewish periodical *Menorah* and by the Protestant multidenominational association, Joint Strategy and Action Committee. The lead article in a 1984 issue of the *JSAC* newsletter began: "If you want to know what eco-justice is, read the Psalms. The dual theme of justice in the social order and integrity in the natural order is pervasive and prominent. The book is, in large part, a celebration of interrelationships, the interaction, the mutuality, the organic oneness and wholeness of it all that is, that is to say, the Creator and the creation, human and nonhuman."

The green-oriented Jewish and Protestant leaders seek to locate justice and ecological wisdom in the Old Testament. Green-oriented Catholics usually turn to the papal encyclicals, especially Pope Pius XI's 1931 encyclical *Quadragesimo anno [Forty Years After],*[15] which established three cardinal principles:

(1) *Personalism* (the goal of society is to develop and enrich the individual human person),

(2) *subsidiarity* (no organization should be bigger than necessary and nothing should be done by a large and higher social unit than can be done effectively by a lower and smaller unit), and

(3) *pluralism* (that a healthy society is characterized by a wide variety of intermediate groups freely flourishing between the individual and the state).[16]

Andrew Greeley argues in No *Bigger Than Necessary* that Catholic social theory is firmly rooted in the communitarian, decentralist tradition and that Catholics who drifted into Marxism in recent decades are simply unaware that their own tradition contains a better solution. Joe Holland, a Catholic activist with the Center of Concern in Washington, D.C., argues, however, that Left-oriented Catholics have never embraced "scientific Marxism" and the model of a machinelike centralized government and economy. They are attracted, rather, by communitarian ideals and are uncomfortable with the modernity of many socialist assumptions.[17] Hence, we may assume, to Joe Holland's, agreement, that many of these lukewarm leftists in Catholic circles would readily become green.

On Religious Orientation of Green-Oriented Activism

The possibilities for locating and working with green-oriented activists in mainline religions have never been better. For example, a task force of the Presbyterian Church in Pennsylvania, Ohio, and West Virginia has been instrumental in introducing Rodale Press's Regeneration Project in economically depressed communities. The project's goals are to stimulate local economic vitality and to improve the overall quality of life.[18] Within our own green political organizations, however, the question remains of how much religious content is proper in pluralistic meetings and publications. It is not known how much overt spirituality the "market will bear" in green conferences and statements.

It is true that no green, whatever his or her spiritual orientation, could object to our structuring our groups according to the Deep Ecology principles of diversity, interdependence, openness, and adaptability—as well as the spiritual principles of cultivating wisdom and compassion. These can be our guidelines as we evolve the everchanging forms of green politics. There is no end to what we could do to promote spirituality based awareness to save our environment.

NOTES

1. Paul Ryan, "Relationships," *Talking Wood* 1, no. 4 (1980).
2. One example, although by no means the only one, is Murray Bodo, O.F.M., *The Way of St. Francis* (Garden City, N.Y.: Doubleday, 1984).
3. "Pagan" is from the Latin word for "country people," *pagani*. It has nothing to do with Satan worship.
4. Collections of Thomas Berry's papers, such as *The Riverdale Papers on the Earth Community,* are available from the Riverdale Center for Religious Research, 5801 Palisade Avenue, Riverdale, N.Y. 10471. His work is also presented by the physicist Brian Swimme in The Universe *is a Green Dragon* (Santa Fe, N.M.: Bear and Co., 1984).

5. Arthur Waskow, *Seasons of Our Joy: A Celebration of Modern Jewish Renewal* (New York: Bantam Books, 1982).
6. See, for example, Mary Evelyn Jegen and Bruno V. Manno, eds., *The Earth is the Lord's: Essays on Stewardship* (New York: Paulist Press, 1978); Wesley Granberg-Michaelson, *A Worldly Spirituality: The Call to Take Care of the Earth* (New York: Harper and Row, 1984); John Hart, *The Spirit of the Earth: A Theology of the Land* (New York: Paulist Press, 1984); John Carmody, *Ecology and Religion: Toward a New Christian Theology of Nature* (New York: Paulist Press, 1983); and Ian G. Barbour, ed., *Earth Might Be Fair: Reflections on Ethics, Religion, and Ecology* (Englewood Cliffs, N.J.: Prentice Hall, 1972).
7. In addition to the scores of books by the creation theologians cited in the text, there is a relevant anthology, Philip N. Joranson and Ken Butigan, eds. *Cry of the Environment: Rebuilding the Christian Creation Tradition* (Santa Fe, N.M.: Bear and Co., 1984).

   A partial "family tree of creation-centered spirituality" may be found in Matthew Fox, Original Blessing (Santa Fe, N.M.: Bear and Co., 1983).
8. Alice Walker, *The Color Purple* (New York: Harcourr Brace Jovanovich, 1982), 167.
9. "Prayer for the Great Family" may be found in Gary Snyder's Pulitzer Prize-winning volume of poetry. *Turtle island* (New York: New Directions Books, 1974).
10. See Byron Kennard, "Mixing Religion and Politics," Ecopinion, *Audubon,* 86, no. 2 (Mar. 1984)- 14-19
11. "Power, Glory —and Politics? *Time.* 17 Feb. 1986, 65
12. Center for Religion Research. Galiup Organisation. Princeton, N.J. (Information given via telephone to the author on 16 Oct. 1984.)
13. Ruth Bleier, *Science and Gender (*New York: Pergamon Press, 1984).
14. See Charlene Spretnak, "Naming the Cultural Forces That Push Us toward War," *Journal of Humanistic Psychology* 23 no. 1 (Summer, 1983), 104-14; also in *Nuclear Strategy and the Code of the Warrior Face of Mars and Shiva in the Crisis of Human Survival* ed. Richard Grossinger and Lindy Hough (Berkeley, Calif.: Atlantic Books, 1984). Also .see the chapters on "The Soldier" and "War" in Mark Gerzon, *A Choice of Heroes* (Boston: Houghton Mifflin, 1982).
15. *Quadragesima anno* was a commemoration and expansion of Pope Leo XIII's 1891 encyclical *Rerum Notarum (Of the New Situation of the Working Class).*
16. Andrew M. Greeley, *No Bigger than Necessary* (New York: New American Library, 1977), 10.
17. Joe Holland, *The Postmodern Paradigm Implicit in the Church's Shift to the Left* (Washington. D.C.: Center of Concern, 1984).
18. Regeneration Project, Rodale Press, 33 East Minor St., Emmaus, Penn. 18049.

2

The Geography of Religion

Religion is part of culture. It involves a set of beliefs and practices, a social system, through which people seek mental and physical harmony with the powers of the universe, through which we attempt to influence the awesome forces of nature, life, and death. As such, religion has been an essential attribute of culture, and the geographer would be foolish to ignore it. For some cultural groups, religion is little more than a protective buffer between humans and the mysterious, potentially destructive forces of nature. Others have, over centuries, developed highly articulated systems of belief with elaborate moral codes. Your first reaction to a chapter on the geography of religions may well be: "What does geography have to do with religious faith?" The study of religion in its entirety may be the subject for philosophers and theologians—after all, the word theology means literally "the study of God," while the exact original Greek meaning of *geography* is "description of the earth."

The appropriateness of the study of religion in cultural geography will be revealed through our five themes. Religion differs from one place to another, producing variations that can be mapped as culture regions. These spatial variations were produced by cultural diffusion and reflect a complex interplay among religion, the environment, and other aspects of culture. In turn, the spatial pattern of religion is visibly imprinted on the cultural landscape. Religion is an essential hue in the human mosaic.

RELIGIOUS CULTURE REGIONS

Both functional and formal religious culture regions abound. The smallest administrative unit, the congregation, is a functional social unit with spatial dimensions and constraints. Perhaps the most basic spatial act by religious groups is the functional designation of sacred space, including areas and sites recognized as worthy of devotion, loyalty, fear, or esteem. By virtue of their sacredness, these special religious regions can be avoided by the faithful, sought out by pilgrims, or barred to members of other religions.

Often sacred space contains the site of supposed supernatural events or is viewed as the abode of gods. Conflict can result if two religions venerate the same space, as in Jerusalem, where the Muslim Dome of the Rock, the site of Muhammad's ascent to heaven, stands above the Wailing Wall, the remnant of a great Jewish temple. Cemeteries are generally regarded as a type of sacred space. We can devise all kinds of formal culture regions based cm religion. One might, for instance, define culture regions on the basis of a single religious trait. An example would be a map of all areas where monotheism, the worship of a single god, is prevalent. Much of the world is in such a culture region, since monotheism is typical of a number of major religions.

We may choose instead to set up religious culture regions based on a combination of traits. The most basic kind of multitrait formal religious culture region depicts the spatial distribution of generally acknowledged religious groups, such as Christians, Jews, Muslims, and Hindus. The boundaries of formal religious culture regions like most cultural borders, are rarely sharp. Persons of different faiths live in the same province or town, and individuals can belong to a number of different religious sects in a lifetime.

Ethnic and Universalizing Religions

There are two major categories of religion, both of which are further divided into various groups, sects, and denominations. The first category includes universalizing religions, those that actively seek new members and have as a goal the conversion of all humankind. Universalizing religions instruct their faithful to spread the word to all the Earth, using one method or another to convert the heathen.

Contrasted to universalizing religions are ethnic religions, each of which is identified with some particular ethnic or tribal group and does not seek converts. Universalizing religions grow out of ethnic religions — the evolution of Christianity from its parent Judaism is the primary example. This change usually occurs within an ethnic religion when a charismatic leader or reformer emerges whose revelations are so profound and whose personality is so dynamic that persons beyond the immediate cultural group are attracted. Once the evangelical spirit of such a universalizing religion is spent, a fragmentation and reversion to ethnic status sometimes occurs.

Christianity

Christianity is the largest universalizing religion, both in area and number of adherents, with about 1.7 billion people (32 percent of humanity), though it has long been fragmented into separate churches. The single greatest division is between Western and Eastern Christianity, each of which is further subdivided. Belonging to the Eastern group are the *Coptic* Church, originally the nationalistic religion of Christian Egyptians and still today a minority faith there, as well as being the dominant church among the highland people of Ethiopia; the *Maronites,* Semitic descendants of seventh-century heretics who retreated to a mountain refuge in Lebanon; the *Nestorians,* who live in the mountains of Kurdistan and in India's Kerala State; and *Eastern Orthodoxy,* originally centered in Greek-speaking areas and focused upon the city of Constantinople (currently Istanbul).

After converting many Slavic groups, Eastern Orthodoxy also split into a variety of national sects, such as Russian, Greek, and Serbian Orthodoxy. Western Christianity splintered also, most notably in the Protestant breakaway of the 1400s and 1500s. Since then, the Roman Catholic Church has remained strongly unified, but Protestantism, from its beginnings, tended to divide into a rich array of sects.

Mapping Formal Religious Regions Denomination Wise

The denominational map of the United States and Canada vividly reflects the fragmented nature of Western Christianity and the resulting complex pattern of religious culture regions. Numerous faiths imported from Europe were later augmented by Christian sects developed in America.

The American frontier was a breeding ground for new religious groups, as individualistic pioneer sentiment found expression in splinter Protestant denominations. In numerous parts of the country, a relatively small community may contain the churches of half a dozen religious groupings, with individual families sometimes split along religious lines.

As a result of this local fragmentation and mixing, religious geography of United States displays less regionalization of faiths than is found in much of the rest of Christendom. In a broad "Bible Belt" across the South, Baptist and other conservative fundamentalist denominations are dominant, and Utah is at the core of a Mormon realm. A Lutheran belt stretches from Wisconsin westward through Minnesota and the Dakotas, and Roman Catholicism dominates southern Louisiana, the southwestern borderland, and the heavily industrialized areas of the Northeast. The Midwest is a thoroughly mixed zone, though Methodism is generally the largest single faith. In a recent study in American religious geography, Roger W. Stump found a twentieth-century trend toward Protestant denominational-regional divergence. Baptists in the South, Lutherans in the upper Midwest, and Mormons in the West each dominate their respective regions more thoroughly today than early twentieth century. Each of the three denominations is conservative and has a long-standing, strong infrastructure.

In an age when many social scientists proclaim that Americans are becoming homogenized, with a national culture supplanting traditional regional cultures, Stump's findings reassure us that the ancient message of geography, "different place, different people," remains true. At the same time, we need to be aware that certain denominations, in particular Methodism, are very important on a national scale but are dominant in only a small number of counties.

Mapping Formal Religious Regions Ideology Wise

Another way of mapping formal religious regions in the United States is to cut across denominational lines, grouping churches and sects by philosophy, ideology, intensity, and local diversity. Geographer James R. Shortridge used such an approach. Dr. Shortridge divided the individual churches into "liberal" and "conservative" categories. Some Baptist, Methodist, and Lutheran sects, for example, were judged to be liberal, while others, such as the Lutheran Church-Missouri Synod, the Southern Baptist, and the Free Methodist, were placed in the conservative category. Measurements were made to determine how many churches were present in each county and how strong religious belief or commitment was. The results revealed a Lower Southern "Bible Belt" of intense, conservative. Protestantism; a northern belt of diverse, liberal, low-intensity Protestantism; and several "Super Catholic" areas, where the Roman Catholic Church was overwhelmingly dominant.

Not just denominational traits, religious ideology, intensity, and diversity vary spatially. Geographer Stump also found that regional variations in religious behavior extend "into the very motivations of religious participation," reflecting the variable cultural importance of religion. In the Bible Belt, for example, the great importance of religion leads to "the expectation that higher-status individuals will actively support and participate in religious institutions."

Islam

Islam, another great monotheistic, universalizing faith, claims perhaps as many as 820 million followers, centered mainly in the great desert belt of Asia and northern Africa, but extending as far east as Indonesia and the Philippines. Although not as severely fragmented as Christianity, Islam too has split into separate groups. Two major sects prevail. The *Shiite* Muslims, 11 percent of the Islamic total, form the majority in Iran, Iraq and Bahrain. Substantial Shiite groups also live in Afghanistan, Pakistan, North Yemen, Kuwait, Turkey, India, and Lebanon. A fundamentalist revival *is* occurring among the Shiites, under Iranian leadership, producing religious and political tension. *Sunni* Muslims form most of the remaining majority within Islam. Their strength is greatest in the Arabic-speaking lands, a reflection of the fact that Islam arose in Arabia, though non-Arabic Indonesia now contains the world's largest Sunni Islamic concentration, and other large clusters occur in Indo-European Bangladesh and Pakistan. The Shiite group, by contrast, is strongest among Indo-European groups.

Judaism

Judaism, another monotheistic faith, is the parent of Christianity and closely related to Islam, as well. It has close to 14 million adherents throughout the world. At present, almost half of the world's Jewish population lives in the United States; another 30 percent in Europe and the western Soviet Union; and 20 percent in Asia, mainly Israel. The large majority of American Jews settled in cities and towns rather than rural areas. Most Jews in the larger urban centers, such as New York City, are descendants of Ashkenazim from eastern Europe, especially Poland and Russia, who immigrated between 1880 and 1915. Those found in towns and small cities of the Midwest and the South immigrated largely from Germany in the period before 1880. The Hebrew prophets and leaders, such as Moses, are recognized in all three religions. In contrast to the other monotheistic faiths, Judaism does not actively seek new converts and has remained an ethnic religion through most of its existence. It has split into a variety of subgroups, partly as a result of the dispersal of the Jews in Roman times and the subsequent loss of contact among the various colonies. Jews, scattered to many parts of the Roman Empire, became a minority group wherever they were found. In later times, they spread through much of Europe, North Africa, and even southern Arabia.

Those Jews who resided in the Mediterranean lands were called the *Sephardim,* while those in central and eastern Europe were known as the *Ashkenazim.* The late nineteenth' and early twentieth centuries witnessed large-scale Jewish migration from Europe to America. The disaster that befell European Judaism during the Nazi years involved the systematic murder of perhaps a third of the entire Jewish population of the world, mainly Ashkenazim. Europe ceased to be the primary homeland of Judaism as many of the survivors fled overseas, mainly to Israël and America.

Hinduism

Hinduism, a religion closely tied to India and its ancient culture, claims about 650 million adherents. A decidedly polytheistic religion, involving the worship of hundreds of deities, Hinduism is also linked to the *caste system,* a rigid segregation of people according to ancestry and occupation; *ahimsa,* the veneration of all forms of life, involving noninjury to all sentient creatures; and a belief in reincarnation. The faith straddles a major linguistic divide, including both India Indo-Europeans and Dravidians. The skin color of the Hindu population ranges from dark to light, and the faith takes many local forms.

No standard set of beliefs prevails, and some Hindus eat fish, venerate military prowess, or even practice monotheism. These internal contrasts suggest, correctly, that Hinduism was once a universalizing religion, but it long since reverted to the status of a regional, biethnic faith.

Buddhism

Buddhism is the most widespread religion of the Orient, dominating a culture region stretching from Sri Lanka to Japan and from Mongolia to Vietnam. Along with Christianity and Islam, Buddhism remains one of the three great universalizing religions in the world. It began in India as a reform movement within Hinduism, much as Christianity did within Judaism, based in the teachings of Prince Siddhartha, the Buddha. He promoted the four "noble truths": life is full of suffering; desire is the cause of this suffering; cessation of suffering comes with the quelling of desire; and an "Eight-Fold Path" of proper personal conduct and meditation permits the individual to overcome desire. The resultant state of escape and peace is known as Nirvana.

Variant Forms of Buddhism

While Buddhism was being spread, particularly in China and Japan, Buddhism fused with native ethnic religions such as Confucianism, Taoism, and Shintoism to form composite faiths. Southern Buddhism, dominant in Sri Lanka and mainland Southeast Asia, retains the greatest similarity to the religion's original form, while a special variation known as Lamaism prevails in Tibet and Mongolia. Buddhism's tendency to merge with native religions; particularly in China, makes it difficult to determine the number of its adherents. Estimates range from 300 million to 800 million people. While Buddhism in China has become enmeshed with local faiths to become part of an ethnic religion, elsewhere it retains a decidedly universalizing character.

Buddhism has won some converts in the United States, making inroads mainly among well-educated young intellectuals. Perhaps the most popular form of Buddhism in America is Zen, derived from Japan and ultimately from China. The essence of Zen Buddhism is acquiring a new way of looking at life and things generally. Zen Buddhists seek to realize the nature of things, the nature of being, and their oneness with the universe. In their search they try to break from the everyday, logical thought processes that, as they see it, shackle and confine the human mind.

Buddhism in China

The diffusion of Buddhism into China profoundly changed society and culture. Yet China also fundamentally modified Buddhism. In short, Chinese culture presented a permeable barrier to the diffusion of Buddhism.

A few examples will illustrate what happened. Early Chinese translations quickly changed the relatively high position Buddhism had granted women. The "husband supports his wife" became, in Chinese, "The husband controls his wife." "The wife comforts her husband" became "The wife reveres her husband." In addition, the Chinese cult of the family was soon interwoven with Buddhist observances. A typical inscription from a Buddhist temple of the fourth century might read: "We respectfully make and present this holy image in honor of the Buddhas, Bodhisattvas, and pray that all living creatures may attain salvation, and particularly that the souls of our ancestors and relatives may find repose and release."

Among the Chinese masses, Buddhism fused with other popular cults. The Buddhist heavens and hells of India, for instance, were retained, but given a Chinese bureaucratic structure. Over time, Chinese artists transformed the Indian sculptural ideal, the half-naked ascetic, into the potbellied, earthy "happy Buddha" that can be bought in gift shops today.

Such merging of religions is a common occurrence when adherents of one faith attempt to supplant a traditional religion. In this way, spatial variation develops even within the same religious faith, and each culture or subculture places its own distinctive mark on the belief system.

Animism

Tribal peoples who do not adhere to any of the world's major ethnic or universalizing religions are usually referred to collectively as animists. Animists, currently numbering about 28 million, believe that certain inanimate objects possess spirits or souls. These animistic spirits live in rocks and rivers, mountain peaks and heavenly bodies, forests and swamps. Each tribe has its own characteristic form of animism and has vested a particular set of objects with spirits. Usually a tribal religious figure serves as an intermediary between the people and the spirits. To some other animists, the objects in question do not actually possess spirits, but rather are valued because they have a particular potency to serve as a link between a person and the omnipresent god. It is easy but deceptive to classify such systems of belief as primitive or simple, but they can be extraordinarily complex.

Animism is in retreat almost everywhere. It survives in remote areas where tribal peoples have found refuge, such as interior Africa, the Amazon Basin, and the mountains of New Guinea.

Secularized Areas

In some parts of the world, especially in urban and industrial areas, traditional religions are declining. Secularization — the discarding of religious faith—is taking place in lands as different as India, the Netherlands, and the Soviet Union. Typically, secularization displays a vivid regionalization on a variety of scales. Areas of surviving religious vitality lie alongside secularized districts, in a disorderly jumble. Such patterns once again reveal the inherent spatial variety of humankind and invite analysis by the cultural geographer. The retreat from organized religion has resulted from a government's active hostility towards a particular faith or religion in general. We can also attribute the decline to the failure of religions oriented to the needs of rural folk to adapt to the urban scene.

Shift in Role of Religion in U.S.A.

For many Americans, religion today plays a minimal role in their daily lives. To some extent, this change is reflected in the way churches are built. Unlike the great cathedrals of Europe's past and the churches in Quebec or Mexico today, churches in the United States are almost never built at the functional center of a city. Instead, they are usually constructed on peripheral sites where land values are lower or in the suburbs where fragmenting urban congregations have moved in large numbers. This suggests that our lives, like our cities, revolve around business and commerce, not religious activities.

Quasi-religions, or systems of belief similar to religions but lacking worship services, often fill the emotional vacuum produced by secularization. Perhaps the most widespread quasi-religion is communism, which owes much to the Judeo-Christian world from which it sprang. The Communist image of a victorious proletariat parallels the Christian belief that "the meek shall inherit the earth," and both Communists and Christians value sexual morality and hard work. A quasi-religion can also take a nationalistic form, as in Nazi Germany. In Israel, Judaism may be evolving toward quasi-religious nationalism.

RELIGIOUS DIFFUSION

The distribution of religions and denominations is the product of innovation and cultural diffusion. To a quite remarkable degree, the origin of the major religions was concentrated spatially, occurring in two principal Asian hearth areas.

The Semitic Religious Hearth

All three of the great monotheistic faiths — Christianity, Judaism, and Islam — arose among Semitic-speaking peoples in or on the margins of the deserts of southwestern Asia, in the Middle East. Judaism, the oldest of the three, originated 4000 years ago, probably along the southern edge of the Fertile Crescent. Only later did its followers acquire dominion over the lands between the Mediterranean and the Jordan River—the territorial base of modern Israel. Christianity, child of Judaism, originated in this "Promised Land" about halfway through the temporal existence of Judaism. Seven centuries later, the Semitic hearth once again gave birth to a major faith when Islam arose in western Arabia.

Religions spread by diffusion either through relocation or expansion. Expansion diffusion can be divided into *hierarchical* and *contagious* subtypes. In hierarchical diffusion, ideas are implanted at the top of a society, leapfrogging across the map to take root in cities, bypassing smaller villages and rural areas. The use of missionaries, by contrast, involves relocation diffusion.

Spread of Christianity

Obviously, universalizing faiths are more likely to diffuse than ethnic religions, and it is not surprising that the spread of monotheism was accomplished largely by Christianity and Islam, rather than Judaism. From Semitic southwestern Asia, both of the universalizing monotheistic faiths diffused widely. Christians, observing the admonition in the Gospel of Matthew, "Go ye therefore and teach all nations, baptizing them in the name of the Father, and of the Son, and of the Holy Ghost, teaching them to observe all things whatsoever I have commanded you," initially spread through the Roman Empire, using the splendid system of imperial roads to diffuse the faith. In its early centuries of spread, Christianity displayed a spatial distribution that clearly reflected *hierarchical* expansion diffusion. The early congregations were in cities and towns, temporarily producing a pattern of Christianized urban centers and pagan rural areas. Indeed, traces of this process remain in our language. The Latin word *pagus,* "countryside," is the root of both *pagan* and *peasant,* suggesting the ancient heathen connotation of rurality.

Once implanted in this manner, Christianity spread further by means of *contagious* diffusion. When applied to religion, this method of spread is called contact conversion and is the result of everyday association between believers and nonbelievers. Of course, the scattered urban clusters of early Christianity were created by *relocation* diffusion, as missionaries such as the apostle Paul moved from town to town bearing the news of the emerging faith. In later centuries, Christian missionaries often used the technique of converting kings or tribal leaders, setting in motion additional hierarchical diffusion. The Russians and Poles were converted in this manner. Some Christian expansion was militaristic, as in the reconquest of Iberia and the invasion of Latin America. This process involves a mixture of contagious expansion and relocation diffusion.

Spread of Islam

The Islamic faith also spread from its Semitic hearth area in a militaristic manner. Obeying the command in their holy book, the Koran, that they "do battle against them until there be no more seduction from the truth and the only worship be that of Allah," the Arabs exploded westward across North Africa in a wave of religious and linguistic conquest. The Turks, once converted, carried out similar Islamic conquests. In a different sort of diffusion, Muslim missionaries followed trade routes eastward to implant Islam in the Philippines, Indonesia, and the interior of China. Tropical Africa is the current major scene of Islamic expansion, an effort that has produced competition with Christians for the remaining animists.

The Indus-Ganges Hearth

The second great religious hearth area lay in the plains fringing the northern edge of the Indian subcontinent. This lowland, drained by the Ganges and Indus rivers, gave birth to Hinduism and Buddhism. The earliest faith to derive from this hearth was Hinduism, at least 4000 years old. Its origin lay in the Punjab, from where Hinduism diffused to dominate the subcontinent. Missionaries later carried the faith, in its universalizing phase, to overseas areas, but most of these convert regions were subsequently lost. Buddhism began in the foothills bordering the Ganges Plain about 500 B.C., branching off from Hinduism. For centuries it remained confined to the Indian subcontinent, but missionaries later carried Buddhism to China (100 B.C.-A.D. 200), Korea and Japan (A.D. 300-500), Southeast Asia (A.D. 400-600), Tibet (A.D. 700), and Mongolia (A.D. 1500). Like Christianity, Buddhism developed many regional forms and eventually died out in its area of origin, reabsorbed into Hinduism.

Barriers to Religious Diffusion

Religious ideas move in the manner of all innovation waves. They weaken with increasing distance from their places of origin and with the passage of time. Barriers often retard or halt their spread. Similarly, religion itself can act as a barrier to the spread of nonreligious innovations. Religious taboos occasionally function as absorbing barriers, preventing diffusion of foods and practices that violate the taboo. In this way, cigarette smoking, an innovation introduced into the United States mainly during World War I, has been unable to penetrate Mormon communities in Utah.

Similarly, the relocation diffusion of a religious doctrine encounters an absorbing barrier if laws are passed to forbid immigration by the doctrine's believers. More commonly, barriers are of the permeable type, allowing part of the innovation wave to diffuse through it, but weakening it and retarding its spread. The partial acceptance of Christianity by various Indian groups in Latin America and the western United States, serving in some instances as a camouflage beneath which many aspects of the tribal religions survive, is an example. A permeable barrier can also be seen in the commercial cultivation of tobacco by certain Pennsylvania farmers who belong to sects that forbid smoking.

Relocation Diffusion: The Chinese Example

The attempt to introduce Christianity into China provides a good example of barriers to diffusion, barriers not just of a religious nature, but also a linguistic one. Unlike Buddhism, for which Chinese culture presented a permeable barrier to diffusion (see box, "Buddhism in China: Passing a Permeable Barrier"), Christianity faced there, in effect, an absorbing barrier. When Catholic and Protestant missionaries reached China from Europe and the United States in the nineteenth century, they expected to find fertile ground for conversion — millions of people ready to receive the word of God. However, they had crossed the boundaries of a culture region thousands of years old, in which the basic social ideas left little opening for Christianity. For instance, the missionaries were left in a quandary about how to translate sin into Chinese for no equivalent concept existed in the Chinese language. They tried a word meaning "not good"; a Chinese negative particle, the equivalent of the word *not;* and a word carrying the idea of something abhorrent or corrupt. Finally, they settled on the word *tsui,* borrowed from popular Buddhist sects. It meant to do something wrong and was tied to a newly developing Buddhist idea of keeping personal internal ledgers of merit and demerit. Even *tsui,* though, could not solve the problem. Centuries before, the Chinese had settled to their own satisfaction the question of what is basic human nature. As they saw the matter, humans were basically good. Evil desires represented merely a deviation from that natural state. People only had to shrug them off and they would return to the basic nature that they share with heaven. Consequently, the idea of "original sin" left the Chinese baffled.

The Christian image of humankind as flawed, of a gap between creator and created, of the Fall and the impossibility of returning to god-hood, was culturally incomprehensible to the Chinese. Other aspects of Christianity added to the cultural gap. How could the fall from grace come from too much knowledge, a commodity highly prized in China? What was wrong with a giant snake in the garden of Eden to a people whose art was filled with reptilian dragons, the imperial symbol? Even an adequate word for Jehovah, the personalized, single god of the West, was lacking. In short, many concepts of Christianity fell on rocky soil in China. Moreover, Westerners first appeared neither as conquerors nor as superior beings, but as crude barbarians. The thought that they would have anything to offer in the realm of ideas did not occur to the Chinese, secure in their own civilization. Only in the early twentieth century, as China's social structure crumbled under Western assault, did a significant, though still small, number of Chinese convert to Christianity. Many of these were "rice Christians," poor Chinese who were willing to become Christians for the rice the missionaries could give them. For the geographer, this is a good example of an attempted relocation diffusion of a major religion that did not work because of absorbing cultural barriers.

CULTURAL INTEGRATION IN RELIGION

While the interaction between religious belief and the environment can shape both religions and the land, religious faith is similarly intertwined with other aspects of culture. Spatial variations in religious belief influence and are influenced by social, economic, demographic, and political patterns in countless ways. Religions and languages often travel together, and religious belief is sometimes at the root of nationalism. Notice, for example, the high degree of spatial correlation between Christianity and the Indo-European languages. Belief systems can interfere with the demographic transition, as in many Islamic areas, and can even influence urban structure. In the economic sphere, religion can guide commerce; determine which crops and livestock are raised by farmers, and what foods and beverages people consume and even help decide the type of employment a person has.

Religion and Economy

People make their livings in many different ways, and these forms of livelihood vary greatly from one area to another. Religion is partially responsible for these variations. Try to place yourself in the position of the Hindu street sweeper of Kolkata, whose religion discourages him from aspiring to any higher position in life. Try to imagine what job you might get if your town suddenly attracted religious pilgrims from all over the country. Consider the possible economic effect of religious-based food taboos on the agriculture of your area. In these ways and many more, religion and economics are bound together (see box, "A Marriage of Religion and Economy"). This relationship is evident in agriculture.

Religion and Agriculture

Within some religions, certain plants and livestock, as well as the products derived from them, are in great demand because of their roles in religious ceremonies and traditions. When this is the case, the plants or animals tend to spread with the faith. For example, in some Christian sects in Europe and the United States, celebrants drink from a cup of wine that symbolizes the blood of Christ during the sacrament of Holy Communion. The demand for wine created by this ritual aided the diffusion of grape growing from the sunny lands of the Mediterranean to newly Christianized districts beyond the Alps in late Roman and early medieval times.

Wine and Religion in Germany

When you drink German Rhine wine, you are benefiting from this diffusion, because the vineyards of the Rhine were the creation of monks who arrived from the south between the sixth and ninth centuries. Even back into prehistoric times in Europe, wine has been linked to religion. In early Christian times, vineyards were introduced into southwestern Germany by Roman monks, who desired ceremonial wine for the holy sacrament. This dose attachment of church to wine in Germany left vestiges discernible even today. Among these vestiges are the religious names given to many individual vineyards, names that in turn appear on the wine bottle labels. Some are listed below. Certain generic wine names also reveal the link to religion. One of the most famous of these is *Liebfraumilch,* a mild, semisweet blend from German Rheinhessen. The name means "milk of the Holy Virgin."

Catholic missionaries introduced the cultivated grape to California. In fact, wine was associated with religious worship even before Christianity arose. Vineyard keeping and wine making spread westward across the Mediterranean lands in prehistoric times in association with worship of the god Dionysus

Food Taboos

Impact on Pork Industry: Religion also can often explain the absence of individual crops or domestic animals in an area. The environmentally similar lands of Spain and Morocco, separated only by the Strait of Gibraltar, show the agricultural impact of food taboos. On the Spanish, Roman Catholic side of the strait, pigs are common, but they are not found in Muslim Morocco on the African side. The Islamic avoidance of pork underlies this contrast. Judaism also has restrictions against pork and other meats, as is stated in the following passage from the Book of Leviticus:

> *These shall ye not eat, of them that chew the cud, or of them that divide the hoof: as the camel, because he cheweth the cud, but divideth not the hoof; he is unclean unto you. And the coney, because he cheweth the cud, but divideth not the hoof; he is unclean unto you. And the hare, because he cheweth the cud, but divideth not the hoof; he is unclean unto you. And the swine, though he divide the hoof, and be cloven-footed, yet he cheweth not the cud, he is unclean unto you.*

Scholars have attempted to explain the Islamic and Judaic pork taboos in various ways. Some have suggested that these two cultures were primarily concerned with the danger of intestinal parasites (trichinosis)- or that they considered pigs unclean. However, it is unlikely that the cause-and-effect relationship between poorly cooked pork and intestinal parasites could have been detected prior to the days of modern medical technology. Other scholars have suggested a theory based on economy and ecology, after observing that pork avoidance is characteristic of the monotheistic faiths that arose among desert nomads. The proponents of this view believe that nomadic herding originated on the borders of the great farming areas of the ancient Middle East, near the Tigris, Euphrates, Nile, and other rivers. Population pressures forced people to settle farther and farther from the river banks, so that eventually some groups lost access to irrigation waters. These people were forced to abandon most crop farming and turn to animal husbandry. The poor quality of the range required them to wander from place to place in the desert, in nomadic fashion, seeking forage for their livestock.

Pigs, valuable animals to the sedentary farmers of the river valleys, could not travel long distances, and there was little for them to eat in the desert. As a result, the nomad relied instead on sheep, goats, horses, camels, and, in some areas, cattle. Since environmental conditions prevented the nomads from owning pigs, they may have declared pork undesirable in a "sour grapes' reaction. In time, this declaration may have found religious expression as a taboo. Ages later, as a final "revenge" in the seventh century A.D., the Muslim nomads imposed their religion, complete with the pork taboo, on the farming people of the river valleys.

Impact on Alcohol Industry: Muslims are also not permitted any alcoholic beverages. The Koran states: "O ye who have believed, wine, games of chance, idols, and divining arrows are nothing but an infamy of Satan's handiwork. Avoid them so that ye may succeed." Christians, however, have failed to reach a consensus on this taboo. Some Christian denominations prohibit all consumption of alcohol, in the belief that it is detrimental to health, welfare, and behaviour, while others, as described above, even use wine in religious ceremonies. In the United States, such groups as the Baptists, Methodists Mormons, and Seventh-Day Adventists support prohibition, while Roman Catholics, Lutherans, and several oilier churches tolerate alcohol, The economic imprint of these different attitudes can be seen through "wet" and "dry" areas in the United States. Texas provides an excellent example, since it is religiously diverse and by law allows each community to decide in local-option elections whether alcohol may be sold or served. Almost without exception, Catholic and Lutheran areas in Texas are "wet," while Baptist and Methodist counties are "dry."

Impact on Fish Industries: Food taboos also strongly affect the fishing industry. Practices such as the traditional Roman Catholic avoidance of meat on Friday greatly stimulated fishing, since fish became the standard Friday fare in Catholic areas. Indeed, the Christian tradition has always honored fishermen. We can perhaps trace this back to the apostle Peter, a fisherman by profession. The fish was an early symbol of Christianity initially exceeding the cross in importance. Use of this symbol stimulated the fishing industry, particularly in Catholic countries, and a lively trade in shipping preserved fish from coast to interior developed.

Other cultures place religious taboos on fish consumption and produce an opposite economic result. Most Hindus will not eat fish. India regularly suffers food shortages and dietary deficiencies while the nearby ocean teems with protein-rich fish. Among Christians, the Seventh-Day Adventists have a finless fish taboo and also will not eat pork. When missionaries of this church converted the population of Pitcairn Island in the South Pacific to their faith, the island's economic self-sufficiency collapsed, because the people had previously depended heavily on pork and finless fish in their diet.

Religious Tourism: The Pilgrim Trade. Religion provides the stimulus for pilgrimage by offering those who participate the reward of soul purification or the attainment of some desired objective in their lives. Pilgrims often come from great distances to see major shrines. Other sites, of lesser significance, draw pilgrims only from local districts or provinces. Pilgrimages can have tremendous economic impact, since the movement of pilgrims amounts to a form of tourism. In some favored localities, the pilgrim trade provides the only significant source of revenue for the community. For many religious groups, sites of particular importance to the faith have become the goal of pilgrimages. Journeys to these places often involve the movement of large numbers of people. Pilgrimages are typical of both ethnic and universalizing religions. They are particularly significant to followers of Islam, Hinduism, Shintoism, and Roman Catholicism.

The sites vary in character. Some have been the setting for miracles; some are the source regions of religions or areas where the founders of the faith lived and worked; others contain sacred physical features such as rivers and mountain peaks; and still others are believed to house gods or are religious administrative centers where leaders of the church reside. Examples include the Arabian cities of Mecca and Medina in

Islam; Rome and the French town of Lourdes in Roman Catholicism; the Indian city of Varanasi on the holy Ganges River, a goal of Hindu pilgrims; and Ise, the hearth of Shintoism in Japan.

Lourdes, a town of 18,000 in the south of France, attracts between 4 and 5 million pilgrims each year, many seeking miraculous cures at the famous grotto where the Virgin Mary supposedly appeared. Not surprisingly, among French cities, Lourdes ranks second only to Paris in number of hotels, although most of these are small. Mecca, a small city of 367,000 residents, attracted 1,950,000 Muslim pilgrims in 1982 from every corner of the Islamic culture region. By land, sea, and air, the faithful come to this hearth of Islam, a city closed to all non-Muslims. As you might expect, such massive pilgrimages have a major impact on the development of transportation routes and carriers. To facilitate the pilgrimage to Mecca and Medina, steamships connect the Arabian port of Jidda with overseas Muslim areas in East Africa, Indonesia, Malaysia, and other lands. Chartered and scheduled airline service is also available to Mecca pilgrims. In medieval Europe, many roads and bridges were built to accommodate pilgrims. Monks often helped maintain these routes and established shelters at regular intervals as way stations. Some of these hospices still survive, as at the summit of St. Gothard Pass in the Swiss Alps.

Religion and Profession. Often religion and employment are closely connected. In medieval Europe, Christians were generally restricted from lending money for interest. Jews, outcasts in Christian Europe, found most professions closed to them by law. As a result, while most of the Jewish population remained in poverty, individual Jews found an economic niche as moneylenders. They then used this occupation as a capitalist foothold from which they developed skills as retailers, and in time some became important businessmen. In Hinduism, persons in each caste traditionally had a pre- scribed economic role to play. To follow any occupation other than that dictated by caste was a violation of moral obligations. In southern India alone, over 2000 castes and subcastes developed, most with rigidly determined occupational requirements The caste system apparently originated about 1500 B.C., when Indo-Europeans invaded and conquered northern India.

These conquerors formed a light-skinned, elite upper class, while the vanquished native population was kept by law in a subservient position. From this segregation of conqueror and native grew the caste system. More recently, however, this systems has been made illegal, and a total correspondence between caste and occupation no longer exists. However, the caste system has by no means disappeared in rural India, where the greater part of the population lives although it has waned in urban areas.

Religion and Political Geography

In some nations, religion has been the rallying point for nationalistic sentiment and has even provided a justification for national existence. In 1947, when Britain granted independence to her colonial holdings in India, the area split to form a Hindu state (India) and a Muslim state (Pakistan). Those who created this division felt that the two religious groups could not coexist peacefully within the same state. Time has since shown that Hindus and Muslims have difficulty in living together on the same subcontinent, even in separate states. However, the sizable muslim population left in India has lived rather peacefully in the dominantly Hindu state in the last three decades, Israel and the Republic of Ireland are two other nations based on religion. In Israel, automatic citizenship is available only to Jews. In cases where religion is an important basis of nationalism, a state church is often created. Such a church is recognized by law as the only one in the state, and the government controls both church and state. In Norway, for example, the constitution establishes the Lutheran faith as the state church, and pastors and officials are appointed government employees.

In still other cases, the church is actively involved in governing countries. Such a government is known as a theocracy seen in Mormon Region. Initially, and through most of the nineteenth century, a theocratic government ruled in the Mormon culture region, in the Great Basin of the American West, giving a political expression to the faith. The church leader, Brigham Young, was also the territorial governor of Utah. Repeated efforts were made to create the state of Deseret, to be part of the United States but still under church administration. While the power of the United States government was finally employed to destroy the Mormon theocracy, the tie between church and government remained strong for many years.

The head of the church is often also the head of state. Vatican City, ruled by the Pope, is a fully independent state occupying parts of Rome. Similar to theocracies, but less rigid are countries where the secular ruler is the nominal head of the state church, as was true of prerevolutionary Russia. Until 1974, Greek Orthodox bishops, were actively involved in the government of Cyprus. The danger for the church in such a situation is that the religion may fall with the government.

Americans, accustomed by their heritage to the doctrine of separation of church and state, are usually unaware how closely religion and politics are intertwined in much of the world. Religious practices and traits often change abruptly at political boundaries, as along parts of the Franco-Belgian border in western Europe, and political parties are often identified with religious denominations.

The presence of the hostile religious groups within the same country can lead to disruption, and perhaps even civil war. States currently threatened by religious divisions include Cyprus where Turkish Muslims, with Turkey's help, seceded in 1983 from the dominantly Greek Orthodox state to form an independent nation; Lebanon, where Christians and Muslims are fighting a civil war; the United Kingdom, which has sought unsuccessfully to reconcile waning Catholics and Protestants in Northern Ireland; and the Philippines, where Catholics are at war with a Muslim minority on the island of Mindanao.

In some nations, political parties are linked to particular church groups. As a result, voting returns often duplicate the religious map. Such ties are particularly common in Europe, where political parties have names like Catholic People's Party or Christian Democrats. It is common in these countries for churchgoers to be advised from the pulpit on how they should vote. Even in countries like the United States, where legal separation of church and state is maintained, voting patterns often correspond to religion.

RELIGIOUS LANDSCAPES

The role played by religious motive in the transformation of landscapes is very striking producing what we might call sacred landscapes. At the opposite extreme are areas almost purely secular in appearance. Religions, then, differ greatly in visibility, but even those least apparent to the eye normally leave some mark on the countryside. The content of religious landscapes is varied, ranging from houses of worship to cemeteries, wayside shrines, and place-names. Moreover, religion can help shape other landscape features such as settlement patterns.

Religious Structures

The most obvious religious contributions to the landscape are the buildings erected to house divinities or to shelter worshipers. These structures vary greatly in size, function, style of architecture, construction material, and degree of ornateness. Among Roman Catholics, for example, the church building is literally the house of God, and the altar is the focus of vitally important ritual. Partly for these reasons, Catholic churches are typically large, elaborately decorated, and visually imposing, In many towns and villages, the Catholic house of worship is the focal point of the settlement, exceeding all other structures in size and grandeur. To many Protestants, particularly the traditional "chapel-goers" of British background, including Methodists and Baptists, the church building is, by contrast, simply a place to assemble for worship. God visits the church but does not live there. The result is an unsanctified, smaller, less ornate structure. The simpler church buildings of these Protestants appeal less to the senses and more to the personal faith. For this reason, their traditional structures are typically not designed for comfort, beauty, or high visibility, but instead appear deliberately humble. The building materials chosen for a religious structure often demon-strate the value a religion places on its visibility in the landscape. Sects that wish to call attention to their sacred structures typically build them of different materials than those used in the construction of houses and other nonreligious buildings.

In some parts of Europe, for example, churches are built of stone, while secular structures in the same communities are made of brick or wood. In Islam, mosques are normally the most imposing items in the urban landscape, while the visibility of Jewish synagogues varies greatly. Hinduism has produced large numbers of visually striking temples for its multiplicity of gods, but much worship is practiced in private households. Traditional religious architecture takes varied forms. St. Basil's Church or Red Spuare in Moscow reflects a highly ornate Russian landscape presence, while the plain board chapel in rural Georgia, in the American South, demonstrates an opposite tendency favouring visual simplicity on the part of British-derived Protestants. The domed mosques and minarets of Islam, in turn, offer still another very distinctive visual religious presence.

Religious structures can also become mere facades. In rural areas and secularized regions, churches are often abandoned and taken over by very different functions. Along the United States-Canada border west of the Great Lakes, some former churches are now used as granaries, clinics, American Legion halls, garages, and apartments. In the Soviet Union, many have been converted into museums. What appear to be functioning religious landscapes are, in fact, relic. Most tribal ethnic religions do not stand out in the cultural landscape. Animistic groups regard many objects as sacred, but these items are commonplace and would not reveal their religious significance to the eyes of an outsider. Tribal religions often do not have separate houses of worship.

Paralleling this contrast in church styles are attitudes toward wayside Shrines and similar manifestations of faith. Catholic culture regions typically abound with shrines, crucifixes, crosses, and assorted visual reminders of religion, as do some Eastern Orthodox Christian areas. From part of German Catholic religious landscape. Protestant areas, by contrast, are bare of such symbols and do not startle the night driver. Their landscapes do, however, occasionally display such features as signboards advising the traveller to "Get Right With God," *a* common sight in the southern United States. A billboard on the interstate highway near Montgomery, Alabama, advises the traveler: "Go to Church or the Devil will get you."

Landscapes of the Dead

Religions differ greatly in the type of tribute they award to the dead. This variation appears in the cultural landscape. Hindus and Buddhists cremate their dead. Having no cemeteries, their dead leave no obvious mark on the land. In the same way, the few remaining Zoroastrians, called Parsees, who preserve a once-widespread Middle Eastern faith now confined to parts of India, have traditionally left their dead exposed to be devoured by vultures. In Egypt, on the other hand, spectacular pyramids and other tombs were built to house dead leaders. These monuments were generally placed on land not suitable for crop farming.

Christians and Muslims, as well as Chinese who practice the composite Confucianist-Buddhist religion, typically bury their dead, setting aside land for that purpose and erecting monuments to the deceased kin. A striking landscape of the dead has been created in the Sahara Desert by the Nubian peoples of the Sudan. The burials are mounded and covered with hundreds of small rounded rocks. A very different landscape is seen in the French cemeteries of southern Louisiana, including New Orleans, where the dead rest in above ground crypts. In parts of pre-communist China, as much as 10 percent of the land in some districts was covered by cemeteries and ancestral shrines greatly reducing the acreage available for agriculture. Traditionally, Chinese grave sites were geomantically chosen for their *Feng Shui,* literally "wind and water," the perfect combination of tangible and intangible elements that would leave the dead in harmony with their surroundings. It is believed that if the *Feng Shui* of a grave site is wrong, the dead will be restless and their descendants will suffer. Ideally, for a grave site in China, the configuration of the earth should be perfect—neither featureless and flat, nor steep and rugged. The active and passive forces of Chinese cosmology, *Yin* and *Yang,* should correctly surround the site. As Chuen-yan David Lai, a Canadian geographer, has written: "The *Yang* energy is expressed as a lofty mountain range, symbolically called the 'Azure Dragon,' and the *Yin* energy as a lower ridge called the 'White Tiger.' The most auspicious model of *Feng Shui* topography is a secluded spot where these two energies converge, interact vigorously, and are kept together in abundance and in harmony by surrounding mountains and streams."

Cemeteries often preserve truly ancient cultural traits, for people as a rule are reluctant to change practices relating to the dead. The traditional rural cemetery of the southern United States provides a case in point. All grass is chopped from the southern cemetery, exposing the bare earth, and freshwater mussel shells are placed atop elongated grave mounds. Rose bushes and cedars are planted through the cemetery. Recent research suggests that the use of roses may be derived from the worship of the ancient, pre-Christian mother goddess of the Mediterranean lands. The rose was a symbol of this great goddess, who could restore life to the dead. Similarly, the cedar evergreen is an age-old Mediterranean and Germanic symbol of death and eternal life, and the use of shell decoration apparently derives from a pagan custom in West Africa, the source of southern slaves. While the present Christian population of the South is unaware of the origins of their cemetery symbolism, it seems likely that their landscape of the dead contains animistic elements thousands of years old.

Religion and Rural Settlement Patterns

Most farming peoples live either in clustered villages or in dispersed farmsteads separated from one another. Religion often helps determine which of these patterns will prevail. In the United States and Canada, many highly cohesive religious groups have traditionally formed village settlements, in contrast to the more typical American pattern of dispersed farmsteads.

The farm village tradition in Anglo-America was introduced by the Puritans of New England and later perpetuated by Mennonites in Canada, Mormons in the Great Basin of the American West, and the Amana colonists in Iowa. The large majority of utopian communities, so common on the American frontier, also utilized the farm village pattern. These sects, religious and Utopian alike, typically placed a high value on group interaction and mutual support, and they felt that the clustered village was necessary to provide the daily contacts essential to the practice and perpetuation of their faiths.

If the sect weakened and declined, or if factionalism developed, the clustered farm settlements often broke up/in colonial New England where some Puritan settlements had developed as villages, the power of church leaders in Boston waned after about 1700, and the Puritan movement began to fragment. Thereafter the farm villages gave way to scattered farmsteads, for religious individualism and scattered farmsteads had replaced the cohesive, village-based theocracy.

Religious Names on the Land

Religion often inspires the names people place on the land. Within Christianity, the use of saints names for settlements is very common in Roman Catholic and Greek Orthodox areas, especially in overseas colonial lands settled by Catholics such as Latin America and French Canada. In areas of the Old World that were settled long before the advent of Christianity saints' names were often grafted onto pre-Christian names, as in Alcazar de San Juan, in Spain, which combines Arabic and Christian elements. As a part of the French Canadian Landscape we come across:

> "St.-Jean," "St.-Aubert," "St.-Damase-des-Aulnaies," "Ste. Perpetud de l/Islet," "St.-Pamphile," "St.-Adalbert," "Ste.-Lucie," "St.-Fabien-de Panet," "St.-Juste-de-Bretenieres," "Ste.-Camille-de-Bellechasse" —so read the town-name placards as one drives from the St. Lawrence River south on Highway 24 in Quebec, paralleling the Maine border.

Toponyms in Protestant regions display less religious influence, but some imprint can usually be found. In the southern United States, for example, the word *chapel* as a prefix or suffix, as in Chapel Hill and Ward's Chapel, is very common in the names of rural hamlets. Names like this accurately convey the image of the humble, rural Protestant churches that are so common in the South.

CONCLUSION

Religion is firmly interwoven in the fabric of culture, a bright hue in the human mosaic, for religions and individual religious elements vary greatly from one area to another. Several major religions and many minor ones form variety of culture regions. The cultural landscape abounds with expressions of religious belief places of worship—temples, churches, and shrines — differ in appearance, distinctiveness, prominence, and frequency of occurrence from one religious culture region to another. These buildings provide a visual index to the various faiths. Cemeteries and religious place-names also add a special effect to the landscape that tells us about the religious character of the population. Such religious spatial variation led us to ask how these distributions came to be, a question best answered through the methods of cultural diffusion.

Some religions, universalizing denominations, actively encourage their own diffusion. Most Christian churches, for example, send out missionaries to "spread the word." Other religions erect barriers to expansion diffusion by restricting membership to one particular ethnic group Jews, for instance, do not seek converts.

The spatial diffusion of religious ideas often parallels and accompanies other, nonreligious elements of culture, such as language, crops, and political systems. The theme of cultural ecology reveals some fundamental ties between religion and the physical environment.

One major function of many religious systems, particularly the animistic faiths, is to appease and placate the forces of nature and to achieve harmony between the people and the physical environment. Religions differ in their outlook on environmental modification by humans. Some religious groups view such alterations as an affront to the gods. We need to face the question of whether the Christian ecological outlook is leading us to environmental disaster.

Religion is systemically related to economy and politics, among other things everything from tourism to nationalism can have a religious component. This further strengthens the view of culture as a functioning whole with religion being culturally integrated.

SUGGESTED READINGS

Surinder M. Bhardwaj. *Hindu Places of Pilgrimage in India.* Berkeley and Los Angeles: University of California Press, 1973.

Michael E. Bonine. "Islam and Commerce: Waqf and the Bazaar of Yazd, Iran," *Erdkunde,* 41 (1987), 182-196.

Stanley D. Brunn and James O. Wheeler. "Notes on the Geography of Religious Town Names in the United States," *Names: Journal of the American Name Society,* 14, No. 4 (1966), 197-202.

Manfred Buttner. "Religion and Geography," *Numen,* 21 (1974), 163-196.

Joseph Chamic. *Religion and Fertility: Arab Christian-Muslim Differentials.* New York: Cambridge University Press, 1981.

John I. Clarke. "Islamic Populations: Limited Demographic Transition," Geography, 70(1985), 118-128.

Daniel Doeppers. "The Evolution of the Geography of Religious Adherence in the Philippines Before 1898," *Journal of Historical Geography, 2* (1976), 95-110.

R.A. Donkin. *The Cistercians: Studies in the Geography of Medieval England and Wales.* Toronto: Pontifical Institute of Mediaeval Studies, 1978.

Robin W. Doughty. "Environmental Theology: Trends and Prospects in Christian Thought," *Progress in Human Geography,* 5 (1981), 234-248.

L. Alan Eyre. "Biblical Symbolism and the Role of Fantasy Geography Among the Rastafarians of Jamaica," *Journal of Geography,* 84 (1985), 144-148.

Isma'il R. al-Faruqi and David E Sopher. *Historical Atlas of the Religions of the World.* New York: Macmillan, 1974.

Richard H. Foster, Jr. "Changing Uses of Rural Churches: Examples from Minnesota and Manitoba," *Yearbook of the Association of Pacific Coast Geographers,* 45(1983), 55-70.

Richard V. Francaviglia. *The Mormon Landscape.* New York: AMS Press, 1978.

Robert H. Fuson. "The Orientation of Mayan Ceremonial Centers," *Annals of the Association of American Geographers,* 59 (1969), 494-511.

John D. Gay. *The Geography of Religion in England.* London: Gerald Duckworth, 1971.

Clarence J. Glacken. *Traces on the Rhodian Shore.* Berkeley: University of California Press, 1967.

Peter L. Halvorson and William M. Newman. *Atlas of Religious Change in America, 1952-1971.* Washington, D.C.: Glenmary Research Center, 1978; and their accompanying volume, *Patterns in Pluralism: A Portrait of American Religion.* Washington, D.C.: Glenmary Research Center, 1980.

Manfred Hannemann. *The Diffusion of the Reformation in Southwestern Germany, 1518-1534.* Chicago: University of Chicago, Dept. of Geography, Research Paper No. 167, 1975.

Charles A. Heatwole. "The Unchurched in the Southeast, 1980," *Southeastern Geographer, 25 (1985), 1-15.*

Sara Hershkowitz. "Residential Segregation by Religion: A Conceptual Framework," *Tijdschrift voor Economische en Sociale Geografie,* 78 (1987), 44-52.

Richard H. Jackson. "Religion and Landscape in the Mormon Cultural Region," in K. W. Butzer (ed.), *Dimensions of Human Geography.* Chicago: University of Chicago, Dept. of Geography, Research Paper No. 186,1978, pp. 100-127.

Richard H. Jackson and Roger Henrie. "Perception of Sacred Space," *Journal of Cultural Geography,* 3 (Spring-Summer 1983), 94-107.

Terry G. Jordan. "Forest Folk, Prairie Folk: Rural Religious Cultures in North Texas," *Southwestern Historical Quarterly,* 80 (1976), 135-162.

Terry G. Jordan. *Texas Graveyards: A Cultural Legacy.* Austin: University of Texas Press, 1982.

Jeanne Kay and Craig J. Brown. "Mormon Beliefs About Land and Natural Resources, 1847-1877," *Journal of Historical Geography,* 11 (1985), 253-267.

Florence R. Kluckhohn et al. *Variations in Value Orientations.* Evanston, 111.: Row, Peterson, 1961.

Gregory J. Levine. "On the Geography of Religion," *Transactions of the Institute of British Geographers,* 11 (1986), 428-440.

David N. Livingstone. "Environmental Theology: Prospect in Retrospect," *Progress in Human Geography,* 7 (1983), 133-140.

Deryck O. Lodrick. *Sacred Cows, Sacred Places: Origins and Survivals of Animal Homes in India.* Berkeley and Los Angeles: University of California Press, 1981.

Emanuel Maier. "Torah as Movable Territory," *Annals of the Association of American Geographers,* 65 (1975), 18-23.

Joseph T. Manyo. "Italian-American Yard Shrines," *Journal of Cultural Geography,* 4 (1983), 119-125.

Donald W. Meinig. "The Mormon Culture Region: Strategies and Patterns in the Geography of the American West, 1847-1964," *Annals of the Association of American Geographers,* 55 (1965), 191-220.

William M. Newman and Peter L. Halvorson. "American Jews: Patterns of Geographic Distribution and Change, 1952-1971," *Journal for the Scientific Study of Religion,* 18 (1979), 183-193.

Hans-Jurgen Nitz. "The Church as Colonist: The Benedictine Abbey of Lorsch and Planned Waldhufen Colonization in the Odenwald," *Journal of Historical Geography,* 9 (1983), 105-126.

Mary Lee Nolan. "Irish Pilgrimage: The Different Tradition," *Annals of the Association of American Geographers,* 73 (1983), 421-438.

Mary Lee Nolan and Sidney Nolan. *Religious Pilgrimage in Modern Western Europe.* Chapel Hill: University of North Carolina Press, 1989.

Ellen Churchill Semple. *Influences of Geographical Environment.* New York: Henry Holt, 1911.

Yosseph Shilhav. "Principles for the Location of Synagogues: Symbolism and Functionalism in a Spatial Context," *Professional Geographer*, 35 (1983), 324-329.

James R. Shortridge. "Patterns of Religion in the United States," *Geographical Review*, 66 (1976), 420-434.

James R. Shortridge. "The Pattern of American Catholicism," *Journal of Geography*, 77(1978), 56-60.

Frederick J. Simoons. *Eat Not This Flesh: Food Avoidances in the Old World.* Madison: University of Wisconsin Press, 1961.

Paul Simpson-Housley. "Hutterian Religious Ideology, Environmental Perception, and Attitudes Toward Agriculture," *Journal of Geography, 77* (1978) 145-148.

John H. Sims and Duane D. Baumann. "The Tornado Threat: Coping Styles of the North and South," *Science*, 176 (1972), 1386-1392.

Rana P.B. Singh. "Distribution of Castes and Search for a New Theory of Caste Ranking: Case of the Saran Plain," *National Geographical Journal of Indian* 21. (March 1975), 20-46.

David E. Sopher. *The Geography of Religions*. Englewood Cliffs, N.J.: Prentice-Hall, 1967.

David E. Sopher. "Geography and Religions,", Progress *in Human Geography 5* (1981), 510-524.

David Spring and Eileen Spring (eds.). *Ecology and Religion in History*. New York Harper & Row, 1974.

Dan Stanislawski. "Dionysus Westward: Early Religion and the Economic Geography of Wine," *Geographical Review*, 65 (1975), 427-444.

Roger W. Stump (ed.). "The Geography of Religion." Special issue, *Journal of Cultural Geography*, 7, No. 1 (Fall-Winter 1986), 1-140.

Roger W. Stump. "Regional Divergence in Religious Affiliation in the United States," *Sociological Analysis*, 45 (1984), 283-299.

Roger W. Stump. "Regional Migration and Religious Commitment in the United States," *Journal for the Scientific Study of Religion*, 23 (1984), 292-303.

Roger W. Stump. "Regional Variations in Denominational Switching Among White Protestants," *Professional Geographer, 39* (1987), 438-449.

H. Tanaka. "Geographical Expression, of Buddhist Pilgrim Places on Shikoku-Island, Japan," *Canadian Geographer,21 (1977)*, 111-133.

Yi-Fu Tuan. "Discrepancies Between Environmental Attitude and Behavior: Examples from Europe and China," *Canadian Geographer, 12* (1968), 176-191.

Yi-Fu Tuan. "Sacred Space: Explorations of an Idea," in Karl W. Butzer (ed) *Dimensions of Human Geography: Essays on Some Familiar and Neglected Themes*. Chicago: University of Chicago, Dept. of Geography, Research Paper No. 186, 1978, pp. 84-99.

Stephen W. Tweedie, "Viewing the Bible Belt," *Journal of Popular Culture, 11* (1978), 865-876.

Ingolf Vogeler. "The Roman Catholic Culture Region of Central Minnesota", *Pioneer America*, 8 (1976), 71-83.

S. Waterman and B. A. Kosmin. "The Distribution of Jews in the United Kingdom," *Geography, 71* (1986), 60-65.

Lynn White, Jr. "The Historical Roots of our Ecologic Crisis," *Science,* 155, 3767 (March 10, 1967), 1203-1207.

Hong-key Yoon. *Maori Mind, Maori Land: Essays on the Cultural Geography of the Maori People from an Outsider's Perspective.* Bern, Switzerland: Peter Lang 1986.

Wilbur Zelinsky. "An Approach to the Religious Geography of the United States Patterns of Church Membership in 1952," *Annals of the Association of American Geographers, 51* (1961), 139-167.

3

Interpretation of Buddhist Teachings

If the Third Truth means saying no to the urge to stray, then the Fourth Truth means saying yes to joining the path. This path is, the Middle Path. This Middle Path includes both no and yes. It avoids the extremes. In the extremes we are dominated either by yes alone or by no alone. The Fourth Noble Truth is *Marga,* the path. When we are lost in the woods and we come across a path we feel such relief. Suddenly we feel hope and confidence again. Now we can start going somewhere. We may not yet know exactly where the path will take us, but we know people have been there before. To be on the path means to start going in a consistent direction.

The ordinary way of thinking is that yes and no are mutually exclusive. This leads either to a struggle for control or to despair. We were recently discussing the Noble Truths in a Dharma group when one member, Anna, shared the following:

> A few years ago I suffered from cancer. I had treatment which seemed to have been successful. Recently I reached a place where I sensed the cancer had recurred. The uncertainty that I had been struggling to live with for eighteen months became, for a while, overwhelming and intolerable and was accompanied by feelings of doom and fear. I was fighting to get in control, going to see alternative practitioners and doctors, having a scan. I became totally identified with the fight for life-and stopped living.
>
> Ironically, the scan did not yield any information about the very organ I had been concerned for. It had been a waste of time and resources. I realised that I had sunk into a state of panic, had been chasing my own tail, and all to no avail. No amount of activity on my part was going to change the status quo. I realised that it was not within my power to determine the outcome: not in my hands.

> With this came a sense of relief and release. It was not, after all, my responsibility to stay alive. I had a feeling of what I describe as spiritual confidence-something like Julian of Norwich's 'All shall be well and all manner of things shall be well.' I felt like I had something that could not be taken away from me. Marvellous.
>
> With hindsight, it is clear to me that it was sheer hubris to imagine that I had or could aspire to mastery of my own fate. The experience reminds me of something a friend said to me early on when I was first diagnosed. She said: 'What have you done to deserve God's favour?' It is true that I have received many blessings.

Saying no to the, urge to be unrealistically in control allowed Anna to say a real yes to the life she actually does have.

In another group, we were discussing the state of society, the scale of the social problems we face and the difficulty for a citizen alone to effect meaningful change. Richard came in on the discussion with:

> I got burnt out with it. For many years I felt as though it was down to me to put the world right. I went on marches and protests and got involved with many organisations. I felt very angry about capitalism and nuclear bombs and ecology and consumerism. It was as though everywhere I looked everything was wrong. I just got overwhelmed. So eventually I stopped. I still send money to a few good causes, but that's it. I am still recovering. It is like a kind of convalescence, getting over the devastating effect of realising that I could not change it all.

Richard too has tried the extremes of yes ('I will control it all') and no ('I can't do anything'). He is now evolving a new, happier life and has once again begun to become involved in projects to improve the world, but this time free from the desperate quality that formerly drove him.

The Buddha was offering a Middle Path which enables us to go on *being effective without feeling defeated* just because we do not sweep all before us. The Four Noble Truths say, in effect, 'This is what you cannot do anything about and this is what you can do something about.' At one extreme is the idea that 'Because I can do something about some things, it must be possible to do everything about everything.' In the modern world this is a popular fallacy. Having lost their religion, many people feel the responsibility for everything now rests entirely upon them. At the other extreme is the thought that 'Because there are some things I will not be able to do anything about -in this lifetime at least- there is no point in doing anything.' This is also a common apathy that afflicts many. It, too, is related to the loss of religion. People are no longer willing to act on faith that the quality of the action alone will ensure that it contributes to good in the world.

The control fallacy is shaped for us by modern history. Religion in the West has been about relating to a God who was a powerful father figure. God was the creator and controller of the universe. What we have tended to do as modern society has emerged is to replace God by Man. It is not so much that people have stopped believing in the God idea. It is that they have put humankind up as a new God. There is current a kind of humanism that puts people centre stage and expects humankind, either individually or collectively, to solve all problems and right all wrongs. The modern person thus harbours a guilt whenever they are failing to be perfectly happy and successful which is all the time. In the modern mentality it is not so much that God has disappeared from our consciousness as that God has been internalised and we have become our own God. The self has to be appeased because it is now God

The Buddha taught *a path which relies neither upon an external nor an internal all powerful god.* In the tradition, it is said that a Buddha is 'teacher of gods and people'. This means that it is more important to be enlightened than to be all-powerful. God is a power play. If we see God as outside ourselves, then we ally ourselves with him or her and this makes us the chosen people who have superior status and rights over others. If we see ourselves as gods, then we either fall into dissipative selfishness or we wear ourselves out trying to do the impossible. When we do wear ourselves out we can fall into despair.

Teachings of Buddha

Buddha taught us that it is necessary to take the *first step* which is to share and recognise how we and others are afflicted. It is necessary to take the *second step* of sharing and recognising how that makes us feel. These are two essential steps. It is then necessary to take the other two steps. The *third step* is to see that in these feelings lies the energy we need. We can trust the process of self-transformation as long as we can provide a container for it. We need to hold these feelings securely. This is nirodha. Then we need to take the *fourth step* which is to say yes to a positive path of living. Actually, if we can do the first three steps, the fourth follows naturally. By the time we have got to the fourth step, if we have done the first three well, we already have the necessary momentum. The Buddha, therefore, taught: *firstly,* that affliction is real and noble; *secondly,* that the feelings that come up in us in response to it are also real and noble; *thirdly,* that we can capture and harness those feelings-just as one might capture and harness a wild horse; and, *fourthly,* that by doing so we can enter upon a wholesome, constructive and satisfying way of life. In other words, he taught us, on the one hand, to recognise what we cannot do anything about and stop feeling frustrated about that and to recognise what we can do something about and start doing it.

Despair

This means doing something about ourselves. Often this begins with facing our own despair. Anna and Richard both had to go through the despair which arose when they faced the overwhelming scale of what afflicted them. Since different parts of us do not all grow up at the same rate, we may need to go through this birth channel of despair several times in the course of our lives. The Four Noble Truths describe this process. They are not a prescription for escape but for maturity. There is a need within Dharma practice communities to create time and space for this despair work, as Joanna Macy calls it in her book, *Despair and Personal Power in the Nuclear Age* (1983).

If we can understand the Buddha's first talk, then we can see the need for this very clearly. The Buddha was not saying that we should not have such feelings. He was saying that in these very feelings lies the energy which can provide the motive force for the spiritual life, for walking the Noble Path. We should have groups to do this work. We should be willing in our Dharma discussions to share these feelings and to listen deeply to one another. Despair is Samudaya. Samudaya is not the cause of suffering. Samudaya is the essential *second step* of a four-step process which leads to the wholesome life.

The Middle Path, the Eightfold Way, is not the means to eliminate suffering. It is the noble outcome of facing the reality of affliction and working through what then comes up for us in a courageous and authentic way. When we do so, the eight elements of the path described by the Buddha are not means to an end. They are simply a description of our authentic life. The Eightfold Path emerges from the spiritual work described in the first three Truths.

LOOKING BACK ON LIFE AND ITS BIG STORY

What story are you living? What kind of story is it? Is it a story that you will feel glad to have lived? Will you, when old, look back down the years without regret? These are important questions. Many people feel as though their lives have not really begun yet. They are waiting for the right conditions to begin. Others feel as though it is all over already. Some feel a sense of purpose, but many feel that their lives are disjointed, inconsequential or seriously compromised.

Big and Little Story

In each life there is a big story and a little story. The little story is the story of the ego. The other day I was asked: 'What was the little story of Jesus Christ?' I suppose the answer is that he was a carpenter's son who never managed to get himself either a wife or a proper job and finished up being executed for a rather trivial offence. If this were all there were to it, history would not have noticed. The satisfactions of the ego are real enough, but they are exceedingly transitory. It is nice to be praised, or to meet with success and acclaim, and it is painful to be ridiculed and to meet with failure and frustration. Such vicissitudes, however, contain nothing lasting or substantial unless we can conserve the energy from them to serve some greater purpose.

What is there to carry us through when the little story comes apart? Real satisfaction arises when the little story is integrated into or even subsumed within a big story that is itself worthwhile. Most people who have made a great contribution in life have gone through a period of disenchantment-a time in the wilderness-during which they not only came to terms with the defeats in their little story, but also found their place in the big one. This conversion in the wilderness, whereby a little life comes out of its individual backwater and enters the mainstream of the big river, is what is meant by enlightenment. By this step, the little ego is overcome. The circumstances of our birth affect our story deeply.

The Buddha was driven by the fact that his mother died when he was seven days old. If this had remained a little story he might simply have felt sorry for himself. He would have grown up and sought solace here and there and nothing very consequential would have come of it.

He would probably have become a rather depressed old man who took out his frustrations on those around him while secretly regretting that he had not had the courage to throw over the traces. As it was, he went out in search of the answer to a fundamental life problem-the meaning of suffering-not just for himself, but for all humankind. He found a solution and spent his life in service to the cause of bringing this message of hope to others. In the process he set in motion a great story -the story of the tradition we call Buddhism-which has given meaning to millions of other people's lives and provided a vehicle for untold good in the world.

Carving Out a Big Story in One's Life

A person who has integrated his life into the big story may come to be regarded as a great being and, in retrospect, people then think it was all fore-ordained. This is how we sell ourselves short. We think that our own lives are not so great. Whether our lives amount to anything or not however, depends upon whether we find the courage to put them in the service of a big story and whether the big story we choose is a wholesome one. Among big stories some are wholesome and some are not. It is likely that, if we do not deliberately give ourselves to a wholesome story, we will get caught up in an unwholesome one.

Personal Experience

In my own case, I was born shortly after the last world war. The post-war period has been a time in which there has been a great growth in psychological research and understanding in the western world. The original impetus for this research was the question that was left in people's minds after the war: why did ordinary German citizens, not very different from English, French or American ones, participate in the holocaust? Could it happen again? Of course, we now know that the answer is definitely in the affirmative. Genocide has not been uncommon in the post-war period. Having been born into the generation of hope following the world's largest war, I grew up participating in the idea that, there having been two world wars, a third was a distinct possibility. With the advent of nuclear weapons it is apparent that a third world war would be catastrophically destructive. It would take a very long time for the planet to recover, if indeed it did. There has been a big story running during my lifetime and this big story is about the prevention of war and the survival of the human race.

In the last few decades this story has taken on an added twist. This is summed up in the word ecology. It has become increasingly clear that the threat to humankind is not just from war. It is also from pollution and ecological damage. We are using the planet up at more than replacement rate. War and famine hover over us, just as they have done throughout human history. The difference is that now there is nowhere else to go and, as a result of technological 'advance', the stakes are much higher.

Remaining Trapped in Little Stones

A big story brings a big task. The great work requires something of all of us. If we neglect this, then we remain trapped in our little stories. Modern society tends to operate in ways that isolate us in our littleness. We are encouraged to be consumers and economic units. We are assailed by advertising which carries the constant message that individual indulgence is all that matters. All this serves to weaken our spirit and put our world at risk. As our society becomes more and more spiritually impoverished, it is like a forest drying out in the heat of summer. The danger of a forest fire grows. Accustomed to getting our whims fulfilled, untrained in containing our fire, we too become vulnerable to the kind of social conflagration that has consumed Yugoslavia, brought, misery to Northern Ireland and destroyed Chechnya.

Harvesting Our Energies Together for a Big Story

The Buddha offered his followers the opportunity to become part of a big story. This is the story of how afflictions are to be met with a noble response so that people may feel complete, satisfied that they have lived a full and enlightened life. It is the story of how the energies within us, that can sometimes seem so destructive, are to be transformed into the driving power for the salvation of the world. It is a great story, not a trivial one. It is not just the story of one individual. It is also the story of the creation of a community of people who live by a higher calling and it is, therefore, also the story of a home-coming: of people returning to their spiritual roots, their 'original nature'. In psychotherapy, people are often struggling to find a place for themselves in a meaningful story, or trying to pick up the pieces of a story that came undone. It is not true, however, that one story is just as good as another.

There is a serious danger in a complex society like our own that the quest for democracy and equality leads to a kind of moral relativism which is destructive of society, families, groups and individuals alike. If we believe that all stories are as good as one another, then no story can be important. If the story we are living is not important, then our life will peter into apathy and we will be defenceless against tyranny and oppression.[1]

There will always be bad big stories waiting to sweep us away. Indeed, we are already involved in them. By being consumer citizens we collude with all manner of ill: factory farming, armaments production, environmental damage, wars to protect oil supplies, third world debt, to name but a few. It is important to do better than this, to find a more noble story.

Buddhas Inspiration

The Buddha enabled many people to see possibilities for their lives that they had not perceived before they met him. That is the function of a sage. He was able to speak the other person's language and to see their life in terms of the bigger picture -how new meaning could be injected into the person's little story so that it began to serve the great story of peace and compassion in the world. He was an inspirer.[2] Being part of the big story is what is meant by being on a path or way. The Fourth Noble Truth is the Truth of the path. The big story, the story of the spreading of peace and harmony in the world, of constructive and spirited response to obstacles encountered, and of harmony and co-operation, is what he invites us to take refuge in. Without such a path, we are unable to rise to the needs of our time. With it, we can become the kind of people whose lives become consequential in a great variety of wholesome ways. The Middle Way-the mainsteam-emerges directly from the practice of the first three Noble Truths. The four together constitute one whole. There is adversity. Recognising adversity we feel our passion rise. Protecting our passion from the wind of ego-centred concern we can turn it to the service of good in the world. That service constitutes the path. The path is described from eight perspectives. We will now look at each in turn.

THE EIGHT FOLD PATH OF BUDDHA

(i) Right View

Right view is the first step to the Eight fold path. We all know how dangerous views and opinions can be. People come to blows over them. Co-operation between people breaks down over them. The human animal is notable for its skill in communication, but also for its skill in dispute and hostility. It is doubtful whether there is any view that one could hold which would not carry this danger of setting one into conflict with others. The Buddha was acutely aware of the inflammatory potential of clashes of opinion.

Therefore, the Buddha would say: 'All views are wrong views,'[3] by which he meant to warn us about how dangerously opinions can hinder the spiritual path. If I am attached to an opinion, then it inevitably gets in the way of clear perception, both of objective and subject phenomena alike.[4] He wanted his followers to have the kind of steady mind that can cope with a crisis and impart strength to others when it is needed.

If all views are wrong views, what about the Buddha himself? Did he not have views? Certainly he did. But he was also capable of that inner stillness that makes fresh perception possible. Stillness enables innocence and experience to merge. This is a practical not a philosophical matter. It is not a matter of definition of words. The point that the Buddha is making is that what he is offering is something to do rather than something to spend a long time thinking about. He is saying 'Don't spend ages philosophising. Try it and see.' We should not elevate his statements into absolutes. It is absolutes that he is preaching against. All his teaching is practical advice.

Not to be opinion area: The sayings of the Buddha are recorded in five lengthy collections called the *Sutras.* At the very beginning of this huge collection of writings is the Sutra called Brahma's Net. This begins with a description of two wandering holy men, teacher and disciple, walking along the road some distance behind the Buddha and his companions. The teacher and disciple are arguing about the merits and defects of the Buddha's teaching. The Buddha's own disciples hear this argument and start talking about it. The Buddha overhears them and he says: 'If anyone should speak in disparagement of me or of my teaching or of our community, please do not be angry, resentful or upset by it. To become upset in that way would only be a hindrance to you. For if when others criticise me you become angry or upset, you will be unable to judge clearly whether what they are saying is true or false.'

This very practical declaration summarises the Buddha's teaching on views. Getting upset and taking what has been said personally causes unnecessary suffering and clouds the mind. It is a case of the fire being caught by the ego wind. The Buddha believes in and is completely behind the teaching he gives. He is not arguing that one view is as good as another. Yet he is also open to hear what the other person has to say, to receive criticism and to consider what is right and wrong dispassionately.

As the *Zenrin,*[5] a classic collection of Buddhist wisdom, says

Be one who sleeps well.
Undisturbed by 'true or false'.

The mind which is free and unburdened is naturally inquiring. To be free and unburdened does not mean a restriction of activity so much as a lightness in regard to it. An enlightened person thinks about the future sometimes, but does not become oppressed by a sense of what must be achieved or of what could happen. An enlightened person thinks of the past sometimes, but does not become weighed down by agonising over what has 'gone wrong'. They do not hang onto past hurts. An enlightened person thinks about the present state of things sometimes, but they do not become burdened by what they see.[6]

It is important, therefore, not to invest our ego in our views, however strong our conviction may be. Even Buddhist views are subject to the danger of becoming the justification for intolerance and conflict. As a result of the Buddha giving this teaching on views such prominence, the Buddhist record on tolerance has actually been remarkably good over the centuries, but it is by no means perfect. All systems of thought have their dangers, even the most benign.

Opinionatedness is very close to what most people mean by ego. It is attachment to opinions that leads to the fire of our passion getting out of control, just as much as or even more than attachment to the pleasures of the senses.

Willingness to listen and see: What then is Right View? Outwardly, Right View is total attention. Inwardly, it is stillness. The word 'right' here means wholehearted. Right View is not an opinion, it is willingness to look listen and flow. The path begins with deep listening and deep seeing.

Such listening and seeing, however, is not devoid of intelligence. Innocence is not ignorance. The Buddha was a practical person. He adapted his teaching to the mentality and experience of each person he met, while still staying true to the bigger story of which we are all a part. If a priest of another religion came to see him he did not say 'Give up your faith and accept mine,' but rather found ways of injecting greater meaning into the practice which the person already followed. Wisdom was set within empathy. Thus, Right View avoids both relativism, at one extreme, and dogmatism at the other.

Getting caught in point-scoring is simply a waste of energy. It is like getting burned by the very fire which could have cooked your dinner or, as the Buddha put it on another occasion, like picking up a snake by the tail and getting bitten.[7] There are safe ways to handle fires and snakes, but they need to be learned.

If we approach life with an open yet dedicated mind, what do we experience? We experience the Noble Truths. We experience the suffering that is in the world in all its particular manifestations. This is how the fire begins and this is why Right View is the first step. The *Eightfold Path* is an eight-step training in fire management. *Right View* enables us to see and deeply feel the suffering in the world, to notice our heartfelt response, to see the possibility for harnessing and directing that response. You have to be alert when you are playing with fire. To make a useful fire, we begin by creating a sheltered fireplace, and bringing together fuel and a spark. All of these initial steps fall within Right View. Our inner life must be sheltered from the ego wind. The inflammable material within us must be managed correctly. The spark is provided by our openness to the suffering in the world. Perceiving dukkha, both within us and around us, is the spark that lights the fire of our spirit. And there is no shortage of sparks.

None of us knows what is going to happen next. Later today we might discover that one of our children had a terrible accident, or we might discover a lump in your body which indicated that you have cancer, or a war might break out in some part of the world, killing thousands of innocent people. Things like this are happening all the time. On the one hand we live in a beautiful paradise. We inhabit this exquisite blue planet with all manner of quite miraculous wonders all around us. On the one hand ... on the other hand ... Life is like that.

Jain Yourself to Face Suffering: We can be ambushed. We are going along happily enough perhaps, when suddenly our world is turned upside down. The moment when three large men have jumped on you in a back alleyway is not the time to start learning self-defence.

It is much better to have trained oneself to the point where one can handle the situation without a second thought. The path which the Buddha advocated increases our capacity to cope with life's ambushes. Actually, just about anything can be an ambush. The more aware we become of our lives, the more we realise just how blind we have been. Every time that greed or hate gets the better of us, we have suffered another injury to our spirit.

So, in practical terms, Right View is about resolving to do something about the compulsiveness in our lives in all the thousand and one ways that it pops up in the course of an ordinary day. If we work at this, then when the big ambushes arrive we will be prepared. What we can be sure of is that they will indeed arrive. Disease, decay and death will come. Disappointment, failure and loss may seem to be things that we might be cunning enough to circumvent, but if we think so, then we are deceiving ourselves. Nobody gets away unscathed in these respects. Often clients in therapy nowadays believe that their lives have been irremediably damaged by their having been abused in some way in the past. However, everybody gets abused in one way or another. To say this is not to diminish the experience, but to emphasise the universal aspect.

The suffering in the world is not something for us each to solve on our own. It is of concern to us all. It is by reaching out to one another that we can respond to our collective pain in a noble and constructive way.

None of this is hidden. We all know full well that death will come. We are all exposed to transiency. It is clear as daylight. Yet all too often we live our lives pretending it will not happen to us. We try to find a refuge in self-deception and search for security. We turn even religion into a bulwark against reality, when its only real function is to help us to live authentically.

> Nothing is hidden;
> It has always been clear as day.
>
> For divine wisdom: look at the old pine tree;
> For eternal truth: listen to the birds sing.
>
> Seeking the mind: there is no place to look;
> Can you see the footprints of flying birds?

Above, not a single tile to shelter under;
Below, not a morsel of ground for support

The *Zenrin* is full of such good advice. Right View is to have this kind of freedom that looks for nothing in the way of support or shelter from the existential reality of our lives. When we have the courage to live life as it is, no longer running away, well grounded, then we experience a profound relaxation in our heart. We put down the burden and no longer have to live defensively.

In life, seek no heaven;
In death, fear no hell.

Enter the woods without disturbing a blade of grass;
Enter the water without making waves.

Meet the enlightened one on the street;
Do not greet him with words nor silence.

Just laugh and laugh -
In the forest, so many fallen leaves.

For so long, like a bird in a cage;
Now fly free like a cloud in the blue sky.

Hold the hoe with empty hands;
Ride the ox by standing on your own feet.

These verses point to an innocence of mind that is yet fully mature. The enlightened person is mature enough to enjoy life as it is and by doing so liberates the creative fire within. The ox is an age old symbol for the wildness in us that is also the basis for our spiritual life. If we can catch and tame the ox, we will be in command of our power.[8]

(ii) Right Thought

Right thought is the second step to the Eightfold Path. What should we think? What should we not think? The Buddha was very clear about this.

> 'He abused me, he beat me, he defeated me, he robbed me.' In those who harbour such thoughts hatred is not appeased. 'He abused me, he beat me, he defeated me, he robbed me.' In those who do not harbour such thoughts hatred is appeased. Hatreds never cease through hatred in this world; through love alone they cease. This is an eternal law.[9]

Right Thought follows directly from Right View. If we view others as our enemy, then we will think harmful thoughts. We will plot and scheme against them. Our secret life will be full of terrible imaginings. Just as there is a radiant, innocent, creative child in each of us, so there is also a murderous, hateful, greedy, tyrannical child as well.

The Good and Bad Side of All

It is important to recognise both sides of our nature and not expect to be too good. The novelist Fay Weldon suffered from nightmares as a child and until well into her twenties. Later she came to the conclusion that: 'Nightmares happen, I now believe, to people who think they are good, and fail to acknowledge their own dreadfulness. Children are always the heroes of their own lives: as one grows older one comes to realise one is the villain too.' One night when on holiday, she put her children in a room of a hotel that she was frightened to sleep in herself because it reminded her of her nightmare. 'I am not proud of it. Mothers should not behave like this. They should give up their lives and sanity for their children. I knew the better way, but chose the worse. I was not a good person.' After this incident, she never had the nightmare again. What had changed was that she admitted her 'dark side' into her life.[10] To be proud of ourselves while devaluing others is simply self-deception. If we have some special talent or some particular virtue, then we have it for a purpose, which is to benefit the world. If we see it as a platform from which inwardly to assert our superiority, we defeat our real purpose immediately.

The Hidden Rage: Along with the light there will always be shadow. This is the inner aspect of the fact that along with bliss there will always be *dukkha* in the world. The introspective side of the First Noble Truth is to see clearly just how much negativity there is within us. There may be rage and grasping hidden behind the exterior that we present to public view. In civilised people this hidden rage mostly creeps out in sly criticism and subtle angling for advantage rather than in bloody feuds. It is always waiting in ambush, always on the look out for opportunities to create greater mayhem. After all, Bosnia was a civilised country full of civilized people, not so very different from ourselves and so was the pre-war Germany that put the Nazis into power.

When we are able to see our own negativity clearly we will be less complacent and we will not stand in judgement over others. We will know that we too have all the seeds in us to be every possible kind of saint or sinner. We are not made of different stuff from the people we might choose to scorn.

Getting Control Over Thought: Dealing with affliction is only possible if we can get some control over our thoughts, but this does not mean that our thoughts should always be good ones. Horrible thoughts also arise. This is samudaya. The shadow must be admitted. If we can live with the devil in us as well as the angel we will be a lot healthier. The Buddhist way is not necessarily always nice. When we first adopt this practice, our thoughts include a lot of wrathful energy. We feel angry about the injustices in the world. We think we would like to destroy the torturers with their own instruments-rather as King Ashoka, on first learning about the Buddhist principles of non-oppressive government, is reputed to have boiled the state torturer in his own glue pot![11]

Hatred, however, does not cease with hatred. We have to husband the fire in such a way that it becomes love rather than hate. This is achieved by seeing deeply into the hearts of others. This is what is required of one who would be a therapist for the world.

When a person who is following this path conscientiously feels anger or disappointment or greed or any such impulse rising up, they do not immediately start to look for someone or something outside themselves to blame. They smile to themselves and think, 'Ah, now the energy is rising,' and they welcome it. For spiritual training this is very profitable, provided that we can keep our nerve. Then we can see that the person who insulted us or cheated us has actually done us a favour. The habit of angry thought, when seen clearly, becomes a source of fire for our furnace.

The Thought of Enlightenment

It is only possible to think like this if following the path of spiritual training or enlightenment is more important to us than short-term personal advantage. If we are just interested in selfishness, we are soon out of control and reduced to a thoroughly ignoble way of being. Spirituality requires a longer view. Or we may say it requires us to attend to a different dimension of the situation in hand. We might talk loosely about there being a horizontal and a vertical dimension to life.

The horizontal dimension is the mundane aspect. It is concerned with the preoccupations of money, relationships, work, personal security, advancement and danger. It is about 'having'. The vertical dimension is all about 'being', it is the province of spirituality and meaningfulness. Our modern society is all about 'having'. We even call it the consumer society. The Buddha's renunciation was a dramatic enactment of the shift from 'having' to 'being'. He simply gave up everything material and adopted the homeless life. When we give up 'having', then we put ourselves in a position of having nothing to defend and so the basis for attachment to negative states of mind is cut away.[12]

Simply being is what Buddhism is about. When we simply are, then we find that we are not cut off from the existence of everything. The enlightenment experience is an experience of being one with everything.

The Vertical Dimension: The thought of enlightenment, or the thought of the vertical dimension, or the higher purpose of life, or whatever other name one wishes to give to it, is, therefore, a supremely important thought. It is the thought which enables us to focus on being rather than having, on the quality of our moment by moment living rather than on the quantity of what we are getting. This thought is important enough in Buddhism to have a name. It is called *bodhichitta.* In the Mahayana schools of Buddhism, the bodhichitta is regarded as of supreme importance. It is by keeping the thought of higher purpose in mind that we are able to let go of all the trivia that otherwise would constantly lead to greed, hate and delusion in our everyday lives.

The path described in the Four Noble Truths is that of transformation. The horrible thoughts can be harnessed, too. In fact, they are the makings of the inner fire that becomes our enlightened nature. The Chinese Dhyana Master Yuan Miao (1238-95) taught that it was essential to discover 'the mind of great anger', 'the mind of great ferocity' and 'the mind of great doubt' within ourselves and to cultivate these qualities in the service of our quest for enlightenment.[13]

The bodhichitta may also be called 'the thought of great compassion'. It is the essence of the transformation in human mentality which the Buddha was working for. The transformed human being is called a Bodhisattva. In Buddhist mythology there is an ideal Buddha and an ideal Bodhisattva. These ideals exist to help us aspire to a better life and to find the vertical dimension of existence. In Buddhist iconography, the ideal Buddha is called Amida and the ideal Bodhisattva is called Quan Yin.[14] Amida means 'measureless'. This draws our attention to the fact that the vertical or spiritual dimension is unconditional. When we think of it, we are not thinking about things that we can calculate. When we give a gift with an ordinary mind, some calculation goes on. We measure out our generosity. When we give a gift with an enlightened mind there is no calculation. We just give, without any ulterior motive.

Unconditional Positive Regard

In Buddhism we say that this latter kind of giving is 'empty'. This leads to many seemingly puzzling statements in Buddhist writings which are not really as odd as they first seem. We read of 'no mind' and 'the thought of no thought' and so on. Actually this is all quite close to common usage which is a practical and not a literal use of language. When we say that the best kind of friend is 'one who would help you without a thought', we do not mean that they literally would not think. We mean that they would act in our interests without reservation. They would not count the cost to themselves. There would be no self in their decision.

The name Quan Yin means 'hearer of the cries', and it refers to a heart moved to compassion. She 'regards all beings with a compassionate eye'.[15] Quan Yin always hears the cry in the heart. When a person acts badly, it is because there is a cry of pain in their heart. Quan Yin hears this cry. She is thus able to regard everybody with deep empathy because she has this ability to see deeply. This is what is required of a helper. The great American psychologist Carl Rogers coined the term 'unconditional positive regard' for the attitude that a psychotherapist needs to have toward their client.[16] This term, unconditional positive regard, is very close to an amalgam of the names Amida and Quan Yin.

When we recognise, acknowledge and contain our own afflictions and are no longer afraid of the shadows that arise within ourselves, we put ourselves in a position to think well of others and to become useful in the world. Right Thought is the thought that puts the higher purpose at the centre of our existence and does not exclude anything from its orbit.

(iii) Right Speech

Right Speech is the third step to the Eightfold path. The Buddha did not waste words. His words were well chosen and to the point. They came from his depths. They were sincere and beautiful. They touched people's hearts and moved them to positive action. The speech of a Buddha is both a healing and a creative force in the world. Not only that, but it puts the hearer in touch with what is beyond the ordinary world, what is on the vertical dimension. The words of a Buddha, although intrinsically beautiful, may therefore sometimes be shocking to the ordinary mind. They challenge its most basic assumptions. They place no value on having, getting, accumulation nor security. They do not laud power and privilege, nor do they carry any assumption that the goal is the pursuit of pleasures. If we consider our own speech in this light, we may well see that it is very different from that of a Buddha. Buddha saw the potential of communication. What has come down to us is the example of his life and much of it was spent communicating. He was an exceptionally effective and purposeful communicator. The purpose was to convey the message of peace in the world through peace in the heart.

He advocated that we should be reconcilers of those at variance, encouragers of those at one, rejoicing in peace, loving it, delighting in it, speakers of words that make for peace.[17] The Buddha put his passion into bringing peace to the world. This was his life and we can continue his life by doing likewise. He knew that the attainment of such peace requires great courage. It requires courage to change one's ways. In this respect the Buddha was a great therapist. His words gave people the courage to make major changes. Often these changes were not easy. Just as nowadays, parents and relatives were not always enthusiastic about their children leaving home to follow a wandering meditation teacher and more than one would-be disciple had to go on hunger strike to obtain parental permission. In those days, parents had more power than today, extending to adult children as well as minors.

The Buddha taught a lot about Right Speech. There are many instances of people coming to him and being enlightened by a single conversation. People met him, talked with him and then changed their lives. Many of them then went on to inspire others. Thus there was a ripple effect. The Buddha's greatest disciple, Shariputra, became a disciple after hearing another quite inexperienced monk, Assaji, give a very sketchy account of Gautama's teachings.[18] Centuries later the great Zen Master Hui Neng had his first enlightenment experience by hearing a man reading a sutra in the street.[19] Words can have great power.

Inspiration and Aspiration

Many of the people the Buddha enlightened spent very little time with him. Others spent years by his side. It is not that they learned a method whereby to obtain something called enlightenment as though this were a possession one could acquire. If we think of spirituality in this worldly way, we simply bring the sublime down to the level of the mundane. What is required is the reverse: to raise everything mundane to the level of the sublime. When a person is inspired, every situation becomes a stimulus for joy and creativity. When a person is not inspired, even the most elevating circumstances are converted to dross. Cynicism for instance is the cancer of spirituality.

Inspiration is closely associated with aspiration. When we are inspired, we aspire. When we aspire it is much easier for things to inspire us. The two go together. Right Speech is the utterance of inspiration and aspiration. In Buddhism, the utterance of aspiration is called the vow.

Vows and Promises

Vows are out of fashion in the modern materialistic world because they do not fit into the horizontal dimension. A vow is an unconditional commitment. It goes beyond calculation. It is a statement that 'I will...' no matter what the odds against me may be. When we vow something we take it in a total way. A vow is not a prediction of success. Modern people tend to say, 'I will not promise something until I am sure that I can deliver it.' This is a conscientious thought and it is related to a concern for fair dealing. Really it is, however, still part of the conditional, contractual, horizontal way of thinking. It also, in western culture, has as its backdrop the fear of punishment. In the Judeo-Christian tradition the wrath of God is to be feared. If you promise something to God and you do not deliver, he will punish you. So the thought arises, 'better not promise in the first place.' This 'better not', however, tends to make for a spiritually limp existence. It is like shooting oneself in the foot.

In Buddhism, the meaning of vows is different because the context is different. In the first place, there is no God. In the second place, consequences will follow from your actions whether you promised or not. Whether you promised to stop smoking or did not promise to, the chance of contracting cancer is still the same. The chance of getting cancer is related to whether you do or do not smoke, not to whether you do or do not promise. The same is true with ethical commitments. Actions have consequences. If you steal, you harm yourself and others, whether or not you had previously promised to be honest.

Thirdly, a vow, in the Buddhist sense, is not quite the same thing as a promise. I promise to pay you back the money you gave me is really part of a contractual culture which belongs to the horizontal dimension. In the language of Jesus, we might say that it belongs to Caesar. A vow is something different. For example: A person lives in a country that has been overrun by an enemy. There are soldiers in the street. The people are everywhere oppressed. The person feels the injustice of the situation very deeply. This depth of feeling is expressed in a vow: 'I will free our land of these invaders.' This is a vow because it is made unconditionally. As a matter of fact, the person does not know whether it is possible to fulfil the vow. The enemy may be too strong. That, however, is not the point. A vow is not conditional upon possibility. A vow comes from depth of feeling. A vow connects our little life to a big story. It becomes a central organising force. It sets a person on a path. All effort is directed toward its accomplishment. The person's sense of identity changes. In this case, he has become a freedom-fighter. The quality of even the ordinary things of life changes. He is constantly aware of the way in which every action does or does not contribute to the cause. He is in the grip of a powerful inspiration. People who are inspired in this way, like Gandhi, for instance, often achieve seeming miracles. Their energy all flows one way. The vow has an organising effect upon character.

The difference between a person who lives by vow and a person who does not is like the difference between a piece of ordinary iron and a magnet. In the ordinary piece of iron, the atoms are all higgledy-piggledy so their individual forces cancel each other out. The overall effect is neutral. This is like the ordinary person who drifts about dissipating their energy on things that arise by chance. In the magnet, all the atoms are aligned so that their forces reinforce one another. The overall effect is to create a powerful force field that draws in other pieces of iron and magnetises them too. A person who lives by vow has a magnetised life. The Buddha was a great magnet. Many of the most talented people of his day went to see him and this is one reason why we still, twenty five centuries later, feel his effect upon the world.

A person who has vowed to free his country may meet with many setbacks. It will not be plain sailing. He or she may be defeated many times. They may sometimes fall into despair. Sometimes there will be triumphs. Much of the time it will be a long hard slog. Intense relationships will form from which will come the most intense emotions. It will not be secure, but it will be intense. It will not be an easy life. The person will not be able to count on success, and will have to be willing to sacrifice anything in the cause. They will, by making such a vow, have relinquished all the things that ordinary people cling to. Although they will have, in one sense, lost everything, they will, in a more important sense, have found the meaning of their life.

The Buddhist as Freedom Fighter

Jean Paul Sartre wrote, reflecting upon his time working in the French Resistance during the war, 'it was when we were most oppressed that we were most free.' The vow, in one sense, coerces every aspect of life yet, in a more important sense, it liberates. The more important sense is that it liberates a person from attachment to trivia. If a fighter in the French Resistance were required to give up her house she would do so without calculation of personal advantage, because it served the cause. The vow gives life coherence and meaning and frees the person to do things they would never contemplate in more settled times. The vow unsettles our old life.

The Buddha inspired people to become freedom fighters. He used the military metaphor a good deal. He had been brought up to be a warrior. He saw that the true victory was to conquer oneself rather than to conquer others.[20] The epitome of Buddhist speech, therefore, is the vow. There is a sense in which the Buddhist is a kind of freedom fighter. When we look around, we see that our land is indeed overrun by a powerful enemy. The soldiers of the enemy are greed, hate and delusion. When we are constantly being pushed around by greed, hate and delusion, we are everywhere oppressed and our lives remain on the flat horizontal plane. In this circumstance we may put our energy into distracting ourselves from the inauthenticity of our existence: a depressing prospect. Or, we may strike out for liberation.

The Story of Amida: The Buddha also used the metaphor of

creating a land which was free from the enemy: a Pure Land. When the Buddha talked about Amida,[21] he told a story, like a fairy story, of how, long long ago, Amida had formerly been a king called Dharmakara.[22] At that time, a Buddha appeared in the world. This Buddha was called Lokeshvararaja. Dharmakara immediately gave up his throne and went to meet this Buddha. He was so impressed by what he saw that he exclaimed, 'I announce that the aspiration of highest enlightenment has awakened in me. Please tell me what I should do to establish a pure land.' Lokeshvararaja said: 'You must already know what to do.' Dharmakara was confused and asked again for instruction. Lokeshvararaja then said: 'There is no vow which cannot be fulfilled!' And he went on to describe the perfection of the world perceived by a Buddha. Dharmakara was inspired to adopt the Noble Path without reservation. He then expressed his inspiration by proclaiming a list of forty-eight vows and a verse which ends, 'If these vows are to be fulfilled, let the universe shake and the devas send down cascades of heavenly flowers!' And according to the story this is what happened and Dharmakara in due course became Amida Buddha.

Dharmakara was enlightened by his own words just as much as by those of his teacher. The Buddha's words point us toward what we already know and give us the inspiration to do something about it. The attention of ordinary people is generally upon endpoints. Ananda, who was listening to this story, naturally wanted to know whether Dharmakara did become enlightened and establish a pure land. The story, however, takes place in mythical time and so is intended to be applicable to all people at all times. When the Buddha says, 'Yes, Dharmakara fulfilled his vow,' he means that we can fulfil our vows.

Knowing that 'There is no vow which cannot be fulfilled' is inspiring. The aspect of the story which is of immediate relevance to us is that it suggests that we must find the vow in ourselves. Dharmakara found his vow. We must find our own and speak it out just as he did. The idea here is that there is a vow already buried deep within each of us, a 'primal vow' which is just crying for an opportunity to come out. When Dharmakara saw the Buddha, he cried out his vow. This was not really a case of a pupil being given instruction which he then follows and so achieves something. It was a case of a person, Dharmakara, who had a pent up longing to be all that he could be, coming in contact with another person, Lokeshvararaja, who inspired him to get on with the task he already knew was right and necessary.

Enlightenment is not the end point. Enlightenment is the beginning. Dharmakara became fully alive as soon as he saw what needed doing. His speaking out his vow was his declaration of his new life. Similarly, Kondañña cried out with joy. Actually, the pure land of bliss exists as soon as a person starts to let their energy flow in this way.[23] What could be more blissful than knowing one is on the right path?

The point at which we get in touch with our own primal vow, our own deepest longing, and dare to believe that it is possible to live it, and make this the open declaration of our lives, is the turning point. That is when we shift from the horizontal to the vertical dimension. That is enlightenment. After that one is a freedom fighter. In this new life there are many ups and downs. That is what having a vertical dimension is all about. This is a passionate path: 'impassioned for peace' said the Buddha.

(iv) Right Action

Right Action is the fourth step to the Eightfold path. Right Action begins with self-restraint. This seems paradoxical to the person caught on the horizontal dimension. In the flat world, more means better. The more choice we have, the happier we think we will be. The more we get, the more pleased we think we will be. That is horizontal thinking. The spiritual path begins with giving some things up. On the vertical dimension, most of the things the flat-landers cherish seem like unnecessary baggage. How can one rise to the heights while carrying so much ballast? The enlightening effect of contact with a Buddha is due to the fact that the way such a person is in itself demonstrates that we too can be all that we have the potential to be. This does not mean that a Buddha goes round doing spectacular things all the time in a showy sort of way. A Buddha simply is what he or she is. They are not pretentious. They simply live out their truth unabashedly. They do not expect life to be easy, particularly. They do not expect praise all the time. There is hardship and affliction. These afflictions bring up many feelings. That is natural. We do not have to be overwhelmed, however. These invasions can be contained by the primal vow.[24] They put fire in our belly.

When we are guided by our aspiration to the highest purpose, every situation, good or ill, becomes more fuel for the fire. A meaningful life has this quality of working with whatever is to hand. It is not a matter of creating a particular state of affairs. An enlightened person might live in riches or in poverty, in a time of peace or a time of war. Nowadays, most of us live in what would have seemed extreme riches to our ancestors. Materially society progresses, but spiritually, the challenge is still the same.

Code of Conduct of a Buddhist

When a person becomes a Buddhist they make certain declarations. These are generally in the form of 'Refuges' and 'Precepts'. Different schools of Buddhism word them somewhat differently from one another but the essential meaning is much the same throughout the Buddhist world.

The Three Refuges: The Three Refuges are the first vow. They are a declaration that from now on one will take refuge in the Buddha, the Dharma and the Sangha. Buddha here means both the historical Buddha and the Buddha nature in oneself and all beings. Dharma means both the historically given teachings and the truth as it manifests in everything all the time. Sangha means both the great teachers of the past who are our spiritual ancestors and the community of all people in the present time who are following the Middle Way. By implication, this means that one will not take refuge in money, security, status and all the other things that constitute the worldly way. Taking refuge therefore, effects one's shift from what we have been calling a horizontal life to a vertical one. It means waking up and getting onto one's feet. The precepts are a summary of the moral code taught by the Buddha. Taking Refuge is to express one's primal vow. Taking Precepts is to say 'And this is going to make a difference to my life.'

The ethics of Buddhism are extensive. The Buddha taught at great length about what we should and should not do. None of this is new to us. It is simply important for it to be said and acted on. We already know that hurting people is not good. We already know that dishonesty and theft are not good. We know that improper sexual relations lead to no end of trouble. We know that consuming intoxicants does us no good and opens the door to behaviour we later regret. Right action means taking our life in hand.

Lokeshvararaja said to Dharmakara: 'You must already know what to do.' Even though this was true, Dharmakara still found it inspiring to hear it said. We need inspiration to show us what is possible. We know intuitively what is right, but we need help to actualise what we know or it just remains an unrealised potential.

Right Action is the fourth step of the Eightfold Path. It does not stand alone. Morality should not be taken out of its spiritual context. When we live from our vow, moral action is a natural corollary. Morality that is not rooted in right view, right thought and right speech, however, can rapidly degenerate into repression.

The Buddha's standard is simple and direct: Cease from harm; do only good; do good for others. Do not kill. Do not create the cause for others to kill. Do not collude in killings, either of people or of other sentient beings. Do everything possible to avert war. Do not support the meat trade. Do not take what should belong to others. Share. Use what you have for the good of the world. Be hospitable. Respect others. Do not engage in sexual relations without love and commitment. Be responsible in bringing new life into the world. Encourage one another in what is good. Speak truthfully. Speak well of others and not of their faults. Avoid all drugs and alcohol. Treat the world and all its creatures with loving care. Live simply and perform actions that benefit individuals, families, society and the natural world.

The Diamond Sutra: He lived what he taught. The Diamond Sutra is a discourse on profound wisdom. It may be considered one of the Buddha's most advanced teachings. The text deals with the attitude of mind of the bodhisattva who saves all sentient beings while not himself considering that he is doing anything special or out of the ordinary. The text begins like this:

> Thus have I heard. Once Buddha was staying at Anathapindika's Park near Shravasti along with many monks. One day, at the time for breaking fast, the Blessed One put on his robe, took his bowl, and made his way into the great town of Shravasti to beg for his food. In the city he begged from door to door according to rule. This done, he returned to his place and ate his meal. When he had finished, he put away his robe and his bowl, washed his feet, arranged his seat and sat down.

Then his disciple Subhuti approaches him and the dialogue unfolds. We might think that this paragraph is insignificant: mere scene setting. However, what it demonstrates is that the Buddha himself lived in exactly the same simple way as all his nuns and monks. He was a beggar. Right Action begins, therefore, with a radical simplification of life brought about by applying some basic moral precepts. This gives life a new vigour. Initially, this simplification frees up a vast amount of energy. If all that happens, however, is that a person then remains within a straitjacket of rules without significant outlet for the energy, the whole spiritual enterprise may turn sour.

The Mission of the Bodhisattva

Enlightenment is inspiration. Inspiration needs expression. Otherwise it is like breathing in without breathing out. The Buddha was a charismatic teacher who radiated a powerful field of energy. Those who start to be carried along by this energy, need to apply it for the good of the world. It is a path and a path goes somewhere. The bodhisattva-the enlightenment being-has the transformation of the whole world in view. This is not in the sense of an ambition. It is simply that once the energy is liberated it has to be used. It is like the fairy tales in which a genie has been trapped in a bottle for a thousand years. Once the genie is out of the bottle, it is very hard to put it back. Not only does the bodhisattva need to express their 'passion for peace', but the world needs such people.

Enthusiasm is infectious. The spirit of the world must not be allowed to curdle and die. Spirited people are needed to kindle it. We need a corps of inspired people who will work together for the betterment of the world. There is a great work to be done. What is needed is for us to demonstrate by our actions that a good big story is possible. Such was the Buddha's mission: that all the energy generated by the affliction that is in the world should be turned to the work of creating a path for the good of the many, for the happiness and well being of all beings.

There are plenty of people who do not know how to handle the hurt inside themselves who are devoting great energy and discipline toward some very destructive purposes in this world. If the effect of human presence on this planet is to be benign rather than malignant there is a great need for even more dedicated people to be working for the cause of great compassion. If we do not put ourselves forward to become part of the solution, we will remain part of the problem. More, however, is required than simple enthusiasm. It is important to find a place for ourselves in the big story, but it is also important to make sure it is the right big story. There are many big stories around that are cruel, greedy and built on delusions. They will carry us along if we do not find a firmer footing. War, for instance, is a big story. Many people remember the war as 'The best time of my life'. It was the best time because it was a big story that lifted them out of their little self and gave meaning to life. However, it was a terrible story and one we should not wish to repeat. Many people settle for little inconsequential lives precisely because the only big stories they know about are terrible ones.

V. Right Livelihood

Right Livelihood is the fifth step to the Eightfold Path. Right Livelihood is not just about how one earns one's money. It is about finding the lifestyle which will further the great work.

Enlightenment in Adverse Circumstances

Yelui Chu Tsai[25] was a young man of the Khitan race, living in Beijing in the early thirteenth century. This was the time of Genghis Khan's invasion of northern China. Beijing was under siege. Yelui studied Buddhism inside the city and went on an intensive retreat. In 1215 he experienced a breakthrough in his understanding of the Dharma. He felt completely inspired. A few days later the city finally fell to the Mongol armies. Yelui, was rounded up, along with many other talented young people that the Mongols thought might be useful to them, and marched back to Mongolia where he was brought before the Khan. Yelui was still radiant in the effects of his enlightenment experience. Genghis was struck by the young man's demeanour and even more by the fact that he was unwilling to speak in criticism of or disloyalty to his former Chinese masters, despite being in the presence of the Khan who had just defeated them and who had the power to have him executed.

The Khan respected fearlessness and loyalty and decided to take Yelui into his service. Yelui was appointed astrologer to the court. Very rapidly he was promoted to become Genghis' chief advisor. Yelui, an enlightened Buddhist, was now chief minister to one of the most savage characters of history. In this position he participated in all the affairs of state of the rapidly expanding Mongol empire. He always argued for the long-term view: if you destroy a city it will pay no taxes; if you decimate a country, it will not help you in future wars; if you practise unnecessary oppression, you breed rebellion.

There are probably several whole nationalities which owe their continued existence on this planet to Yelui's skill and human-heartedness. Yelui also used his position to protect Confucianism and Taoism. Genghis' empire became one of the first on earth to practise genuine religious toleration and the codes of law that came into effect under

Yelui's influence were far in advance of their time. Yelui did not become rich. When he died, he left behind only books, musical instruments and a cabinet of medicines. So it is not necessary to be a monk to carry out the Buddha's intention, nor should we despair of practising on account of adverse circumstance. In fact, we may surmise that it was facing of such adversity that drove Yelui's realisation so deep. If he had lived in a time of peace and ease, would he have had so meaningful a life? Perhaps not. The path to enlightenment begins with facing the reality of affliction.

It is difficult for a person to see the meaning of work unless they perceive the need. In our society things have become so sophisticated that it is often difficult to see the connection between what one does and the good that comes of it. Zen Master Dogen wrote: 'It is an act of charity to build a ferry or a bridge and all forms of industry are charity if they benefit others.[26]

Alienation in Works

However, it is difficult for many people in modern society to see their work as contributing anything useful or valuable, even when it does. People feel as though they are working simply for the money, for an extrinsic reward. Work, therefore, becomes a utilitarian or selfish necessity rather than an offering. The question of Right Livelihood thus becomes perplexing.[27] Not only is this true at the level of the individual. On a large scale in our society there is a concern with whether there is enough employment as though employment were something quite divorced from its outcome. There are demands for job creation. Really this is a very strange idea. The truth is that certain things need to be done if people are not to go hungry, if dwellings are to be built and maintained, if the sick are to be cared for and so on. In a simple society, the connections between work and outcome are much easier to see. If a village in the mountains in Vietnam does not have a school, the village people may get together and build one. They cut the bamboo to make the walls themselves. Everybody who is involved can see what they are doing and why it matters. The person sitting in county hall in a modern western city dealing with planning applications and fire regulations, processing advertisements to recruit education department staff, or writing reports, does not generally' have the same sense of involvement in something important.

Mindful Livelihood

Being divorced from the direct perception of need creates a deadening alienation in the worker. Really this is just another facet of the same Noble Truths that the Buddha described. Unless we have full awareness of the affliction that our work is designed to allay, we have little sense of meaningfulness in our occupation. Right Livelihood is not just a question of doing the right job. It is also a matter of consciousness of what the job really means.

The Amida Trust seeks to implement Buddhist principles in the contemporary world. Contributing to a debate with other members of the Trust, a participant recently wrote:

> One of the many questions I would be happy to discuss is 'mindful livelihood'. Since I am still engaged in the treadmill of work-pay-mortgage and have a completely irrational fear of being unemployable (I sometimes think no one will ever want to employ me because I am 'over' qualified), the question often arises for me of why it is that I do what I do and what should I do with the money that I earn and the time that I have. What is the right balance between what I give to myself and what I give to others (in terms of time, presence and financial assistance)? I have just recently bought a house, but is this a wise 'investment' (not in the sense of 'will it pay off financially', but in the sense 'perhaps I should have (a) given the money away to those who need it more than myself, (b) spent it on an Amida Therapy Training course and changed careers ... etc.)?'

This frank piece of sharing by a very sincere modern Buddhist highlights the difficulty. The modern person so often feels that they are on 'the treadmill of work-pay-mortgage' and that their work serves only to bring in necessary money. The analysis that Karl Marx made to the effect that the modern worker necessarily feels alienated from their work is not so far from the truth. Marx believed that religion served the function of keeping the workers from complaining about this situation. It was perhaps because Marx failed to see that religion has revolutionary potential that his efforts to bring about a social renewal have largely petered out. Historically, it is religious groups, on the whole, that have practised communism and the communalistic ethos is strong in Buddhism.

On Why it is that I do what I do we learn from our experience. This question of Right Livelihood has been one of the main motivators of my life. I gave up a career in accountancy, not because I did not think that accountancy is an honourable profession — it can be — but because at the time I was engaged in it, I was, via my employers, busy helping to make a number of armaments manufacturers and meat farmers more efficient, which did not sit easily with me as a pacific vegetarian. So I went and worked for an organisation called Children's Relief International which has since become part of Save the Children Fund. That gave me a taste for social work and I subsequently qualified as a social worker. At that time, Throssel Hole Priory Soto Zen Monastery was just getting off the ground, so I applied for and got a job as a social worker in Northumberland so that I could be close to the monastery.

Initially, when I became a disciple of Dhyana Master Jiyu Kennett Roshi three decades ago, she was part of an order in which there was a married priesthood. There were then, just after she settled in the USA, plans for a community of married ordained Zen practitioners. For a short time they had a centre in north California called Kannon Dell (after Quan Yin, the pre-eminent lay bodhisattva in Buddhist mythology). This community foundered for a time. Roshi's new order moved steadily in the direction of adopting the Chinese rather than the Japanese standard for its priests. Celibacy became the rule, and the venture in an ordained married sangha came to a halt. Although they had changed in their goals, I had not.

I am not alone. There is increasing interest in the west in the creation of intermediate status roles: more committed than an ordinary lay person but not a celibate monastic set up. The Tiep Hien Order of Zen Master Nhat Hanh is just one venture in this direction.

Regarding the dilemma, *what should I do with the money that I earn and the time that I have, I* would simply say, use everything for good purposes. The Buddhist lay person is not expected to give everything away. They are encouraged to use whatever they have for good ends. My wife Caroline and I make our house available. We use our time for things that help. We apply our minds to finding the best ways to advance the great work. We practise Dharma together and with others. We do our best. Often this is far short of perfect, but that is not the point.

As for, *I have just recently bought a house, but is this a wise 'investment',* to me, the answer to this question depends entirely upon what one then uses the house for. Hospitality is one of the foremost

Buddhist virtues. If the great work is to be advanced, there will certainly be a need for houses somewhere in it.

And *the right balance between what I give to myself and what I give to others* — for me, this has become an increasingly false dichotomy as I have become more deeply committed. I do not think in these terms. It does not seem like two different directions to me. Most activities could be said to have something of both in them, but it does not seem to be a useful way of approaching life to think that way. My needs are quite well met. I have faith, most of the time, that I will get by one way or another. I am actively engaged in many ventures. For myself or for others? It is all of a piece. It may be different if one spends all day doing a job that one does not think is part of the great work. If this is the case then I would say change the job. It might be replied that is easier said than done, but it is possible. I know. There is also, of course, a gradient, rather than a black and white contrast. Some work contributes more, some less, no doubt. Our task is to move toward the light, not to worry about where we happen to be starting from.

We need a transformation in our society and this needs to come from a shift of consciousness. In order to bring this about there will need to be people committed to a new view, a non-alienated and non-alienating approach to social life. We have to evolve a new form of post-industrial society in which what people spend their time doing is meaningful and is experienced as being so. The idea that market forces will create this situation of their own accord—Adam Smith's 'invisible hand'—is not totally wrong, but it is woefully inadequate.

While the socially approved motivations are variants of greed, competition and the delusion of status, the 'neutral' mechanism of market forces will simply go on reproducing these oppressive factors unrestrictedly. A full treatise on Buddhist economics is beyond the scope of this article, but if we are to understand Right Livelihood, we must begin again to experiment with forms of sharing, communalism, hospitality, generosity, and small scale non-alienating organisation. We must create an environment in which we work together toward purposes that matter and that further the emergence of a new kind of civilisation. We must avert the decay of community and the spread of civil strife.

(vi) Right Effort

Right effort is the sixth step to the Eightfold Path. The fire needs attention. It needs a supply of fuel and it needs constant care to ensure both that the fuel gets completely burned up and also that the fire does not get out of hand. Burning the fuel up means that there is no residue of regret from our actions. We do not come away thinking, 'if only I had . . .' Right Effort means intensity. 'You must be as audacious as someone trying to grab the eyebrows of a living tiger or to snatch the whiskers of a flying dragon.[28] Things come up in us. We should be immediately aware of what has arisen. The sixth step of the Eightfold Path is Right Effort or Right Diligence. You could call it tuning in because what is meant is the effort involved in noticing what is coming up in the mind. The traditional formula is that it is the effort:

(1) to prevent unwholesome states of mind from arising;

(2) to eradicate those that have arisen;

(3) to bring about wholesome states not yet arisen; and

(4) to sustain wholesome states already arisen.

In less traditional mode, we can say that it is the effort to face obstacles, achieve full awareness of arising feelings and commit ourselves to positive action. In the analogy of fire, Right Effort is the activity of tending the fire once it is underway.

The last three steps of the Eightfold Path are closely correlated with the last three Noble Truths. The sixth, Right Effort, is concerned with becoming aware of samudaya. We set ourselves to notice what comes up as it comes up. The seventh, Right Mindfulness, is concerned, as we shall see, with protecting the fire by the art of stopping, nirodha. The eighth step, Right Samadhi, is that subjective experience of the transformed life.

Awareness of Feelings Through Meditation

Right effort, in the sense that the Buddha used the term, is the means to the setting up of mindfulness. It means being observant of everything that arises. The practitioner notices what comes out of the storehouse of the mind as it emerges into consciousness. This is the awareness of feelings in the midst of feelings: the practice of meditation. It is for this reason that the Zen school, which places such central emphasis upon meditation, is considered to be the school of effort or 'self-power'. The Zen practitioner makes great effort sitting still upon his or her cushion. Zen can be very hard work.

In the practice of Zen meditation-called 'sitting zen'—one sits very still, in the lotus position, left foot on right thigh and right foot on left thigh, watching the mind. Whatever arises is noted and allowed to pass. The practitioner does not budge from the spot, no matter what comes up.

In Theravada Buddhism there is a similar practice called 'choiceless awareness' and most schools of Buddhism have something similar. In one sense, this is very hard work as anyone who has attended an intensive Zen retreat will testify. On the other hand it is simply a matter of sitting doing nothing. This is the interesting paradox. The challenge is to do nothing. We are so programmed to react to stimuli that not doing so requires the highest degree of self-mastery.

Right effort is a fine tuning of one's effort in cultivating the mind. The Buddha uses the analogy of tuning a stringed musical instrument.[29] If the strings are too taut or too slack, it will be impossible to make good music. If a person is either too idle or over-zealous, they will not live a truly spiritual life. The too zealous person is unnecessarily hard on themselves. This is the extreme of asceticism. The slacker lets their life pass without having really been there.

A Personal Experience: Recently I was ill. A particularly unpleasant attack of influenza sent me to my bed. Most of the other members of the family had already had their turn at falling prey to this malady and were, by then, on the road to recovery. I became very drowsy and slept a good deal which was to the good. When I was awake, my body was very uncomfortable. I took stock of pains arising in my legs, my arms, the back, the shoulders, the front of the head, the back of the head, the chest-just about everywhere, in fact. In this situation there was little to do but endure. I recognised an important spiritual opportunity, nonetheless. Sickness is a great leveller. While it lasts one is just as incapacitated whether one is the least of creatures or king of the world. 'One fever will quench your pride.[30] There is no opportunity to pursue any of the schemes that one's ego delights in. There is nothing for it but to be patient.

Patience[31] is one of the characteristics of a bodhisattva. The bodhisattva is somebody with a big mind, a big heart, a lot of capacity to take life in their stride and to reach out to people, both in joyful and in difficult times. Each contact with suffering is an opportunity for increasing our capacity for compassion and understanding. Many feelings come up when we are ill. It is not pleasant. Accepting each 'arising' and not allowing it to get caught by the ego which would sweep us away into self-pity or resentment, requires poise.

The Experience of Meditation: Sitting on the meditation cushion is an exercise in expanding one's capacity. We set ourselves to sit still for a time. Quite quickly the mind finds all manner of compelling reasons for us to abandon our seat. These impulses afflict us and we are inclined to struggle with them. It is very easy to become enmeshed in a sequence of thoughts that carries us away into a kind of unconsciousness.

The person who has done even a limited amount of such meditation soon comes to recognise the difference between the clear awareness of being in touch with here and now reality on the one hand and the dull opaqueness of a mind lost in thought or struggle on the other. In fact, one is only really aware of the latter on the point of waking up from it. As soon as the mind is entranced in this way, however, the spiritual path has been, at least momentarily, lost.

The Experience of Illness: We sit on our cushion by choice. Illness is not chosen, but the effort required, while lying on the sickbed, is similarly that of simply being there. When the body wants to sleep, sleep. When the body is awake, be awake. Being awake, I notice the arising of pain in some part of my anatomy. I notice what arises in my mind in relation to it. I am not carried away by what arises. All these things are ephemeral. It is not comfortable. It is not the end of the world. It simply is what it *is.* This is what is meant by effort.

Sometimes we think that simply to be would mean to live effortlessly and you will, indeed, come across descriptions of the enlightened state as effortless. We should be careful not to be trapped by the limitations of language here. Life without effort is a contradiction of terms. The enlightened state is not one of idleness. For a living being, effort is part of being. The finely tuned kind of effort that the Buddha has in mind, however, is a kind of pure awareness. Sometimes it is called 'effortless effort'. It is the effort of drawing our attention to what is there. We are all conditioned in a million ways by our experience. We do not live naturally. We live according to our programming. The effort needed to live the Eightfold Path is that of applying ourselves to seeing what is going on in us, as it is going on. We might think that simply to be would not involve us in any character-training, but in Buddhism we discover that only the developed character has the capacity simply to be.

Inner Stillness in Crisis

Everybody else is too readily panicked by circumstances to be able to remain calm in the midst of the whirlwind of life. The effort that it takes simply to sit still is a good measure of the extent to which we have become alienated from our true nature. So the practice of Right Effort, of tending the spiritual fire, of learning to sit still no matter what wind may blow up, is the basic training of the spiritual aspirant. It gives us the ability to operate effectively under fire, as it were.

When Mahatma Gandhi founded his first Ashram at Ahmedabad in 1915 he made it plain that the Ashram would be open to anybody who was willing to abide by its rules, irrespective of caste. A number of local people gave financial support to the project and it got off to a good start. A few months later an Untouchable family applied to join and Gandhi accepted them. Suddenly, all financial support to the project stopped. Gandhi had anticipated this possibility and told his companions that if the project were brought to a halt by this boycott, they were not to leave Ahmedabad, but were all to go and live in the Untouchables' quarter themselves. Money ran out. When the ashram treasurer came to Gandhi and said that they had nothing for the next month, Gandhi became quiet and simply said again, Then we shall go to the Untouchables' quarter.' A few days later an unknown donor arrived and made a gift of 13000 rupees -enough to support the main expenses of the ashram for many months and so the project was saved.

The world needs spiritual leadership. The kind of leadership which is not necessarily a matter of stirring preaching from pulpits, but is rather to be found in the kind of stillness that Gandhi evinced in this moment of crisis. In a life like his there were innumerable such moments. They all called for inner stillness. Gandhi had his fire under control. The great Buddhist teachers had the same quality. If we are going to change the world, the peace starts within ourselves.

(vii) Right Mindfulness

Right Mindfulness is the seventh step to the Eightfold Path. Mindfulness really means remembrance. The point that Buddha is making in setting these two items, Effort and Mindfulness, next to each other in the Eightfold Path is exactly the same point as he is making with the Second and Third Noble Truths.

We meet with affliction. We react. The first moment of this reaction is beyond our control. There is therefore no shame in either perceiving affliction or in the first impulse of response. It is at the next step that the will can come into play. Effort is required to notice what is happening. That is the sixth step of the Eightfold Path. As soon as we notice our reaction we are faced with choice. If I feel angry, say, what will I do with this feeling? To be mindful is to keep in mind. This operates in two different ways. On the one hand, what has arisen is contained and not allowed to spill out in a destructive way. On the other hand, wholesome states are cultivated. New ones are planted in the garden of the mind and we help them to grow and flourish.

Cultivating of the Wholesome Stage: The juxtaposition of the wholesome and the unwholesome is the means to hand for managing the mind. If an unwholesome state, like greed, say, arises, it is no use resorting to denial. Pretending that it is not there really just leaves it outside conscious control and is an abdication of responsibility. Besides, denial-dishonesty-is a second weed alongside the first one. What is needed is to bring up a wholesome state alongside it. We learn to love our greed, but not to indulge it. We learn to love the child within us and we do not let the child get burned. We can look after our greed, or our grief, or our hate, or whatever it is in an appropriate way.

Living in the Present: Another important aspect of mindfulness is to live in the present moment. A freshness of perception is possible to us that most people only rarely experience. Enhanced awareness of the immediate natural environment is a very powerful healing influence upon the wounded psyche. To gaze at the setting sun, to touch a flower, really to hear the bird sing or to feel the weight of a stone in your hand is to come in contact with reality in a way that little else can match. In such perfect moments, we are fulfilling our purpose in being here.

Keeping in Mind a Mantra: Mindfulness is more, however, than acute awareness and observation. It is also the practice of faith. To be mindful is to keep in mind. What is to be kept in mind is some sense of the vertical dimension, the larger story, the possibility of transcendence. It does not really matter a great deal what form of words one uses for this. In Buddhism a great many formulas exist to serve this purpose. Such formulas are sometimes called *mantras.* A mantra is a word or phrase which is held in mind to protect the mind from unwholesome influences and to cultivate awareness of the higher purpose. A mantra is a spell. Mostly people live in a kind of trance. The mantra is a spell which breaks the trance.

Mindfulness is taking refuge. This phrase is congruent with the imagery of nirodha, already discussed, which implies taking shelter. Refuge is kept in mind by means of a phrase which expresses commitment. Thus the word 'Buddha' alone may be used. Another very commonly used formula is *Namo Amida Buddha,* or some variant thereon which is the mantra of Amida Buddha. Another is *Om Mani Padme Hum* which is the mantra of Quan Yin, the Bodhisattva of Great Compassion. These phrases are invocations. They conjure up particular associations in the mind and so act as cultivation tools of great power. For Buddhists, the story of Amida Buddha is the big story *par excellence.* It symbolises what the spiritual path is all about, namely the salvation of all beings and the creation of a pure land of bliss where all are able to progress to the fulfilment of their highest potential. To recite *Namo Amida Bu',* therefore, is to affirm one's connection to the biggest story of all. It helps us wake up to our real reason for being here. Simply to keep a particular mantra in mind for as much of the day as possible and to recite it out loud frequently may be sufficient formal practice. The effect of this practice should, however, also be visible in the way we live our lives. To say the words is important, but then they must be put into practice.[32]

Kindling the fire of Enlightenment: Mindfulness which is simply a technique can aid inner healing, but it does not go very deep. The really deep mindfulness comes out of conviction—inner change—a kind of catharsis. Enlightenment is a cathartic experience: an inner cleansing. There is no way that we can ensure that such an experience will occur. Often it is triggered by something unexpected. Sometimes it comes out of a feeling of contrition. Sometimes out of gratitude or grief. The emotional element is never missing. The fire of enlightenment is kindled from the fire of our passion. It is only strong authentic emotion that has the power to penetrate to the core of our being. No intellectual procedure will ever reach deep enough.

After deep cathartic experience we may be surprised to look around the familiar sights in our environment and see them as if for the first time. In a major enlightenment experience, however, the condition of brilliant reality can persist for weeks or even months. Perhaps there are some accomplished practitioners for whom it is their all-the-time experience. Perhaps the Buddha was one such.

What happens on enlightenment experience is unbelievable. The environment around one turns to fire and ice. Everything is transformed by an unexpected radiance and the feeling of Tightness is complete. Even though the initial effect fades after a few weeks or months, one never returns to how one was before. Something is different inside. This 'something different' becomes a constant companion.

Mindfulness, then, does not just mean awareness. It is not just a matter of becoming scientifically objective. Mindfulness means to recollect our true purpose and deeply and fully live all that entails. Remembering that there is a higher, nobler life available than that of subjection to base desires and ego maintenance, frees us to be happy. We rise above the inevitable afflictions that flow into our lives. If we have something more important to base ourselves upon, then the hurts and assaults of circumstance do not have such effect. It is not so difficult to know what we should be doing and to do it. For a long time we have been seeking an impossible immunity to the ups and downs of life, and have found ourselves repeatedly capsized as a result. Our efforts have been misdirected. There is, however, another better way that does work.

To have Freedom from being oppressed of what others would say: Much modern psychology asserts that values are completely relative and that we should (sic) get away from a life based on 'shoulds' and 'oughts'. The germ of truth in this idea is that many people are seriously oppressed by their fear of what others will think about them. To live our lives just trying to appease other people is surely a recipe for disaster. On the other hand, realising this should not send us to the opposite equally pernicious extreme of thinking that it does not matter what we do. It is very obvious that some courses of action do have destructive consequences. Some stories are bad stories and it is important that we do not get recruited by them.

Enjoy the little things and saster cravings: The Third Noble Truth tells us that the fire of craving is mastered by bringing to mind what is lovely and satisfying. Yesterday I was walking into town on my way to meet a friend. I was walking quite slowly. There was no hurry. I had left in plenty of time so that I could fully experience walking. It was getting dark and there was a slight chill in the air. It was very pleasant to notice the other people all going about their business.

Overhead, the sky was turning a deep ultramarine blue as the light faded away. My footfall on the pavement was gentle. I enjoyed my walk. To act mindfully means to remember to enjoy the simple things that we do.

To enjoy walking enriches our lives greatly since, unless we have serious health problems, we all spend some time walking. Take my hand and we will walk together. We will look at flowers and smile at passers-by. Our walking will be like a beautiful song, a melody that flows on without haste. The point is not to get somewhere. The point is to enjoy something lovely and satisfying. If we do so, then we are fulfilling the higher purpose.

Mindfulness, therefore, is to be happy. It is not so much the case that by overcoming craving we will overcome dukkha and find release from suffering. It is more the case that the energy provoked by dukkha will be continuously converted into bliss. We do not like to admit that we have been wrong or that we have made ourselves suffer unnecessarily. When we are first around happy people who practise mindfulness, we may start to hate them! 'Why are they smiling all the time?' we say to ourselves viciously. We find ourselves picking fault with all sorts of trivial things in an attempt to discredit what they are doing. All this, however, is really quite unnecessary.

Kondanna was made so happy by the Buddha's teaching because it was attainable. He felt happy straight away and he felt confident that he would be able to continue to practise in this way. He would not forget. We have the option to be happy if we choose. The cost may be that we have to give up everything that we have used to defend ourselves with in the past, but this is a small price.

(viii) Right Samadhi

Right Samadhi is the eighth step to the Eightfold Path. Here we come to the quintessence of the Buddha's teaching. It is very easy sometimes to begin to think that what the Buddha was describing was a kind of dry psychological technique. In fact, what he offered was a transformative vision opening on to an authentic life. It is the fate of most innovators in the realm of psychology and spirituality that those who count themselves the truest disciples enshrine the founders' innovations without ever realising the source of the innovativeness. When the Buddha said that he had no teachers, he was not being literally accurate in a historical sense. He had at least two important teachers. He had gone beyond them however, to the point where he saw for himself. He was authentic. He hoped his own disciples would become authentic in the same way, but he could not do it for them.

The Hindrances to Enlightenment

The Buddha's cousin, Ananda, accompanied him everywhere he went and was present at every talk he gave. Ananda knew all the Buddha's teachings off by heart. However, Ananda was not enlightened during the Buddha's lifetime. From this we know that the enlightenment of Buddhism is not a matter of learning or believing a doctrine. It is an experience. The very extent of Ananda's knowledge may well have obstructed his final enlightenment. Twenty years after the Buddha died, Ananda was enlightened after a dialogue with the Buddha's successor, Kashyapa. It is said that Ananda was eventually able to enter the room of the teachings by appearing in a very small body and entering through the keyhole. We can imagine that Ananda must have attracted a great deal of envy, being always at the Buddha's side. Ananda was handsome and his brilliant intellect was greatly admired. As soon as the Buddha was dead, however, the other monks called Ananda before them and found a long list of things to criticise him for publicly.

Pride and Intellect' as a Barries to Enlightenment: Pride in intellect stands in the way of enlightenment. It also attracts envy. Ananda had to chop down the mast to which he had metaphorically nailed his colours, to eat humble pie and genuinely assume a smaller form before he could enter the storehouse of the Dharma. In the story of Ananda, as recorded by Dhyana Master Keizan, it says: Ananda was fond of intellectual learning, and that is why he had not yet truly realised enlightenment. Shakyamuni, on the other hand, cultivated energy, whereby he attained true enlightenment. Many of the people whom the Buddha called to be his disciples were already people with a considerable achievement and following of their own. He called people who had their own light. The aim of Buddhism is not to produce replica Buddhas, but to enable each person to find their light.

On the other hand, for people who have achieved something there is always a danger of pride in achievement. Like Ananda, they may have to find a small body to replace their inflated one. Kondanna was able to understand directly because he had no difficulty in admitting he had been wrong. By the night of his enlightenment the Buddha-to-be was almost completely alone. He had left everyone. Only the milk maid Sujata was still supporting him. Indeed, it was she who had brought him back from the brink of total isolation. It was she, in fact, who showed him the thing he really needed to see.

Buddha Towards Enlightenment: We read of the Buddha's four sights-the invalid, the old person, the corpse and the wandering holy man-that inspired his going forth from the palace. The sight of Sujata's unaffected kindness was the fifth and most important sight, the one which precipitated enlightenment. Everybody else only showed the Buddha actions which were tainted with greed, hate or delusion. There was always an ulterior motive. The most elevated spiritual practices were still just ways of getting something and so were tainted with greed to get salvation, hatred for the flesh and the delusion of ego. Sujata was on the way to give her offering to the forest gods when she saw Gautama in need. Without a second thought she gave him the food. It was an authentic action. That was what he had been looking for all these years.

Authentic Vision Received by Buddha on Enlightenment

Action free of greed, hate and delusion became the weapon with which Gautama knew he could combat all the afflictions of the world. This was then deeply confirmed for him on the night of his enlightenment by a vision. He had the vision of Mara's host being transformed into celestial flowers. Samadhi means concentration or rapture and refers to the vision of the purpose of life. Mara represents everything that tends toward death. Mara's representatives are all the instances of inauthentic action that crowd our ordinary lives. Newly armed with the confidence of realness, Gautama saw them all transformed into opportunities for spiritual growth.

This vision was the samadhi of the Buddha. The basic meaning of the term samadhi is concentration, but to say that the samadhis of Buddhism are concentrations is a bit like saying that the works of Shakespeare are books: true, but not revealing the quality that matters. The Buddha's enlightenment is a visionary experience. There are many indications in the texts that visionary experience was not simply something that happened to the Buddha once and for all. The transformative vision is part and parcel of the Buddha's practice on-goingly. The modern person may also be inclined to read the passages about the Buddha's converse with gods and *devas* in this way.

Enlightenment changes what a person sees and experiences. The fact that modern people prefer to call visions 'inner' experiences is simply a contemporary convention of speech. A vision is certainly not experienced inwardly. When a person sees a god, the god stands before them and is in no sense 'inner'. The Buddha often talked with gods, visited heavens and preached to assemblies which included celestials as well as humans. These details are not just a superstitious addition by the Buddha's biographers. They are an indication of the quality of his lived experience. To be enlightened is to talk daily with the gods and to visit the heavens at will. In the Mahayana approach to Buddhism, many of the texts are simply attempts to give some indication of the nature of these visionary experiences. There is something which is passed down outside the scriptures that will never be available simply through reading books. But the books, nonetheless, are replete with indications of its nature for those willing to risk themselves.

The eighth step of the Eightfold Path, therefore, is authentic vision. What distinguishes an authentic vision from any other sort of vision? An authentic vision is inspired, not constructed. There is no point in trying to have the same vision that Siddhartha had, for instance.

Authentic Vision Received by Queen Vaidehi on Enlightenment

There is a sutra called *The Sutra on Visualisation of the Buddha of Infinite Life.*[33] This includes the story of Queen Vaidehi. Vaidehi was the consort of King Bimbisara, a patron of the Buddha, who had been overthrown by his son Ajatashatru. Queen Vaidehi had interceded between her husband and son and had tried to thwart Ajatashatru's intention to starve his father to death. In consequence she herself was imprisoned without food to await the same fate. In the extremity of her distress she addressed a prayer to the Buddha who she knew would be preaching at a place not far away.

The Buddha and two of his disciples appeared to her: 'he was the colour of purple gold and was seated on a lotus flower of a hundred jewels. He was attended by Maudgalyayana on his left and Ananda on his right. Shakra, Bramah, the guardian gods of the world and other devas were in the air about him. Scattering heavenly blossoms like rain, they paid homage to the Buddha.'[34] Such was the first vision she saw. Then she again falls into tears. She laments her fate and particularly the fact of having a son who is so wicked as to be in process of murdering both his parents. She feels a point of kinship here with the Buddha since he, the Buddha, has a cousin, Devadatta, who has tried, unsuccessfully, to overthrow his leadership of the Buddhist community and assassinate him. She longs for a better world in which one will not have to 'hear evil words or see wicked people'. She agonisies over the question that so many human beings have asked in so many circumstances: What have. I done to deserve this? She does not, however, do so in the spirit of asserting her innocence or of rhetorically expressing her indignation. She kneels down to repent.

At this point there is a flood of light in which she sees Buddha lands in every direction. She has an authentic vision. The vision emerges from the depth of her emotion (samudaya) which, in turn emerges from the extremity of her plight (dukkha). From amongst these varied Buddha lands, she chooses the Land of Amitayus, the Buddha of Infinite Life, the Western Land of Utmost Bliss. This is the story of how Vaidehi found peace and meaning in the time prior to her death.

It is easy to see the moral of the story. There is not much worse that can happen to a person than to be stripped of everything important and slowly destroyed by their only child, while knowing that the same thing is happening to the spouse they love. This must rank at the extremity of torments. Yet in such a place, Vaidehi, could find peace through samadhi which became possible through her faith in the Buddha and her willingness to let go of any sense of self-righteousness. Abandon self and have faith. The vision was triggered by an act of contrition. If a woman of no particular spiritual advancement could, simply through faith, reach such a point in such an extremity, then, in principle, there is nothing that the human spirit cannot surmount.

Means to Have on a Vision: The Sutra then goes on, interestingly, to describe a means to have a vision approximating to that which Vaidehi experienced. This description is a kind of do-it-by-numbers version which begins with 'Visualise a sunset ...' Such an approach provides us with a means to achieve a replica via the imagination of Vaidehi's experience. Of course, there is as much in common between this replica and Vaidehi's original as there is between a real tree and a plastic model of one. The purpose of giving a description of how to achieve such an imitation is simply to inspire people to go and find their own vision.

We can read about the vision received by Gautama on the night of his enlightenment, or by Queen Vaidehi prior to her death or, indeed, the visions of Mary the mother of Jesus or of the saints of any religion. Such visions are part of the conversion experience of all spiritual traditions. What matters is not so much the content of the precise vision-whether we see angels or bodhisattvas, for instance-as whether the vision is authentic. Does it come from the true spontaneous source? Does it show a true path? Is it both inwardly and outwardly authentic? If so, then it is a genuine spiritual experience. The real measure of such an event, however, is not in the experience itself but in the effect it has upon the life of the person.

The Visionary Experience: A spiritual teacher will have no end of people come along and describe all manner of visionary experiences. Sometimes the motive of the teller is simply to impress, in which case the telling, let alone the vision itself, is inauthentic. Sometimes the person genuinely wants to know what the meaning may be of what they have experienced. The test of validity, however, always lies in the lived life. If a vision leads a person to a more unified, wholesome, constructive and kind way of living, then the vision is sound. If it leads to estrangement, artificiality, pride or confusion, then it is delusion. Not all visions are the same. The Buddha specifies right samadhi in the Eightfold Path because there are also wrong samadhis that do no good.

Samadhi, right or wrong, has great spiritual power. Wrong samadhi may lead to the most terrible consequences. This kind of negative enlightenment is what leads to a person becoming a megalomaniac. Hitler and Stalin certainly had their visions and great powers of concentration. The results, however, were terrible. The highest and the lowest lives are inspired by visions.

The Necessity of Suffering

Looking back at the Four Noble Truths and to draw out some implications. We have seen that this is a four-step teaching. The first step is the *inevitability of affliction*. The second is the *naturalness of the arising of passion in us when affliction is perceived.* The third step is to do with the *art of mastering that passion and rendering it useful*. The fourth step is the *path or purposeful life* which unfolds for a person who has mastered their passions in the manner prescribed.

Common Misconceptions Regarding Buddhist Teachings

We have seen that this interpretation leads to the rejection of many commonly made assertions about what the Buddha is supposed to have taught. In particular we have rejected all of the following propositions:

1. That the Buddha taught the cessation of suffering.
2. That dukkha refers primarily to mental suffering.
3. That the doctrine of rebirth is an essential implication of the Four Noble Truths.
4. That passion and enlightenment are mutually exclusive.
5. That buddhas are not sentient and do not have personal problems after their enlightenment.
6. That the Eightfold Path leads to enlightenment.
7. That attaining enlightenment necessarily takes a long time.
8. That the Second Noble Truth is about the cause of suffering.
9. That the Third Noble Truth is about bringing the cause of suffering to an end.
10. That nirvana means extinction.

We have seen that enlightenment is a cathartic experience which occurs when a person deeply realises the extent to which they have been running away from reality and surrenders to this possibility of living a full and meaningful life in whatever circumstances they find themselves. Such an awakening reveals to them the compelling desirability of the 'noble life' and the corresponding necessity for the form of self-training implied by the Third Noble Truth. Such an experience stops persons in their tracks. They discover a deep *inner stillness,* the mind becoming like crystal clear water and, as the inner interference drops away, they experience the world around them transfigured in radiance. This experience is called perceiving a 'Buddha land'. It occurs naturally to many people on their deathbed. It is available, however, at any time. The sincere spiritual seeker is likely to have at least one and sometimes several profound experiences of this kind which will stand out as landmarks in their lifetime. Although such major awakenings fade, they leave the person significantly changed. Their personality has been magnetised. Their energies are more unified and their senses more acute. Life becomes more vibrant in every way.

Such a transformation inspires inner stillness and outer purpose. *Nirvana* is the mastery of passion by sheltering it from ego-driven disturbance. *Enlightenment* is cathartic, both because it involves a climb down by the ego and because it involves an opening up to the impact of affliction not just upon oneself, but upon everyone. It most characteristically manifests as a profound sense of relief: a 'who would have thought that everything is so wonderful just as it is!' One abandons one's individual concerns as one becomes carried up into the bigger story. In this bigger story both bliss and suffering have their proper parts: a time to be born and a time to die.

The practices of Buddhism which have come down through the centuries are very compatible with the interpretation of the Dharma that we have arrived at. In fact they are, in a number of respects, more compatible with this interpretation than with that of the traditional commentaries. It may well be that the Buddha's message has been better preserved in the practices than in the texts. Bodhidharma's assertion that the truth is handed down outside the scriptures may be more literally true than many have realised.

Suffering as Strarting Point to Spirituality

The Buddha, we know, rejected the extremes of self-indulgence and of asceticism. However, there is no doubt that he also encouraged a number of practices that are in the nature of privations. Fasting every day after noon is not designed for comfort. Begging for your food and going hungry if none is forthcoming would be a strange practice, if the aim were to eliminate suffering from your life. The Buddha did intend that his followers experience a certain amount of adversity daily, some suffering was part and parcel of his prescription. He did not encourage extremes, but he did encourage a degree of experimentation with fasting and with reducing the amount of sleep taken, and generally advocated an attitude of stoicism in regard to unanticipated misfortunes that might arise. Even the fundamental practice of meditation involves sitting in a posture that most people find uncomfortable until they have been doing it for many years and staunchly resisting every impulse to move. This practice is a training in fortitude as well as a quest for insight.

If we consider once again our summary of the Four Noble Truths at the beginning of this chapter, we can see why this might be so. If the Four Noble Truths are to be read in this A leads to B leads to C leads to D fashion, then it is clear that the desirable goal, namely the path, depends upon the initial factor, namely affliction. No suffering, no passion. No passion, no mastery thereof. No mastery, no path. From this perspective we can see affliction, dukkha, not as an unavoidable evil, let alone as the curse of mankind that the path is designed to eliminate, but rather as the essential starting point without which the spiritual life would not be possible. Suffering is necessary.

Suffering as Fuel to Inner Five

The analogy used throughout this study is that of fire. This analogy was given by the Buddha himself. The spiritual life consists of mastery of the fire. Affliction is the fuel for the fire. If I need a fire I need fuel. The disciple of the Buddha tends his or her inner fire. This fire needs a supply of fuel. The fuel is the affliction in the world. In order to get the fire to the appropriate heat there needs to be the right amount of fuel. Sometimes this is readily to hand. The circumstances of life provide plenty to work on. The koan arises naturally in daily life, as they say in Soto Zen temples. Sometimes, however, the practitioner needs to feed the fire. This is where a modest degree of privation or ascetic practice starts to make sense. Not too much and not too little. This way of thinking is completely congruent with the behaviour of serious Buddhist practitioners as we witness it in the world today and as it has no doubt always been. The practitioner tends the inner fire. This is not the way toward enlightenment. It already is enlightened action. Keeping the fire healthy and under control is a matter of balance — a middle way. In this process, affliction plays an essential part.

This way of thinking suggests a significant shift of perspective. Buddhism is not about eliminating suffering. It is about noble living. Noble living requires the existence of a moderate amount of hardship. This has nothing to do with punishment and even less to do with indulgence. It is simply a practical matter. Suffering is no longer a problem, it is absorbed into the noble life by being given its proper role which is to feed the spirit. This is only possible for a person who has learned the art of husbanding passion. The Third Noble Truth is thus the vital one in terms of practice. The Third leads to the Fourth, not *vice versa.* If the traditional interpretation were correct they would probably have been said the other way round.

This rehabilitation of suffering in the scheme of things does not mean that Buddhists seek martyrdom. That would be an extreme. Martyrdom is a rare phenomenon in Buddhism. There have been Buddhist martyrs, but they are not particularly glorified. Suffering is not glorified.

It has its place, that is all. Suffering is not a measure of our virtue and is not to be carried to extreme. That would, the Buddha says, be quite counterproductive. When the bodhisattva vows to take all beings with him to the other shore, what is implied? If the other shore is not the abolition of suffering in the world, what is it?

Interpretation of Buddhist Perspective

What sort of world are these Buddhists trying to create? The Buddhist ideal is summed up in the two key adjectives 'noble' and 'true'. A Buddha is not someone who has no personal problems and certainly not someone who never suffers. To stand on the other shore is not so much to go to a different world as to see this world from a different standpoint. The bodhisattva is not saying, 'This world is terrible: let me help you escape from it.' He or she is saying, 'Come and look at it this way and you will have a quite different and much more satisfactory experience.'

When Shakyamuni was enlightened he is supposed to have said, 'When I am enlightened, all beings are enlightened with me.' What can this mean? When a person is enlightened, they see the noble truth of others' lives as well as of their own. The person who practises Right View, listens deeply and, like Quan Yin, hears the cry in the person's heart. When we perceive a person in this way, we cannot help respecting them and seeing how that cry expresses a deep and universal truth. We see how their life naturally grows out of their struggle. We see that they are also noble in their own way and that their truth is unfolding as it should.

It was because the Buddha had this *deep empathy* for everyone who came to see him that he was able to be such an effective teacher-or perhaps nowadays we might say, therapist. He could tune into the other person's world. *When we look at a person superficially,* we may find much to criticise. We cannot see why they act in such a foolish way. If only they would see sense and realise what we can see so clearly. *When we look deeply,* however, we get a quite different feeling for the person. The reason for their foibles becomes clear to us. We can imagine ourselves being just the same, had we been born with their temperament and brought up in their circumstances. The deeper our empathy, the more readily comes our positive regard.

While we think that enlightenment is total freedom from suffering, we cannot understand the meaning of the Buddha's statement, since the world is undeniably full of suffering beings. If we abandon this idea, however, and see that affliction has a necessary part to play in the sustenance of the noble life, this obstacle dissolves. Buddha was not saying, 'When I am free from suffering all beings are free from suffering.' He was saying, 'When I am noble and true, all beings are noble and true.' A noble person is one who sees the nobility of others-the courage of ordinary lives. To see what is noble and true in others is not a product of seeing our own perfection so much as of seeing our own humanity. That the Buddha was enlightened does not mean that he ceased to be human — quite the contrary.

The noble life which the Buddha advocated is not dependent upon circumstances. It is easier if we have noble friends to inspire us, of course, and we are advised to seek them out, support them and associate with them, but even if we finish up, like Yelui Chu Tsai, surrounded by butchers, it is not impossible.

What Buddha Did after Receiving Enlightenment

Soon after his enlightenment, the Buddha realised that he had a job to do. He changed completely. Instead of becoming more and more isolated, as he had done before, he became more and more engaged. He reached out to everybody. He brought forth love. He touched and inspired many people. He still had a few personal matters to sort out-like his relationship with the wife and the child he had deserted, the father he had defied and the mother for whom he mourned-so he got on with that, too. He started a movement which in due course needed a lot of practical organisation. A big story began to unfold that is still running. It had its ups and downs. There was a time when the Buddha so despaired of the wrangling going on among his followers that he left them to it and retired to the forest for a few months. But his capacity to keep his nerve even in this situation paid off, just as it later did when attempts were made to split the order and even to assassinate him. He had his fire and he had it under control.

If we want to see a Buddha land, it is right here. This is the mandala-the big story. Nobody is excluded save by their clinging to their own little story. The gates of enlightenment are wide open. It is not a matter of accumulating merit. We are all quite acceptable to the Buddhas already, just as we are. It is not a matter of eliminating grief. Grief is essential to the process of spiritual growth. It is not a matter of solving all our personal problems. They are grist to the mill. There is therefore nothing to be done other than to wake up and embrace reality and opportunity. If we do wake up, however, it is apparent that there is something to be done after all. This something is what the Four Noble Truths describe: the necessity of affliction; the value of passion; the sheltering of it from the ego wind; and the unfolding of the noble life: Right View, Right Thought, Right Speech, Right Action, Right Livelihood, Right Effort, Right Mindfulness, and Right Samadhi. If we follow this path, the birds will sing for us more clearly than before, the sunset will be more magnificent and the peace in our heart will be fathomless.

In sum we can say that the Four Noble Truths provide the basis of Buddhism. They constitute a practical approach to the problem of life. They define spirituality as the art of converting base passion into noble engagement. On the one hand, we live in a wonderful world in which there is the potential for immense satisfaction. On the other hand, at every turn we come up against obstacles, restrictions, limits and frustrations. Both these things, called 'sweet spaces' and 'bitter spaces', *sukha* and *dukkha,* are inherent aspects of existence. We live in a world which is both bliss and affliction. This is the transformative vision offered us by the Buddha. It contains no element of escapism, nor is it dependent upon belief in a particular system of metaphysics. The poetry necessary to convey the workings of the spirit should not be reified into dogma. It is available to people of all races, classes, genders, and creeds. It is capable of translation into the language of different social groups because it speaks to the basic existential condition of our lives which transcends all membership categories.

Limitation is part of life and is actually the part that gives it meaning, tenor, vitality and aliveness. The affliction we come up against is the basis of our consciousness and our capacity for awareness, without which bliss would not be possible. This is the basis of the problem which constitutes our main spiritual work. We do not get everything we want. Affliction is part and parcel of life. In response to affliction, feelings arise. These feelings are capable of making our life hell. They are also an energy source which can be harnessed to put us onto a constructive life path.

The Buddha describes what such a path would be like. It would be one in which we were free from self-defeating views. Our heads would not be full of either arrogance or self-deprecation. Our thoughts, speech, and action would all flow together in a constructive way to create a positive lifestyle. This in itself brings a major degree of peace of mind. This mental cultivation however, can be carried further through right effort and mindfulness, until we enter into the condition of mind that Buddhists call samadhi: a mind which naturally finds the bliss in all the eventualities of everyday life and so enables us to fulfil our purpose in being alive.

This purpose is to contribute our energy to the creation of 'the pure land of bliss' which is not an other-worldly paradise entered after physical death, but a here and now state of psychological maturity, through which the obstacles we meet are, like the army of Mara in the Buddha's enlightenment vision, continuously transformed into celestial flowers.

It provides a workable basis for a therapy of individuals, families, societies and the strife torn world in which we live. Affliction is both individual and collective and so is our response to it. Buddhism is not just a private affair. It is the so very simple yet all embracing basis for the creation of mature lives and civilised societies in which harmony and awareness prevail. The tendency to distance ourselves from the realities and hard work of life is understandable, but it cuts us off from our bliss.

We have seen how it emerged from the life experience of Siddhartha Gautama who lost his mother at birth, who was driven by inner anguish to wander the world, who drove himself to the limits of endurance, who was moved to enlightenment by an act of kindness, who dedicated the remainder of his life to the service of others, and who came to be called the Buddha, but who called himself 'the one who had been there'.[35] He went to see for himself. His self-chosen epithet carries the implication of having found out the hard way. The Buddha was a human being and a person with a passion. The momentum of that passion is still very much alive today.

Here we have the essence of his whole message. If we are moved by its spirit, simplicity and power, then we may follow his final advice to 'seek out our own salvation with all diligence' and to 'go forth for the benefit of the many'. The world needs people who have become fully alive. The cost of becoming so is high in that it involves facing the inherent insecurity of our situation and realising that we do not stand alone, but are indissolubly involved in the fate of one another and of the world around us. The potential reward is, however, commensurate with the cost.

REFERENCES

1. See, for instance, W. Mikulas' article 'Mindfulness, Self-control and Personal Growth', in M. G. T. Kwee (editor) *Psychotherapy, Meditation and Health* (East-West Publications, 1990), pp. 151-65.
2. The phrase *Namo Amida Bu* is called the *nembutsu* (in' Japanese) which means Buddha-impulse or Buddha-thought. It is an expression of the fact that there is an impulse toward buddha-hood occurring in us every moment. It is also an expression of faith in the saving power of the Buddha's aspiration to help all beings.
3. See Nhat Hanh's manual of guided meditations *The Blooming of a Lotus,* Beacon Press.(1993), for many similar valuable reflections.

NOTES

1. See an interesting discussion of this point in chapter 7 of D. Taylor's *The Healing Power of Stories* (Gill & Macmillan, 1996).
2. The Buddha's great energy is apparent in passages such as the following: 'Then the blessed One instructed, inspired, fired and delighted the lay people of Pataligama with discussion of Dharma until far into the night.' *Mahaparinibbana Sutta, Digha Nikaya* 2.87.
3. There is good discussion of the Buddha's view about views in Phra Khantipalo book, *Tolerance* published by Rider (1964).
4. The method which the Buddha is advocating by his idea that 'all views are wrong views' is similar to the approach of those western philosophers who call their approach phenomenology. Edmund Husserl, the German philosopher who founded phenomenology, showed how, if we are to see reality, we have to 'bracket' our preconceptions. Husserl was originally a mathematician. In algebra variables are put in brackets to keep them apart from the other operations that are going on. This idea is not to be confused with 'moral relativism' which is the idea that all views are right views, an idea that the Buddha, like any sensible person, rejected.
5. The "*Lenrin* is a collection of two-line poems compiled by Toyo Eicho (142.9-1504).
6. The *Bhaddekaratta Sutta, Majjhima Nikaya* 131 provides a clear account of the unburdened mind. There is a translation by Bhikkhu Nanananda published by the Buddhist Publication Society (1973} under the title *Ideal Solitude.*
7. The comparison with catching a snake is found in the *Alagaddupama Sutta, Majjhima Nikaya* 22. There is a translation by Nyanaponika Thera published by the Buddhist Publication Society (1973) under the title *The Snake Simile* and another by Thich Nhat Hanh, *Thundering Silence: Sutra on Knowing the Better Way to Catch a Snake,* Parallax Press (1993).

8. A review of the background to the Zenrin can be found in Alan Watts's *The Way of Zen,* Penguin (1957). The symbol of the ox finds expression in a well known series of Zen paintings with accompanying poems known as the 'Ox Herding Pictures'. The latter can be found in translation in *Zen Flesh, Zen Bones* by Paul Reps (Penguin, 1957) and in Katsuki Sekida's *Zen Training: Methods and Philosophy,* published by Weatherhill (1985).
9. *Dhammapada* V3-5. Many translations of this favourite Buddhist anthology are available. Juan Mascaro's translation, *The Dhammapada: The Path of Freedom,* published by Penguin (1973), is easily obtained, as is Eknath Easwaran's *The Dhammapada,* published by Arkana, and there are many others,
10. Fay Weldon, 'The Enemy Within', *Prospect,* February 1997, p. 15.
11. *The Biographical Scripture of King Ashoka, Taisho* 50, 2043. A translation by Li Rongxi is published by the Numata Centre (1993).
12. R. E. Buswell *The Zen Monastic Experience* published by Princeton University Press (1992), p. 155.
13. For these observations I am indebted to Stephen Batchelor's book *Alone With Others,* Grove Press (1983).
14. The name Amida derives from the Sanskrit *Amitabha* meaning 'Buddha of infinite light' and *Amitayus,* Buddha of infinite life. Amida, in one or other of these forms appears in a great many Buddhist scriptures. Quan Yin, the Buddha or bodhisattva of great compassion is a female form in Chinese Buddhism but in India was male. His (or her) Sanskrit name is *Avalokiteshvara.* These two figures show the interaction between different spiritual traditions in their attempt to represent archetypal forces. The origins of Amida probably owe something to the Persian god of light, *Ahura Mazda,* and the female form of Quan Yin something to Marian Christian influence.
15. This is a quotation from the 25th chapter of the Lotus Sutra. This chapter of the Sutra is often treated as a scripture in its own right.
16. C. R. Rogers, The necessary and sufficient conditions of therapeutic personality change', *Journal of Consulting Psychology* 21, (1957), pp. 95-103.
17. This sentence is taken from the Buddhist scripture *Digha Nikaya* 1.4.
18. An account of this famous incident is given by Z. Isigami in his book *Disciples of the Buddha* published by Kosei (1989), pp. 18-19.
19. *The Sutra of Hui Neng.* See Price and Wong 1969, part II, pp. 11-12.
20. This point is made repeatedly in the Buddha's teachings. See, for example, *Dhammapada* v.44-45 and 103-105.
21. See the Larger Sutra on Amitayus, the Longer *Sukhavativyuha Sutra.* The Pure Land Sutras have been translated and extensively commented upon by Hisao Inagaki.
22. The name Dharmakara means one for whom the Dharma is their fixed purpose in life. There is a probably intentional parallel between this name

and the word *samskara* which indicates having the mind fixed to things other than Dharma.

23. In chapter one of the *Vimalakirti Sutta* we are told that the spirit of the bodhisattva path beginning with wholeheartedness is the pure land. See the translation by Burton Watson published by Columbia University Press (1997) pp. 26-30.

24. Or, we could say, they are contained by the grace of Amida which is within and all around us. It is this sense of the omnipresence of this saving power that makes Buddhism a religion. This should not, however, be thought of as something supernatural, but rather as a dramatic way of describing one of the basic laws of the universe. This is not magic. It is simply the way reality works.

25. Yelui lived 1189-1243.

26. Jiyu Kennett, *Zen Is Eternal Life,* Dharma Publishing (1976), p. 160.

27. The progressively increasing divorce between the activities of life in modern society and their intended ends was perceived and elegantly documented by the sociologist Georg Simmel who pointed out how this trend leads to an atrophy of the capacity for acts of will. See Peter Lawrence's translations of selections from Simmel's work, *Georg Simmel, Sociologist and European,* published by Nelson (1976), especially the section called 'The Style of Life' on pages 173-2.2.1

28. This saying by the Korean Dhyana Master Kusan is reported by R. E. Buswell in *The Zen Monastic Experience,* published by Princeton University Press (1992.).

29. *Anguttara Nikaya 6.55.*

30. 'You are a mortal man ... today you live, and tomorrow you are dust; one fever will quench your pride': spoken by Romanus, emperor of Constantinople to the invading Bulgarian king Symeon. See, D. Obolensky, *The Byzantine Commonwealth.* London: Car-dinal (1974), p. 153

31. Zen Master Nhat Hanh, in a lecture given at Plum Village, France, in September 1996, suggested that we should translate the term *ksanti* by the word 'capacity' since it indicates our capacity to cope with the vicissitudes of life in a constructive way.

32. *Namo Amida Buddha* literally means 'I call upon (or I take refuge in) the Buddha of Infinite Light'. Sometimes it is said *na-mo-a-mi-da-bu'* with just six syllables. *Om Mani Padme Hum* is-all but untranslatable. A rough rendering would be 'hail to the jewel in the lotus', but with these phrases what is important is the stringing together of a number of individual words or syllables each of which has a wealth of resonance and association. Many other mantras exist, each generally associated with the invocation of one of the many figures who, in Buddhism, personify the qualities of enlightenment and help us realise them in ourselves. For simplicity, the discussion in this book has been limited to Amida and Quan Yin, two of the best known and most loved.

33. The Visualisation Sutra is one of the Pure Land Sutras already referred to in note 5 to chapter 2.3.
34. H. Inagaki, *The Three Pure Land Sutras*, published by Nagata Bunshodo (1994), p. 320.
35. The name the Buddha used for himself is *Tathagata*. Opinions vary about its correct translation. I have taken it as implying 'been there' but it could equally mean 'thus gone', though what the implication of the latter term might have been in the context of his time is guesswork.

4

Spiritual Perspectives of Natural Environment

The Power of Nature

The five great elements that constitute are environment are evoluts of prakin, they are distinctive elaborations of primal energy. Every element has its own life, form and location, but all are interconnected and interdependent. These five elements according to Hindu scriptions are—space, air, fire, water and earth. Throughout the centuries, humans have had a love-hate relationship with the natural environment within which we live. We depend on nature for the air we breathe, the water we drink, the food we eat, the materials and resources to clothe and shelter our bodies. From the natural environment, we obtain the resources to be transformed to meet our material needs. In turn, the natural environment serves as the repository for our waste products. The aesthetic beauty of nature in all its forms is a source of spiritual and cultural inspiration as well as emotional sustenance. The powerful forces of nature are also the harbingers of destruction and death. A less benevolent nature brings the droughts, floods, fires, hurricanes, and earthquakes against which humanity is virtually powerless. There are aspects of nature, living and non-living, with which contact is dangerous for humans. Nature reminds us in innumerable ways of our mortality, that individual lives are but preciously brief journeys in time.

> And God said, Let us make man in our image, after our likeness: and let them have dominion over the fish of the sea, and over the fowl of the air, and over the cattle, and over all the earth, and over every creeping thing that creepeth upon the earth. (Genesis 1: 26.)

While this biblical passage has often been used to justify human beings' right to dominate and exploit the natural world, history has taught us much about the complex and intricate 'web of life' that humankind has woven with the natural environment (Wall 1994; Worster 1994). It has been a tale, in one respect, of humankind's struggle to survive with nature; in another, of humankind's search to find spiritual meaning and purpose of life within Nature. It is this quest that will be explored in this study on the spiritual dimension of global environmental change. Thomas Berry writes of the urgent need for modern societies to find a 'new story', a new sense of the universe, to take humankind into the twenty-first century.

> This universe itself, but especially the planet Earth, needs to be experienced as the primary mode of divine presence, just as it is the primary educator, primary healer, primary commercial establishment, and primary lawgiver for all that exists within this life community. The basic spirituality communicated by the natural world can also be considered as normative for the future ecological age. (Berry, 1988:120)

Berry is not alone in his call for fundamental and transformational changes in humankind's currently dysfunctional relationships with the natural environment at spiritual, cognitive and behavioural levels (Carroll, Brockelman, and Westfall, 1997; Hull, 1993). There are many 'old stories'—stories forgotten, distorted, or marginalized within modern Western societies—which can provide guidance during these times of change. One can also learn from many newer stories informed by an environmentalist ethic.

History of Nature Worship

Nature worship has been present in traditional and primitive societies since five immemorial. Archaeological evidence of prehistoric hunter-gatherer and agrarian societies depicts an era when humans strove to live in harmony with nature which was all-powerful (Eisler, 1987). From that time to the present, nature and its forces have been personified as deities to be worshipped and revered. In the horticultural societies of south-eastern Europe in the period 7000 to 3500 BCE, female deities represented the natural fertility and generative power in nature (Gimbutus, 1982). In many aboriginal and Native American societies, Mother Earth or the Great Mother was regarded as 'the beginning and end of all life on earth' (Walker, 1988: 339). The reverence for nature deities was/is present in the spiritual traditions of shamanism, pantheism, paganism, and Hinduism (Wall, 1994). In the ancient cradle of western civilization, the fertile Mother Goddess or Earth Goddess took the mythological forms of goddesses such as Isis (Egypt), Ishtar (Mesopotamia), Demeter and Gaia (Greece), Ceres (Roman) who were regarded as the creators and sustainers of life within the cosmos. However, in time, these ancient urban civilizations challenged the belief that humans needed to be subservient to an all-powerful and sacred nature.

Advent of Humanism

In ancient Mesopotamia, humans claimed a divine right to tame the 'monstrous chaos' of nature while classical Greek humanists (Aristotle, Plato) and the early Stoics claimed that the resources of nature were there for the exclusive use of humankind (Hughes 1975; Wall 1994). The emergence of anthropocentrism (human-centredness) in spiritual, religious, and philosophical thought on humankind's relationship with nature would be central to Judaeo-Christian edicts for humans to 'be fruitful and multiply' as well as to 'have dominion over every living thing that moveth upon the earth' (White, 1973). Even though the universe was still seen as organic, living and spiritual, humankind's place in that universe was regarded as separate and above that of nature and all that was nonhuman (Merchant, 1980).

In western societies, the 'ascent of man' over nature was advanced by seventeenth-century Enlightenment philosophers (Bacon, Descartes Newton, Hobbes) as essential for scientific and social progress (Ehrenfeld, 1978; Merchant, 1980). Mechanistic materialism, rationality and scientific reductionism became the ideological cornerstones of the Scientific and Industrial Revolutions of western societies (Bramwell, 1989; W. Fox, 1990) Human intellect and will would produce the science and technology to master and manage a chaotic nature. Ehrenfeld describes this ideology as the 'religion of humanism'.

> The core of the religion of humanism: a supreme faith in human reason—its ability to confront and solve the many problems that humans face, its ability to rearrange both the world of Nature and the affairs of men and women so that human life will prosper. Accordingly, as humanism is committed to an unquestioning faith in the power of reason, so it rejects other assertions of power, including the power of God the power of supernatural forces, and even the undirected power of nature in league with blind chance. (Ehrenfeld 1978: 5)

Although environmental exploitation and degradation have always been one consequence of human activity, the current nature, scale, and rate of humankind's impact on the planet is unprecedented in our history. Humankind can no longer ignore or deny its role in creating an ecological crisis which touches all aspects of the natural environment. Fundamental to the industrial-materialist-scientific world-view has been the exorcism of a nature which is organic, living, and spiritual. Instead, nature is regarded and treated as a machine in the service of humankind. In this mechanistic hierarchical world-view, both persons and non-human nature are objectified and valued only in utilitarian instrumental terms (as inputs or consumers of production) rather than for any intrinsic or spiritual value (Devall and Sessions 1985).

There is no doubt that the modern industrial age has been a period of unprecedented scientific and technological achievement. Members of western industrialized societies enjoy the highest material standard of living, economic prosperity, and physical security known to date. And yet, as we approach the twenty-first century, this same science and technology is also revealing how this course is endangering the long term survival of humans and other entities on this planet (Brown 1991; Daly and Cobb 1994).

There are many in science and industry who are working to find scientific, technological, and industrial solutions to environmental problems (Hawken, 1993; Schmidheiny 1992). There are also many in government, communities, and the environmental movement who are working to find political and institutional remedies at local, national, and international levels (Sitarz, 1993; World Commission on the Environment and Development, 1987). However, there are others who speak of finding spiritual or religious ways to make peace with the planet which humankind has abused (Berry, 1988; Gottlieb, 1996; Hull, 1993). As written by Matthew Fox (1988-89: 50), 'Mother Earth is in jeopardy, caused by the anthropocentrism of religion, education, and science during the past three centuries. A new beginning is required, centred on the sacredness of the planet.'

Transformational changes of the kind which many believe are required cannot happen or endure without going deep into the realm of values and beliefs—the spiritual consciousness of humanity. Developing a sustainable relationship with the environment requires a deep awareness not only of the biophysical environment within which we live but also of one's spirituality (Schwarz and Schwarz, 1987).

Spiritual Traditions Based on Nature

Nature-centred spiritualities have existed since before the advent of modern human civilization. Although the early Greek and Roman deities have been relegated to the status of mythology, the reverence for nature-based entities or deities remains in many spiritual traditions. Two are shamanic spiritual traditions (specifically, in indigenous cultures), goddess spirituality and neopaganism.

Shamanic Spiritual Traditions

For over 20,000 years, shamanic spiritual traditions have guided indigenous peoples throughout the world. In this holistic and integrative tradition, 'spirituality is not a religion with a fixed set of dogmas but rather, spirituality pervades and infuses all forms of existence—human, animate and inanimate' (Frost and Egri, 1994: 7). It informs the view that all that exists in nature is living and sacred therefore deserving of respect and care (Halifax, 1990).

There are three assumptions which underlie the shamanic belief system: (1) the existence of numerous coexisting and interpenetrating worlds of experience; (2) the need for holistic balance amongst these worlds; and (3) that change is a continuous transformational process (Egri and Frost, 1991).

In regard to human relationships with the natural environment, most important is the need for holistic balance between the ordinary world of material reality, the symbolic and social world of human societies, and the spiritual world of the universe. To ignore or deny the spiritual, cultural, emotional and physical interconnections between humans and the rest of creation is not only disrespectful but also self-destructive.

> Several different traditions talk about four or five different worlds and say that the Creator made all these worlds with one simple law: that we shall be in harmony and in balance with all things, including the sun. And time and again people have destroyed that harmony; we have destroyed that harmony. And we have done it again needlessly. Unless we bring about that balance again, this is our last chance. (Brooke Medicine Eagle, Crow Nation shaman, as cited by Halifax 1979: 91)

Shamanic spiritual traditions identify multiple sources of spiritual and practical information which can assist in healing a destructive imbalance between human societies and the natural environment (Egri and Frost, 1991). However, the transformational process of healing out-of-balance relationships is not the sole responsibility of the shaman but one shared by all human beings. Native American spiritual teachers often tell of the importance of 'place' to maintain one's spiritual connection to the earth. The Native American land ethic teaches that spiritual connections to the earth are born from the heightened awareness and identification that comes from staying in one place long enough to experience, learn from and care for the spirit of the place one is in (Kelly, 1993). The assumption of care and responsibility for the environment within which one lives thereby becomes natural and inevitable.

Goddess Spirituality

Goddess spirituality also celebrates the cycles of regeneration, diversity within unity, and humans' essential connectedness with nature (Nicholson, 1989). The image of Gaia, the Greek goddess of the earth, has been adopted by those who envision the world as a living spiritual organism within which life is "holistic, systemic, symbiotic, connective and participatory' (Spangler, 1993: 93). This in turn has informed the practice of Gaian meditations and rituals to rediscover one's connections with nature (Seed, Macy, Fleming, and Naess 1988). While in one respect contemporary Goddess spirituality represents a resurgence of pantheism, neopagan spirituality (or the Old Religion) remains truer to the rituals and practices of ancient Celtic and indigenous societies (Gimbutus, 1982; Merchant, 1992).

Pagan Spirituality

Pagan spirituality (or Wicca) is based on the core concepts of: *immanence* wherein everyone and everything in nature has inherent value and power; *interconnection* among the human and natural worlds; and *integrity of* thoughts, words, and practice (Starhawk, 1990).

In summary, nature-centred spiritual traditions such as shamanism, goddess spirituality, and neopaganism emphasize human beings' physical and spiritual connections with an animate and sacred nature. As an ecological belief system, they teach of the need for respect for all that exists in the natural environment as well as the need for transformational change to regain holistic balance and harmony in the cosmos.

Asian Religions and Philosophies Connection with Nature

The ancient Asian religions and philosophies of Hinduism, Buddhism, and Taoism offer much to ponder concerning the spiritual and metaphysical connections between humans and nature.

Hinduism

The Hindu religion teaches that earth is the Universal Mother with the rivers and earth being personified as goddesses and the winds and fire as male deities (Chapple, 1993; Klosterrnaier, 1989). Nature is the spiritual guide and teacher in a religion which has codified environmentally beneficial practices in its rituals, proverbs and stories (Gadgil and Guha, 1992). For example, respect and even reverence for other species is based on Hindu beliefs that the Supreme Being is incarnated in various species and that humans themselves can be reincarnated as animals and birds. In Hindu religion, trees and plants are seen as possessing divine powers and thus are to be protected from destruction (Dwivedi, 1996).

Buddhism

The Buddhist principle of reciprocity and interdependence is based on the belief that 'all events and beings are interdependent and interrelated' in a universe which is 'a mutually causal web of relationship' as in the image of the Jewel Net of Indra (Kaza 1993: 57). Buddhism proposes that *nirvana* is a higher ultimate spiritual reality and truth which transcends all else. The 'Middle Way' of Buddhism teaches the importance of simplicity in living, that attachment and craving for material wealth and goods stands in the way of liberation (Badiner, 1990; Schumacher, 1973). The Buddhist principle of the truth of personal experience emphasizes the importance of experiential learning, practising the 'art of mindfulness' to resensitize oneself to hear, see, and feel the web of life rather than limiting oneself to abstract ideas of reality (Kaza, 1993; Martin, 1993).

Buddhist relational ethics teach that moral actions are those which are informed, sensitive to and respectful of all beings (sentient or not) within interdependent relationships. In both Buddhism and Hinduism, violence to other beings within the biotic community is immoral and given the precept of interdependence, self-destructive. The principle of non-violence is also central to both traditions' concept of *Dharma* which has been interpreted to mean 'moral duty', 'right action' and 'the truth about right living' (Bhatt, 1989'). The Buddhist and Hindu doctrine of *karma* (fate or destiny) also teaches the importance of taking responsibility for moral action in all of one's relationships.

Taoism

Belying its early roots in Shamanism, Taoism teaches of the need for balance with nature and the spirit world (Palmer, 1991) with the relationship between humans and the environment being one of holistic interdependence, interpenetration and interaction. Furthermore, interference with the delicately balanced natural order will lead to upset and disorder (Lau, 1963).

Lao Tzu, the sixth-century Chinese philosopher wrote of the *Tao* as being the creator of the universe as well as 'the way' followed by all that exists in the universe (human, animate, and inanimate). Rather than being the product of a transcendent God, the *Tao* is the infinite energy of the cosmos—a totality and unity of being and becoming which 'embraces every thing, large or small, in the universe and imparts a unity of relationships in our environment' (Cheng, 1986: 355).

In Taoism, reality is conceived in terms of *Tao* (the way of transformation and change), *sheng-sheng* (life creativity), and *ch'i* (the vital force or energy that creates, connects, flows, and balances forms and experience). *Yin* and *yang* are the two dialectical polarities of *ch'i* which are complementary and together, represent the fundamental forces in the universe which cause the cyclic process of change (Callicott and Ames, 1989; Lau, 1963). Whereas yin is part of *K'un/The Receptive* associated with earth, death, mother, and being devoted and yielding; *yang* is part of *Ch'ien/The Creative* which is associated with heaven, life, father, and strong action in the universe (Wilhelm, 1977). When there is a dynamic balance between *yin* and *yang,* harmony within and with the natural environment is attained. When there is imbalance working against the natural flow of the *Tao,* then there is disharmony and harm. As related in the *I Ching* (Book of Changes), *T'ai* or Peace is achieved when *K'un* (earth) is above *Ch'ien* (heaven) for this is 'a time in nature when heaven seems to be on earth. Heaven has placed itself beneath the earth, and so their powers unite in deep harmony. Then peace and blessing descend upon all living things ... In the world of man, it is a time of social harmony' (Wilhelm, 1977: 48). Alternatively, *P'i/Standstill* (stagnation and decline) results when *Ch'ien* is above K'un for during these times, 'Heaven and earth are out of communion and all things are benumbed. What is above has no relation to what is below, and on earth confusion and disorder prevail' (Wilhelm 1977: 52).

> In harmony with the Tao
> the sky is clear and spacious,
> the earth is solid and full,
> all creatures flourish together,
> content with the way they are,
> endlessly repeating themselves,
> endlessly renewed.
> When [humanity] interferes with the Tao,
> the sky becomes filthy,
> the earth becomes depleted,
> the equilibrium crumbles,
> creatures become extinct.
>
> Lao Tzu (1988: 39)

One important lesson to be learned from the I *Ching* concerns the means by which 'peace' or 'standstill' are achieved and maintained. Peace, prosperity, and order do not happen automatically but require continuous efforts and a creative attitude on the part of humans. Otherwise, peace will change and disintegrate into stagnation and decline. In contrast, times of standstill or disorder do not change of their own accord to peace and order. While not lasting forever, human effort is required to end stagnation in order to regain peace and order. Thus, purposeful action is needed to attain peace and harmony, whereas lack of action results in standstill and disorder.

Balance with Nature

Asian religions and philosophies teach that there is an intricate web of cyclic relationships within and between the spiritual and material realms, the human and the non-human environment. Asian philosophies tell us that: "The environment is a perfect mirror of man' (Cheng, 1986: 367). If humans abuse or misuse the natural environment, then the environment responds in a harmful way. Obversely, if humans act in ways which preserve life and enhance health in the environment, then the environment responds in kind Peace and harmony in the natural order requires active and creative effort on the part of human beings. Whether it is through disciplined meditation personal observation and reflection or through community practice, such action needs to be informed by the principles of compassion, nonviolence and the 'virtue of non-contention' (passive resistance). The restoration of harmony and balance with nature can only be achieved through subjective and objective understanding as well as self-transformation in all aspects of human existence—spiritual, intellectual, social, and material.

Monotheist Religions Views on Links of Human with Nature

Judaic, Christian, and Islamic theologies teach that there is one omnipotent God who was the creator of all in the universe (Armstrong, 1993; Rodwell, 1994). Within that universe, there is a hierarchy of existences with a transcendent God, human beings, and nature. Biblical scholars have identified that this God (Yahweh, the God of Moses and of Israel) is a pure spiritual being in a realm apart from the forces of nature and matter (Armstrong, 1993). Human beings are a 'microcosm of the universe' in that they have both bodies (belonging to the earth) and souls (akin to God). The human soul is the divine gift of the intellect which permits wisdom to raise humans above the flawed and mortal realm of animals and plants in nature. In turn, nature is conceived of as wilderness which man is commanded to master, subdue and transform in accordance with God's laws. The strong anthropocentrism (or more accurately, androcentrism) of the traditional Judaeo-Christian tradition notwithstanding, there have been alternative Christian views of the relationship between humans and nature.

Christian Views

St Francis of Assisi has been identified as one who 'tried to substitute the idea of the equality of all creatures, including man, for the idea of man's limitless rule of creation' (White, 1973: 28). Early Celtic Christianity also advanced a view of the mystical intimacy of human, nature and the divine in which there was a human partnership with the natural world (Hull 1993) The Christian mystics of eleventh-thirteenth-century Rhineland Germany (Hildegard of Bingen, Mechtild of Magdeburg, Meister Eckart, and Julian of Norwich) wrote of a creation-centred philosophy premised on a holistic and blessed cosmos in which a loving and compassionate God was both mother and father, the earth was holy and there was a unity of body and soul (M. Fox 1994; Merchant 1992). More recently, Matthew Fox has adapted this western mysticism to formulate an ecological creation spirituality while

Christian theologists John Cobb and David Ray Griffin propose an eco-theology based on an ecosystems perspective (Cobb and Griffin 1976). In these ways, nature is conceived of as the sacred creation of God which ennobles the human stewardship of nature and all its creatures.

Islamic Views

In Islam where there has been less of a separation between the sciences of nature and religion, the Islamic principle of unity *(al-tawhid)* links humans with nature (Nasr 1968). In the Qur'an, the principles of *khalifa* (trusteeship) and *akhrah* (accountability) underlie Mohammed's edicts to humans: 'He hath appointed you his viceregents in the earth' (Sura 35); 'And commit not disorder on the earth after it hath been well ordered' (Sura 7). (Rodwell 1994) As stated by Farhadi (1989: 6-7): 'No religion on earth is so clearly vocative against destruction of domestic and wild life and against decimation of the God-granted natural wealth.' Thus while humankind is the master and custodian of nature, their role is to care for and protect God's creation.

Judeo Christian Views

Although the traditional Judeo-Christian ethic for the domination of nature has often been criticized as anti-ecological (Kinsley 1994; White 1973), some of this may be attributed to narrow interpretations of scriptural writings which deny the need for the stewardship of nature (Nash 1989). As observed by Wall (1994: 192): The Judaeo-Christian concept of original sin may have given rise to the doctrine that, far from being sacred and worthy of reverence, the Earth is a fallen realm that deserves little care.' The Very Reverend James Park Morton (1993: 124), dean of the Episcopal Cathedral of St John the Divine in New York City observes that, 'We forgot that *dominion* has its root in *dominus*—dweller in the house or caretaker, the Latin equivalent of the *oikos* in ecology.'

In response, the importance of humankind's ecological stewardship rather than domination and exploitation has led modern theologians to focus more on biblical passages such as the following.

> The earth dries up and withers,
> the world languishes and withers,
> the heavens languish together with the earth.
> The earth lies polluted under its inhabitants,
> for they have transgressed laws,

violated the statutes,
broken the everlasting covenant.

(Isaiah 24: 4-5)

Recent developments within contemporary western religions demonstrate that divine concern for all of creation (and not just for humans) is not incompatible with Judaeo-Christian theology (Daly and Cobb, 1994; McFague, 1993). There are those who are working towards an ecological Judaism which integrates environmental principles into Judaic laws and rituals (Lerner 1994; Swartz 1996). Both Protestant and Catholic religious leaders and theologians have made the ecological crisis a central concern in their writings and meetings. Most noteworthy has been Pope John Paul II's papal addresses on ecology: 'Peace with God the creator, peace with all of creation' in December 1989 (Beyer, 1992) and "The ecological crisis: A common responsibility' message for the Celebration of the World Day of Peace on 1 January 1990 (Pope John Paul II 1990). While not totally abandoning their anthropocentric worldview, mainstream religions are endeavouring to create a theology which advances the 'integrity of creation' for both environmental and social justice (Beyer 1992; Gottlieb 1996).

Spirituality and Environmental Change

Spiritual traditions; and religions provide alternative ways of perceiving and understanding the world. To the degree that spiritual belief systems influence individual and collective values and beliefs, they create the ideational motivation to change the ecological status quo. That said, there still remains the question of whether transformational changes in the human psyche are enough to inspire changes in human action. Pessimists would highlight the numerous contradictions between espoused spiritual values and ecologically destructive behaviours of various cultures throughout history (Callicott and Ames 1989; Timm 1993). They would also point to the power of deeply rooted social and economic institutional systems to resist transformational changes of the type which are proposed (Dobson 1995).

> Human identity and personal fulfillment somehow depend on our relationship to nature. The human need for nature is linked not just to the material exploitation of the environment but also to the influence of the natural world on our emotional, cognitive, aesthetic, and even spiritual development.
>
> (Kellert, 1993: 42)

As proposed by the biophilia hypothesis which seeks to explain humans' instinctual and learned responses toward the natural environment (Wilson, 1984), humans' spiritual, mental, and physical well-being is innately and intimately connected to nature. The biophilia hypothesis also proposes that humankind's evolutionary experience (past, current, and future) is deeply dependent on the well-being or health of all aspects of the natural environment. However, ecopsychologists contend that before the earth can be healed, one must first heal oneself (Roszak, Gome, and Kanner, 1995). Developing a sense of ecological perception or awareness is the first step towards overcoming the destructive myopia and denial which is at the foundation of the modern ecological crisis (Sewall, 1995).

There have been several ways in which the spiritual communities and religious have been forces for environmental change. Some of there have been discussed in the following pages.

(A) Environmental Activism of Spiritual Communities and Religions

> Earth-based spirituality provides both an imperative toward action in the world and a source of strength and renewal of the energies that often burn out in political action.
>
> (Starhawk, 1989: 176)

As expressed by Starhawk, environmental activism is not inconsistent with neopagan or goddess spirituality. During the 1980s, members of Starhawk's Matrix affinity group organized political demonstrations to protest California's Lawrence Livermore Laboratory's research on nuclear weapons (Merchant, 1992). They employed Wiccan rituals, chants and spells throughout this large-scale non-violent protest which resulted in numerous arrests (at one point in 1983, 1,000 persons were detained for 15 days).

Approaches of Nature Centred Spiritual Traditions

In terms of the impetus and logic for political activism for environmental change, believers in neopaganism and goddess spirituality differ from those in shamanic communities. Shamanic spiritualities discourage such organized political activism. The approach of the Shamanic spiritual tradition is to look into one's own culture, community, and environment for spiritual guidance and to offer only examples of how one can live according to nature-centered spiritual principles (A. Smith, 1993). The uniqueness of each place's natural environment and culture requires that those who live there develop their own ways, stories and rituals (Gaard, 1993). Even so, this has not precluded indigenous peoples from joining together to address common environmental problems. One example is the Indigenous Environmental Network, an alliance of fourteen North American indigenous grassroots organizations formed in 1991 to share information on environmental problems that face their communities and to work for environmental protection and sovereignty on their lands.

The Buddhist Concept

Kaza (1993) recounts a number of arenas of Buddhist environmental education and activism. For example, the Buddhist Peace Fellowship (founded in 1978) has worked within the peace and environmental movements to enhance environmental awareness as well as engage in non-violent anti-nuclear protests. Buddhists Concerned for Animals have worked to stop the inhumane treatment of animals in scientific research as well as in factory-farms. Buddhist values have been identified as being closest to that of an environmentally sustainable society (Badiner 1990). Schumacher (1973) adapted the Buddhist concept of 'Right Livelihood' to develop a Buddhist economics for environmental and industrial change. Specifically, he proposed an environmental ethic based on liberation through simplicity and non-violence; attaining ends with the minimum of means; and holding a reverent and non-violent attitude to all beings and entities in nature. In this way, Buddhism provides a blueprint for individual and collective efforts to effect environmental change.

Initiatives by Mainstream Religions

Mainstream religions have also endeavoured (singly and in collaboration) to translate their theology into practice and policy for ecological change at local, national, and international levels. Christian and Jewish organizations, seminaries, and divinity schools have initiated numerous environmental projects and task forces. Among the most notable is the National Religious Partnership for the Environment which includes the US Catholic Conference, the Coalition on the Environment and Jewish Life, the National Council of Churches of Christ, and the Evangelical Environmental Network to provide educational programmes, advocate environmental legislation and policies, and organize environmental projects and action campaigns. Other noteworthy initiatives include the Friends Committee on Unity with Nature (Quakers), the Eco-Justice Project of the Center for Religion, Ethics, and Social Policy at Cornell University, the Commission on Stewardship of the National Council of Churches of Christ, and the North American Conference on Christianity and Ecology (Washington, DC, and San Francisco). The Eco-Justice Project of the United Methodist Church has set out specific principles for Christian stewardship of the environment. Other Christian denominations which have environmental projects include the American Baptist Churches, Lutheran Church, Presbyterian, United Methodist Church, the United Church of Christ, and the Reformed Church in America. (Gottlieb 1996; Merchant 1992)

The Jewish ecological movement has identified several means for recovering an ecological consciousness (Lerner 1994). This includes: developing a code of eco-kosher practices relating to consumption (avoiding food produced with chemical pesticides, paper from old-growth forests, products derived from the exploitation of non-renewable resources and polluting technologies) and investment; observing *shabbat* as a seventh year of rest for the land; and celebrating *sukkot* as the Jewish thanksgiving ritual for a living planet.

At a global level there have been several interfaith initiatives focusing on ecological issues. In July 1979, the World Council of Churches addressed environmental issues at their meeting on 'Faith, science, and the future' (Brown, 1981). The 300 delegates from fifty-six countries proposed that an ecological theology be developed to heal the destructive relationship between humanity and nature. They also proposed that there be an international moratorium on construction of nuclear power plants as well as remedies to resolve food shortages and hunger. Since then, environmental stewardship has been a frequent theme at gatherings of the World Council of Churches (which represents over 400 million Christians). In 1990 at Seoul the theme was 'Justice, peace, and integrity of creation' (Beyer, 1992) and the 1991 General Assembly held in Canberra, Australia focused on 'Come Holy Spirit, Renew the Whole Creation' (Oelschlaeger, 1994).

In Central and South America, liberationist Catholicism provides the impetus for aiding peasants and workers in their struggle against environmental degradation. One example is the Commisao Pastoral da Terra (CPT) created by the Organization of Brazilian Bishops. The

CPT has helped local tribal communities' efforts to save the inland lakes along the Amazon River by providing ideological, technical, financial, and organizational assistance (Hadsell 1995). Another example of how organized religion can promote ecological stewardship is provided by the Association of African Earth-keeping Churches (AAEC) (Daneel, 1994). Over 100 African Independent Churches (representing 2 million congregants) belong to the AAEC which serves as the thinktank and fundraiser for the Zimbabwean Institute of Religious Research and Ecological Conservation (ZIRRCON). In addition to their work on afforestation, wildlife conservation and protection of water resources projects, the AAEC has brought the environmental ethic into church teachings and liturgy through innovations such as tree-planting eucharists performed in AAEC congregations.

In June 1991, the Joint Appeal in Religion and Science (leaders of major American faith groups, scientists and US senators) convened a 'Summit on the Environment' and concluded that 'social justice and environmental integrity are inseparable' (Morton 1993: 130). And during the 1992 United Nations Conference on Environment and Development (UNCED) in Rio de Janiero, the World Council of Churches convened an interfaith gathering to draft ethical principles on the environment and development for consideration in the proposed UNCED Earth Charter (Hallman 1994). Although governments could not negotiate an agreement on an Earth Charter,[1] work continued on what became the *One Earth Community* document to be 'used as a guide for church programmes and for advocacy with government and industry' (Hallman, 1994: 265). Thus, much of mainstream religions' environmental activism (especially within the northern hemisphere) could be regarded as rites of renewal (Trice, 1985) in which symbolic discourse and action serve to rejuvenate and reinforce existing systems of power and authority rather than radically transforming them.

In totality, these examples of spiritual environmental activism illustrate a wide variety of symbolic, behavioural, institutional, and political strategies of actions to effect environmental change. However, to what degree do these examples of spiritual environmentalism challenge the modernist status quo? Many of mainstream religions' environmental initiatives such as their reinterpretations of religious texts, creation of environmental rituals and ceremonials, and development of education programmes (cognitive and experiential) indicate an assumption of cultural continuity (Swidler, 1986). Similarly, it could be argued that the political advocacy being undertaken at national and international levels represent an extension of previous social justice activities. Although the global interorganizational initiatives represent collaboration of previously separate organizations, there is less evidence that fundamental changes in internal organizational arrangements are occurring.

In contrast, during periods of cultural transformation, alternative ideologics provide coherent belief and ritual systems which 'model new ways to organize action and to structure human communities' (Swidler, 1986: 280). However, the long term effectiveness of these strategies of cultural change is largely dependent on the development of supportive structural arrangements (Swidler, 1986). In this respect, environmental activism by mainstream religions within the southern hemisphere may have the advantage whereas neopagan activism could be regarded as too radical and Buddhist activism could be regarded as too diffuse to be at the forefront of social transformation. In this respect, the assumption that this is a period of cultural transformation appears to underlie more of the environmental activism of neopagan and Buddhist spiritual organizations as well as mainstream religious organizations in the southern hemisphere. These organizations' grassroots protest and resistance activities explicitly challenge existing socio-political arrangements. There also appears to be a greater unity of words and deeds in the everyday lives of their followers. That these forms of environmental activism are more often found in places where the evidence of ecological threat is most visible cannot be taken as coincidental.

(B) Spirituality in Eco-Philosophies and the Environmental Movement

Spirituality has been integrated into contemporary eco-philosophers as well as informed environmental activism to promote ecolosical consciousness. While not all eco-philosophers are receptive to the idea of a spiritual ecology or an ecological spirituality,[2] many have found inspiration and guidance from various spiritual and religious traditions for developing their philosophies of the socio-natural relationship. They recognize that human values and beliefs concerning the natural environment do not emerge *sui generis* but rather have a long cultural and spiritual heritage. One of the central tenets of radical eco-philosophies is the recapturing of a pre-Enlightenment world-view in which the universe is seen as organic, living and spiritual (Devall and Sessions, 1985; Drengson and Inoue, 1995). The following explores how the eco-philosophies of deep ecology, transpersonal ecology, and eco-feminism propose this should be accomplished.

Spirituality and the Deep Ecology Philosopher

Deep ecology philosophers (Devall and Sessions 1985; Drengson and Inoue 1995) have drawn from Asian and Native American spiritual traditions in their writings on biocentrism, biospherical egalitarianism (intrinsic value of all life forms), and the need for holistic balance with nature. Deep ecology proposes the moral goal of *self-realization* wherein 'the interest or interests of another being [which] are reacted to as our own interest or interests' (Naess, 1988: 261). Deep ecology's radical biocentrism advocates the restriction of individual human freedoms (in particular, neo-Malthusian restrictions on human reproduction) in favour of the rights of wildlife and nature.

Spirituality and Transpersonal Ecology

Transpersonal ecology extends deep ecology's focus on the alienation caused by the mechanistic and dualistic worldview of modern industrialized society which can only be healed by recapturing humanity's sacred connections with all aspects of creation (W. Fox 1990). Drawing from the work of Abraham Maslow, Stanislav Grof, and Anthony Sutich, transpersonal psychology offers proposals for personal growth or eco-actualization through a holistic identification (personal, ontological, and cosmological) with all life forms including the non-human world.

Spirituality and Eco-Feminism

Nature-centred spiritual traditions (especially goddess spirituality) and Asian philosophies have been particularly influential in the development of ecofeminist philosophy (Adams, 1993; Warren, 1994). As identified by Ruether (1993), spirituality provides ecofeminists with the energy to challenge and survive (at both conceptual and behavioural levels) oppressive hierarchical systems to create new systems based on the principles of egalitarianism, inclusiveness, communitarianism, consensual decision making, mutual care and responsibility (Cheney, 1987). Ecofeminism posits that humankind is different from, but not equivalent to, other life forms within the ecological community. The central position of ecofeminism is that the achievement of social justice is integral to environmental justice to end all forms of hierarchical domination within patriarchal cultures.

Radical Environmental Activism

Within the radical environmentalist literature, there are other proposals for how intentional community and communal strategies can facilitate environmental change (Dobson, 1995; B.R. Taylor, 1995). Ecotopian communities founded on bioregional ideals serve as exemplars from which the rest of society can learn how to live an ecologically sustainable lifestyle. However, networks of such communities can only succeed as revolutionary alternatives to the degree that they operate outside of conventional society (thereby avoiding co-opration and compromise). As the operating philosophy of radical environmental activist organizations such as Earth First!, the Sea Shepherd Society, Friends of the Earth, and Greenpeace, deep ecology provides the rationale for direct action campaigns (including ecological sabotage) and civil disobedience against those interests viewed as the enemies of nature (Manes, 1990). It has been observed that radical proponents of deep ecology have quasi-religious aspirations to promote ecological consciousness as a spiritual quest (Bookchin, 1994; W. Fox, 1990).

One could question deep ecologists' justification of the use of violent means to effect ecological balance and harmony. While professing to be guided by Taoist, Buddhist, and Native American spiritualities, deep ecologists who advocate and engage in violent acts are violating these traditions' fundamental principle of non-violent thoughts and deeds to all beings in creation. It should be noted that not all radical environmentalists who subscribe to a deep ecology perspective condone the use of violence to effect environmental change.

Grassroots advocacy groups in the environmental movement have more often organized campaigns of civil disobedience and passive resistance (Merchant 1992). On several occasions, the more pacifist ecofeminist approach has been adopted by environmental activists such as the protesters who during the summer of 1993 strove to stop clear-cut logging in British Columbia's Clayoquot Sound (Maclsaac and Champagne, 1994).

The 'virtue of non-contention' common to both Hinduism and Buddhism was present in the passive resistance of the women's Chipko movement in northern India to prevent logging in the Himalayan foothills

(Shiva, 1989). Green Party candidates in Europe and North America eschew violence in favour of working within existing political systems for a peaceful transition to an ecological world (Jancar-Webster, 1993; Sale, 1993; Spretnak and Capra, 1986). Whether informed by eco-feminist philosophy or not, the approach of the majority within the environmental movement has been one of non-violence (Day, 1989; Sale, 1993). While the tactics of a few 'eco-terrorists' have garnered much media attention, the majority are working in peaceful ways that involve bearing witness to environmental destruction and hazards, developing environmental educational and information programs as well as working collaboratively with legislators and industry to initiate environmental change.

Religious monastic orders have also served as models for radical environmentalist proposals for ecologically sustainable communities. In a spiritual extension of the deep ecology concept, Devall (1990) proposes that Buddhists develop ecocentric *sangha* communities within bioregions. Bahro (1994: 90) contends that 'we need a new Benedictine order' of small self-sufficient bioregional communities which will create a critical mass of spiritual consciousness to effect transformational change in society.

(C) Implications for Organizing for Environmental Change

The magnitude and urgency of current environmental problems requires both institutional and personal changes in envisioning and enacting an ecologically sustainable world. To the degree that organized religions constitute consensus movements, change strategies which eschew conflict or confrontation may hinder their effectiveness in mobilizing their members to take personal committed action to achieve espoused environmental goals.

> Whatever the tradition, religions are malleable. In the face of environmental deterioration, they have been mutating into forms capable of inspiring (or reinforcing) ecological activism, both by articulating ideals that participants find compelling ... and by providing concrete institutional resources for ecological struggles.
>
> (B.R. Taylor 1995: 335-7)

Advantages of Spiritual Ideals for Ecological Activism

Spiritual principles and teachings provide personal inspiration and guidance for those seeking ecologically sustainable lifestyles. Spiritual and religious organizations provide information and educate about the principles of environmental stewardship and respect for the natural environment. Leading by example, these organizations have translated words into action by initiating environmental projects and providing organizational support and resources for direct action campaigns to stop environmental degradation. Spiritual ideas have also inspired eco-philosophy and ecological activism in the wider environmental movement.

Rold of Mainstream Religions in Ecological Activism

Mainstream religions demonstrate the potential of hierarchical institutions to forge another path for change. Mainstream religions have the institutional infrastructure, knowledge, and resources to organize ecological conservation initiatives. These organizational competencies also facilitate the development and implementation of environmental initiatives with similarly organized economic, political, cultural, and religious institutions. Recent examples of interfaith dialogue and collective action illustrate the potential of adopting a global partnership approach to develop a world environmental ethic. As exemplified by the 1993 Second Parliament of the World's Religions which gathered together 8,000 individuals representing over 200 religious organizations (Tobias, Morrison, and Gray 1995) and the 1996 United Religions Initiative Summit (Khalsa and Kaczmarski 1996), disparate parties can work towards the common good despite fundamental ideological differences. In these ways religious organizations model the new forms of collaboration needed for transformational social and ecological change that transcend cultural and political factionalism (Brulle 1995). Spiritual traditions such as Buddhism, Taoism, and shamanism suggest that ecological transformation will be realized by letting 'a thousand flowers bloom'. That is, an accumulation of changes in individual ecological consciousness will over time, create a critical mass within groups, societies, and populations to effect a change in the collective ecological consciousness. It is a way that requires active personal commitment to work for ecological sustainability in ever-widening circles of concern (oneself, one's home, community, bioregion, nation, planet). This is a path that requires high levels of dedication, patience, and faith to achieve integrity in means and ends. To this end, modern communication and transportation technologies can accelerate the speed and broaden the scope of collaborative connections among people and organizations in disparate parts of the globe (Bilimoria *et al.,* 1995).

Even so, the question remains as to the potency of such organizational initiatives to mobilize personal and institutional change. Snow and Benford (1992) argue that 'collective action frames' have greater mobilizing potential if they are more elaborated and more central to the ideology of the targets of mobilization. Thus, the reinterpretation and reintegration of the natural environment in religious teachings and edicts bode well for creating an environmental metanarrative to organize experience and guide action to challenge the status quo (Brulle, 1995, Tarrow, 1992). New social movement theorists (Morris and Mueller, 1992) also identify that pre-existing social relationships are a critical part of the mobilization process for social change. In this regard, spiritual and religious communities also appear to be well suited as focal points for environmental activism. However, Schwartz and Paul (1992) observe that consensus social movements which have broad attitudinal support, developed social infrastructures and considerable institutional resources have lower rates of membership mobilization and greater strategic rigidity than conflict movements. Thus, the role that spiritual organizations and their leaders have to play in this process is to: Primarily, it is to facilitate the development of ideational motivation of individuals and collectives by offering information and guidance, by providing encouragement and support, and by providing spiritual, intellectual, and social linkages for people.

Spiritual Pathways for Environmental Change?

> The human community and the natural world will go into the future I is a single sacred community or we will both perish in the desert.
>
> (Thomas Berry, as quoted by Martin 1993: 43)

Berry's (1993) agenda for healing the earth community is far reaching and encompasses the spiritual, technological, educational, economic, and institutional dimensions of the human community. It is also an agenda that requires changes at individual, organizational, societal, and global levels.

In *The Dream of the Earth,* Berry (1988) writes about creating an earth community (the whole planetary ecosystem) based on a 'functional spirituality' or 'functional cosmology'. He calls for a new story, a new sense of the universe, to take humanity forward from the mechanistic orientation of the scientific world and the pathologies of modern industrial society. Interestingly, Berry (a Passionist priest) calls for a new shamanic personality, not a prophet, to help discover this story.

> The shamanic type is the person that goes deep into the mystery of the universe and brings back power and direction to a society. It brings back healing, because the power is frequently healing power but supportive power. But the main thing about the shamanic personality is that it's dealing more with the powers of the natural world. We are not accustomed to dealing with the powers of the natural world.
>
> (Berry, 1990: 20)

Current global interfaith initiatives to address environmental issues demonstrate that there can be a unity in purpose (peace and justice ideals irrespective of a diversity of spiritual and religious perspectives. This in turn can serve as an important counterbalance to the instrumental orientation (progress, efficiency, technical rationality) and individuation of functionally specialized, globally homogeneous economic and social systems (Beyer, 1992).

The nature-centred and Asian concept of 'place' is a critique of the universalist meaning structures underlying modern science and technocratic societies. On the other hand, the concept of place could also serve as an exclusionary mechanism to pre-empt open debate regarding actions needed to resolve environmental problems which transcend physical and cultural boundaries. Thus, these approaches to spiritual environmentalism posit a potential dialectical tension between inclusion and exclusion which necessitates reflexive discourse.

The linkage between spirituality and environmental activism may be uncomfortable for those who believe in the importance of a strictly secular society. To be sure, history has taught us that the politicization of spirituality in the advocacy of environmental change warrants a degree of caution (Deudney, 1995). However, there is little evidence that the goals of spiritual and religious leaders engaged in environmental advocacy and projects extend to a rejoining of Church and State. Instead, their agenda has been more to facilitate environmental change by re-examining their spiritual teachings, being exemplars of environmental responsibility, and working in parallel and collaboratively with existing political and economic institutions (Oelschlaeger, 1994).

> This passage into the twenty-first century is a social invention. It is an act of cultural imagination, and as such it provides a catalyst for other similar acts of imagination on which our collective prosperity and health—and even our survival—may rest. It is an invitation to reexamine, reevaluate, and where necessary, change attitudes and habits of culture that increasingly prove dysfunctional on the inter-connected planet that we inhabit.
>
> (Spangler, 1993: 70)

While there is a richness within each spiritual tradition and religion that remains to be further explored, we need to trigger our imagination and our thinking about what these spiritual traditions and religions have to offer, in terms of guiding modern secular societies during this time of ecological crisis.

We have thus seen the role which spiritual values and beliefs can play in recapturing connections with the natural environment and guiding humankind through the modern ecological crisis. In one sense, this has been an exploration about *being* as well as *doing*. It is based on the assumption that action which is not grounded in and guided by one's values and beliefs is superficial and transitory. If, as many have observed, there need to be fundamental changes in the ecological consciousness of humankind, then one important starting point for those changes is from within. To the degree that religions and spiritual traditions influence social norms and behaviours, they provide the inspiration and personal commitment so needed for ecological self-discipline and activism (Carroll *et al.,* 1997; Deudney, 1995).

> God has made different religions to suit different aspirations, times, and countries. All doctrines are only so many paths, but a path is by no means God Himself. Indeed, one can reach God if one follows one of the paths with whole-hearted devotion. (Ramakrishna, as cited by H. Smith 1991: 74)

There is no universal environ-mental belief system nor is there one best way to relate to nature, what we need is to be cognizant and respectful of the many significant and fundamental differences amongst these traditions, particularly in regards to their spiritual practices. As there is need for biodiversity on the planet, there is also a need for diversity in human expression and action which reflects the unique historical, cultural, and biophysical realities which have co-evolved throughout the world

(Roberts, 1990; Warren, 1994). It is required that spiritual perspectives on the natural environment and ways of effecting environmental change are complementary to other necessary cognitive and behavioural initiatives which are currently envisioned and underway.

This chapter has presented a variety of spiritual values and beliefs concerning the relationship between humankind and the natural environment Nature-centered and Asian spiritual traditions emphasize the need for holistic balance and harmony within the interdependent and interpenetrating webs of relationships between humans and the natural environment. They teach that thoughts and actions towards others and nature need to be respectful and informed by the principle of non-violence. Asian philosophies tell of the requirement for continuous effort and a creative attitude to achieve and maintain this peace and harmony. Both teach of the importance of experiential knowledge—that knowing one's physical place within the natural world is integral to attaining an intellectual and spiritual understanding of the universe. Monotheist religions emphasize the divine concern of God for all in creation and humankind's role as stewards of the natural world. Many environmental thinkers, writers, and activists (even the most secular) view the natural world and unity of life on the planet with awe respect, and love. That is to say, they view life on earth as sacred and, hence having a spiritual dimension to it even if they don't use those terms.[3]

NOTES

1. It is noteworthy that the official Agenda 21 for global environmental change bears no mention of religious organizations or spirituality in its goals and strategies for change (Sitarz 1993).
2. Perhaps the most vocal critic has been social ecologist, Murray Bookchin (1994) who advocates a strictly secular ecological theory which has no place for the 'spiritualism' proposed by 'ecomystics', 'ecotheists' and deep ecologists.
3. I am indebted to Don Wolfe of Case Western Reserve University for these words and thoughts on the spiritual dimension of environmental thinking and writing.

5

The Assertion of Power of Women and Godde Symbol

The affirmation of female powers through Goddess symbol is part of a legacy of patriarchal oppression, bringing with it authoritarianism, hierarchicalism and rigid dogmas associated with monotheistic religions.

At the close of Ntosake Shange's stupendously successful broadway play "For Colored Girls Who Have Considered Suicide When the Rainbow Is Enuf," a tall beautiful black woman rises from despair to cry out, "I found God in myself and I loved her fiercely."[1] Her discovery is echoed by women around the country who meet spontaneously in small groups on full moons, solstices, and equinoxes to celebrate the Goddess as symbol of life and death powers and waxing and waning energies in the universe and in themselves.[2]

> It is the night of the full moon. Nine women stand in a circle, on a rocky hill above the city. The western sky is rosy with the setting sun; in the east the moon's face begins to peer above the horizon. . . . The woman pours out a cup of wine onto the earth, refills it and raises it high. "Hail, Tana, Mother of mothers!" she cries. "Awaken from your long sleep, and return to your children again!"[3]

What are the political and psychological effects of this fierce new love of the divine in themselves for women whose spiritual experience has been focused by the male God of Judaism and Christianity? Is the spiritual dimension of feminism a passing diversion, an escape from

---

From: *Womanspirit Rising: A Feminist Reader in Religion* by Carol P. Christ and Judith Plaskow (San Francisco: Harper and Row, 1979), 273-89. Also printed in Carol P. Christ, *Laughter of Aphrodite: Reflections on a journey to the Goddess* (San Francisco: Harper and Row, 1987), 117-32. First published in Heresies No. 5: The Great *Goddess*, 1978.

difficult but necessary political work? Or does the emergence of the symbol of Goddess among women have significant political and psychological ramifications for the feminist movement?

Religious Symbols

To answer this question, we must first understand the importance of religious symbols and rituals in human life and consider the effect of male symbolism of God on women. According to anthropologist Clifford Geertz, religious symbols shape a cultural ethos, defining the deepest values of a society and the persons in it. "Religion," Geertz writes "is a system of symbols which act to produce powerful, pervasive, and long-lasting moods and motivations' in the people of a given culture. A "mood for Geertz is a psychological attitude such as awe, trust, and respect, while a "motivation" is the social and *political* trajectory created by a mood that transforms mythos into ethos, symbol system into social and political reality. Symbols have both psychological and political effects, because they create the inner conditions (deep-seated attitudes and feelings) that lead people to feel comfortable with or to accept social and political arrangements that correspond to the symbol system.

Because religion has such a compelling hold on the deep psyches of so many people, feminists cannot afford to leave it in the hands of the fathers. Even people who no longer "believe in God" or participate in the institutional structure of patriarchal religion still may not be free of the power of the symbolism of God the Father. A symbol's effect does not depend on rational assent, for a symbol also functions on levels of the psyche other than the rational. Religion fulfills deep psychic needs by providing symbols and rituals that enable people to cope with limit situations' in human life (death, evil, suffering) and to pass through life's important transitions (birth, sexuality, death). Even people who consider themselves completely secularized will often find themselves sitting in a church or synagogue when a friend or relative gets married, or when a parent or friend has died. The symbols associated with these important rituals cannot fail to affect the deep or unconscious structures of the mind of even a person who has rejected these symbolisms on a conscious level—especially if the person is under stress. The reason for the continuing effect of religious symbols is that the mind abhors a vacuum. Symbol systems cannot simply be rejected, they must be replaced. Where there is not any replacement, the mind will revert to familiar structures at times of crisis, bafflement, or defeat.

Male God

Religions centered on the worship of a male God create "moods" and "motivations" that keep women in a state of psychological dependence on men and male authority, while at the same legitimating the *political* and social authority of fathers and sons in the institutions of society. Religious symbol systems focused around exclusively male images of divinity create the impression that female power can never be fully legitimate or wholly beneficent. This message need never be explicitly stated (as, for example, it is in the story of Eve) for its effect to be felt. A woman completely ignorant of the myths of female evil in biblical religion nonetheless acknowledges the anomaly of female power when she prays exclusively to a male God. She may see herself as like God (created in the image of God) only by denying her own sexual identity and affirming God's transcendence of sexual identity. But she can never have the experience that is freely available to every man and boy in her culture, of having her full sexual identity affirmed as being in the image and likeness of God. In Geertz's terms, her "mood" is one of trust in male power as salvific and distrust of female power in herself and other women as inferior or dangerous. Such a powerful, pervasive, and longlasting "mood" cannot fail to become a "motivation" that translates into social and political reality.

In *'Beyond God the Father',* feminist theologian Mary Daly detailed the psychological and political ramifications of father religion for women. "If God in 'his' heaven is a father ruling his people," she wrote:

> "then it is the 'nature' of things and according to divine plan and the order of the universe that society be male dominated. Within this context, a mystification of roles takes place: The husband dominating his wife represents God 'himself.' The images and values of a given society have been projected into the realm of dogmas and 'Articles of Faith,' and these in turn justify the social structures which have given rise to them and which sustain their plausibility."[6]

Philosopher Simone de Beauvoir was well aware of the function of patriarchal religion as legimater of male power. As she wrote:

> "Man enjoys the great advantage of having a god endorse the code he writes; and since man exercises a sovereign authority over women it is especially fortunate that this authority has been vested in by the Supreme Being. For the Jew, Mohammedans, and Christians, among others, man is Master by divine right; the fear of God will therefore repress any impulse to revolt in the downtrodden female."[7]

Goddess Symbolism

The Goddess symbol has emerged spontaneously in the dreams, fantasies, and thoughts of many women around the country in the past several years. Kirsten Grimstad and Susan Rennie reported that they were surprised to discover widespread interest in spirituality, including the Goddess, among feminists around the country in the summer of 1974.[8] The sources for the symbol of the Goddess in contemporary spirituality are traditions of Goddess worship and modern women's experience. The ancient Mediterranean, pre-Christian European, Native American, Mesoamerican, Hindu, African, and other traditions are rich sources for Goddess symbolism. But these traditions are filtered through modern women's experiences. Traditions of goddesses, subordination to gods, for example, are ignored. Ancient traditions are tapped selectively and eclecticly, but they are not considered authoritative for modern consciousness. *Woman Spirit* magazine, which published its first issue in 1974 and has contributors from across the United States, has expressed the grass-roots nature of the women's spirituality movement.

In 1976, a journal, *Lady Unique,* devoted to the Goddess emerged. In 1975, the first women's spirituality conference was held in Boston and attended by eighteen hundred women. In 1978, a University of California Santa Cruz course on the Goddess drew over five hundred people. Sources for this essay are these manifestations of the Goddess in modern women's experiences as reported in *Woman Spirit, Lady Unique,* and elsewhere, and as expressed in conversations with women who have been thinking about the Goddess and women's spirituality.

Meaning of Goddess Symbol

(1) Affirmation of Female Power: The simplest and most basic meaning of the symbol of Goddess is the acknowledgment of the legitimacy of female power as a beneficient and independent power. The internationally acclaimed novelist Monique Wittig captured the

novelty and flavor of the affirmation of female power when she wrote, in her mythic work *Les Guerilleres,*

> There was a time when you were not a slave, remember that. You walked alone, full of laughter, you bathed bare-bellied. You say you have lost all recollection of it, remember. . . you say there are no words to describe it, you say it does not exist. But remember. Make an effort to remember. Or, failing that, invent.[9]

While Wittig does not speak directly of the Goddess here, she captures the "mood" of joyous celebration of female freedom and independence that is created in women who define their identities through the symbol of Goddess. Artist Mary Beth Edelson expressed the political "motivations" inspired by the Goddess when she wrote,

> The ascending archetypal symbols of the feminine unfold today in the psyche of modern Everywoman. They encompass the multiple forms of the Great Goddess. Reaching across the centuries we take the hands of our Ancient Sisters. The Great Goddess alive and well is rising to announce to the patriarchs that their 5,000 years are up—Halleluiah! Here we come.[10]

A woman who echoes Ntosake Shange's dramatic statement, "I found God in myself and I loved her fiercely," is saying "Female power is strong and creative." She is saying that the divine principle, the saving and sustaining power, is in herself, that she will no longer look to men or male figures as saviors. The strength and independence of female power can be intuited by contemplating ancient and modern images of the Goddess. This meaning of the symbol of Goddess is simple and obvious, and yet it is difficult for many to comprehend. It stands in sharp contrast to the paradigms of female dependence on males that have been predominant in Western religion and culture.

The affirmation of female power contained in the Goddess symbol has both psychological and political consequences. Psychologically, it means the defeat of the view engendered by patriarchy that women's power is interior and dangerous. This new "mood" of affirmation or female power also leads to new "motivations"; it supports and undergirds women's trust in their own power and the power of other women in family and society. If the simplest meaning of the Goddess symbol is an affirmation of the legitimacy and beneficience of female power, then a question immediately arises: Is the Goddess simply female power writ large, and if so, why bother with the symbol of Goddess at all? Or does the symbol refer to a Goddess "out there" who is not reducible to a human potential? The many women who have rediscovered the power of Goddess would give three answers to this question:

(1) the Goddess is divine female a personification who can be invoked in prayer and ritual.

(2) the Goddess is symbol of the life, death, and rebirth energy in nature and culture in personal and communal life; and

(3) the Goddess is symbol of the affirmation of the legitimacy and beauty of female power (made possible by the new becoming of women in the women's liberation movement).

If one were to ask these women which answer is the "correct" one, different responses would be given. Some would assert that the Goddess definitely is not "out there." that the symbol of a divinity "out there is part of the legacy of patriarchal oppression, which brings with it the authoritarianism, hierarchicalism, and dogmatic, rigidity associated with biblical monotheistic religions. They might assert that the Goddess symbol reflects the sacred power within women and nature, suggesting the connectedness between women's cycles of menstruation, birth, and menopause, and the life and death cycle of the universe. Others seem quite comfortable with the notion of Goddess as a divine female protector and creator and would find their experience of Goddess, limited by the assertion that she is not also out there as well as within themselves and in all natural processes. When asked what the symbol of Goddess means feminist priestess Starhawk replied, "It all depends on how I feel When I feel weak, she is someone who can help and protect me, When I feel strong, she is the symbol of my own power. At other times I feel her as the natural energy in my body and the world."[11] How are we to evaluate such a statement? Theologians might call these the words of a sloppy thinker. But my deepest intuition tells me they contain a wisdom that Western theological thought has lost.

(2) Affirmation of Female Body and Life Cycle: A second important implication of the Goddess symbol for women is the *affirmation of the female body and the life cycle* expressed in it. Because of women's unique position as menstruants, birthgivers, and those who have traditionally cared for the young and the dying, women's connection to the body, nature, and this world has been obvious. Women were denigrated

because they seemed more carnal, fleshy, and earthy than the culture-creating males.[12] The misogynist antibody tradition in Western thought is symbolized in the myth of Eve, who is traditionally viewed as a sexual temptress, the, epitome of women's carnal nature. This tradition reaches its nadir in the *Malleus Maleficorum* (The Hammer *of Evil-Doing Women),* which states, "All witchcraft stems from carnal lust, which in women is insatiable."[13]

The Virgin Mary, the positive female image in Christianity, does not contradict Christian denigration of the female body and its powers. The Virgin Mary is revered because she, in her perpetual virginity, transcends the carnal sexuality attributed to most women.

Menstruating Women: The denigration of the female body is expressed in cultural and religious taboos surrounding menstruation, childbirth, and menopause in women. While menstruation taboos may have originated in a perception of the awesome powers of the female body,[14] they degenerated into a simple perception that there is something "wrong" with female bodily functions. Menstruating women were forbidden to enter the sanctuary in ancient Hebrew and premodern Christian communities. Although only Orthodox Jews still enforce religious taboos against menstruant women, few women in our culture grow up affirming their menstruation as a connection to sacred power. Most women learn that menstruation is a curse and grow up believing that the bloody facts of menstruation are best hidden away. Feminists challenge this attitude toward , the female body. Judy Chicago's art piece "Menstruation Bathroom" broke these menstrual taboos. In a sterile white bathroom, she exhibited boxes of Tampax and Kotex on an open shelf, and the wastepaper basket was overflowing with bloody tampons and sanitary napkins.[15] Many women who viewed the piece felt relieved to have their "dirty secret" out in the open.

Woman as Birth Giver: The denigration of the female body and its powers is further expressed in Western culture's attitudes toward childbirth.[16] Religious iconography does not celebrate the birthgiver, and there is no theology or ritual that enables a woman to celebrate the process of birth as a spiritual experience. Indeed, Jewish and Christian traditions also had blood taboos concerning the woman who had recently given birth. While these religious taboos are rarely enforced today (again, only by Orthodox Jews), they have secular equivalents. Giving birth is treated as a disease requiring hospitalization, and the woman is viewed as a passive object, anesthetized to ensure her acquiescence to the will of the doctor. The women's liberation movement has challenged these cultural attitudes, and many feminists have joined with advocates of natural childbirth and home birth in emphasizing the need for women to control and take pride in their bodies, including the birth process.

Aging Woman: Western culture also gives little dignity to the postmenopausal or aging women. It is no secret that our culture is based on a denial of aging and death, and that women suffer more severely from this denial than men. Women are placed on a pedestal and considered powerful when they are young and beautiful, but they are said to lose this power as they age. As feminists have pointed out, the "power" of the young woman is illusory, since beauty standards are defined by men, and since few women are considered (or consider themselves) beautiful for more than a few years of their lives. Some men are viewed as wise and authoritative in age, but old women are pitied and shunned. Religious iconography supports this cultural attitude toward aging women. The purity and virginity of Mary and the female saints is often expressed in the iconographic convention of perpetual youth. Moreover, religious mythology associates aging women with evil in the symbol of the wicked old witch. Feminists have challenged cultural myths of aging women and have urged women to reject patriarchal beauty standards and to celebrate the distinctive beauty of women of all ages.

Moods and Motivations Created by the Symbols of Goddess: The "mood" created by the symbol of the Goddess in triple aspect is one of positive, joyful affirmation of the female body and its cycles and acceptance of aging and death as well as life. The "motivations" are to overcome menstrual taboos, to return the birth process to the hands of women, and to change cultural attitudes about age and death. Changing cultural attitudes toward the female body could go a long way toward overcoming the spirit-flesh, mind-body dualisms of Western culture, since, as Ruether has pointed out, the denigration of the female body is at the heart of these dualisms. The Goddess as symbol of the revaluation of the body and nature thus also includes the human potential and ecology movements. The "mood" is one of affirmation, awe, and respect for the body and nature, and the "motivation" is to respect the teachings of the body and the rights of all living beings.

The symbol of Goddess aids the process of naming and reclaiming the female body and its cycles and processes. In the ancient world and among modern women, the Goddess symbol represents the birth, death, and rebirth processes of the natural and human worlds. The female body is viewed as the direct incarnation of waxing and waning, life and death, cycles in the universe. This is sometimes expressed through the symbolic connection between the twenty-eight-day cycles of menstruation and the twenty-eight-day cycles of the moon. Moreover, the Goddess is celebrated in the triple aspect of youth, maturity, and age, or maiden, mother, and crone. The potentiality of the young girl is celebrated in the nymph or maiden aspect of the Goddess.

The Goddess as mother is sometimes depicted giving birth, and giving birth is viewed as a symbol for all the creative, life-giving powers of the universe.[17] The life-giving powers of the Goddess in her creative aspect are not limited to physical birth, for the Goddess is also seen as the creator of all the arts of civilization, including healing, writing, and the giving of just law.

Women in the middle of life who are not physical mothers may give birth to poems, songs, and books, or nurture other women, men, and children. They too are incarnations of the Goddess in her creative, life-giving aspect. At the end of life, women incarnate the crone aspect of the Goddess. The wise old woman, the woman who knows from experience what life is about, the woman whose closeness to her own death gives her a distance and perspective on the problems of life, is celebrated as the third aspect of the Goddess. Thus, women learn to value youth, creativity, and wisdom in themselves and other women.

The possibilities of reclaiming the female body and its cycles have been expressed in a number of Goddess-centered rituals. Hallie Mountainwing and Barby My Own created a summer solstice ritual to celebrate menstruation and birth. The women simulated a birth canal and birthed each other into their circle. They raised power by placing their hands on each other's bellies and chanting together. Finally they marked each other's faces with rich, dark menstrual blood saying, "This is the blood that promises renewal. This is the blood that promises sustenance. This is the blood that promises life."[18] From hidden dirty secret to symbol of the life power of the Goddess, women's blood has come full circle.

Other women have created rituals that celebrate the crone aspect of the Goddess. Z. Budapest believes that the crone aspect of the

Goddess is predominant in the fall, especially at Halloween, an ancient holiday. On this day, the wisdom of the old woman is celebrated, and it is also recognized that the old must die so that the new can be born.

(3) Positive Valuation of will in Goddess Centred Ritual: A third important implication of the Goddess symbol for women is the positive valuation of will in a Goddess-centered ritual, especially in Goddess-centered ritual magic and spellcasting in woman-spirit and feminist witchcraft circles. The basic notion behind ritual magic and spellcasting is energy as power. Here the Goddess is a center or focus of power and energy; she is the personification of the energy that flows between beings in the natural and human worlds. In Goddess circles, energy is raised by chanting or dancing. According to Starhawk, "Witches conceive of psychic energy as having form and substance that can be perceived and directed by those with a trained awareness. The power generated within the circle is built into a cone form, and at its peak is released—to the Goddess, to reenergize the members of the coven, or to do a specific work such as healing."[19] In ritual magic, the energy raised is directed by willpower. Women who celebrate in Goddess circles believe they can achieve their wills in the world. The emphasis on the will is important for women, because women traditionally have been taught to devalue their wills, to believe that they cannot achieve their will through their own power, and even to suspect that the assertion of will is evil.

Faith Wildung's poem "Waiting," sums up women's sense that their lives are defined not by their own will, but by waiting for others to take the initiative.

> Waiting for my breasts to develop
> Waiting to wear a bra
> Waiting to menstruate
> ...
> Waiting for life to begin, Waiting—
> Waiting to be somebody
> ...
> Waiting to get married
> Waiting for my wedding day
> Waiting for my wedding night
> ...
> Waiting for the end of the day
> Waiting for sleep. Waiting...[20]

Patriarchal religion has enforced the view that female initiative and will are evil through the juxtaposition of Eve and Mary. Eve caused the fall by asserting her will against the command of God, while Mary began the new age with her response to God's initiative, "Let it be done to me according to thy word" (Luke 1:38). Even for men, patriarchal religion values the passive will subordinate to divine initiative.

The classical doctrines of sin and grace view sin as the prideful assertion of will and grace as the obedient subordination of the human will to the divine initiative or order. While this view of will might be questioned from a human perspective, Valerie Saiving has argued that it has particularly deleterious consequences for women in Western culture. According to Saiving, Western culture encourages males in the assertion of will, and thus it may make some sense to view the male form of sin as an excess of will. But since culture discourages females in the assertion of will, the traditional doctrines of sin and grace encourage women to remain in their form of sin, which is self-negation or insufficient assertion of will.[21] The reason the will is denigrated in a patriarchal religious framework is that both human and divine will are often pictured as arbitrary, self-initiated, and exercised without regard for other wills.

In a Goddess-centered context, in contrast, the will is valued. A *woman is encouraged to know her will, to believe that her will is valid, and to believe that her will can be achieved in the world,* three powers traditionally denied to her in patriarchy. Moreover, a woman's will is not subordinated to the Lord God as king and ruler, nor to men as his representatives. Thus, a woman is not reduced to waiting and acquiescing in the wills of others as she is in patriarchy. But neither does she adopt the egocentric form of will that pursues self-interest without regard for the interests of others.

While providing a different understanding of the will than that available in the traditional patriarchal religious framework, the Goddess framework, will can be achieved only when it is exercised in harmony with the energies and wills of other beings. Wise women, for example, raise a cone of healing energy at the full moon or solstice when the lunar or solar energies are at their high points with respect to the earth. This discipline encourages them to recognize that not all times are propitious for the achieving of every will. Similarly, they know that spring is a time for new beginnings in work and love, summer a time for producing external manifestations of inner potentialities, and fall or winter times for stripping down to the inner core and extending roots. Such awareness of waxing and waning processes in the universe discourages arbitrary ego-centered assertion of will, while at the same time encouraging the assertion of individual will in cooperation with natural energies and the energies created by the wills of others.

Wise women also have a tradition that whatever is sent out, will be returned and this reminds them to assert their wills in cooperative and healing, rather than egocentric and destructive, ways. This view of will allows women to begin to recognize, claim, and assert their wills without adopting the worst characteristics of the patriarchal understanding and use of will. In the Goddess-centered framework, the "mood" is one of positive affirmation of personal will in the context of the energies of other wills or beings. The "motivation" is for women to know and assert their wills in cooperation with other wills and energies. This of course does not mean that women always assert their wills in positive and life-affirming ways. Women's capacity for evil is, of course, as great as men's. The purpose here is simply to contrast the differing attitudes toward the exercise of will per se, and the female will in particular, in Goddess-centered religion and in the Christian God-centered religion.

Revaluation of Woman's Bonds and Heritage: The fourth and final aspect of Goddess symbolism that I will discuss here is the significance of the Goddess for a revaluation of woman's bonds and heritage. As Virginia Woolf has said, "Chloe liked Olivia," a statement about a woman's relation to another woman, is a sentence that rarely occurs in fiction. Men have written the stories, and they have written about women almost exclusively in their relations to men.[22] The celebrations of women's bonds to each other, as mothers and daughters, as colleagues and co-workers, as sisters, friends, and lovers, is beginning to occur in the new literature and culture created by women in the women's movement. While revaluing of each of these bonds is important, here we will focus on the mother-daughter bond, in part because it may be the key to the others.

Adrienne Rich has pointed out that the mother-daughter bond, perhaps the most important of woman's bonds, "resonant with charges ... the flow of energy between two biologically alike bodies, one of which has lain in amniotic bliss inside the other, one of which has labored to give birth to the other,"[23] is rarely celebrated in patriarchal religion and culture. Christianity celebrates the father's relation to the son and the mother's relation to the son, but the story of mother and daughter is missing So, too, in patriarchal literature and psychology, the mothers and the daughters rarely exist. Volumes have been written about the Oedipal complex, but little has been written about the girl's relation to her mother. Moreover, as de Beauvoir has noted, the mother-daughter relation is distorted in patriarchy because the mother must give her daughter over to men in a male-defined culture in which women are viewed as inferior. The mother must socialize her daughter to become subordinate to men, and if her daughter challenge patriarchal norms, the mother is likely to defend the patriarchal structures against her own daughter.[23] These patterns are changing in the new culture created by women in which the bonds of women to women are beginning to be celebrated.

Holly Near has written several songs that celebrate women's bonds and women's heritage. In one of her finest songs she writes of an "old-time woman" who is "waiting to die." A young woman feels for the life that has passed the old woman by and begins to cry, but the old woman looks her in the eye and says, "If I had not suffered, you wouldn't be wearing those jeans / Being an old-time woman ain't as bad as it seems."[25] This song, which Near has said was inspired by her grandmother, expresses and celebrates a bond and a heritage passed down from one woman to another.

In another of Near's songs, she sings of "a hiking-boot mother who's seeing the world / For the first time with her own little girl." In this song, the mother tells the drifter who has been travelling with her to pack up and travel alone if he thinks "travelling three is a drag" because "I've got a little one who loves me as much as you need me / And darling, that's loving enough."[26] This song is significant because the mother places her relationship to her daughter above her relationship to a man, something women rarely do in patriarchy.[27]

Almost the only story of mothers and daughters that has been transmitted in Western culture is the myth of Demeter and Persephone that was the basis of religious rites celebrated by women only, *the Thesmophoria*, and later formed the basis of the Eleusian mysteries, which were open to all who spoke Greek. In this story, the daughter,

Persephone, is raped away from her mother, Demeter, by the God of the underworld. Unwilling to accept this state of affairs, Demeter rages and withholds fertility from the earth until her daughter is returned to her. What is important for women in this story is that a mother fights for her daughter and for her relation to her daughter. This is completely different from the mother's relation to her daughter in patriarchy. The "mood" created by the story of Demeter and Persephone is one of celebration of the mother-daughter bond, and the "motivation" is for mothers and daughters to affirm the heritage passed on from mother to daughter and to reject the patriarchal pattern where the primary loyalties of mother and daughter must be to men.

The symbol of Goddess has much to offer women who are struggling to be rid of the "powerful, pervasive, and long-lasting moods and motivations" of devaluation of female power, denigration of the female body, distrust of female will, and denial of the women's bonds and heritage that have been engendered by patriarchal religion. As women struggle to create a new culture in which women's power, bodies, will, and bonds are celebrated, it seems natural that the Goddess would reemerge as symbol of the newfound beauty, strength, and power of women.

To theologians, these differing views of the 'meaning" of the symbol of Goddess might seem to threaten a replay of the trinitarian controversies. Is there, perhaps, a way of doing theology, which would not lead immediately into dogmatic controversy, which would not require theologians to say definitively that one understanding is true and the others are false? Could people's relation to a common symbol be made primary and varying interpretations be acknowledged? The diversity of explications of the meaning of the Goddess symbol suggests that symbols have a richer significance than any explications of their meaning can express, a point literary critics have long insisted on. This phenomenological fact suggests that theologians may need to give more than lip service to a theory of symbol in which the symbol is viewed as the primary fact and the meanings are viewed as secondary. It also suggests that a thealogy[28] of the Goddess would be very different from the theology we have known in the West. But to spell out this notion of the primacy of *symbol* in thealogy in contrast to the primacy of the *explanation* in theology would be the topic of another paper.

NOTES

1. From the original cast album, Buddah Records, 1976.
2. See Susan Rennie and Kristen Grimstad, "Spiritual Explorations Cross-Country," *Quest* 1, no. 4 (1975): 49-51; and *Woman Spirit* magazine.
3. See Starhawk, "Witchcraft and Women's Culture," in *Womanspirit Rising: A Feminist Reader in Religion,* ed. Carol P. Christ and Judith Plaskow (San Francisco: Harper and Row, 1979), 259-68.
4. Clifford Geertz, "Religion as a Cultural System," in *Reader in Comparative Religion,* ed. William L. Lessa and Evon V. Vogt, 2d ed. (New York: Harper and Row, 1972), 206.
5. Geertz, "Religion as a Cultural System," 210.
6. Mary Daly, *Beyond God the Father,* (Boston: Beacon Press, 1974), 13; emphasis added.
7. Simone de Beauvoir, *The Second Sex,* trans. H. M. Parshleys (New York: Alfred A. Knopf, 1953).
8. See Grimstad and Rennie, "Spiritual Explorations Cross-Country."
9. Monique Wittig, *Les Guerilleres* trans. David LeVay (New York: Avon Books, 1971), 89. Also quoted in Morgan MacFarland, "Witchcraft: The Art of Remembering," *Quest* 1, no. 4 (1975): 41.
10. Mary Beth Edelson, "Speaking for Myself," *Lady Unique* 1 (1976): 56.
11. Personal communication.
12. This theory of the origins of the Western dualism is stated by Rosemary Ruether in *New Woman: New Earth* (New York: Seabury Press, 1975), and elsewhere.
13. Heinrich Kramer and Jacob Sprenger (New York: Dover, 1971), 47.
14. See Rita M. Gross, "Menstruation and Childbirth as Ritual and Religious Experience in the Religion of the Australian Aborigines," in *Journal of the American Academy of Religion,* 45, no. 4 (1977): supplement 1147-81.
15. Judy Chicago, Through the *Flower* (New York: Doubleday, 1975), Plate 4, pp. 106-67.
16. See Adrienne Rich, of Woman Born (New York: Bantam Books, 1977), Chaps. 6 and 7.
17. See James Mellaart, *Earliest Civilizations of the Near East* (New York: McGraw-Hill, 1965), 92.
18. Barbry My Own, "Ursa Maior: Menstrual Moon Celebration," in Moon, Moon ed. Anne Kent Rush, (Berkeley, Calif: Moon Books, Random House, 1976), 374-87.
19. Starhawk, "Witchcraft and Women's Culture."
20. In Judy Chicago, *Through the Flower,* 213-17.
21. Valeric Saiving , "The Human Situation: A Feminine View," *Journal of Religion,* 40 (1960): 100, and reprinted in this volume.
22. Virginia Woolf, *A Room of One's Own* (New York: Harcourt Brace Jovanovich, 1928), 86.

23. Rich, *Of Woman Born,* 226.
24. De Beauvior, *Second Sex,* 448-49.
25. "Old Time Woman," lyrics by Jeffrey Langley and Holly Near, from *Holly Near: A Live Album,* Redwood Records, 1974.
26. "Started Out Fine," by Holly Near, from *Holly Near: A Live Album.*
27. Rich, *Of Woman Born*, 223.
28. A term coined by Naomi Goldenberg to refer to reflection on the meaning of the symbol of goddess.

6

Hindu Perspective of Environmental Ethics

Man and Environment

The harmonious relationship between Man and environment has been grossly upset by Man's exploitative attitude towards Nature and its resources. Under the impact of the materialistic culture created by the Industrial Revolution, Man has unwittingly slipped into the vortex of wasteful consumption through the widespread misutilization of exhaustible and non-renewable resources in the name of the modern civilized life style.

This extreme consumerism has come to the East from Western ideology, which grants Man absolute rights over Nature and its resources and treats him as "master of the universe". Lynn White Jr. (1967), the greatest supporter of this thesis, holds Christianity responsible for the emergence of the exploitative, acquisitive, materialistic culture. According to White, what individuals and communities do to their environment depends upon how much they see themselves in relation to Nature. He maintains that the exploitative view that has generated much of the present environmental crisis, particularly in Europe and North America, is a result of the teachings of Christianity, which conceives of Man as superior to all God's creations and that everything else has been created for Man's use and enjoyment. In White's opinion, the only way to reduce the ecological crisis facing mankind is to reject the Christian view that Nature has no reason to exist except to serve Man. This proposition shook Western scientists, theologians and environmentalists and evoked academic debate throughout the world.

Ecologists widely made use of White's criticism of Christianity as "the most anthropocentric religion the world has seen" in organising ecological movements in industrial towns of the West (Derr, 1975). Derr posed a counter-question:

> "If Christian doctrine has produced technological culture and its environmental troubles, one would be at a loss to understand the absence of the same results in equally Christian Eastern Europe. And conversely, if ecological disaster is a particularly Christian habit, how can one explain the disasters non-Christian cultures have visited upon their own environments?"

Derr's challenge did not go unnoticed. A number of scholars in the Eastern world started examining their religious scriptures afresh to prepare an answer to his question.

Oriental religions, such as Hinduism, Buddhism, Jainism, Taoism and Confucianism, have well established norms determining Man's behaviour towards Nature and its resources. Since his origin, Man has lived through the ages in harmony with Nature and has held Nature in awe and reverence. The holy scriptures of various religions, faiths and beliefs uphold the need for harmony with the universe, which is the habitat not only of Man but also of all animals, birds, insects, plants and vegetation. The mutually supportive role of all living beings is often mentioned as a crucial factor for a balanced social existence. However, under the impact of the culture of colonisers, the traditional view of Man and environment came to be undermined and people in the colonies accepted the Western view as scientific and suitable to modern times.

International Awakening to Environmental Protection

The awakening in the United Nations to the urgency of environmental protection and the insertion in the constitution of India of a Constitutional Provision regarding the protection and improvement of the environment and the safeguarding of the forests and wildlife of the country (Article 48-A) more or less coincided.

The Club of Rome in 1972 had published a report after the Stockholm Conference (UN), 1972 which stated:

> "If the present growth trends in world population, industrialisation, pollution, food production and resource depletion continue unchanged, the limits to growth in this planet will be reached sometime within the next one hundred years."

U Thant, the United Nations Secretary-General from 1967 to 1971, had also expressed similar fears which actually put the entire Western world on alert. The Eastern world had, however, still not bothered to take the environmental threats seriously and considered them a part of the West's conspiracy to keep the East under-developed. U Thant said:

> "I do not wish to seem over-dramatic, but I can only conclude from the information that is available to me as Secretary-General that the members of the United Nations have perhaps ten years left in which to subordinate their ancient quarrels and launch a global partnership to curb the arms race, to improve the human environment, to defuse the population explosion and to supply the required momentum to development efforts. If such a global partnership is not formed within the next decade, then I very much fear that the problems I have mentioned will have reached such staggering proportions that they will be beyond our capacity to control."
>
> (Meadows, 1972)

The International Environmental Workshop, held in Belgrade, Yugoslavia in October 1975 and co-sponsored by the UN and UNESCO, issued a Charter, which called for a new global ethic and identified two main goals of environmental action:

1. For each nation, according to its culture, to clarify for itself the meaning of such basic concepts as "quality of life" and "human happiness" in the context of the total environment.
2. To identify which "actions" will ensure the preservation and improvement of humanity's potentials and develop social and individual well being in harmony with the bio-physical and man-made environment.

(UNESCO-UNEP, 1976).

The twin goals prompted a research in Hindu scriptures and philosophy which could help in redefining the real meaning of "quality of life" and "proper actions" in consonance with Indian culture and beliefs, for the improvement of environment by striking a balance between Man's needs and Nature's resources.

Hindu Tradition View on Man and Environment

Of all the living religious traditions, Hinduism is the oldest. Hindu religious scriptures are, in fact, teachings about Man's relationship with the environment and his attitude towards ecology. The Hindu religion is in a way a religion of "human ecology". The oneness of all living and non-living beings and the concept of non-violence are the essence of the Hindu religion. The basic concept of peace and harmony on earth is beautifully depicted in the *Vedas*. Its origins lie in the *Vedas,* the marvellous hymns sung by seers and sages many thousands of years before the birth of Christ. The *Vedas* are the bedrock of Hindu religion and philosophy. They provide a world view with regard to the ecological situation which is startlingly relevant today, based as it is on the premise that mankind is an integral part of Nature itself, linked to the rest of creation by indissoluble bonds. The Vedic hymns deal with natural phenomena, animals and birds, flora and fauna, pollution and its prevention. The magnificent *Hymn to the Earth* in the *Yajurveda* speaks of the Hindu religion's concern for peace and harmony in the environment:

> *May there be peace in the celestial region*
> *May there be peace in the atmosphere*
> *May peace reign on earth*
> *May the waters be soothing*
> *May the medicines be healing*
> *May the plants be source of peace to all*
>
> (*Yajurveda* 36.17)

Environmental ethics have been taught through religion. It has set a proper, well-defined code of conduct, according to which human beings are required to make use of the resources of the earth. They have been taught the art of conservation and protection of the environment and *Vanaspati* and also how to make their own contribution in promoting and enhancing its wealth and virtues.

Respect for "all life" has been, a part of Indian religious philosophies since history was first recorded. Non-violence and reverence for all living creatures has been preached by Hinduism, Buddhism and Jainism. The Ashoka edicts confirm the presence of non-violent thinking in Indian religions. However, despite the presence of such magnificent ideas and knowledge, environmental awareness came to India in the early Seventies, i.e.. after the Stockholm Conference of 1972 (United Nations, 1972).

In essence, Hinduism is an environmental religion. Its scriptures are full of environmental ethics and have prescribed norms for Man's behaviour towards Nature. The Hindu religion looks at Man as an integral part of Nature, as other non-human species are. Man and Nature are both the creation of God Almighty and He Himself is present in all His creations—from ants to human beings. In order to understand the relationship of Man and Nature, a study of the Hindu theories of the creation of the Universe may be helpful.

The Creation of the Universe

There is a great similarity between the biological theory of the origin of the environment, its survival and relationship with Man and the Hindu religious theories of the origin of the Universe and Man's place in it. Environment comprises the whole range of external influences acting on an organism, of both physical and biological forces of Nature surrounding the human individual. All living beings are a part of a balanced and interacting ecosystem. They draw sustenance from the solid, liquid and aerial resources on the earth. They pass through the phases of reproduction, sustenance and extinction.

Ecosystem: The ecosystem consists of sub-systems such as sea, forests, water reservoirs, plants, trees, insects and animals—all of which are inter-connected in a network of devourer-devoured relationships. None of the elements in the network is useless or without purpose; each of them helps to regulate the balance of the sub-system. The ultimate source of energy for the entire ecosystem is solar energy. Bio-gas chemical cycles are essential for the process of reproduction in the physical environment. Examples are cited from the natural cycles of water, carbon, oxygen and nitrogen. The elements in each of these cycles are fused into the environment, absorbed and used in the biological constituents and again emitted into the environment (Bhagwat, 1989). This is one of the finest descriptions of the ecosystem and the entire Hindu view of Man and environment can be explained around it.

Creation of the World: There are several theories of the creation of the world propounded in the *Vedas, Puranas, Upnishads,* Epics *(Ramayana* and *Mahabharata), Bhagwatgita* and *Smriti* ("memorised wisdom"). *Shruti* ("transmitted wisdom") is also a source of knowledge about the creation of the Universe. A number of Sanskrit scholars, such as Bharatarihari and Kalidasa, have given the interpretation of these theories. In modern times too, Swami Ramtirtha, Ramkrishna Paramahansa, Vivekanand, Swami Dayanand Saraswati and Shri Aurbindo have given several interpretations of the theories of the creation of the *Srishti* (Universe) propounded by various Indian religions.

The *Taittriya Upnishad* deals with the course of evolution of *Srishti* from *Brahma* (another name of *Hiranyagarbha,* the sole creator). He is also called *Atman*. The *Upnishad says:*

> "From *Atman* space (sky) arose, from space wind (gaseous conditions), from wind fire, from fire water, from water the earth, from the earth herbs, from herbs food, from food semen, from semen human beings."
>
> *(Taittriya Upnishad* Brahmanand Valli Anuvak I)

This verse explains the evolutionary process. Food is the main requirement of all beings in the universe, including human beings. Therefore, food is called a panacea from which energy is gained. Food is produced on the earth and thus earth is called "mother", as it sustains the entire creation *(Taittriya Upnishad* Brahmanand Valli Anuvak 2).

Existence of God: Almost all religious scriptures agree about the existence of God prior to the creation of the *Srishti, Rigveda* says that God created the world by transforming the *Asat* (non-existent) into Sat (existent). It is also said that prior to the creation, there was darkness all over. Darkness was surrounded by water. There was nothing around. Then "That one" *(Tadekam)* arose through the power of heat. "That one" cannot be described. It is beyond time, beyond space, beyond age, beyond death, and beyond immortality. One cannot explain what it is. One only knows that "It is".

From the desire of "That one" arose *Purush* and *Mul Prakriti* (the matter). With the help of *Maya* (material cause), *Purush* and *Prakriti* interacted and "That one" incarnated himself as *Hiranya Barbha* (the cosmic mind). *Yajurveda* calls him *Prajapati* and *Vishvakarma,* who is considered the great progenitor of the entire universe [see *Yajurveda* Chapter XXXI (Verse 2), *Rigveda* Mandal 10, *Sukta* 121 (Verse 1) and *Sukta* 81 (Verses 2-4)].

Evolution of the Human Race: The *Brihadaranyaka Upnishad* presents a systematic process of evolution of the human race and also of non-humans. It says that *Atman* (self) transformed into a man and then into a cow and bull, mare and stallion, she-goat and he-goat, ewe and ram, and every other creature in the universe. In this way, he created everything that exists in pairs from human beings down to ants.

The Upnishads maintain equality of all human and non-human beings, as all have been created by the same *Atman* (self), no one is superior to the other and no one can command authority over the other. *Bhagwatgita* also maintains the same theory. The universe has been created by Him (God) and at the end of it, it will once again merge with Him so that it can reappear at His will. In *Gita,* Lord Krishna says:

> "The entire cosmic order is under me. It is at my command that it manifests again and again. And at my command it becomes extinct at the end."
>
> *(Bhagwatgita,* Chapter 9 (Verse 8))

> "Man has no control over his life. He can control his deeds because deeds are very important. Those who do not perform their duties towards the world, Nature and its inhabitants take birth in the animal kingdom in the next life."
>
> *(Bhagwatgita,* Chapter 14 (Verse 15))

Concept of Rebirth: The concept of "rebirth" is a regulating device which compels a man to be pious and dutiful. Besides, the very idea that all the birds and animals must have been human beings in the earlier life and have become animals because of their unpious deeds establishes a bond of oneness between the human and non-human inhabitants of the earth. The great epics, *Ramayana* and *Mahabharata,* also affirm the theory of "rebirth" and the elevation of Man through various species.

It is said that, after one hundred and eighty-four lives in the form of various living species, one gets into the human form and life. Hence, one has to be respectful and grateful to all those species in whose world he has held a place. The theory of the creation and extinction is also explained in the *Bhagwatgita,* which says that this cycle is of a *Kalpa* (a millennium). In this cyclical process the *Atman* (self) creates, protects and dissolves himself by himself, the *Kalpa* after *Kalpa.*

The Elements of the Universe

In Hindu theory, there are five elements created by *Hiranyagarbha* (the cosmic being). They are space (sky), air, fire, water and earth. The theories of incarnations *(avtars)* also explain the evolution of the human race through various species.

Puranas are also a good source of knowledge about the theories of evolution. *Brahma Puran, Narsingh Puran, Vishnu Puran,* and *Varah Puran* substantiate the Vedic concepts and teach righteousness. It is maintained that, when righteousness disappears from the earth, it starts moving towards decay. To save it from annihilation, He incarnates in some or other form, restores the balance and saves the earth from becoming extinct.

Human nature consists of the qualities of the five elements, together with three attributes—*Man, Ahankar* and *Buddhi.*

1. Sky (Space)

'Sky' is called *Dyouh, Svah, Akash, Kham* etc. In *Rigveda* sky is called "Father" and the earth "Mother". Sky gives water and with water earth reproduces the entire *Prakriti* and the living beings of Nature. It is said in *Rigveda:* "Sweet be our father heaven (sky) to us". The mantra *Bhur, Bhuvah, Svah* means "God is present in earth, atmosphere and sky."

Atharvaveda (2.11.2) maintains that sky is a dwelling place of the forces of Nature (air, water and fire). Sky is also accepted as a nourishing place of all good things. The prayer says: "May they, whom the beautiful objects in the sky nourish, who are manifold in air's mid-regions, who preserve lightning in their womb and are beautiful in appearance, bring felicity and bliss to us".

2. Water

'Water' was the only thing that existed prior to the Creation and it surrounded the all-pervading darkness. From the water emerged the "golden egg", the cause of *Hiranyagarbha.* Water is treated as propitious and an enhancer of energy in the body. *Agni* and *Soma* are part of water and within the waters are all medicines that heal. *Agni* blesses them all. Water is the best physician. According to the Hindu scriptures, water is the best drink ever created by God for men *(Atharvaveda,* 3.13.5; *Rigveda,* 1.23. 20 and 6.50.7; *Yajurveda,* 2.20.7).

Hydropathy was a developed science in ancient times. It was the duty of every human being to protect the "purity" of water. *Yajurveda* is the book of *Havans* and *Yajnas. Yajnas* are considered necessary for the purity of the atmosphere and water. It is said that the human.

offerings to *Yajnas* purify the water sucked by the sun into clouds with air. The same water after evaporation rains and makes the growth of herbs and medicines on the earth possible. All sources of water are worshipped by the Hindus. *Atharvaveda* (19.2.1-2) says:

May the waters from the snowy hills be peace giving to you.
May the waters from the springs bring peace to you.
May the flowing waters be pleasant to you.
May the rain water be the source of prosperity to you.

and

Sweet be the waters of the oasis
So may be the waters of the pool.
May the waters dug from the earth be sweet
As well as those stored in the tanks during the rains.

Water is the cause of the birth of *Vanaspati* and a number of living beings of the non-human category. The *Chandogya Upnishad* (7.10.1) says:

This earth, the air, the heavens, the mountains, gods and men, domestic animals and birds, vegetables and trees, wild creatures down to worms, flies and ants, are nothing but water under sol id conditions.

The great epic *Mahabharata* (*Moksha Parva,* 183.2-4) says "the god first produced water for the survival of life on the earth. That water has enriched life and its absence would be killing for all the creatures and the plant life."

3. Vayu (Air)

Vayu Devta is considered most reverend among the Hindus. The *Pran* (life, soul) depends on air, i.e. *Pran Vayu* (the breath). The moment air is not entering the body and Man is not breathing, he is dead. It is also called *Vat* in *Rigveda* (10.186.1):

May vata blow in soothing manner
And bring well being and health to body and heart
And lengthen our life.

Chandogya Upnishad (1.11.5) says that:

With breath one takes birth and with the loss of breath they depart from the earth.

Upnishads maintain that, if a person adheres to the path of morality and leads a virtuous life, then all elements of the universe—earth, water, air, nature *(Vanaspati)*—bring him prosperity and good health and he lives longer.

The ancient scriptures maintain that the *pran* is not only a psychic but also a cosmic principle, that is, it is not only the breath of life in men, but also the universal breath of life that prevails throughout Nature. Thus *Vayu* is essential to the survival of all human, non-human and plant life on earth (*Traittreya Brahman,* 3.2.5.11; *Manusmriti,* 3.77).

4. Agni (Fire)

Agni has a wider meaning in the Hindu scriptures. It is fire (burnt through wood etc.); it is energy; it is power; it is stimulation leading to strength. *Agni* is the cause of water as it facilitates evaporation and produces aerial waters. *Agni* is worshipped by the Hindus in many forms. Whatever is cooked in the kitchen is first offered to *Agni.* It means offering the same that has been given to us by the mother earth produced with the help of water given to it by *Agni.* It is said (*Satpatha Brahman,* 5.3.5.17) that:

> *Agni causes steam (evaporation)*
> *From evaporation are formed clouds*
> *And from cloud comes rain.*

Manusmriti (3.76) says:

> *Every offering made to Agni reaches the sun and from sun is born rain which brings prosperity, peace and beauty to the earth.*

In the Hindu rituals the *Havans* and *Yajnas* hold an important place. Through *Yajnas* all nutritious and healthy things are sent to the atmosphere and after becoming part of condensation, through rains they come to the earth and improve the fertility and quality of the soil, leading to the best agricultural production. Before the commencement of the rainy season, the *Yajna* for rain is performed. It is done even now in this age of science. It is widely believed that the *Yajnas* bring rains and good rains which are good for human beings and the *Vanaspati,* *(Yajurveda* is the book of various kinds of *Havans* and *Yajnas* and speaks at length of their utility for Man and environment.)

5. Earth

Prithvi (earth) is worshipped as mother, as it is the source of that which is cherished by human beings for good life—*Mata Bhumih Putroham Prithviyam* ("Earth is mother, we are children of the mother Earth"). *Atharvaveda* says that we pray to *Prithvi* which bears trees, plants and medicinal herbs and protects them for the wellbeing of the human being. It possesses oceans, rivers and other bodies of water which give us land to produce food grains to eat and survive. Mother earth and its wealth give meaning to life. Its characteristics—*roop* (form), *ras* (taste), *gandh* (smell), *sparsh* (touch or feel) and *Shabd* (sound)—have a deep impact on human life and Man inherits these qualities in his own being or personality *(Mahabharat, Mokshparva* Chapter 184 (Verses 27-29) and see also *Atharvaveda,* 12.1.3 and 12.1.27).

A Vedic prayer says:

> *Earth, our mother on whom is grown food grains like wheat, rice, barley, on whom are born all human races (five in all) is nourished by clouds, loved by rains; we worship her for she bears in her womb all precious things.*

The Hindu philosophy believes in the equality of human beings and looks at them as soul-parts of the same God. Vedic scriptures maintain that earth does not belong to any individual or set of people or races. It belongs to everyone, to all races regardless of their language, colour, religion and place of birth. It belongs to humans and non-humans alike and pampers them both with love, care and concern. Human beings and all other creatures inherit the qualities of the mother earth in the same way they inherit the qualities of their own mother *(Atharvaveda,* 12.1.27, 12.1.3, 12.1.42-43, 12.1.15, 12.1.45 and *Mahabharat,* 184, 27-29). As children of the mother earth, human beings have to have an attitude of love, peace, harmony and mutual co-existence towards all that belongs to earth, namely *Vanaspati,* wildlife, plants, birds, insects, rivers, mountains, springs, lakes and waterfalls. Man's survival and well-being depend on the survival of the ecosystem of which he is an integral part.

Provision in Scriptures for Protection of Flora

The importance of trees, their planting and preservation, has been enumerated in various scriptures such as *Vedas, Puranas, Upnishads* and epics. Trees and green surroundings were considered as symbols of a well-kept village and such villagers were respected. The Hindus were careful observers of both the internal and external properties of plants and furnished copious lists of vegetables with sensible notices of their uses and names significant of their peculiarities. *Varah Puran* (Chapter 172, Verse 39) advocates planting as a sure means to attain *Swarga* (heaven):

> *One who plants one peepal, one neem, one ber, ten flowering plants or creepers, two pomegranates, two oranges and five mango trees goes to heaven.*

In order to make trees safe, *Puranas* have preached the presence of some or other form of God in various trees. Owing to their association with God, people worshipped and protected them from being cut or destroyed. The basil plant *(Tulsi)* is regarded as so sacred that its presence is considered essential in every household and married ladies worship it every morning and evening. *Vat Vriksha* is associated with Hindu *sanskaras,* so are peepal, amla, palas, ashok and gooler. *Bilva* leaves are offered to Lord Shiva during the rainy season. *Kusha* (a kind of grass) is very sacred and its stems are used for making a mat for sitting on during *puja* (worship). Wild flowers and fruits like *Dhatura, Ankra, Mandara* are also offered to Lord Shiva. The wood of palas, shami, pipal, bar, gooler, mango, bilva, kasturi, keṣhar and sandal are used in *Yajnas. Skand Puran* gives a comprehensive list of the trees which should not be cut while they are green. Verse 227 of the *Yagyavalakya Smriti* says that in ancient India the cutting of green trees was a punishable crime:

> *If a person cuts the branches of the trees full of green leaves, stems or the whole of it and if that is not the source of livelihood, he should be punished for twenty or forty or eighty panas* [a gold coin].

According to *Charak Samhita,* the destruction of forests is most dangerous for the nation and human beings. *Vanaspati* has a direct relationship with the wellbeing of society. The destruction of *Vanaspati may* cause many serious diseases and ruin the prospects of human life. With the destruction of medicinal plants, there may not remain any means to save the health and life of human beings on this earth *(Rigveda,* 1.91.22, 5.41.11-12, 3.8.11 and 4.57.3).

Chandogya Upnishad (6.11.1-2) describes trees as living beings. It says that when a tree is cut at the root, it trickles sap because it lives. When cut in the middle, it trickles sap, which means it lives. When it is cut at the top, it trickles sap because it lives. It stands erect because that is its glorious self-confident profile. If life goes out of one branch, it withers away. If life goes out of the entire tree, the entire tree will wither away. It is so because a tree is a living thing with life.

In the Vedic period people had respect for flora and fauna and their environmental consciousness and knowledge about their uses are depicted in wall carvings and the carvings on utensils of the Indus Valley civilisation period. Even the coins have trees and plants carved out on them. On a seal of the Harappan period a woman is shown with a plant coming out of her womb, which may be seen as a flamboyant depiction of fertility.

Atharvaveda has prayers for trees who are worshipped as lords:

> *We call on trees, cords of forests, herbs and plants, on the learned teacher, a Vedic scholar and the sun; may they deliver us from sin.*

Mahabharat (184.10-14, 18.15-17) advocates the protection of trees in a very beautiful manner with elaborate illustrations. Bhishma explains to Pandavas that:

> *Although trees are solid, they have the properties of sky. They have life, they flower and bear fruit. They feel warmth and get dry when the sun is too hot and water is scarce. It shows that they have a sense of touch. Fruits and flowers of the tree fall down under the effect of thunder, air and fire. It shows that they can hear. Creepers grow around trees and encircle them to go up. It shows that they can see and they do know how to climb up. The bad smell or pollution makes them suffer as it changes their colour and flavour. It shows that they can smell. They live like humans and also die like them.*
>
> *They have sensory nerves. They take water from the roots. If they have any disease the sprinkling of medicine cures them. On cutting they feel sorrow and when new branches appear they feel happy. This shows that they have sense to feel happy and sorry and have rasendriyas* [sensory nerves].

Vriksharopan (tree planting) and *Vrikshapuja* is not a new practice. In *Mohinjodaro* culture, too, tree worship was a tradition. Every village had a *Vriksha Devta,* worshipped with prayers and offerings of water, flowers and sweets. In Hindu families, particularly in a tribal society, women even married trees. The 80% of India's population which lives in villages, hills and tribal areas still believes in these age-old customs and traditions.

In *Matsaya Puran* the process of planting a tree is described. It shows that 1,500 years ago India had an environmental culture and ecological ethics which people observed with commitment and conviction. *Matsaya Puran* says:

> *Clean the soil first and water it. Decorate the tree with flowers, burn guggulu* [incense] *perfume in front of them and place one pitcher, filled with water, by the side of each tree, offer prayers and oblations and then sprinkle holy water on trees. Recite prayers from Rigveda, Yajurveda and Samveda and kindle fire. After such worship the actual plantation should be celebrated. He who plants even one tree goes straight to heaven.*

Kautilya's *Arthshastra* has strictly prohibited the destruction of forests and prescribed punishment for destroying the woods by cutting trees and plants. For cutting off the green, tender, blooming trees in the parks, public places and streets a fine of six panas was imposed. *Charak Samhita* also warns against cutting the trees:

> *... destruction of forests is most dangerous for the nation and for human beings. Vanaspati has a direct relationship with the well being of society. Due to the pollution of the natural environment and the destruction of Vanaspati, many diseases might crop up to ruin the nation. In such circumstances only Vanaspati and herbs with medicinal qualities can cure the people and save their life.*

Even the Buddhists have preached that one person in his entire lifetime should plant at least five trees and each tree after planting should be looked after for at least five years.

Provision in Scriptures for Protection of Animals and Birds

Ahisma, or non-violence, is the essence of all Indian religions. *Ahisma* means respect for all living beings and a duty to protect them. In some Indian religions, such as Jainism, *Ahisma* is extended to plant life and insects too and the devotees take care to protect them. Austerity in the use of Nature's resources, particularly food and water, is also a watchword of Jainism, which is in essence an offshoot of the Hindu religion.

Karuna, or compassion, is another essential characteristic of Hinduism. *Vaishnava Jan* is the person who is kind to all human beings, animals, birds, insects, plants, trees and things of Nature, and feels hurt by seeing any of these exploited, misused or destroyed. Gandhiji's *Vaishnava Jan* felt the pain of others in his heart and with compassion tried to lessen it by sharing it and if possible by eradicating it.

Yajurveda (34.13.94) has elaborate verses about the protection of various animals and birds. It advises the king that:

> *You should never kill animals like bullocks useful for agriculture or cows which give us milk or any other helpful animals and must punish those who kill or harm them.*

Manusmriti (5.45) categorically declares the killing of animals a punishable crime:

> *He who gives permission, he who kills the animals, he who sells the slaughtered animal, he who cooks the animal, he who administers the distribution of such food stuff and at last he who eats such cooked animal food are all murderers and liable to be punished according to the law of Nature.*

King Ashoka the Great, after seeing so many people killed in the battle of *Kalinga,* turned to *Ahisma* and adopted the Buddhist religion. All his life he preached *Ahisma* and constructed pillars and on them had the rules of *Ahisma* written so that the people would learn about them and observe them strictly in their life. Ashoka declared the following animals inviolable: parrots, mynahs, ruddy geese, wild ducks, the nandimukhas, the gelata, bats, the amba kapilika, tortoise, boneless fish, porcupines, squirrels, deer, bulls, wild asses, white and grey pigeons, she-goats, ewes and cows. He prohibited the burning of husks as they might contain insects. The burning of forests and grass was also strictly prohibited.

Hindus even see their God in various animals and show reverence to them. Many of them are worshipped. Some of them are carriers of various Gods and, being associated with them, they are treated as sacred—for example, the cow is holy. It is associated with Lord Krishna, who is known as the Shepherd God. Besides giving milk and butter, cows also give bulls, which are useful in agriculture. The bull is the carrier of Lord Shiva and immune from killing. The elephant is associated with the Goddess Laxmi, the Goddess of Wealth. They are also associated with Lord Ganesha, who is known as the Elephant God, as his face (head) is that of an elephant. Like Ganesh, the elephant is also the symbol of *Buddhi,* i.e., intellect and wisdom.

Perhaps the Hindu religion is the only religion whose scriptures have such elaborate provisions for the maintenance, protection and conservation of the environment—nature, plant life and animal life.

Provisions in Anti-Pollution Scriptures on

Indian religious scriptures, particularly the *Vedas,* are the "comprehensive code", having rules for all aspects of life on earth. *Vedas* maintain that cities should develop along the flowing rivers. All the large cities of India are around the Indus, Ganges, Yamuna, Brahmputra, Kaveri, Narmada, Mahanadi, Chambal etc. The next choice was near hills or forests. Natural surroundings and scenic beauty were considered essential for a happy life and healthy disposition. *The* description of *Indraparastha,* the capital of Pandavas, in *Mahabharata (Adiparva,* 199.77) is that:

> *The city of Indraparastha abounded in lakes full of water, lotus and cranes and beautiful gardens.*

Kautilya's *Arthshastra* (2.20, 2.145, 2.45) has detailed provisions about maintaining cleanliness and sanitary conditions:

> *The punishment of one eighth pana should be awarded to those who throw dust on the roads; for muddy water, one fourth pana. If both are thrown, the punishment should be double.*

It disallowed the disposal of dead bodies near human habitats. Kautilya even suggested sites for cities saying that:

> *Boundaries should be denoted by a river, mountain, forests, bulbous plants, caves, artificial bridges, trees of salmali* [silk], *Sami and Khsirvriksha* [milk tree].

Vishnu Smriti, Charak Samhita, Chandogya Upnishada, Manusmriti, Rigveda have discussed the problems of pollution and its adverse impact on human life and *Vanaspati* and have suggested means to counter them. *Charak Samhita* (3.2) says:

> *It seems possible that all stars, planets, moon, sun, air agni, nature and all dishas* [direction] *may get polluted. Then seasons will appear against nature. Prithvi, in spite of being full of its virtues,*

> *may lose its ras* [quality] *and render plants, herbs and medicinal shrubs useless. When such pollution occurs, human beings will suffer from various diseases. Due to the pollution of nature and seasons, several types of diseases will crop up and they will ruin the country. Therefore, 0 Man, collect all medicinal plants before the commencement of such terrible diseases to save Mankind from their evil effects.*

In ancient scriptures pollution is called *Vikriti,* which means change in the original form, nature, feel, taste, appearance and quality of certain things. *Charak Samhita* (3.6) further says:

> *When air is mixed with bad elements, it gets polluted and brings harm to the body. The air which is against the virtues of season, full of moisture, windy, hard icy cool, hot dry, harmful, terribly roaring, colliding from two or three sides, bad smelling, oily, full of dust, smoke sand and steam creates diseases in body and it is polluted.*

Taittraiya Aranyak (5.101), *Manusmriti* (4.151) and *Vishnu Puran* (3.11.11-12) have written that drinking water and water of rivers, ponds, springs, wells and tanks should be kept clean from dirt and pollution. *Shuchita,* i.e. cleanliness, was considered a means to reach God as it was believed that God is always present in clean, healthy, beautiful, loving, peaceful and harmonious surroundings.

For those who, being uneducated and unconcerned, may not care for environmental ethics, Hindu scriptures have given an environmental God-Lord Datatreya, who is the patron saint of ecology and one of the twenty-four incarnations of Hindu Gods. (The twenty-four Avatars are Sanak, Varah, Narada, Nar Narayan, Kapil, Dattatreya, Yagya, Rishbha, Prithu, Matsya, Kaschap, Dhanvantri, Mohini, Narsimha, Vamana, Parashuram, Vyas, Rama, Balrama, Krishna, Hansa, Hayagriva, Buddha and Kalki.) He pleads that to save the environment and revive ecological culture, the resurrection of Lord Dattatreya is essential. This would help particularly those who have no awareness of environmental degradation. The presence of an environmental God may restrain them. (The God Dattatreya accepted the following twenty-four creatures and elements as his "Guru"—Pingala, Boa, Arrowmaker, Madhukara, Woodpecker, Virgin, Earth, Water, Fire, Sky, Air, Moon, Sun, Child, Sea, Insect, Elephant, Deer, Fish, Pigeon, Snake, Bee, Spider and Butterfly.)

Revival of Traditional Environmental Ethics

In order to maintain a balance between the environment and the materialistic-scientific-technological culture, a revival of environmental ethics is essential. It is distressing to see that, despite such glorious traditions of preservation of the environment, India and other developing countries (those with the impact of Buddhism and Hinduism in South and South-East Asia) are faced with serious environmental problems, such as deforestation, desertification, soil erosion, extinction of rare species of plants and wildlife, drought, famine, water scarcity, unemployment, malnutrition, diseases and pollution of air, water and human environment through noise. There are several reasons for this environmental decay.

To some extent it is true that the invasion of foreign culture has pushed the local or indigenous culture into the background and, following the styles of the ruling classes, the local people tend to undermine the traditional ways of living. In the changed circumstances, the traditional system of education in *Gurukuls* in the open surroundings came to an end. Traditional wisdom became confined to a few people who felt indifferent to imparting it to the common man.

Thus, the loss of traditional knowledge about the relationship of Man with Nature and Man's responsibility towards the preservation of the environment led to the present state of degradation and almost total decay.

Modern education has alienated Man from the environment, as most of it is imparted in closed buildings and laboratories. With this detachment, Man has gradually become indifferent to Nature and looks at it as one of the means to satisfy his needs.

Scientific and technological developments have enabled man to establish superiority over Nature. With the use of technology, Man has mastered oceans, rivers, wild falls and natural springs. He can control the flow of a river, divert its route or totally dry it up. Man has mastered space and outer space. He can determine and change the course of seasons, alter weather, and turn the rainy season into hot summer by eliminating the clouds and humidity.

In his eagerness to control Nature, Man has ruined the environment to the extent that now his own survival is threatened. Several studies have come out with such frightening calculations that now the attention of the entire world has focused on these issues (World Commission on Environment and Development, 1987; Council on Environmental Quality and the Department of State, 1982; UNEP, 1989; Mintzer, 1987). Efforts are being made to check further environmental deterioration by adopting preventive measures. While these measures are taken at Government level and at international institutions, it is also worthwhile to generate some kind of environmental ethics. If this can be done by resorting to religious scriptures and the traditions of ancient societies, it is worth the effort.

REFERENCES

Bhagwat, Ravi. 1989. Paryavaran (in Marathi language of India) In *Bhartiya Samaj Vidhyan Kosha,* Vol. III, pp. 212-213 (Pune).

Council on Environmental Quality and the Department of State, 1982. The Global 2000 Report to the President: Entering the Twenty-first Century (Penguin).

Derr, Thomas Sieger. 1975. Religion's responsibility for ecological crisis. *World View.*

Meadows, Donella H. 1972. *The Limits to Growth* (Signet Books).

Mintzer, Irving M. 1987. *A Matter of Degrees: The Potential for Controlling the Greenhouse Effect* (World Resources Institute).

United Nations, 1972. *Year Book of the United Nations,* Vol. 26, pp. 319-21 and pp. 330-31.

UNEP. 1989. *Action on Ozone.*

UNESCO-UNEP. 1976. *Environmental Education Newsletter,* No. 1 (January).

WHITE Jr., Lynn. 1967. The historical roots of our ecological crisis. *Science,* Vol. 155, No. 3767, pp. 48-56.

World Commission on Environment and Development, 1987. *Our Common Future* (Oxford University Press).

7

Interpreting Rgveda in Todays Environ-mental Context

The celebration of beauty in the Vedas accompanies the offering of part of that beauty (cows, representing light, as the primary animal sacrifice) up for slaughter. The balance of the universe, of such natural elegances as the sun, the weaving together of heaven and earth, and the power of speech to sustain the earth, all depend on the integration of cosmology and killing.

The correspondence between cosmogony and the detailed specifics of the ritual action of animal sacrifice has not, been much remarked upon by scholars and therefore may be of some use in the present day environmental context.

Sacralizing Nature

Both ecologists and Indologists have resorted to ancient texts to describe Indian ideas about the cosmological workings of nature and to recover an understanding of balance and harmony within that world. As we shall see below, both appeal to a kind of Romantic ideal of "nature in the abstract," which is in fact only part of the picture suggested by the ancient Indian milieu itself. A more realistic glance at that textual tradition is the object of this chapter our readings will teach us lessons about how and why we use ancient texts and what they in turn can teach us about human relationship to the natural world.

What does it mean to sacralize nature? How and why do we sue ancient texts in the service of an idea of nature or ecology? As Norman Crowe puts it in his most recent theory of the environment, *Nature and the Idea of a Man-Made World,*[1] to claim something about ecology is, in pan, to claim a certain kind of unity: to invoke nature is to invoke primordial balance, holism, biological economy, understanding of interrelationship between things. In the study of religion this description is called a *cosmology*, a story about the origins of the universe, which describes just that interrelationship and balance between the world of nature and the world of humans. To put it succinctly, cosmology is usually in the service of some form of ecology. In the recent study of Indian ecology, the focus has been similar, stressing cosmological texts and ritual practices which, as one recent Indian publication claimed, "sacralize nature, so that man sic can live as an integral part of the universe."[2]

Romanticising India

A voluminous literature is developing about the roots of the Romantic movement, the idea of nature, and present-day ecological philosophy.[3] A lesser, but nonetheless important, literature is developing on the Romanticization of India, particularly in its relationship to its status as a culture in touch with nature and the earth. The literature, taken as a whole, is ambivalent; on the one hand, the last two decades have witnessed a massive postcolonial critique of European Romanticization of India as a place of natural mystery and beauty, a beauty which is essentially female and which should be plundered (raped) and "developed" out of its primitive state.[4] On the other hand, the last decade has also witnessed a reassertion of these same values in Hindu culture as positive ones, to be celebrated as unique and ancient and to be used as resources for future ecological movement.[5]

Dealing with Protection and Destruction of Nature

Herein lies the philosophical question about Nature Romanticism and India. What if the texts that are used to support both of these arguments (both for and against the Romancing of India) are in fact the same texts? What if the "seeds" of a nonviolent, harmonious, relationship to nature also contain explicit (and transcendentally sanctioned) scenes of destruction as well? It is incumbent upon us as ecologically minded readers of texts to acknowledge the presence of both attitudes?

One participant in the Harvard conference on Hinduism and ecology, Harry Blair, made a very eloquent plea on behalf of Romanticization —for without that process of affirmation of harmony between humans and nature, the respect and veneration which could determine our constructive behavior toward nature would be lost. At the same time "leaves something out" of the ancient assessment of nature can lead to a dishonest practice of reading, which ultimately does not help the ecological cause. For if, in fact, balanced harmony can be read into the *Ṛgveda,* so too can the destruction of nature. And such destruction can be seen as equally sanctioned by the Vedic texts. Any citation of ancient texts lands the ecologically minded on a very sticky wicket, and, because of their benign but quite evident selectivity, leaves them open to being less, and not more, persuasive.

An important word of caution is necessary here. Although the texts referred to in this chapter are sacrificial texts which do involve a level of violence to nature, it is not our intention to define sacrifice as inherently violent. As Frédérique Apffel-Marglin has pointed out,[6] there are ways in which the sacrificial paradigm could be used in a nonviolent way to talk about ecological balance and harmony. A definition of sacrifice does not necessarily entail violence. But the sacrificial worldview can inform our ecological reading of ancient India.

Even more importantly, it is the early Indian case, beginning with the sacrificial practices and metaphors of the Vedas and coming to full flower in the Upaniṣads, that teaches us that "everything is eating everything else."[7] Although space does not permit a detailed discussion of a vast scholarly literature, some general review of ancient Indian sacrifice practice might be useful here.

The Concept of Sacrifice in the Rgveda

As many scholars imply the sacrifice (*yajña*) of the *Ṛgveda* was probably a basic offering of hospitality, without the extreme elaboration and detail that the later philosophical and performative texts, the Brāhmaṇas Sutras, describe. Yet, even in those earliest of times, the sacrifice played a crucial role in Vedic religion: it is the religious act par excellence. One might describe its earliest form as an act of homage to the divinities of the Vedic world, consisting of a gift of oblation, called *havis,* made in order to obtain certain benefits, such as prosperity, health, long life, abundance of cattle, male offspring, and, in the later rites, even more elaborate requests.

In the view of the Aryans, the sacrifice also played a major role in the survival of the Aryan group and its ability to conquer enemies, both natural and human, along the way. In a later Vedic work, the *Satapatha Brāhmaṇa,* there is mention of the story of the sacrificial fire, which came out of the mouth of Videgha Mathava and then rolled eastward to the boundary river of Videha in eastern India, purifying as it rolled along. Thus, the image and practice of sacrifice also was integrally bound up with the development of Vedic society.

Offerings in Vedic Sacrifice

What is offered in Vedic sacrifice is what one likes to eat oneself: milk in its various forms of curd, warmed and clarified butter, barley and rice, especially in the form of cakes. In the later ritual literature there are elaborate prescriptions of the preparation of the cakes of the various gods. These edible offerings are also accompanied by scents, seats, and clothing, especially in the domestic rituals. The animal sacrifices *(pasu)* should be contrasted with the vegetable sacrifices *(isti).* The animal victim was usually the goat, but could also have been another animal, such as a bull, a donkey, or a dog, one that is used particularly in the sacrifice to the Raksas. The Asvamedha, or sacrifice of the horse, was one of the most elaborate of Vedic ceremonies, involving rituals lasting up to a year and the political appropriation of land, depending upon where the horse wandered.

Soma Offering: In addition to the vegetable and animal offerings, the Vedic offering par excellence is the *soma,* the intoxicating drink. It promotes an ecstatic state of mind, and is believed to confer immortality. In all of the later ritual texts, and certainly throughout the entire ninth book of the *Rgveda,* the purchase of the plant and the various sacrificial operations connected with it are described in detail the purchase of it, the transportation in carts, the procession of carrying it, the drawing of the water, the pressing of the stems that are swelled by the water and the straining of the juice into the decanter.

Eating the Remains: The sponsor of the sacrifice and the officiant priest usually partake of the remains of the dishes offered. While there is mention of the remains in the *Rgveda,* later in the ritual texts of the Brāhmaṇa the question of the why's and wherefore's of eating the remains becomes one of great speculative importance. In the later ritual, the goddess Iḍā is called to descend to earth and enter that part of the offering, also called *iḍā,* in order to convey to the sacrificer the quality of the victim: this has been called by Hermann Oldenberg an absorption of strength or healing, by Henri Hubert and Marcel Mauss a transubstantiation. It has also been analyzed as a communion or as a ceremony of alliance.

Secrificial Fire: Perhaps the most essential part of the ritual is the sacrificial fire: the fire acts as an intermediary between the sacrificer and the gods, the carrier of food between the worlds. Fire was also from its very inception an agent of purification, which protected against evil spirits.

Circumambulation: A frequent practice is circumambulation about an object, an animal victim, a consecrated instrument, and especially the fire. The movement takes place in the direction the sun circles, with the right side presented to the honored object, thus the name *pradakisna.*

In sum, as many Vedic hymns and later ritual texts discussed above indicate, sacrifice of an animal into the fire was part of the ecological balance in the ancient Vedic world; the killing and distribution of the animal was part of a larger understanding of human harmony with natural forces. Jan Heesterman has constructed a kind of cyclical "potlatch" scenario, wherein animal sacrifice is countered by animal sacrifice from a competing lineage. In the human realm, the stakes involved death to the loser, and, on a higher scale, nothing less than the disruption of cosmological forces. While some scholars might disagree with his more violent interpretation of the ancient Indian world, all do agree that cosmological functions and sacrificial functions are radically interdependent upon each other. The gods are given food and return it through their natural bounty; thus, the ecology of sacrificial food production and consumption is the central, guiding metaphor for the survival of earthly and celestial worlds.

In our ecological readings of the ancient world we very rarely incorporate these sacrificial processes into our ecological sensibilities of the twentieth and twenty-first centuries. Given that this is the case, our responsibility is to a holistic reading that realistically takes in both harmonious and disharmonious, creative and destructive accounts of ecology.[8] If we read ancient sources in this way, we take lessons from the *Rgveda* other than those of constant natural harmony—but these are nonetheless important lessons for us to learn. While as ecological activists we may not want to condone the practice of animal sacrifice today, the Vedic scenario can teach us far more than beatific contemplation of nature. It can teach us what it means to redistribute the natural world in the process of destruction; what it means to hasten the processes of life and death, growth and decay, on behalf of a larger religious perspective; and how ideas of harmony with nature and sacrifice can frequently go hand in hand.

Ancient Texts in the Service of Nature

Let us turn to the texts to see how ecology and sacrifice play themselves out in particular exegetical situations. The most appealing of these texts are the cosmologies found in the *Ṛgveda.* They are poetic and can read like an enigmatic version of Walt Whitman's *Leaves of Grass,*[9] filled with natural imagery of waters being released *(RV* 1.32); cows careening down well-trodden paths *(RV* 3.31); the sun rising like a wife coming to meet her husband *(RV* 1.92) or racing across the sky like a chariot driver *(RV* 1.115); healing plants, which emerge gently and magically from the earth's soil *(RV* 10.97); elements emerging from the human body back into the wind, sun, sky, and water *(RV* 10.16); spirits of the forest who show gentleness and a lack of fear *(RV* 10.146). This ecological appeal brings us back to the heart of the issue: how and why do we use ancient texts in the service of a harmonious idea of nature? In Indological writing since the nineteenth century, this appeal rests on a basic premise: that interaction with, and invocation of the world of nature in cosmological terms goes hand in hand with mystical vision and/or beatific contemplation. Max Müller's understanding of sun worship, the initial human experience of the awesomeness of nature, and thereby of God, was based on the hymn to Sūrya. or sun hymn, RV 1.115.[10]

Willard Johnson and Abel Bergaigne before him, saw the goddess of speech as the essence of *ṛta*, the order of the cosmos, and thereby a kind of goddess in the natural idiom (RV 10.1 25, 10.71, etc.).[11] The basic understanding of balance and harmony is traced by A. B. Keith to the threefold cosmological stride of Viṣṇu, who not only orders the world, but embodies all creatures within himself *(RV* 7.99, 7.100, 1.154).[12] Let us be even more specific: the Rgvedic hymns were seen as concepts and poetic images of contemplation, which we ourselves can also contemplate. They are extractable from the context of contemplation. Indeed, as Karl Figlio points out in his influential article "Knowing, Loving, and Hating Nature,"[13] when nature becomes an extractable "idea," the world of nature is born.

We can contemplate it just as the ancients did and we can use it just as the ancients did, because it exists apart from us and, as such, is manipulatable. This notion of extracting and contemplating is the convergence of Romanticism and science, and, I would argue, the convergence between Indological and some ecological writing about the Veda. In other words, we as scholars do intellectually with texts what we as environmentalists advocate against doing to the world of nature itself: we plunder and use. I want to argue that it is far more instructive to behave in the same environmental way with Vedic texts as we would like to do with the earth itself. If we refrain (as much as is humanly possible) from extraction, we learn a great deal more about ancient modes and forms of interaction with the world of nature than we do if we plunder the image.

The three images most frequently used in the service of the idea of natureare the sun, the idea of eloquence as nature goddess, and the balance of Viṣṇu's stride. Here we place them in their first ecological context: the world of the sacrifice,[14] and even more specifically, the world of their *viniyoga,* or application.

Rgveda 1.115 on the Sun's Form

Our discussion might well begin with RV 1.115, Kutsa's hymn to Surya. It invokes awe and wonder and glorious pastoral imagery, we can see how tempting of would have been to extrapolate from the hymn, as Muller did, into experiential contemplation of the natural world, and thus, of the universe.

Kutsa's Hymn to Surya:

1. The glorious group of rays has arisen; the eye of Mitra, Varuna, and Agni; the sun is the self of the moving and fixed; and has filled the heaven, earth, and the atmosphere.
2. The sun follows the godly and shining dawn, as a man follows a woman, dawn is where god-like men span the ages, that which is auspicious for the sake of good.
3. The auspicious, swift horses of the sun, with beautiful limbs, crossing the roads, well deserving of praise, honored by us, have ascended to the dome of the sky, and quickly

circle around earth and heaven.

4. Such is the divinity and majesty of the sun that, when he has set, he withdraws that which has been spread in the middle of things. When he has unyoked his racehorses from his chariot, then night spreads the veiling darkness over all.
5. The sun, in the sight of Mitra and Varuna, displays his form in the middle of the heavens, and his rays (horses) extend his eternal shining power, and bring on the blackness of night.
6. O gods, this day deliver us from severe wrongdoing, and may Mitra, Varuna Āditi, ocean, earth and heaven, be favorable to this mantra.[15]

Interpretation: One can see why Muller and others favored this hymn: dawn is personified; the sun has his racehorses; the sun is also the "self of all things and therefore the one who has the power to give and withdraw light. In verse two, there is a lovely wordplay on *yugāni,* or "ages," which could also mean "yokes" for ploughs; thus, the sacrificers who invoke the sun and "span the ages" are also agriculturalists who work the plough. The analogy is continued in verse four, where the sun can also cause darkness to be spread over "the middle of things," that is, the cultivator with the plough must stop in the middle of cultivating his field. The hymn is, in one sense, profoundly ecological, presenting levels of human and cosmic activity in delicate and poetic inter-relationship. What of the interpretive frame that idologists and ecologists have given it? Max Muller quotes this hymn in several of his works on the origin of religious ideas.[16] The sun is the beginning of humankind's understanding that there is a power beyond itself, and humans stand trembling before that power in awestruck wonder, stammering out the first few syllables of proto-Indo-European.

In a later vein, Willard Johnson also views this hymn as a kind of description of a contemplative act, filled with aesthetic power (*samvega*).[17] In his book published for the Centre of Advanced Study in Sanskrit, *Ancient Indian Theories of the Earth,* S.R.N. Murthy also describes the sun as one of the many divinities who were "natural powers personified"; the Vedic Aryans worshiped the sun as a kind of geothermal field, and their philosophy was dynamic. According to Murthy, they did not make the mistake of modern science, in seeing these forms and fields as without life.[18] Murthy is right to emphasize the dynamic nature of the sun, and its clear relationship to fire and water, in Vedic texts. Yet, the claim that Vedic natural forces can be interpreted as kinds of geothermal fields is to extract and contemplate in a way similar to those who used the Rgvedic sun as the "origin" of religion.

Ritual Usage of Hymn: Our first question, then, as historians, is to inquire as to how dynamic these forces actually were in their own environments—most particularly, the ritual environment, where one would expect just such texts to be used. At first glance, we can see hymn 1.115 used in two well-known Rgvedic ritual texts, the *Āśvalāyaṇa Śrauta Sūtra* and the *Śāṅkhāyana Śrauta Sūtra.* Both texts claim that *RV* 1.115, the hymn to Surya, is used in the Āśvinaśāstra—the offering to the healing deities the Aśvins, at the first soma-pressing, just before sunrise. (The soma-pressing is the physical crushing of a sacred plant into a sacred drink—a process which is a basic building block of Vedic sacrificial procedure.) Once again we can see the balance between human and cosmic activity reflected here, and thence the appeal of this hymn to ecologists. As is basic to the Agniṣṭoma rite, the *soma* drink is offered in a kind of bridge between the worlds of human and natural activity.

Hymn Used before Sacrificing an Animal: However, there is another, lesser-known, ritual usage, one which suggests a much different scenario: *Āsvalāyaṇa Śrauta Sūtra* 3.8 also states that verses one through three are recited as the "inviting" verses for the god Sūrya, when an animal is about to be sacrificed to him. Verse one, describing the rising of the sun, invites one to the *vapa.* or roasting of the omentum, or abdominal membrane, of a cow on a spit of *udumbura* wood and the spreading of clarified butter over and under the omentum. Verse two describing the sun following the maiden dawn, invites one to the *puroḍāśa,* or grain offering of barley cakes, which typically follows the offering of the limbs or the omentum of the animal. Verse three, describing the limbs of the steed, invites one to the *havis,* or main offering usually, in the case of a *paśu* sacrifice, the limbs of the animal, which follows the offering of the omentum. Verses five and six of *RV* 1.115, describing the onset of darkness, are sung not as prefatory verses, as the earlier ones are, but when the *vāpa* and *puroḍāśa* offerings are made. They are sung as the animal is actually sacrificed.

What is revealed when the hymn is put into this context? First, we learn that, in the Vedic time and context, the praise of nature is intimately associated with killing animals for food, and that eating animals, both symbolically and literally, is a function of ecology. Second, we see that each poetic image of the movement of the sun is linked, metonymically, with the movement and actions of the sacrificer engaged in the immolation of a sacrificial victim. Verses one through three illustrate this fact. And, at verse four, at the actual offering of the victim, there is a kind of break in thematic imagery—in this case, the introduction of darkness, which interrupts a task left unfinished.

Rgveda 7.99

Let us move to another case study. *Ṛgveda* 7.99, a hymn to Viṣṇu, is a companion hymn to *RV* 7.100, which depicts the three wide strides of Viṣṇu mentioned above. Both together are frequently invoked as a kind of ecological hymn representing preserving and sustaining action and the balance of the earth in the three strides of the god.

A Hymn Depicting the Three Wide Strides of Vishnu

1. Widening with a body beyond measure, Viṣṇu, men don't understand your greatness; we know your two worlds from the earth, but you, divine Viṣṇu, know the highest.
2. No being that exists, or that has been born, divine Viṣṇu, has reached the utmost limit of your magnitude, which you have held up in wide and beautiful heaven; you have sustained the eastern horizon of the earth.
3. Heaven and earth, abounding with cattle, yielding rich fodder, you are ready to be liberal to man. You. Viṣṇu, have helped up these two, heaven and earth, and secured the earth around with mountains.
4. You two. Indra and Viṣṇu, have made the expansive world for the sake of sacrifice, giving birth to the sun, the dawn, and the fire; you leaders have confounded the machinations of the *dāsa* Vṛṣaśipra in the battles of armies.
5. Indra and Viṣṇu, you have destroyed the ninety-nine strong

cities of Sambara, you have killed in one moment the hundred thousand heroines of the demon Varchin.

6. This ample praise magnifies you both. You are mighty, striding wide, and imbued with the power to you two, Viṣṇu and Indra offer praise at sacrifices, grant us food in battles.
7. I offer Viṣṇu the oblation placed before you with the exclamation *vaṣaṭ,* be pleased, Śipiviṣṭa, with my offering. May my hymns of praise magnify you; value us always with blessings.[19]

Interpretation: As before, we can see the ecological import of this hymn in its first three cosmological verses. Viṣṇu holds up the highest heaven, the meeting point in the eastern horizon, and gives birth to the sun, the dawn, and fire. He secures the entire earth with mountains as a kind of ecological carpenter. Alfred Hillebrandt agrees with the earliest of Indologists in dubbing Viṣṇu a solar god who is combined with a vegetation demon.[20] Jaan Puhvel speaks of Viṣṇu's deeds as part of the concept of "the meadow of the otherworld" in Indo-European tradition.[21] Moreover, the hymn has its less controversial ritual uses; according to the *Āśvalāyana Śrauta Sūtra,* in one part of the Agnistoma sacrifice, which is focused on recitation, the Ukthya ceremony, *RV* 7.99 is used as a special invitation *(acchavaka śastra).*

Sacrificial Side of the Hymn: However, once again there is a sacrificial side to the *viniyoga,* or application, of this hymn. The same verses, one through three, are used in exactly the same pattern as the previous hymn, dedicated to Surya. They are recited when a victim is immolated for Viṣṇu (itself a rather startling idea given our own understanding and reception of Vaiṣṇavism in classical Hinduism).

Verse one is the invitation to the *vapa,* or cooking of the omentum, when the animal is killed, and describes the wide expanse of Viṣṇu. Verse two, describing the vastness of his magnitude, accompanies the barley-cake offering. And verse three, describing the giving of cattle, accompanies the offering of the limbs of the cattle. Even more interestingly, *RV* 7.99 reveals another pattern similar to *RV* 1.115, the hymn to Sūrya. There is a "break" in verse four and onwards: the acts of battle and war, like the introduction of the interrupting darkness in the previous hymn, *RV* 1.115, occur at verse four. Verses four and five are recited at the actual offerings, following the pattern of the hymn previously discussed. Thus, the cosmological dimensions (VV. 1-3) involve the invitation to the animal sacrifice, and the mention of slaying and battle (VV 4-5) accompanies the actual offering of the animal.

Rgveda 10.125

Let us turn to one final well-known Vedic hymn, cited many times by ecological and Indological sources alike as a kind of beautiful description of "nature" in the Vedas. *Ṛgveda* 10.125 is a hymn on the creation of the world by the goddess of speech. It, too, is an excellent lens onto the uses of cosmological descriptions in ritual. The hymn consists of eight verses; while speech herself is not named, she is named in the commentarial literature as the "seer" of the hymn—literally, the sage who sees the hymn in a vision and then utters it out loud.

A Hymn on the Creation of the World by the Goddess of Speech

1. I move with the Rudras, the Vasus, with the Ādityas and the All-Gods. I carry both Mitra and Varuna, both Indra and Agni, and both of the Aśvins.
2. I carry the swelling soma, and Tvaṣṭṛ and Pūṣaṇ. I give wealth on the diligent sacrificer who presses the soma and offers the oblation.
3. I am the queen, the gatherer of riches, the artful one who is first among those worthy of the sacrifice. The gods divided me up into many parts; I abide in many places and enter into many forms.
4. The one who eats food, who really sees, who breathes, who hears what is said, does so through me. Though they do not realize it, they dwell in me.
5. Listen, you whom they have heard: I tell you something which should be heeded. I declare, by myself, that which gives joy to gods and men. The one whom I love I make formidable, I make him a sage, a wise man, a brahmin.
6. I stretch the bow for Rudra so that his arrow will strike down the enemy of prayer. I incite the contest among the people. I have pervaded sky and earth.

7. I gave birth to the father on the head of this world. My womb is in the waters, within the ocean. From there I spread through all creatures and touch the sky with the crown of my head.
8. I am the one who breathes forth like the wind, embracing all creatures. Beyond the sky, beyond this earth, so vast am I in my greatness.[22]

Usage of Hymn in Rituals: Many Vedic texts cite *RV* 10.125 as one to be recited at the beginnings of things The *Kauṣītaki Brāhmaṇa* (57.31,139.15) requires it to be recited at the beginning of the Upanayana cremony, the investiture of the scared thread, and the Utsarjana of the beginning of Vedic study. The hymn is about the relationship between eloquence and the beginning of the world thus any ritual of "centrance" into the rites of the twice-born, particularly Vedic study would make this hymn an apt one use.

And, *RV* 10.125 has attracted some of the more Romantic interpretations of Indologists and some environmentalists. Indologists, while textually thorough, have nonetheless tended to view the goddess of speech in an "inspiring muse" kind of role, either abstract or concrete; however, they hardly ever acknowledge her as the recipient of an animal sacrifice.[23] S. R. N. Murthy sees the goddess of speech as one example of the "geospheric" theories found in the Rgvedic understandings of the earth, akin to Sarasvati, the river goddess and nurturer of the soil.[24] Many other ecological writers see her as the Vedic equivalent of the "great mother" in early Indian thought.[25] If we look at the ritual application of this hymn, we see a pattern exactly like that of the two earlier hymns.

Interpretation: As *Sāṅkhāyana Śrauta Sūtra* 6.11.11 prescribes, the cosmological description of the first three verses are meant to be an invitation to offer the slaughtered animal to Vāc (again, a rather odd-sounding phrase, given our own predispositions to see the goddess of eloquence as rather more mellow). Verse one describing the activities of all the gods, is used as the invitation to offer the omentum of the cow; verse two, describing the particular wealth-giving action of the goddess, accompanies the invitation to offer the barley cake; and verse three, describing the division of the goddess into various parts, calls for the offering of the limbs of the animal. Once again we see a metonymic relationship between the verses of the hymn and the action of the sacrificer. And here, just as in the two earlier hymns, the later verses describe the tumultuous earthly action after the cosmological beginnings; as verse six says, the goddess stretches the bow for Rudra so that his arrow will strike down the hater of prayer. She also incites the contest, which could mean either war or the *brahmodya,* or verbal contest of the sacrifices. These later verses may also be used for the actual offering of the animal, as in the earlier cases.

Coexistence of Nature and Sacrifice

How then can we best sum up this brief reading of some of the favorite nature hymns of the *Rgveda* and their uses for present-day environmental theory? First and foremost, if we read the texts carefully, with a view to their own "environment" it is clear that an understanding of sacrifice followed close on the heels of an appreciation of the natural world and its ecology. We can see this in two different ways, First in all of the hymns, *RV* 1.115, 7.99, and 10.125, the celebration of the balance and beauty of the creation of the universe in the first three verses is immediately followed by a mention of interruption or breakage, whether it be the onset of darkness, or, more dramatically, of slaying, or of harm done to those who are outside the system.

Second, we can see the integration of sacrifice in the fact that this very intriguing pattern in thematic structure of cosmological hymns reflects the ritual usage found in the Ṛgvedic ritual texts of animal sacrifice. The first three verses of cosmogony accompany the invitation to offer the slaughtered animal, and the following verses of dramatic, interruptive deeds on earth accompany the actual offering.

Thus, what we learn from the Vedas about the environment is not the contemplation of the beauty of nature or the experience of the sun, as Bergaigne and Muller would have it. Nor is it that the Vedas are hymns which describe the action of various geological agencies in their pristine form identifying themselves with nature and with harmony, as Murthy might have it.[26] While these themes are present.

Approach to Read Ancient Text

Three principles of "reading for the environment" are:

1. When we go to ancient texts such as the Vedas, we must be textually environmentalist in our approach: we must take historical milieus, and, therefore, ritual interpretations

of texts involving nature as seriously as we do our own environmental concern.

2. Second and following on this point we can be less romantic (extracting and contemplating) in our hermenteutice of retrieval and emphasize instead our agreement and disagreement with the ancient world. We may in fact disagree with what we see in the ritual interpretation of inspiring Vedic cosmologies, but we cannot *refuse to see it.*

3. Third, we can use ancient texts not to "help" or "hinder" our discussion of the environment, but to relativize our own concerns about it. I want to be very clear here: I am not advocating that the excellent ecological theories built by Hindu philosophers and theologians be undone by a few historical flourishes. Rather, I want to argue that, as Hindu philosophers concerned with the environment, we can ask ourselves more sophisticated questions, ones that are informed by careful textual reading and by history. (Frank Korom, in his multi-layered interpretation of the sacred cow in India, argues for the necessity of a textual as well as an ethnographic perspective in the development of an ecological ethic.)[27]

The Importance of the Ancient Texts

We can ask ourselves, why do we need this authoritative text, and how do its constructions of the natural world teach us something about our own constructions? In the Vedic case, since the ancient Aryans did not think it possible, in fact, to have cosmological balance without the inevitable accompaniment of sacrifice, are our own assumptions similar? Those involved in the present-day issues of the Narmada Dam and deforestation in the lower Himalayas might ask the same questions. If, in fact, we are scholars committed to conservation of natural resources, how might we be more attentive to that factor about which the Veda teaches us so well, that sacrifice has its own powerful aesthetic and, in many systems of thought, is not different from nature's beauty?

Views on Animal Sacrifice

In addition, we can also ask ourselves about how we view the present practice of animal sacrifice in many parts of contemporary India. Here, too, as discussed in the Vedic case, the practice has ecological meanings which tend to be overshadowed in controversies about violence and nonviolence to animals. James Preston, B.B. Lal, and Alf Hiltebeitel. among many others, have recently discussed animal sacrifice as a kind of balancing of the cosmos.[28] In discussing the controversy surrounding sacrifice at the Chandi Temple to the goddess in Cuttack, South India, Preston writes:

> A ritual sacrifice is never meant as a violent act against a particular animal. The ceremonies that surround the event are intended instead to establish relationship between man and god. The animal's life is offered to the diety as an act of love, thanksgiving, and conciliation It would be a mistake to equate everyday slaughter for food, with this higher dimension of the ritual sacrifice. Thus the meaning of sacrifice may be missed by those who find it repulsive or brutal. It is neither "primitive" nor "barbaric," but rather an expression of special significance for devotees who strive to establish a sense of harmony with the cosmic order.[29]

As many local citizens expressed to Preston during his fieldwork, animal sacrifice is seen as human beings willing to play their part in the divine drama, an admission of the tumultuous forces of the universe as part of reality. These principles of textual reading also imply that we develop an ecology of memory: it is only in the memory of what we have lost— the sacrificial price we have paid—that we can truly understand the nature of our greed, and understand the difficult Gandhian distinction between need and greed. If we do not remember what it was like for us (or our ancestors) to have killed, then we will not know the nature of our ethical choice of restraining from killing. For these reasons, we might keep the sacrificial parts of the ancient Hindu tradition before us. The maturity of our ecological thinking depends on our ability to be fully honest about the traditions we embrace.

Ending the Vedic Sacrifice: One particularly salient Vedic procedure gives us imagery more instructive than all the pastoral images of harmony put together. This procedure usually follows those in which the cosmological hymns discussed above would have been sung. As the *Āśvalāyana Śrauta Sutra* states in describing the model animal sacrifice, the sacrifice should end by remembering the particular animal victims. After the stick holding the heart of the animal is driven into the ground, the priests then go out through the *tīrtha* passage, or crossing, without passing through the fire or the animal parts. They then return into the sacrificial arena, with explicit instructions to avert their eyes while passing the heart spit. They build three fires, while still avoiding all physical and visual contact with the central symbol of killing, and, after offering prayers *(RV* 1.23.23), they conclude the animal sacrifice.

The text does not say why the priests are explicitly instructed to look away from the center of the animal immolation. But it does ask us, as ecological readers of ancient India, to contemplate the degree to which a system inexplicably requires looking away from the heart of destruction. The passage also asks us to consider the degree to which a system places psychological and physical distance between the actors and the acted upon in any given ecological system. Its starkness inquires of us: how is a man, enjoying the fruits of his divinely sanctioned sacrifice on a spit of *udumhura* wood, unable to look, even as he enjoys the fruits and the mantras about harmony and balance still ring in his ears? In what ways are we like him, moving in and out of our own postindustrial sacrificial arenas, averting our eyes because it is deemed right, respectful, and customary to do so, while the smoke from the newly burnt food is rising only few feet away?

NOTES

We would like to acknowledge the help of Christopher Chapple, Mary Evelyn Tucker, Julius Lipner, Jack Hawley, David Haberman, Philip Lutgendorf, Frédérique Apffel-Marglin, Kusumita Pederson, Diana Eck, Tara Doyle, Maggie Kulyk, Joyce Flueckiger, Frank Korom, and Shalom Goldman in the preparation of this article. It was first delivered at the conference on Hinduism and Ecology at the Center for the Study of World Religions at Harvard University in October 1997.

1. See especially Norman Crowe's chapter, "Unity and the Idea of Harmony," in *Nature and the Idea of a Man-Made World: An Investigation into the Evolutionary Roots of Form and Order in the Built Environment* (Cambridge, Mass.: MIT Press, 1995), 108ff.
2. From the promotional material for *Prakrti: The Integral Vision,* ed. Kapila Vatsyayan (New Delhi: Indira Gandhi National Centre for the Arts; D. K. Printworld, 1995).
3. See, among many others, Jonathan Bate, *Romantic Ecology: Wordsworth and the Environmental Tradition* (London and New York: Routledge, 1991); Samuel R Levin, *Metaphoric Worlds: Conceptions of a Romantic*

Nature (New Haven: Yale University Press, 1988); Bernard Rosenthal, *City of Nature: Journeys to Nature in the Age of American Romanticism* (Newark: University of Delaware Press, 1980); Paul Henri Thiry. Baron d 'Holbach, *The System of Nature* (New York: Garland Publishers. 1984); H R., Rookmaaker, *Towards a Romantic Conception of Nature: Coleridge' Poetry up to 1803: A Study in the History of Ideas* (Amsterdam and Philadelphia: J. Benjamins, 1984); Desmond King-Hele's *Erasmus, Darwin, and the Romantic Poets* (Basingstoke, Hampshire: Macmillan, 1986); and Christopher Thacker, *The Wildness Pleases: The Origins of Romanticism* (London: Croom Helm; New York: St. Martin's Press, 1983).

4. See A. Leslie Willson, A Mythical Image: The Ideal of India in German Romanticism (Durham, N.C.: Duke University Press, 1964); Joh Drew, Inia and the Romantic Imagination (Delhi and New York: Oxford University Press, 1987) Ronald Inden, *Imagining India* (Oxford: Basil Blackwell, 1990); Bernard S. Cohn, *An Anthropologist among the Historians and Other Essays* (Delhi and New York: Oxford University Press, 1991); Partha Chatterjee, *The Nation and Its Fragments: Colonial and Postcolonial Histories* (Princeton, N.J.: Princeton University Press, 1993); *Orientalism and the Postcolonial Predicament: Perspectives on South Asia,* ed. Carol A. Breckenridge and Peter Van Der Veer (Philadelphia: University of Pennsylvania Press, 1993); *After Colonialism: Imperial Histories and Postcolonial Displacements,* ed. Cyan Prakash (Princeton, N.J.: Princeton University Press, 1995); and Henry Schwarz, *Writing Cultural History in Colonial and Postcolonial India* (Philadelphia: University of Pennsylvania Press, 1997).
5. While the literature on India and the environment is voluminous, the texts which address the use of ancient Indian texts are worth citing here: O.P. Dwivedi and B.N. Tiwari, *Environmental Crisis and Hindu Religion* (New Delhi: Gitanjali Publishing House, 1987); *The Hindu Survey of the Environment* (Madras: Kasturi and Sons, 1992-); Ranchor Prime, *Hinduism and Ecology: Seeds of Truth* (London: Cassell, 1992); Marta Vannucci, *Ecological Readings in the Veda: Matter. Energy, Life* (New Delhi: D.K. Printworld, 1994); Banwari, *Pancavati: India's Approach to Environment,* trans. Asha Vohra (Delhi: Shri Vinayaka Publications, 1992); *Nonviolence to Animals, Earth, and Self in Asian Traditions,* ed. Christopher Chappie (Albany: State University of New York Press, 1993); *An Ecology of the Spirit: Religious Reflection and Environmental Consciousness,* ed. Michael Barnes (Lanham, Md.: University Press of America, 1994); and Christopher Chappie, "Toward an Indigenous Indian Environmentalism," in *Purifying the Earthly Body of God: Religion and Ecology in Hindu India,* ed. Lance E. Nelson (Albany: State University of New York Press, 1998).
6. Frederique Apffel-Marglin, oral communication, October 1997.
7. I am grateful to conversations with Mary Evelyn Tucker in refining my theoretical frame for this material.

8. An excellent overview of the nonviolent possibilities of Asian literature is given in Chappie, *Nonviolence to Animals, Earth, and Self in Asian Traditions:* in Hindu literature more specifically, see Chappie's "Toward an Indigenous Indian Environmentalism."
9. For an intriguing reading of Whitman's influence on contemporary culture, see John Berryman, "On Whitman" in Alfred Kazin's *The Open Form: Essays for Our Time,* 2d. ed. (New York: Harcourt, Brace, and World, 1965)
10. See Max Muller, *Lectures on the Origin and Growth of Religion* (New. York: AMS Press, 1976), 268ff: and *Lectures on the Science of Religion,* 73 ff.
11. Willard Johnson, *Poetry and Speculation of the Rg Veda* (Berkeley and Los Angeles: University of California Press, 1980), 93-94. Abel Bergaigne, *Religion Vedique, d'apres les hymnes du Rig-Veda.* Abel Bergaigne's Vedic Religion, trans. V.G. Paranjpe (Delhi: Motilal Banarsidass, 1978), 314.
12. Arthur Berriedale Keith, *The Religion and Philosophy of the Veda and Upanishads,* 2 vols. (Cambridge, Mass.: Harvard University Press, 1925).
13. Karl Figlio, "Knowing, Loving, and Hating Nature," in *Future Natural: Nature, Science, Culture,* ed. George Robertson et. al., (New York and London: Routledge, 1996), 72-85.
14. Frédérique Apffel-Marglin, *Oral communication,* October 1997.
15.
    1. *citrám devā́nam úd agād ánīkam cákṣur mitrásya váruṇasya agnéh/ ā́prā dyā́vāpṛthivī́ antárikṣaṃ sū́rya ātmā́ jágatas tasthúṣaś ca//*
    2. *sū́ryo devī́m uṣásaṃ rócamānām máryo ná yóṣām abhī́ eti paścā́t/ yátrā̧ náro devayánto yugā́ni vitanvate práti bhadrā́ya bhadrám//*
    3. *bhadrā́ ásvā harī́tah sū́riyasya citrā́ étagvá anumā́diyāsah/ namásyanto divá á pṛṣṭhám asthuḥ pári dyā́vāpṛthivi yanti sadyáḥ//*
    4. *tát sū́ryasya devatvám tán mahitvám madhyā́ kártor vitatam sám jabhāra/ yadéd áykta harī́tah sadhásthād ā́d rā́trī vā́sas tanute simásmai//*
    5. *tán mitrásya váruṇasyābhicákṣe sū́ryo rūpáṃ kṛṇute dyór upásthe/ anantám anyád rúśad asya pā́jaḥ kṛṣṇám anyád dharī́taḥ sám bharanti/*
    6. *adyā́ devā údifa sū́riyasya nī́r áṃhasah pipṛtā́ nī́r adadyā́t/ tán no mitró váruṇo māmahantām áditiḥ sī́ndhuh pṛthivī́ utá dyaúṭḥ//*
16. Müller, *Origin and Growth,* 297.
17. Johnson, *Poetry and Speculation,* 55.
18. S.R.N. Murthy, *Ancient Indian Theories of the Earth* (Pune: Centre of Advanced Study in Sanskrit, University of Poona, 1992), 14.
19.
    1. *paró mā́trayā tanúvā vṛdhāna ná te mahitvám ánu aśnuvanti/ubhé te vidma rájasī pṛthivyā́ vī́ṣṇo deva tvám*

paramásya vitse//

2. *ná te viṣṇo jā́yamāno ná jātó déva mahimnáh páram ántam āpa/*
   úd astabhnā nā́kam rsvám brhántam dādhártha prā́cīṃ kakúbham
   pṛthivyā́h//
3. *ī́rāvatī dhenumátī hī́ bhūtám sūyavasī́nī mánuṣe dasásyā́/*
   vī́ astabhnā ródasī viṣṇav eté dādhártha pṛthvī́m abhī́to mayū́khaiḥ//
4. *urúm yajñā́ya cakrathur ulokáṃ janáyantā sū́ryam uṣā́sam agnī́m/*
   dā́sasya cid vṛṣasiprásya mayā́ jaghnáthur narā pṛtanā́jiveṣu/ /
5. *indrāviṣṇū dṛṃhitā́ḥ sámbarasy náva púro navatī́ṃ ca śnathiṣṭam/*
   śatáṃ varcī́naḥ sahásraṃ ca sākáṃ hathó apratī́ ásurasya vīrā́n//
6. *iyám manīṣā́ bṛhatī́ bṛhántā urukramā́ tavásā vardháyantī/*
   raré vāṃ stómam vidátheṣu viṣṇo pī́nvatam ī́ṣo vṛjáneṣu indra//
7. *váṣaṭ te viṣṇav āsá ā́ kṛṇomi tán me jusasva śipiviṣṭa havyám/*
   várdhantu tvā suṣṭutáyo gī́ro me yūyám pāta suastī́bhih sádā naḥ//

20. Alfred Hillebrandt. Vedic Mythology, vol. 2, trans, Sreeramula Rajeswara Sarma (Delhi: Motilal Banarsidass, 1990): 64-69.
21. Jaan Puhvel, "Meadow of the Otherworld in Indo-European Tradition," *Zeitschrift fur vergleicende Sprachwissenschaft* 83 (1969), 64-69.
22. 1. ahám rudrébhir vásubhis carā̄mi ahám ā̄dityaī́r utá visvádevaiḥ/
       ahám mitrā́váruṇobhā́ bibharmi ahám indrā̄gnī́ ahám aśvī́nobhā́//
    2. aháṃ sómam ā̄hanásam bibharmi aháṃ tváṣṭaram utá pūṣáṇam bhágam/
       aháṃ dadhā̄mi dráviṇaṃ havī́ṣmate suprā̄vī́ye yájamā̄nāya sunvaté//
    3. aháṃ rā́strî samgámanî vásūnam cikitúsî prathamā́ yajñī́yā̄nā̄m/
       tā́m mā̄ devá vī́ adadhuh purutrā́ bhū́risthā̄trám bhū́ri ā̄vesáyantîm//
    4. máyā̄ só ánnam attyó vipásyati yàh prā́nti yá îm sṛnóti uktam/
       amantávo mā́m tá úpa ksiyanu srudhi sruta sraddhivám te vadami//
    5. aháṃ evá svayám idaṃ vadami jústam devébhir utà mā́nuṣedhih/
       yáṃ kā̄máye tám-tam ugráṃ kmomi tám brahmā́ṇaṃ tám ṛṣun tám sumedhā́m//
    6. aháṃ rudrā́ya dhánur ā́ tanomi brahmadvī́ṣe sárave hántavā́ u/
       aháṃ jánā̄ya samádam kṛṇomi aháṃ dyā́vā̄pṛthivī́ ā́ viveśa//

7. ahám̩ suve pitáram asya mū́rdhán máma yónir apsú antáh samudré/

táto vī́ tiṣṭhe bhúvanā́u vī́śvā utā́mū́m̩ dyā́m̩ varṣmánópa spṛśāmi//

8. ahám̩ evá vā́ta iva prá vāmi ārábhamāṇā bhúvanāni vísvā/

paró divá pará enā́ pṛthivyā́ etā́vatī mahinā́ sám bhahūva//

23. In addition to Johnson's discussion of this hymn in *Poetry and Speculation*, see Fritz Staal's allusion to it in his article. "Rg Veda 10:71 on the Origin of Language," in *Revelation in Indian Thought: A Festschrift in Honour of Professor T.R.V. Muni*, ed. Harold Coward and Krishna Sivaraman (Emeryville, Calif.: Dharma Publishing), 3—14; and my own treatment of it in passing, "Vac: Myth or Philosophy?" in *Myth and Philosophy*, ed. Frank E. Reynolds and David Tracy (Albany: State University of New York Press, 1990), 183-214. For earlier treatments see W. Norman Brown, 'The Creative Role of the Goddess Vac in the Rg Veda," in *Pratidanam: Indian, Iranian, and Indo-European Studies Presented to Franciscus Bernardus Jacobus Kuiper on His Sixtieth Birthday*, ed. J. C. Heesterman, G. H. Schokker, and V. I. Subramoniam (The Hague: Mouton, 1968), 393-97; B. Essers, *Vac: Het Woord als godsgestalte en als godgeleerdheid in de Veda* (Assen: Van Gorcum, 1952); Louis Renou, "Les Pouvoirs de la Parole dans le Rg Veda," in *Etudes Vediques et Panineennes*, 1 (Paris: E. De Boccard, 1955): 1-27; C.A. Scharbau, *Die Idee der Schopfung in der vedischen Literatur* (Stuttgart: W. Kohlhammer, 1932), 123.

24. Murthy, *Ancient Indian Theories of the Earth, 22.*

25. See, in particular, *God, Humanity, and Mother Nature*, ed. Gilbert E. M. Ogutu (Nairobi: Masaki Publishers, 1992), among many other examples; Pupul Jayakar, *The Earth Mother*, rev. ed. (Delhi: Penguin Books, 1989); Carol Bolon, *Forms of the Goddess Lajja Gauri in Indian Art* (University Park: Pennsylvania State University Press, 1992).

26. Murthy, *Ancient Indian Theories*, 9.

27. Frank Korom, unpublished manuscript, 19.

28. James Preston, *The Cult of the Goddess: Social and Religious Change in a Hindu Temple* (New Delhi: Vikas Publishing House, 1980), 69. B. B. Lal, "Hindu Perspectives on the Use of Animals in Science," in *Animal Sacrifices: Religious Perspectives on the Use of Animals in Science*, ed. Tom Regan (Philadelphia: Temple University Press, 1986). Alf Hiltebeitel, *The Cult of Draupadi*. vol. 2 (Chicago: University of Chicago Press, 1991).

29. Preston, *Cult of the Goddess*, 69.

8

Cultural Dimension of Religious Analysis

One of the main functions of religions is the maintenance of a harmonious relationship between people and their physical environment. Santayana in his book *Reason in Religion* very rightly opines:

"Any attempt to speak without speaking any particular language is not more hopeless than the attempt to have a religion that shall be no religion in particular .... Thus every living and healthy religion has a marked idiosyncrasy. Its power consists in its special and surprising message and in the bias which that revelation gives to life. The vistas it opens and the mysteries it propounds are another world to live in; and another world to live in—whether we expect ever to pass wholly over into it or no—is what we mean by having a religion."

Accomplishments of Anthropological Study on Religion

Anthropological studies on religion have had very few achievements. Two factors have been observed: First is that it has made no theoretical advances of major importance. It is living off the conceptual capital of its ancestors, adding very little, save a certain empirical enrichment, to it. Secondly, the approach of one or two transcendent figures like Durkheim, Weber, Freud or Malinewski is followed with but a few marginal corrections necessitated by the natural tendency to excess of seminal minds or by the expanded body of reliable descriptive data. Thus the concepts belong to a very narrowly defined intellectual function. But virtually no one even thinks of looking elsewhere—to philosophy, history, law, literature, or the "harder" sciences—as these men themselves looked, for analytical ideas. That these two curious characteristics are not unrelated is well understood.

Results cannot be produced by making minor variation on classical theoretical themes. Only if we abandon, in a phrase of Leo Steinberg's, that sweet sense of accomplishment which comes from parading habitual skills and address ourselves to problems sufficiently unclarified as to make discovery possible, can we hope to achieve work which will not just reincarnate that of the great men of the first quarter of twentieth century, but match it.[1] A meticulous case in point for such well-established propositions as that ancestor worship supports the jurat authority of elders, that initiation rites are means for the establishment of sexual identity and adult status, that ritual groupings reflect political oppositions, or that myths provide charters for social institutions and rationalizations of social privilege, may well finally convince a great many people, both inside the profession and out, that anthropologists are, like theologians, firmly dedicated to proving the indubitable. In art, This solemn reduplication of the achievements of accepted masters is called academicism; and I think this is the proper name for our malady also.

The way to do this is not to abandon the established traditions of social anthropology in this field, but to widen them. At least four of the contributions of the men who, dominate our thought to the point of parochializing it. Durkheim's discussion of the nature of the sacred, Weber's *Verstehenden* methodology, Freud's parallel between personal rituals and collective ones, and Malinowski's exploration of the distinction between religion and common sense—seem to me inevitable starting-points for any useful anthropological theory of religion, But they are starting-points only. To move beyond them we must place them in a much broader context of contemporary thought than they, in and of themselves, encompass. The dangers of such a procedure are obvious arbitrary eclecticism, superficial theory-mongering, and sheer intellectual confusion. But there is no other road of escape from what, referring to anthropology more generally, Janowitz has called the dead hand of competence.[2]

In working toward such an expansion of the conceptual envelope in which our studies take place, one can, of course, move in a great number of directions; and perhaps the most important initial problem is to avoid setting out, like Stephen Leacock's mounted policeman, in all of them at once. Cultural Dimension of Religious Analysis.[3] The term "culture" has by now acquired a certain aura of ill-repute in social anthropological circles because of the multiplicity of its referents and the studied vagueness with which it has all too often been invoked. A cultural concepts denotes historically transmitted pattern of meanings embodied in symbols, a system of inherited conceptions expressed in symbolic forms by means of which men communicate, perpetuate, and develop their knowledge about and attitudes toward life. Of course, terms such as "meaning," "symbol," and "conception" cry out for explication. But that is precisely where the widening, the broadening, and the expanding come in. If Langer is right that "the concept of meaning, in all its varieties, is the dominant philosophical concept of our time," that "sign, symbol, denotation, signification, communication . . . are out [intellectual] stock in trade," it is perhaps time that social anthropology, and particularly that part of it concerned with the study of religion, became aware of the fact.[4]

Religious Symbols

Religious symbols formulate a basic congruence between a particular style of life and a specific (if, most often, implicit) metaphysic, and in so doing sustain each with the borrowed authority of the other. As we are to deal with meaning, let us begin with a paradigm: viz., that sacred symbols function to synthesize a people's ethos—the tone, character, and quality of their life, its moral and aesthetic style and mood —and their world view—the picture they have of the way things in sheer actuality are, their most comprehensive ideas of order. In religious belief and practice a group's ethos is rendered intellectually reasonable by being shown to represent a way of life ideally adapted to the actual state of affairs the world view describes, while the world view is rendered emotionally convincing by being presented as an image of an actual state of affairs peculiarly well-arranged to accommodate such a way of life.

This confrontation and mutual confirmation has two fundamental effects. On the one hand, it objectivizes moral and aesthetic preferences by depicting them as the imposed conditions of life implicit in a world with a particular structure, as mere common sense given the unalterable shape of reality. On the other, it supports these received beliefs about the world's body by invoking deeply felt moral and aesthetic sentiments as experiential evidence for their truth.

The notion that religion tunes human actions to an envisaged cosmic order and projects images of cosmic order onto the plane of human experience is hardly novel. But it is hardly investigated either, so that we have very little idea of how, in empirical terms, this particular miracle is accomplished. We just know that it is done, annually, weekly, daily, for some people almost hourly; and we have an enormous ethnographic literature to demonstrate it.

But the theoretical framework which would enable us to provide an analytic account of it, an account of the sort we can provide for lineage segmentation, political succession, labor exchange, or the socialization of the child, does not exist. Let us, therefore, reduce our paradigm to a definition, for, although it is notorious that definitions establish nothing, in themselves they do, if they are carefully enough constructed, provide a useful orientation, or reorientation, of thought, such that an extended unpacking of them can be an effective way of developing and controlling a novel line of inquiry. They have the useful virtue of explicitness: they commit themselves in a way discursive prose, which, in this field especially, is always liable to substitute rhetoric for argument, does not.

Definition and Analysis

A religion is:

(1) a system of symbols which acts to ...

(2) ... establish powerful, pervasive, and long-lasting moods and motivations in men by ...

(3) ... formulating conceptions of a general order of existence and ...

(4) ... clothing these conceptions with such an aura of factuality that ...

(5) ... the moods and motivations seem uniquely realistic."

In the following pages we analyse parts (1) to (5) to get an explicit picture of the statements in the definition.

(1) A Religion is a system of Symbols which acts to ...

While interpreting the definition we see that such a tremendous weight is being put on the term "symbol" that our first move must be to decide with some precision what we are going to mean by it. This is no easy task, for, rather like "culture," "symbol" has been used to refer to a great variety of things, often a number of them at the same time. In some hands it is used for anything which signifies something else to someone: dark clouds are the symbolic precursors of an on-coming rain. In others it is used only for explicitly conventional signs of one sort or another: a red flag is a symbol of danger, a white of surrender. In others it is confined to something which expresses in an oblique and figurative manner that which cannot be stated in a direct and literal one, so that there are symbols in poetry but not in science, and symbolic logic is misnamed. In yet others, however, it is used for any object, act, event, quality, or relation which serves as a vehicle for a conception— the conception is the symbol's "meaning"—and that is the approach we shall follow here.[5]

The number 6, written, imagined, laid out as a row of stones, or even punched into the program tapes of a computer, is a symbol. But so also is the Cross, talked about, visualized, shaped worriedly in air or fondly fingered at the neck, the expanse of painted canvas called "Guernica" or the bit of painted stone called a churinga, the word "reality," or even the morpheme "-ing." They are all symbols, or at least symbolic elements, because they are tangible formulations of notions, abstractions from experience fixed in perceptible forms, concrete embodiments of ideas, attitudes, judgments, longings, or beliefs.

Cultural Patterns: To undertake the study of cultural activity—activity in which symbolism forms the positive content—is thus not to abandon social analysis for a Platonic cave of shadows, to enter into a mentalistic world of introspective psychology or, worse, speculative philosophy, and wander there forever in a haze of "Cognitions," "Affections," "Connotations," and other elusive entities. Cultural acts, the construction, apprehension, and utilization of symbolic forms, are social events like any other; they are as public as marriage and as observable as agriculture. They are not, however, exactly the same thing; or, more precisely, the symbolic dimension of social events is, like the psychological, itself theoretically abstractable from those events as empirical totalities. There is still, to paraphrase a remark of Kenneth Burke's, a difference between building a house and drawing up a plan for building a house and reading a poem about having children by marriage is not quite the same thing as having children by marriage.[6] Even though the building of the house may proceed under the guidance of the plan or—a less likely occurrence—the having of children may be motivated by a reading of the poem, there is something to be said for not confusing out traffic with symbols with our traffic with objects or human beings, for these latter are not in themselves symbols, however often they may function as such.[7]

No matter how deeply interfused the cultural, the social, and the psychological may be in the everyday life of houses, farms, poems, and marriages, it is useful to distinguish them in analysis, and, so doing, to isolate the generic traits of each against the normalized background of the other two.

So far as culture patterns, that is, systems or complexes of symbols are concerned, the generic trait which is of first importance for us here is that they are extrinsic sources of information. By "extrinsic," mean only that—unlike genes, for example—

"Extrinsic" Meaning

they lie outside the boundaries of the individual organism as such in that intersubjective world of common understandings into which all human individuals are born, in which they pursue their separate "careers, and which they leave persisting behind them after they die. The termindog, "sources of information," indicates that—like genes—they provide a blueprint or template in terms of which processes external to themselves can be given a definite form. As the order of bases in a strand of DNA forms a coded program, a set of instructions, or a recipe, for the synthesis of the structurally complex proteins which shape organic functioning, so culture patterns provide such programs for the institution of the social and psychological processes which shape public behavior. Though the sort of information and the mode of its transmission are vastly different in the two cases, this comparison of gene and symbol is more than a strained analogy of the familiar "social heredity" sort. It is actually a substantial relationship for it is precisely because of the fact that genetically programmed processes are so highly generalized in men, as compared with lower animals, that culturally programmed ones are so important; only because human behavior is so loosely determined by intrinsic sources of information that extrinsic sources are so vital.

To build a dam a beaver needs only an appropriate site and the proper materials—his mode of procedure is shaped by his physiology. But man, whose genes are silent on the building trades, needs also a conception of what it is to build a dam, a conception he can get only from some symbolic source—a blueprint, a textbook, or a string of speech by someone who already knows how dams are built—or, of course, from manipulating graphic or linguistic elements in such a way as to attain for himself a conception of what dams are and how they are built.

It is sometimes argued that cultural patterns are *"models,"* that they are sets of symbols whose relations to one another "model" relations among entities, processes or what-have-you in physical, organic, social, or psychological systems by "paralleling," "imitating," or "simulating" them.[8] The term "model" has, however, two senses—an "of" sense and a "for" sense—and though these are but aspects of the same basic concept they are very much worth distinguishing for analytic purposes.

In the first, what is stressed is the manipulation of symbol structures so as to bring them, more or less closely, into parallel with the pre-established nonsymbolic system, as when we grasp how dams work by developing a theory of hydraulics or constructing a flow chart. The theory or chart models physical relationships in such a way—that is, by expressing their structure in synoptic form—as to render them apprehensible; it is a model of "reality."

In the second, what is stressed is the manipulation of the nonsymbolic systems in terms of the relationships expressed in the symbolic, as when we construct a dam according to the specifications implied in an hydraulic theory or the conclusions drawn from a flow chart. Here, the theory is a model under whose guidance physical relationships are organized: it is a model for "reality." For psychological and social systems, and for cultural models that we would not ordinarily refer to as "theories," but rather as "doctrines," "melodies," or "rites," the case is in no way different.

Unlike genes, and other nonsymbolic information sources, which are only models for, not models of, culture patterns have an intrinsic double aspect: they give meaning, that is, objective conceptual form, to social and psychological reality both by shaping themselves to it and by shaping it to themselves. It is, in fact, this double aspect which sets true symbols off from other sorts of significative forms. Models for are found, as the gene example suggests, through the whole order of nature; for wherever there is a communication of pattern, such programs are, in simple logic, required. Among animals, imprint learning is perhaps the most striking example, because what such learning involves is the automatic presentation of an appropriate sequence of behavior by a model animal in the presence of a learning animal which serves, equally automatically, to call out and stabilize a certain set of responses genetically built into the learning animal.[9] The communicative dance of two bees, one of which has found nectar and the other of which seeks it, is another, somewhat different, more complexly coded, example.[10] Craik has even suggested that the thin trickle of water which first finds its way down from a mountain spring to the sea and smooths a little channel for the greater volume of water that follows after it plays a son of model for funtion.[11] But models of—linguistic, graphic, mechanical, natural, etc. processes which function not to provide sources of information in terms of which other processes can be patterned, but to represent those patternted processes as such, to express their structure in an alternative medium—are much rarer and may perhaps be confined, among living animals, to man. The perception of the structural congruence between one set of processes, activities, relations, entities, and so on, and another set for which it acts as a program, so that the program can be taken as a representation, or conception—a symbol—of the programmed, is the essence of human thought. The intertransposability of models *for* and models *of* which symbolic formulation makes possible is the distinctive characteristic of our mentality.

(2) . . . to establish powerful, pervasive, and long-lasting moods and motivations in men by . . .

So far as religious symbols and symbol systems are concerned: this intertransposability is clear. The endurance, courage, independence, per-severance, and passionate willfulness in which the vision quest of practices the Plains Indian are the same flamboyant virtues by which he attempts to live: while achieving a sense of revelation he stabilizes a sense of direction.[12] The consciousness of defaulted obligation, secreted guilt, and, when a confession is obtained, public shame in which Manus' compunctiousness rehearses him are the same sentiments that underlie the son of duty ethic by which his property-conscious society is maintained: the gaining of an absolution involves the forging of a conscience.[13] And the same self-discipline which rewards a Javanese mystic staring fixedly into the flame of a lamp with what he takes to be an intimation of divinity drills him in that rigorous control of emotional expression which is necessary to a man who would follow a quietistic style of life.[14]

Whether one sees the conception of a personal guardian spirit, a family tutelary, or an immanent God as synoptic formulations of the character of reality or as templates for producing reality with such a character seems largely arbitrary, a matter of which aspect, the model *of or* model *for.* one wants for the moment to bring into focus. The concrete symbols involved—one or another mythological figure materializing in the wilderness, the skull of the deceased household head hanging censoriously in the rafters, or a disembodied "voice in the stillness" soundlessly chanting enigmatic classical poetry—point in either direction. They both express the world's climate and shape it.

They shape it by inducing in the worshipper a certain distinctive set of dispositions (tendencies, capacities, propensities, skills, habits, liabilities, pronenesses) which lend a chronic character to the flow of his activity and the quality of his experience.

A disposition describes not an activity or an occurrence but a probability of an activity being performed or an occurrence occurring in certain circumstances: "When a cow is said to be a ruminant, or a man is said to be a cigarette-smoker, it is not being said that the cow is ruminating now or that the man is smoking a cigarette now. To be a ruminant is to tend to ruminate from time to time, and to be a cigarette-smoker is to be in the habit of smoking cigarettes." [15] Similarly, to be pious is not to be performing something we would call an act of piety, but to be liable to perform such acts. So, too, with the *Plains Indian's bravura,* the *Manus' compunctiousness,* or the *Javanese's quietism,* which, in their contexts, form the substance of piety. The virtue of this sort of view of what are usually called "mental traits" or, if the Cartesianism is unavowed, "psychological forces" (both unobjectionable enough terms in themselves) is that it gets them out of any dim and inaccessible realm of private sensation into that same well-lit world of observables in which reside the brittleness of glass, the inflammability of paper, and, to return to the metaphor, the dampness of England.

So far as religious activities are concerned: (and learning a myth by heart is as much a religious activity as detaching one's finger at the knuckle), two somewhat different sorts of disposition are induced by them: moods and motivations.

Motivation: This is a persisting tendency, a chronic inclination to perform certain sorts of acts and experience certain sorts of feeling in certain sorts of situations, the "sorts" being commonly very heterogenous and rather ill-defined classes in all three cases: On hearing that a man is vain [i.e., motivated by vanity] we expect him to behave in certain ways, namely to talk a lot about himself, to cleave to the society of the eminent, to reject criticisms, to seek the footlights and to disengage himself from conversations about the merits of others. We expect him to indulge in roseate daydreams about his own successes, to avoid recalling past failures and to plan for his own advancement. To be vain is *to* tend to act in these and innumerable other kindred ways. Certainly we also expect the vain man to feel certain pangs and flutters in certain situations; we expect him to have an acute sinking feeling when an eminent person forgets his name, and to feel buoyant of heart and light of toe on hearing of the misfortunes of his rivals. But feelings of pique and buoyancy are not more directly indicative of vanity than are public acts of boasting or private acts of daydreaming.[16]

Similarly for any motivations. As a motive, "flamboyant courage" consists in such enduring propensities as to fast in the wilderness, to conduct solitary raids on enemy camps, and to thrill to the thought of counting coup. "Moral circumspection" consists in such ingrained tendencies as to honor onerous promises, to confess secret sins in the face of severe public disapproval, and to feel guilty when vague and generalized accusations are made at seances. And "dispassionate tranquility" consists in such persistent inclinations as to maintain one's poise come hell or high water, to experience distaste in the presence of even rnoderate emotional displays, and to indulge in contentless contemplations of featureless objects.

Motives are thus neither acts (that is, intentional behaviors) nor feelings, but liabilities to perform particular classes of act or have particular classes of feeling. And when we say that a man is religious, that is, motivated by religion, this is at least pan—though only part—of what we mean.

Moods: Another part of what we mean is that he has, when properly stimulated, a susceptibility to fall into certain moods, moods we sometimes lump together under such covering terms as "reverential," "solemn," or "worshipful." Such generalized rubrics actually conceal, however, the enormous empirical variousness of the dispositions involved, and, in fact, tend to assimilate them to the unusually grave tone of most of our own religious life. The moods that sacred symbols induce, at different times and in different places, range from exultation to melancholy, from self-confidence to self-pity, from an incorrigible playfulness to a bland listlessness—to say nothing of the erogenous power of so many of the world's myths and rituals. No more than there is a single sort of motivation one can call piety is there a single sort of mood one can call worshipful.

Differences between Moods and Mohvations: The major difference between moods and motivations is that where the latter are, so to speak, vectorial qualities, the former are merely scalar. Motives have a directional cast, they describe a certain overall course, gravitate toward certain, usually temporary, consummations. But moods vary only as to intensity: they go nowhere. They spring from certain circumstances but they are responsive to no ends. Like fogs, they just settle and lift; like scents, suffuse and evaporate. When present they are totalistic: if one is sad everything and everybody seems dreary; if one is gay, everything and everybody seems splendid. Thus, though a man can be vain, brave, willful, and independent at the same time, he can't very well be playful and listless, or exultant and melancholy, at the same time.[17] Further, where motives persist for more or less extended periods of time, moods merely recur with greater or lesser frequency, coming and going for what are often quite unfathomable reasons.

Perhaps the most important difference, so far as we are concerned, between moods and motivations is that motivations are "made meaningful" with reference to the ends toward which they are conceived to conduce, whereas moods are "made meaningful" with reference to the conditions from which they are conceived to spring. We interpret motives in terms of their consummations, but we interpret moods in terms of their sources. We say that a person is industrious because he wishes to succeed; we say that a person is worried because he is conscious of the hanging threat of nuclear holocaust. And this is no less the case when the interpretations are ultimate. Charity becomes Christian charity when it is enclosed in a conception of God's purposes; optimism is Christian optimism when it is grounded in a particular conception of God's nature. The assiduity of the Navaho finds its rationale in a belief that, since "reality" operates mechanically, it is coercible; their chronic fearfulness finds its rationale in a conviction that, however "reality" operates, it is both enormously powerful and terribly dangerous.[18]

(3) . . . by formulating conceptions of a general order of existence and . . .

That the symbols or symbol systems which induce and define dispositions we set off as religious and those which place those dispositions in a cosmic framework are the same symbols ought to occasion no surprise. For what else do we mean by saying that a particular mood of awe is religious and not secular, except that it springs from entertaining a conception of all-pervading vitality like mana and not from a visit to the Grand Canyon? Or that a particular case of asceticism is an example of a religious motivation, except that it is directed toward the achievement of an unconditioned end like nirvana and not a conditioned one like weight-reduction? If sacred symbols did not at one and the same time induce dispositions in human beings and formulate, however obliquely, inarticulately, or unsystematically, general ideas of order then the empirical differentia of religious activity or religious experience would not exist. A man can indeed be said to be "religious" about golf, but not merely if he pursues it with passion and plays it on Sundays: he must also see it as symbolic of some transcendent truths, And the pubescent boy gazing soulfully into the eyes of the pubescent girl in a William Steig cartoon and murmuring, "There is something about you, Ethel, which gives me a sort of religious feeling," is, like most; adolescents, confused. What any particular religion affirms about the fundamental nature of reality may be obscure, shallow, or, all too often perverse; but it must, if it is not to consist of the mere collection of received practices and conventional sentiments we usually refer to as moralism, affirm something. If one were to essay a minimal definition of religion today, it would perhaps not be Tylor's famous "belief in spiritual beings," to which Goody, wearied of theoretical subtleties, has lately urged us to return, but rather what Salvador de Madariaga has called "the relatively modest dogma that God is not mad."[19]

Usually, of course, religions affirm very much more than this: we believe, as James remarked, all that we can and would believe everything if we only could.[20] The thing we seem least able to tolerate is a threat to our powers of conception, a suggestion that our ability to create, grasp, and use symbols may fail us, for were this to happen, we would be more helpless, as already pointed out, than the beavers. The extreme generality, diffuseness, and variability of man's innate (that is, genetically programmed) response capacities means that without the assistance of cultural patterns he would be functionally incomplete, not merely a talented ape who had, like some underprivileged child, unfortunately been prevented from realizing his full potentialities, but a kind of formless monster with neither sense of direction nor power of self-control, a chaos of spasmodic impulses and vague emotions. Man depends upon symbols and symbol systems with a dependence so great as to be decisive for his creatural viability and, as a result, his sensitivity to even the remotest indication that they may prove unable to cope with one or another aspect of experience raises within him the gravest sort of anxiety:

> [Man] can adapt himself somehow to anything his imagination can cope with; but he cannot deal with Chaos. Because his characteristic function and highest asset is conception, his greatest fright is to meet what he cannot construe—the "uncanny," as it is popularly called. It need not be a new object; we do meet new things, and "understand" them promptly, if tentatively, by the nearest analogy, when our minds are functioning freely; but under mental stress even perfectly familiar things may become suddenly disorganized and give us the horrors. Therefore our most important assets are always the symbols of our general *orientation* in nature, on the earth, in society, and in what we are doing: the symbols of our *Weltanschauung* and *Lebensanschauung*. Consequently, in a primitive society, a daily ritual is incorporated in common activities, in eating, washing, fire-making, etc., as well as in pure ceremonial; because the need of reasserting the tribal morale and recognizing its cosmic conditions is constantly felt. In Christian Europe the Church brought men daily (in some orders even hourly) to their knees, to enact if not to contemplate their assent to the ultimate concepts.[21]

There are at least three points where chaos—a tumult of events which lack not just interpretations but *interpretability*—threatens to break in upon man: (a) at the limits of his analytic capacities, (b) at the limits of his powers of endurance, and (c) at the limits of his moral insight. Bafflement, suffering, and a sense of intractable ethical paradox are all, if they become intense enough or are sustained long enough, radical challenges to the proposition that life is comprehensible and that we can, by taking thought, orient ourselves effectively within it—challenges with which any religion, however "primitive," which hopes to persist must attempt somehow to cope.

Of the three issues, it is the first which has been least investigated by modern social anthropologists (though Evans-Pritchard's classic discussion of why granaries fall on some Azande and not on others, is a notable exception).[22] Even to consider people's religious beliefs as attempts to bring anomalous events or experiences—death, dreams, mental fugues, volcanic eruptions, or marital infidelity—within the circle of the at least potentially explicable seems to smack of Tyloreanism or worse. But it does appear to be a fact that at least some men—in all probability, most men—are unable to leave unclarified problems of analysis merely unclarified, just to look at the stranger features of the world's landscape in dumb astonishment or bland apathy without trying to develop, however fantastic, inconsistent, or simple-minded, some notions as to how such features might be reconciled with the more ordinary deliverances of experience. Any chronic failure of one's explanatory apparatus, the complex of received culture patterns (common sense, science, philosophical speculation, myth) one has for mapping the empirical world, to explain things which cry out for explanation tends to lead to a deep disquiet—a tendency rather more widespread and a disquiet rather deeper than we have sometimes supposed since the pseudoscience view of religious belief was, quite rightfully, deposed. After all, even that high priest of heroic atheism. Lord Russell, once remarked that although the problem of the existence of God had never bothered him, the ambiguity of certain mathematical axioms had threatened to unhinge his mind. And Einstein's profound dissatisfaction with quantum mechanics was based on a—surely religious—inability to believe that, as he put it, God plays dice with the universe.

But this quest for lucidity and the rush of metaphysical anxiety that occurs when empirical phenomena threaten to remain intransigently opaque is found on much humbler intellectual levels. It is striking to see the animistically inclined informants behaved like true Tyloreans. They seemed to be constantly using their beliefs to "explain" phenomena: or, more accurately, to convince themselves that the phenomena were explainable within the accepted scheme of things, for they commonly had only a minimal attachment to the particular soul possession, emotional disequilibrium, taboo infringement, or bewitchment hypothesis they advanced and were all too ready to abandon it for some other, in the same genre, which struck them as more plausible given the facts of the case. What they were *not* ready to do was abandon it for no other hypothesis at all; to leave events to themselves.

And what is more, they adopted this nervous cognitive stance with respect to phenomena which had no immediate practical bearing on their own lives, or for that matter on anyone's. When a peculiarly shaped, rather large toadstool grew up in a carpenter's house in the short space of a few days (or, some said, a few hours), people came from miles around to see it, and everyone had some sort of explanation —some animist, some animatist, some not quite either—for it. Yet it would be hard to argue that the toadstool had any social value in Radcliffe-Brown's sense, or was connected in any way with anything which did and for which it could have been standing proxy, like the Andaman cicada.[23] Toadstools play about the same role in Javanese life as they do in ours, and in the ordinary course of things Javanese have about as much interest in them as we do. It was just that this one was "odd," "strange," "uncanny"—*aneh*. And the odd, strange, and uncanny simply must be accounted for—or, again, the conviction that it could be accounted for sustained. One does not shrug off a toadstool which grows five times as fast as a toadstool has any right to grow. In the broadest sense the "strange" toadstool did have implications, and critical ones, for those who heard about it. It threatened their most general ability to understand the world, raised the uncomfortable question of whether the beliefs which they held about nature were workable, the standards of truth they used valid.

Nor is this to argue that it is only, or even mainly, sudden eruptions of extraordinary events which engender in man the disquieting sense that his cognitive resources may prove unavailing or that this intuition appears only in its acute form. More commonly it is a persistent, constantly re-experienced difficulty in grasping certain aspects of nature, self, and society, in bringing certain elusive phenomena within the sphere of culturally formulatable fact, which renders man chronically uneasy and toward which a more equable flow of diagnostic symbols is consequently directed. It is what lies beyond a relatively fixed frontier of accredited knowledge that, looming as a constant background to the daily round of practical life, sets ordinary human experience in a permanent context of metaphysical concern and raises the dim, back-of-the-mind suspicions that one may be adrift in an absurd world:

> Another subject which is matter for this characteristic intellectual enquiry [among the Iatmul] is the nature of ripples and waves on the surface of water. It is said secretly that men, pigs, trees, grass—all the objects in the world—are only patterns of waves. Indeed there seems to be some agreement about this, although it

> perhaps conflicts with the theory of reincarnation, according to which the ghost of the dead is blown as a mist by the East Wind up the river and into the womb of the deceased's son's wife. Be that as it may—there is still the question of how ripples and waves are caused. The clan which claims the East Wind as a totem is clear enough about this: the Wind with her mosquito fan causes the waves. But other clans have personified the waves and say that they are a person (Kontummali) independent of the wind. Other clans, again, have other theories. On one occasion I took some Iatmul natives down to the coast and found one of them sitting by himself gazing with rapt attention at the sea. It was a windless day, but a slow swell was breaking on the beach. Among the totemic ancestors of his clan he counted a personified slit gong who had floated down the river to the sea and who was believed to cause the waves He was gazing at the waves which were heaving and breaking when no wind was blowing, demonstrating the truth of his clan myth.[24]

Problem of Suffering

The second experiential challenge in whose face the meaningfulness of a particular pattern of life threatens to dissolve into a chaos of thingless names and nameless things—the *problem of suffering*—has been rather more investigated, or at least described, mainly because of the great amount of attention given in works on tribal religion to what are perhaps its two main loci: illness and mourning. Yet for all the fascinated interest in the emotional aura that surrounds these extreme situations, there has been, with a few exceptions such as Lienhardt's recent discussion of Dinka divining, little conceptual advance over the sort of crude confidence-type theory set forth by Malinowski: viz., that religion helps one to endure "situations of emotional stress" by "open [ing] up escapes from such situations and such impasses as offer no empirical way out except by ritual and belief into the domain of the supernatural."[25] The inadequacy of this "theology of optimism," as Nadel rather dryly called it, is, of course, radical.[26]

Over its career religion has probably disturbed men as much as it has cheered them; forced them into a head-on, unblinking confrontation of the fact that they are born to trouble as often as it has enabled them to avoid such a confrontation by projecting them into sort of infantile fairy-tale worlds where —Malinowski again—"hope cannot fail nor desire deceive."[27] With the possible exception of Christian Science, there are few if any religious traditions, "great" or "little," in which the proposition that life hurts is not strenuously affirmed, and in some it is virtually glorified:

> She was an old (Ba-lla) woman of a family with a long genealogy. Leza, "the Besetting One", stretched out his hand against the family. He slew her mother and father while she was yet a child, and in the course of years all connected with her perished. She said to herself, "Surely I shall keep those who sit on my thighs." But no, even they, the children of her children, were taken from her. . . . Then came into her heart a desperate resolution to find God and to ask the meaning of it all. ... So she began to travel, going through country after country, always with the thought in her mind: "I shall come to where the earth ends and there I shall find a road to God and I shall ask him: 'What have I done to thee that thou afflictest me in this manner? " She never found where the earth ends, but though disappointed she did not give up her search, and as she passed through the different countries they asked her, "What have you come for, old woman?" And the answer would be, "I am seeking Leza." "Seeking Leza! For what?" "My brothers, you ask me! Here in the nations is there one who suffers as I have suffered?" And they would ask again, "How have you suffered?" "In this way. I am alone. As you see me, a solitary old woman; that is how I am!" And they answered, "Yes, we see. That is how you are! Bereaved of friends and husband? In what do you differ from others? The Besetting-One sits on the back of every one of us and we cannot shake him off." She never obtained her desire; she died of a broken heart.[28]

As a religious problem, the problem of suffering is, paradoxically, not how to avoid suffering but how to suffer, how to make of physical pain, personal loss, wordly defeat, or the helpless contemplation of others' agony something bearable, supportable—something, as we say, sufferable. It was in this effort that the Ba-Ila woman—perhaps necessarily, perhaps not—failed and, literally not knowing how to feel about what had happened to her, how to suffer, perished in confusion and despair. Where the more intellective aspects of what Weber called the Problem of Meaning are a matter affirming the ultimate explicability of experience, the more affective aspects are a matter of affirming its ultimate sufferableness.

As religion on one side anchors the power of our symbolic resources for formulating analytic ideas in an authoritative conception of the overall shape of reality, so on another side it anchors the power of our, also symbolic, resources for expressing emotions— moods, sentiments, passions, affections, feelings—in a similar conception of its pervasive tenor, its inherent tone and temper. For those able to embrace them, and for so long as they are able to embrace them, religious symbols provide a cosmic guarantee not only for their ability to comprehend the world, but also, comprehending it, to give a precision to their feeling, a definition to their emotions which enables them, morosely or joyfully, grimly or cavalierly, to endure it.

Navavaho Curing Rites: Consider in this light the well-known Navaho curing rites usually referred to as "sings."[29] A sing—the Navaho have about sixty different ones for different purposes, but virtually all of them are dedicated to removing some sort of physical or mental illness—is a kind of religious psychodrama in which there are three main actors: the "singer" or curer, the patient, and, as a kind of antiphonal chorus, the patient's family and friends. The structure of all the sings, the drama's plot, is quite similar. There are three main acts: a purification of the patient and audience; a statement, by means of repetitive chants and ritual manipulations, of the wish to restore well-being ("harmony") in the patient; an identification of the patient with the Holy People and his consequent "cure."

The purification rites involve forced sweating, induced vomiting, and so on, to expel the sickness from the patient physically. The chants, which are numberless, consist mainly of simple optative phrases ("may the patient be well," "I am getting better all over," etc.). And, finally, the identification of the patient with the Holy People, and thus with cosmic order generally, is accomplished through the agency of a sand painting depicting the Holy People in one-or another appropriate mythic setting. The singer places the patient on the painting, touching the feet, hands, knees, shoulders, breast, back; and head of the divine figures and then the corresponding parts of the patient, performing thus what is essentially a bodily identification of the human and the divine.[30] This is the climax of the sing: the whole curing process may be likened, Reichard says, to a spiritual osmosis in which the illness in man and the power of the deity penetrate the ceremonial membrane in both directions, the former being neutralized by the latter. Sickness seeps out in the sweat, vomit, and other purification rites; health seeps in as the Navaho patient touches, through the medium of the singer, the sacred sand painting.

Clearly, the symbolism of the sing focuses upon the problem of human suffering and attempts to cope with it by placing it in a meaningful context, providing a mode of action through which it can be expressed, being expressed understood, and being understood, endured. The sustaining effect of the sing (and since the commonest disease is tuberculosis, it can in most cases be only sustaining), rests ultimately on its ability to give the stricken person a vocabulary in terms of which to grasp the nature of his distress and relate it to the wider world. Like a calvary, a recitation of Buddha's emergence from his father's palace, or a performance of *Oedipus Tyrannos* in other religious traditions, a sing is mainly concerned with the presentation of a specific and concrete image of truly human, and so endurable, suffering powerful enough to resist the challenge of emotional meaninglessness raised by the existence of intense and unremovable brute pain.

Problem of Evil

The problem of suffering passes easily into the problem of evil, for if suffering is severe enough it usually, though not always, seems morally undeserved as well, at least to the sufferer. But they are not, however, exactly the same thing. Weber was also influenced by the biases of a monotheistic tradition in which, as the various aspects of human experience must be conceived to proceed from a single, voluntaristic source, man's pain reflects directly on God's goodness, did not fully recognize in his generalization of the dilemmas of Christian theodicy Eastward. For where the problem of suffering is concerned with threats to our ability to put our "undisciplined squads of emotion" into some son of soldierly order, the problem of evil is concerned with threats to our ability to make sound moral judgments.

What is involved in the problem of evil is not the adequacy of our symbolic resources to govern our affective life, but the adequacy of those resources to provide a workable set of ethical criteria, normative guides to govern our action. The vexation here is the gap between things as they are and as they ought to be if our conceptions of right and wrong make sense, the gap between what we deem various individuals deserve and what we see that they get—a phenomenon summed up in that profound stanza:

> The rain falls on the just
> And on the unjust fella;

But mainly upon the just,
Because the unjust has the just's umbrella.

Or if this seems too flippant an expression of an issue that, in somewhat different form, animates the Book of Job and the *Bhagavad Gita,* the following classical Javanese poem, known, sung, and repeatedly quoted in Java by virtually everyone over the age of six, puts the point —the discrepancy between moral prescriptions and material rewards, the seeming inconsistency of "is" and "ought"—rather more elegantly:

We have lived to see a time without order
In which everyone is confused in his mind.
One cannot bear to join in the madness.
But if he does not do so
He will not share in the spoils,
And will starve as a result.
Yes, God; wrong is wrong:
Happy are those who forget.
Happier yet those who remember and have deep insight.

Nor is it necessary to be theologically self-conscious to be religiously sophisticated. The concern with intractable ethical paradox, the disquieting sense that one's moral insight is inadequate to one's moral experience, is as alive on the level of so-called primitive religion as it is on that of the so-called civilized. The set of notions about "division in the world" that Lienhardt describes for the Dinka is a useful case in point.[31]

Like so many peoples, the Dinka believe that the sky, where "Divinity" is located, and earth, where man dwells, were at one time contiguous, the sky lying just above the earth and being connected to it by a rope, so that men could move at will between the two realms. There was no death and the first man and woman were permitted but a single grain of millet a day, which was all that they at that time required. One day, the woman—of course—decided, out of greed, to plant more than the permitted grain of millet, and in her avid haste and industry accidentally struck Divinity with the handle of the hoe. Offended, he severed the rope, withdrew into the distant sky of today, and left man to labor for his food, to suffer sickness and death, and to experience separation from the source of his being, his Creator. Yet the meaning of this strangely familiar story to the Dinka is, as indeed is Genesis to Jews and Christians, not homiletic but descriptive.

> Those [Dinka] who have commented on these stories have sometimes made it clear that their sympathies lie with Man in his plight, and draw attention to the smallness of the fault for which Divinity withdrew the benefits of his closeness. The image of striking Divinity with a hoe... often evokes a certain amusement, almost as though the story were indulgently being treated as too childish to explain the consequences attributed to the event. But it is clear that the point of the story of Divinity's withdrawal from men is not to suggest an improving moral judgment on human behaviour. It is to represent a total situation known to the Dinka today. Men now are—as the first man and woman then became—active, self-assertive, inquiring, acquisitive. Yet they are also subject to suffering and death, ineffective, ignorant and poor. Life is insecure; human calculations often prove erroneous, and men must often learn by experience that the consequences of their acts are quite other than they may have anticipated or consider equitable.
>
> Divinity's withdrawal from Man as the result of a comparatively trifling offence, by human standards, presents the contrast between equitable human judgments and the action of the Power which are held ultimately to control what happens in Dinka life. ... To the Dinka, the moral order is ultimately constituted according to principles which often elude men, which experience and tradition in part reveal, and which human action cannot change. . . . The myth of Divinity's withdrawal then reflects the facts of existence as they are known. The Dinka are in a universe which is largely beyond their control, and where events may contradict the most reasonable human expectations.[32]

Thus the problem of evil, or perhaps one should say the problem *about* evil, is in essence the same sort of problem of or about bafflement and the problem of or about suffering. The strange opacity of certain empirical events, the dumb senselessness of intense or inexorable pain, and the enigmatic unaccountability of gross iniquity all raise the uncomfortable suspicion that perhaps the world, and hence man's life in the world, has no genuine order at all—no empirical regularity, no emotional form, no moral coherence. And the religious response to this suspicion is in each case the same: the formulation, by means of symbols, of an image of such a genuine order of the world which will account for, and even celebrate, the perceived ambiguities, puzzles, and paradoxes in human experience.

The effort is not to deny the undeniable— that there are unexplained events, that life hurts, or that rain falls upon the just—but to deny that there are inexplicable events, that life is unendurable, and that justice is a mirage. The principles which constitute the moral order may indeed often elude men, as Lienhardt puts it, in the same way as fully satisfactory explanations of anomalous events or effective forms for the expression of feeling often elude them.

What is important, to a religious man at least, is that this elusiveness be accounted for, that it be not the result of the fact that there are no such principles, explanations, or forms, that life is absurd and the attempt to make moral, intellectual, or emotional sense out of experience is bootless. The Dinka can admit, in fact insist upon, the moral ambiguities and contradictions of life as they live it because these ambiguities and contradictions are seen not as ultimate, but as the "rational," "natural," "logical" (one may choose one's own adjective here, for none of them is truly adequate) outcome of the moral structure of reality which the myth of the withdrawn "Divinity" depicts, or as Lienhardt says, "images."

Problem of Meaning

The Problem of Meaning in each of its intergrading aspects (how these aspects in fact intergrate in each particular case, what sort of interplay there is between the sense of analytic, emotional, and moral impotence, seems to be one of the outstanding, and except for Weber untouched, problems for comparative research in this whole field) is a matter of affirming, or at least recognizing, the inescapability of ignorance, pain, and injustice on the human plane while simultaneously denying that these irrationalities are characteristic of the world as a whole. And it is in terms of religious symbolism, a symbolism relating man's sphere of existence to a wider sphere within which it is conceived to rest, that both the affirmation and the denial are made.[33]

(4) . . . and clothing those conceptions with such an aura of factuality that. . .

There arises here, however, a more profound question: how is it that this denial comes to be believed? How is it that the religious man moves from a troubled perception of experienced disorder to a more or less settled conviction of fundamental order?

Just what does "belief mean in a religious context? Of all the problems surrounding attempts to conduct anthropological analysis of religion this is the one that has perhaps been most troublesome and therefore the most often avoided, usually by relegating it to psychology, that raffish outcast discipline to which social anthropologists are forever consigning phenomena they are unable to deal with within the framework of a denatured Durkheimianism. But the problem will not go away, it is not "merely" psychological (nothing social is), and no anthropological theory of religion which fails to attack it is worthy of the name. We have been trying to stage Hamlet without the Prince quite long enough. It is best to begin any approach to this issue with frank recognition that religious belief involves not a Baconian induction from everyday experience—for then we should all be agnostics—but rather a prior acceptance of authority which transforms that experience.

The existence of bafflement, pain, and moral paradox—of The Problem of Meaning—is one of the things that drives men toward belief in gods, devils, spirits, totemic principles, or the spiritual efficacy of cannibalism (an enfolding sense of beauty or a dazzling perception of power are others), but it is not the basis upon which those beliefs rest, but rather their most important field of application:

> We point to the state of the world as illustrative of doctrine, but never as evidence for it. So Belsen illustrates a world of original sin, but original sin is not an hypothesis to account for happenings like Belsen. We justify a particular religious belief by showing its place in the total religious conception; we justify a religious belief as a whole by referring to authority. We accept authority because we discover it at some point in the world at which we worship, at which we accept the lordship of something not ourselves. We do not worship authority, but we accept authority as defining the worshipful. So someone may discover the possibility of worship in the life of the Reformed Churches and accept the Bible as authoritative; or in the Roman Church and accept papal authority.[34]

This is, of course, a Christian statement of the matter; but it is not to be despised on that account. In tribal religions authority lies in the persuasive power of traditional imagery; in mystical ones in the apodictic force of supersensible experience; in charismatic ones in the hypnotic attraction of an extraordinary personality. But the priority of the acceptance of an authoritative criterion in religious matters over the revelation which is conceived to flow from that acceptance is not less complete than in scriptural or hieratic ones.

Religious Perspective: The basic axiom underlying what we may perhaps call "the religious perspective" is everywhere the same: he who would know must first believe. But to speak of "the religious perspective" is, by implication, to speak of one perspective among others. A perspective is a mode of seeing, in that extended sense of "see" in which it means "discern," "apprehend," "understand," or "grasp." It is a particular way of looking at life, a particular manner of construing the world, as when we speak of an historical perspective, a scientific perspective, an aesthetic perspective, a common-sense perspective, or even the bizarre perspective embodied in dreams and in hallucinations.[35]

The question then comes down to, first, what is "the religious perspective" genetically considered, as differentiated from other perspectives; and second, how do men come to adopt it. If we place the religious perspective against the background of three of the other major perspectives in terms of which men construe the world—the common-sensical, the scientific, and the aesthetic—its special character emerges more sharply.

What distinguishes common sense as a mode of "seeing" is, as Schutz has pointed out, a simple acceptance of the world, its objects, and its processes as being just what they seem to be—what is sometimes called naive realism—and the pragmatic motive, the wish to act upon that world so as to bend it to one's practical purposes, to master it, or so far as that proves impossible, to adjust to it.[36] The world of everyday life, itself, of course, a cultural product, for it is framed in terms of the symbolic conceptions of "stubborn fact" handed down from generation to generation, is the established scene and given object of our actions. Like Mt. Everest it is just there, and the thing to do with it, if one feels the need to do anything with it at all, is to climb it. In the scientific perspective it is precisely this givenness which disappears.[37] Deliberate doubt and systematic inquiry, the suspension of the pragmatic motive in favor of disinterested observation, the attempt to analyze the world in terms of formal concepts whose relationship to the informal conceptions of common-sense become increasingly problematic—there are the hallmarks of the attempt to grasp the world scientifically. The aesthetic perspective, which under the rubric of "the aesthetic attitude" has been perhaps most exquisitely examined, it involves a different sort of suspension of naive realism and practical interest, in that instead of questioning the credentials of everyday experience, one merely ignores that experience in favor of an eager dwelling upon appearances, an engrossment in surfaces, an absorption in things, as we say, "in themselves": "The function of artistic illusion is not 'make-believe'. . . but the very opposite, disengagement from belief—the contemplation of sensory qualities without it their usual meanings of 'here's that chair', 'that's my telephone'. . . etc. The knowledge that what is before us has no practical significance in the world is what enables us to give attention to its appearance as such."[38] And like the common-sensical and the scientific (or the historical, the philosophical, and the artistic), this perspcctive this "way of seeing" is not the product of some mysterious Cartesian chemistry, but is induced, mediated, and in fact created by means of curious quasi objects—poems, dramas, sculptures, symphonies— which, dissociating themselves from the solid world of common sense, take on the special sort of eloquence only sheer appearances can achieve.

The religious perspective differs from the common-sensical in that, as already pointed out, it moves beyond the realities of everyday life to wider ones which correct and complete them, and its defining concern is not action upon those wider realities but acceptance of them, faith in them.

It differs from the scientific perspective in that it questions the realities of everyday life not out of an institutionalized scepticism which dissolves the world's givenness into a swirl of probabilistic hypotheses, but in terms of what it takes to be wider, nonhypothetical truths. Rather than detachment, its watchword is commitment; rather than analysis, encounter. And it differs from art in that instead of effecting a disengagement from the whole question of factuality, deliberately manufacturing an air of semblance and illusion, it deepens the concern with fact and seeks to create an aura of utter actuality. It is this sense of the "really real" upon which the religious perspective rests and which the symbolic activities of religion as a cultural system are devoted to producing, intensifying, and, so far as possible, rendering inviolable by the discordant revelations of secular experience. It is, again, the imbuing of a certain specific complex of symbols—of the metaphysic they formulate and the style of life they recommend—with a persuasive authority which, from an analytic point of view, is the essence of religious action. Which brings us, at length, to ritual.

It is in ritual—that is, consecrated behavior—that this conviction that religious conceptions are veridical and that religious directives are sound is somehow generated. It is in some sort of ceremonial form—even if that form be hardly more than the recitation of a myth, the consultation of an oracle, or the decoration of a grave—that the moods and motivations which sacred symbols induce in men and the general conceptions of the order of existence which they formulate for men meet and reinforce one another. In a ritual, the world as lived and the world as imagined, fused under the agency of a single set of symbolic forms, turn out to be the same world producing thus that idiosyncratic transformation in one's sense of reality to which Santayana refers to in the beginning of this chapter.

Whatever role divine intervention may or may not play in the creation of faith—and it is not the business of the scientist to pronounce upon such matters one way or the other—it is, primarily at least, out of the context of concrete acts of religious observance that religious conviction emerges on the human plane. However, though any religious ritual, no matter how apparently automatic or conventional (if it is truly automatic or merely conventional it is not religious), involves this symbolic fusion of ethos and world view, it is mainly certain more elaborate and usually more public ones, ones in which a broad range of moods and motivations on the one hand and of metaphysical conceptions on the other are caught up, which shape the spiritual consciousness of a people. Employing a useful term introduced by Singer, we may call these full-blown ceremonies "cultural performances" and note that they represent not only the point at which the dispositional and conceptual aspects of religious life converge for the believer, but also the point at which the interaction between them can be most readily examined by the detached observer:

Whenever Madrasi Brahmans (and non-Brahmans, too, for that matter) wished to exhibit to me some feature of Hinduism, they always referred to, or invited me to see, a particular rite or ceremony in the life cycle, in a temple festival, or in the general sphere of religious and cultural performances. Reflecting on this in the course of my interviews and observations I found that the more abstract generalizations about Hinduism (my own as well as those I heard) could generally be checked, directly or indirectly, against these observable performances.[39]

It is not easy to demaicabe always the differences between cultural performances and religious performances, and the line between those that are artistic, or even political, ones is often not so easy to draw in practice, for, like social forms, symbolic forms can serve multiple purposes. But the point is that, paraphrasing slightly, Indians—"and perhaps all peoples"—seem to think of their religion "as encapsulated in these discrete performances which they [can] exhibit to visitors and to themselves."[40] The mode of exhibition is however radically different for the two sorts of witness, a fact seemingly overlooked by those who would argue that "religion is a form of human art."[41]

For a "visitors:" religious performances can, in the nature of the case, only be presentations of a particular religious perspective, and thus aesthetically appreciated or scientifically dissected, for participants they are in addition enactments, materializations, realizations of it—not only models of what they believe, but also models for the believing of it. In these plastic dramas men attain their faith as they portray it.

Let us take for example a spectacularly theatrical cultural performance from Bali—that in which a terrible witch called Rangda engages in a ritual combat with an endearing monster called Barong.[42] Usually, but not inevitably presented on the occasion of a death temple celebration, the drama consists of a masked dance in which the witch —depicted as a wasted old widow, prostitute, and eater of infants—cours to spread plague and death upon the land and is opposed by the monster—depicted as a kind of cross between a clumsy bear, a silly puppy, and a strutting Chinese dragon. Rangda, danced by a single male, is a hideous figure. Her eyes bulge from her forehead like swollen boils. Her teeth become tusks curving up over her cheeks and fangs protruding down over her chin. Her yellowed hair falls down around her in a matted tangle. Her breasts are dry and pendulous dugs edged with hair, between which hang, like so many sausages, strings of colored entrails. Her long red tongue is a stream of fire. And as she dances she displays her dead-white hands,' from which protrude ten-inch claw-like fingernails, out in front of her and utters unnerving shrieks of metallic laughter.

Barong, danced by two men fore-and-aft in vaudeville horse fashion, is another matter. His shaggy sheepdog coat is hung with gold and mica ornaments that glitter in the half-light. He is adorned with flowers, sashes, feathers, mirrors, and a comical beard made from human hair. And though a demon too, his eyes also pop and he snaps his fanged jaws with seemly fierceness when faced with Rangda or other affronts to his dignity; the cluster of tinkling bells which hang from his absurdly arching tail somehow contrives to take most of the edge off his fearfulness. If Rangda is a Satanic image, Barong is a farcical one and their clash is a clash (an inconclusive one) between the malignant and the ludicrous.

This odd counterpoint of implacable malice and low comedy pervades the whole performance. Rangda, clutching her magical white cloth, moves around in a slow stagger, now pausing immobile in thought or uncertainty, now lurching suddenly forward. The moment of her entry (one sees those terrible long-nailed hands first as she emerges through the split gateway at the top of a short flight of stone stairs) is one of terrific tension when it seems, to a "visitor" at least, that everyone is about to break and run in panic. She herself seems insane with fear and hatred as she screams deprecations at Barong amid the wild clanging of the gamelan. She may in fact go amok. Rangdas hurl themselves headlong into the gamelan or run frantically about in total confusion, being subdued and reoriented only by the combined force of a half-dozen spectators; and one hears many tales of amok Rangdas holding a whole village in terror for hours and of impersonators becoming permanently deranged by their experiences.

Barong, though he is charged with the same mana-like sacred power *(sakti* in Balinese) as Rangda, and his impersonators are also entranced, seems to have very great difficulty in being serious. He frolics with his retinue of demons (who add to the gaiety by indelicate pranks of their own), lies down on a metallaphone while it is being played or beats on a drum with his legs, moves in one direction in his front half and another in his rear or bends his segmented body into foolish contortions, brushes flies from his body or sniffs aromas in the air, and generally prances about in paroxysms of narcissistic vanity.

The contrast is not absolute, for Rangda is sometimes momentarily comic as when she pretends to polish the mirrors on Barong's coat, and Barong becomes rather more serious after Rangda appears, nervously clacking his jaws at her and ultimately attacking her directly. Nor are the humorous and the horrible always kept rigidly separated, as in that strange scene in one section of the cycle in which several minor witches (disciples of Rangda) toss the corpse of a stillborn child around to the wild amusement of the audience or another, no less strange, in which the sight of a pregnant woman alternating hysterically between tears and laughter while being knocked about by a group of gravediggers, seems for some reason excruciaingly funny. The twin themes of horror and hilarity find their purest expression in the two protagonists and their endless, indecisive struggle for dominance, but they are woven with deliberate intricacy through the whole texture of the drama. They—or rather the relations between them—are what it is about. Such performances vary widely in detail, consist of several not too closely integrated parts, and in any case are so complex in structure as to defy easy summary. In the present context the main point to be stressed is that the drama is, for the Balinese, not merely a spectacle to be watched but a ritual to be enacted. There is no aesthetic distance here separating actors from audience and placing the depicted events in an unenterable world of illusion, and by the time a full-scale Rangda-Barong encounter has been concluded a majority, often nearly all, of the members of the group sponsoring it will have become caught up in it not just imaginatively but bodily. In one of Belo's examples there were upwards of seventy-five people—men, women, and children—taking part in the activity at some point or other, and thirty to forty participants are in no way unusual. As a performance, the drama is like a high mass, not like a presentation of *Murder in the Cathedral.*

In part, this entry into the body of the ritual takes place through the agency of the various supporting roles contained in it—minor witches, demons, various sorts of legendary and mythical figures—which selected villagers enact. But mostly it takes place through the agency of an extraordinarily developed capacity for psychological dissociation on the part of a very large segment of the population. A Rangda-Barong struggle is inevitably marked by anywhere from three or four to several dozen spectators becoming possessed by one or another demon, falling into violent trances "like firecrackers going off one after the other,[43] and, snatching up krisses, rushing to join the fray. Mass trance, spreading like a panic, projects the individual Balinese out of the common-place world in which he usually lives into that most uncommonplace one in which Rangda and Barong live. To become entranced is, for the Balinese, to cross a threshold into another order of existence—the word for trance is *nodi,* from *dadi,* often translated "to become" but which might be even more simply rendered as "to be." And even those who for whatever reasons, do not make this spiritual crossing are caught up in the proceedings, for it is they who must keep the frenzied activities of the entranced from getting out of hand by the application of physical restraint if they are ordinary men, by the sprinkling of holy water and the chanting of spells if they are priests.

At its height a Rangda-Barong rite hovers, or at least seems to hover, on the brink of mass amok with the diminishing band of the unentranced striving desperately (and, seems, almost always successfully) to control the growing band of the entranced. In its standard form—the performance begins with an appearance of Barong, prancing and preening, as a general prophylactic against what is to follow. Then may come various mythic scenes relating the story—not always precisely the same ones—upon which the performance is based, until finally Barong and then Rangda appear. Their battle begins. Barong drives Rangda back toward the gate of the death temple. But he has not the power to expel her completely, and he is in turn driven back toward the village. At length, when it seems as though Rangda will finally prevail, a number of entranced men rise, krisses in hand, and rush to support Barong. But as they approach Rangda (who has turned her back in meditation), she wheels upon them and, waving her *sakti* white cloth, leaves them comatose on the ground. Rangda then hastily retires (or is carried) to the temple, where she herself collapses, hidden from the aroused crowd which, it is said, would kill her were it to see her in a help-less state. The Barong moves among the kris dancers and wakens them by snapping his jaws at them or nuzzling them with his beard. As they return, still entranced, to "consciousness," they are enraged by the disappearance of Rangda, and unable to attack her they turn their krisses (harmlessly because they are entranced) against their own chests in frustration. Usually sheer pandemonium breaks out at this point with members of the crowd, of both sexes, falling into trance all around the court-yard and rushing out to stab themselves, wrestle with one another devour live chicks or excrement, wallow convulsively in the mud, and so on, while the nonentranced attempt to relieve them of their krisses and keep them at least minimally in order. In time, the trancers sink one by one, into coma, from which they are aroused by the priests' holy water and the great battle is over—once more a complete stand-off Rangda has not been conquered, but neither has she conquered, One place to search for the meaning of this ritual is in the collection of myths, tales, and explicit beliefs which it supposedly enacts. How-ever, not only are these various and variable—for some people Rangda is; an incarnation of Durga, Siva's malignant consort; for others she is Queen Mahendradatta, a figure from a court legend set in eleventh century Java; for yet others, the spiritual leader of witches as the Brahmana Priest is the spiritual leader of men. Notions of who (or "what"] Barong are equally diverse and even vaguer—but they seem to play only a secondary role in the Balinese' perception of the drama. It is in the direct encounter with the two figures in the context of the actual performance that the villager comes to know them as, so far as he is concerned, genuine realities. They are, then, not representations of anything, but presences. And when the villagers go into trance they become—*nodi*—themselves part of the realm in which those presences exist. To ask, a man who has been Rangda whether he thinks she is real is to leave oneself open to the suspicion of idiocy.

The acceptance of authority that underlies the religious perspective that the ritual embodies thus flows from the enactment of the ritual itself. By inducing a set of moods and motivations—an ethos—and defining an image of cosmic order—a world view—by means of a single set of symbols, the performance makes the model *for* and model *of* aspects of religious belief mere transpositions of one another. Rangda evokes fear (as well as hatred, disgust, cruelty, horror, and, the sexual aspects of the performance here, lust); but she also depicts it.

The fascination which the figure of the Witch holds for the Balinese imagination can only be explained when it is recognized that the Witch is not only a fear inspiring figure, but that she is Fear. Her hands with their long menacing finger-nails do not clutch and claw at her victims, although children who play at being witches do curl their hands in such gestures. But the Witch herself spreads her arms with palms out and her finger flexed backward, in the gesture the Balinese call *kapar,* a term which they apply to the sudden startled reaction of a man who falls from a tree. . . . Only when we see the Witch as herself afraid, as well as frightening, is it possible to e-plain her appeal, and the pathos which surrounds her as she dances, hairy, forbidding, tusked and alone, giving her occasional high eerie laugh.[44]

And on his side Barong not only induces laughter, he incarnates the Balinese version of the comic spirit—a distinctive combination of playfulness, exhibitionism, and extravagant love of elegance, which, along with fear, is perhaps the dominant motive in their life. The constantly recurring struggle of Rangda and Barong to an inevitable draw is thus—for the believing Balinese—both the formulation of a general religious conception and the authoritative experience which justifies, even compels its acceptance.

(5). . . that the moods and motivations seem uniquely realistic

But no one, not even a saint, lives in the world religious symbols formulate all of the time, and the majority of men live in it only at moments. The everyday world of common-sense objects and practical acts is, as Schutz says, the paramount reality in human experience — paramount in the sense that it is the world in which we are most solidly rooted, whose inherent actuality we can hardly question (however much we may question certain portions of it), and from whose pressures and requirements we can least escape.[45] A man, even large groups of men, may be aesthetically insensitive, religiously unconcerned, and unequipped to pursue formal scientific analysis, but he cannot be completely lacking in common sense and survive.

The dispositions which religious rituals induce thus have their most important impact — from a human point of view — outside the boundaries of the ritual itself as they reflect back to colour the individual's conception of the established world of bare fact. The peculiar tone that marks the Plains vision quest, the Manus confession, or the Javanese mystical exercise pervades areas of the life of these peoples far beyond the immediately religious, impressing upon them a distinctive style in the sense both of a dominant mood and a characteristic movement. The interweaving of the malignant and the comic, which the Rangda-Barong combat depicts, animates a very wide range of everyday Balinese behavior, much of which, like the ritual itself, has an air of candid fear narrowly contained by obsessive playfulness.

Religion is sociologically interesting not because, as vulgar positivism would have it, it describes the social order (which, in so far as it does, it does not only very obliquely but very incompletely), but because like environment, political power, wealth, jurat obligation, personal affection, and a sense of beauty, it shapes it. The movement back and forth between the religious perspective and the common-sense perspective is actually one of the more obvious empirical occurrences on the social scene, though, again, one of the most neglected by social anthropologists, virtually all of whom have seen it happen countless times.

Religious belief has usually been presented as a homogeneous characteristic of an individual, like his place of residence, his occupational role, his kinship position, and so on. But religious be-life in the midst of ritual, where it engulfs the total person, transporting him, so far as he is concerned, into another mode of existence, and religious belief as the pale, remembered reflection of that experience in the midst of everyday life are not precisely the same thing, and the failure to realize this has led to some confusion, most especially in connection with the so-called primitive-mentality problem. Much of the difficulty between Levy-Bruhl and Malinowski on the nature of "native thought," for example, arises from a lack of full recognition of this distinction; for where the French philosopher was concerned with the view of reality savages adopted when taking a specifically religious perspective, the Polish-English ethnographer was concerned with that which they adopted when taking a strictly common-sense one.[46] Both perhaps vaguely sensed that they were not talking about exactly the same thing, but where they went astray was in failing to give a specific accounting of the way in which these two forms of "thought"—or, as I would; rather say, these two modes of symbolic formulations—interacted, so that where Levy-Bruhl's savages tended to live, despite his postludial disclaimers, in a world composed entirely of mystical encounters, Malinowski's tended to live, despite his stress on the functional importance of religion, in a world composed entirely of practical actions. They became reductionists (an idealist is as much of a reductionist as a materialist) inspite of themselves because they failed to see man as moving more or less easily, and very frequently, between radically contrasting ways of looking at the world, ways which are not continuous with one another but separated by cultural gaps across which Kierkegaardian leaps must be made in both directions.

> "There are as many innumerable kinds of different shock experiences as there are different finite provinces of meaning upon which I may bestow the accent of reality. Some instances are: the shock of falling asleep as the leap into the world of dreams; the inner transformation we endure if the curtain in the theatre rises as the transition to the world of the stageplay; the radical change in our attitude if, before a painting, we permit our visual field to be limited by what is within the frame as the passage into the pictorial world our quandary relaxing into laughter, if, in listening to a joke, we are for a short time ready to accept the fictitious world of the jest as a reality in relation to which the world of our daily life takes on the character of foolishness; the child's turning toward his

> toy as the transition into the play-world and so on. But also the religious experiences in all their varieties—for in stance. Kierkegaard's experience of the "instant" as the leap into the religious sphere—are examples of such a shock, as well as the decision of the scientist to replace all passionate participation in the affairs of "this world" by a disinterested [analytical] attitude.[47]"

The recognition and exploration of the qualitative difference—an empirical, not a transcendental difference—between religion pure and religion applied, between an encounter with the supposedly "really real" and a viewing of ordinary experience in light of what that encounter seems to reveal, will, therefore, take us further toward an understanding of what a Bororo means when he says "I am a parakeet," or a Christian when he says "I am a sinner," than either a theory of primitive mysticism in which the commonplace world disappears into a cloud of curious ideas or of a primitive pragmatism in which religion disintegrates into a collection of useful fictions.

The parakeet example, taken from Percy, is a good one.[48] For, as he points out, it is unsatisfactory to say either that the Bororo thinks he is literally a parakeet (for he does not try to mate with other parakeets), that his statement is false or non-sense (for, clearly, he is not offering—or at least not only offering— the sort of class-membership argument which can be confirmed or refuted as, say, "I am a Bororo" can be confirmed or refuted), or yet again that it is false scientifically but true mythically (because that leads immediately to the pragmatic fiction notion which, as it denies the accolade of truth to "myth" in the very act of bestowing it, is internally self-contradictory). More coherently it would seem to be necessary to see the sentence as having a different sense in the context of the "finite province of meaning" which makes up the religious perspective and of that which makes up the common-sensical. In the religious, our Bororo is "really" a "parakeet," and given the proper ritual context might well mate" with other "parakeets"—with metaphysical ones like himself, not commonplace ones such as those which fly bodily about in ordinary trees. In the common-sensical perspective he is a parakeet in the sense I assumed—that he belongs to a clan whose members regard the parakeet as their totem, a membership from which, given the fundamental nature of reality as the religious perspective reveals it, certain moral and practical consequences flow.

A man who says he is a parakeet is, if he says it in normal

conversation, saying that, as myth and ritual demonstrate he is shot through with parakeetness and that this religious fact has some crucial social implications—we parakeets must stick together, not marry one another, not eat mundane parakeets, and so on, for to do otherwise is to act against the grain of the whole universe. It is this placing of proximate acts in ultimate contexts that makes religion, frequently at least, socially so powerful. It alters, often radically, the whole landscape presented to common sense, alters it in such a way that the moods and motivations induced by religious practice seem themselves supremely practical, the only sensible ones to adopt given the way things "really" are.

Having ritually "lept" (the image is perhaps a bit too athletic for the actual facts—"slipped" might be more accurate) into the framework of meaning which religious conceptions define, and the ritual ended, returned again to the common-sense world, a man is—unless, as sometimes happens, the experience fails to register—changed. And as he is changed, so also is the common-sense world, for it is now seen as but the partial form of a wider reality which corrects and completes it.

But this correction and completion is not, as some students of "comparative religion" would have it, everywhere the same in content. The nature of the bias religion gives to ordinary life varies with the religion involved, with the particular dispositions induced in the believer by the specific conceptions of cosmic order he has come to accept. On the level of the "great" religions, organic distinctiveness is usually recognized, at times insisted upon to the point of zealotry. But even at its simplest folk and tribal levels—where the individuality of religious traditions has so often been dissolved into such desiccated types as "animism," "animatism," "totemism," "shamanism," "ancestor worship," and all the other insipid categories by means of which ethnographers of religion devitalize their data—the idiosyncratic character of how various groups of men behave because of what they believe they have experienced is clear.

A tranquil Javanese would be no more at home in guilt-ridden Manus than an activist Crow would be in passionless Java. And for all the witches and ritual clowns in the world, Rangda and Barong are not generalized but thoroughly singular figurations of fear and gaiety. What men believe is as various as what they are—a proposition that holds with equal force when it is inverted. It is this particularity of the impact of religious systems upon social systems (and upon personality systems) which renders general assessments of the value of religion in either moral or functional terms impossible. The sorts of moods and motivations which characterize a man who has just come from an Aztec human sacrifice are rather different from those of one who has just put off his Kachina mask. Even within the same society, what one "learns" about the essential pattern of life from a sorcery rite and from a commensal meal will have rather diverse effects on social and psychological functioning.

One of the main methodological problems in writing about religion scientifically is to put aside at once the tone of the village atheist and that of the village preacher, as well as their more sophisticated equivalents, so that the social and psychological implications of particular religious beliefs can emerge in a clear and neutral light. And when that is done, overall questions about whether religion is "good" or "bad," "functional" or "dysfunctional," "ego strengthening" or "anxiety producing," disappear like the chimeras they are, and one is left with particular evaluations, assessments, and diagnoses in particular cases. There remains, of course, the hardly unimportant questions of whether this or that religious assertion is true, this or that religious experience genuine, or whether true religious assertions and genuine religious experiences are possible at all. But such questions cannot even be asked, much less answered, within the self-imposed limitations of the scientific perspective.

Importance of Religious Concept's

For an anthropologist, the importance of religion lies in its capacity to serve, for an individual or for a group, as a source of general, yet distinctive, conceptions of the world, the self, and the relations between them, on the one hand—its model *of* aspect—and of rooted, no less distinctive "mental" dispositions—its model *for* aspect—on the other. From these cultural functions flow, in turn, its social and psychological ones. Religious concepts spread beyond their specifically metaphysical contexts to provide a framework of general ideas in terms of which a wide range of experience—intellectual, emotional, moral—can be given meaningful form.

The Christian sees the Nazi movement against the background of The Fall which, though it does not, in a causal sense, explain it, places it in a moral, a cognitive, even an affective sense. An Azande sees the collapse of a granary upon a friend or relative against the background of a concrete and rather special notion of witchcraft and thus avoids the philosophical dilemmas as well as the psychological stress of indeterminism. A Javanese finds in the borrowed and reworked concept of *rasa* ("sense-taste-feeling-meaning") a means by which to "see" choreographic, gustatory, emotional, and political phenomena in a new light. A synopsis of cosmic order, a set of religious beliefs, is also a gloss upon the mundane world of social relationships and psychological events. It renders them graspable. But more than gloss, such beliefs are also a template. They do not merely interpret social and psychological processes in cosmic terms—in which case they would be philosophical, not religious—but they shape them.

In the doctrine of original sin is embedded also a recommended attitude toward life, a recurring mood, and a persisting set of motivations. The Azande learns from witchcraft conceptions not just to understand apparent "accidents" as not accidents at all, but to react to these spurious accidents with hatred for the agent who caused them and to proceed against him with appropriate resolution. *Rasa,* in addition to being a concept of truth, beauty, and goodness, is also a preferred mode of experiencing, a kind of affectless detachment, a variety of bland aloofness, an unshakable calm. The moods and motivations a religious orientation produces cast a derivative, lunar light over the solid features of a people's secular life.

The tracing of the social and psychological role of religion is thus not so much a matter of finding correlations between specific ritual acts and specific secular social ties—though these correlations do, of course, exist and are very worth continued investigation, especially if we can contrive something novel to say about them. Moreover, it is a matter of understanding how it is that men's notions, however implicit, of the "really real" and the dispositions these notions induce in them, colour their sense of the reasonable, the practical, the humane, and the moral How far they do so (for in many societies religion's effects seem quite circumscribed, in others completely pervasive), how deeply they do so (for some men, and groups of men, seem to wear their religion lightly so far as the secular world goes, while others seem to apply their faith to each occasion, no matter how trivial), and how effectively they do so (for the width of the gap between what religion recommends and what people actually do is most variable cross-culturally)—all these are crucial issues in the comparative sociology and psychology of religion.

Even the degree to which religious systems themselves are developed seems to vary extremely widely, and not merely on a simple evolutionary basis. In one society, the level of elaboration of symbolic formulations of ultimate actuality may reach extraordinary degrees of complexity and systematic articulation; in another, no less developed socially, such formulations may remain primitive in the true sense, hardly more than congeries of fragmentary by-beliefs and isolated images, of sacred reflexes and spiritual pictographs. One need only think of the Australians and the Bushmen, the Toradja and the Alorese, the Hopi and the Apache, the Hindus and the Romans, or even the Italians and the Poles, to see that degree of religious articulateness is not a constant even as between societies of similar complexity.

The anthropological study of religion is therefore a two-stage operation: first, an analysis of the system of meanings embodied in the symbols which make up the religion proper, and second, the relating of these systems to social-structural and psychological processes. Dissatisfaction with so much of contemporary social anthropological work in religion is not because it concerns itself with the second stage, but that it neglects the first, and in so doing takes for granted what most needs to be elucidated. To discuss the role of ancestor worship in regulating political succession, of sacrificial feasts in defining kinship obligations, of spirit worship in scheduling agricultural practices, of divination in reinforcing social control, or of initiation rites in propelling personality maturation, are in no sense unimportant endeavors, and it is not recommended that they be abandoned for the kind of jejune cabalism into which symbolic analysis of exotic faiths can so easily fail. But to attempt them with but the most general, common-sense view of what ancestor worship, animal sacrifice, spirit worship, divination, or initiation rites are as religious patterns seems not particularly promising. Only when we have a theoretical analysis of symbolic action comparable in sophistication to that we now have for social and psychological action, will we be able to cope effectively with those aspects of social and psychological life in which religion (or art, or science, or ideology) plays a determinant role. After analysing the system of meanings embodied in religious symbols can we than relate them to social structural and psychological processes.

NOTES

1. L. Steinberg, "The Eye is Part of the Mind," *Partisan Review* 70 (1953): 194-212.
2. M. Janowitz, "Anthropology and the Social Sciences," *Current Anthropology* 4(1963):139, 146-154.
3. T. Parsons and E. Shils, *Toward a General Theory of Action* (Cambridge, Mass., 1951).
4. S. Langer, *Philosophical Sketches* (Baltimore, 1962).
5. Langer, *Philosophy in a New Key.* 4th ed. (Cambridge. Mass., 1960).
6. K. Burke, *The Philosophy of Literary Form* (Baton Rouge, La.: Louisiana State University Press, 1941), p. 9.
7. The reverse mistake, especially common among neo-Kantians such as Cassirer, of taking symbols to be identical with, or "constitutive of," their referents is equally pernicious. [Cf. E. Cassirer, *The Philosophy of Symbolic Forms* (New Haven: 1953-1957), 3 vols.] "One can point to the moon with one's finger" some, probably well-invented, Zen Master is supposed to have said, "but to take one's finger for the moon is to be a fool."
8. K. Craik, *The Nature of Explanation* (Cambridge, 1952).
9. K. Lorenz, *King Solomon's Ring* (London, 1952).
10. K. von Frisch, "Dialects in the Language of the Bees," *Scientific American,* August 1962.
11. Craik, *Nature of Explanation.*
12. R. H. Lowie, *Primitive Religion* (New York, 1924).
13. R. F. Fortune, *Manus Religion* (Philadelphia, 1935).
14. C. Geertz, *The Religion of Java* (Glencoe, 111., 1960).
15. G. Ryle, *The Concept of Mind* (London and New York, 1949).
16. *Ibid.,* p. 86. Quoted by permission of Barnes & Noble Books and Hutchinson Publishing Group Ltd.
17. *Ibid.,* p. 99.
18. C. Kluckhohn, "The Philosophy of the Navaho Indians," in *Ideological Differences and World Order,* ed. F. S. C. Northrop (New Haven, 1949), pp. 356-384.
19. J. Goody, "Religion and Ritual: The Definition Problem," *British Journal of Psychology* 12 (1961):143-164.
20. W. James, *The Principles of Psychology.* 2 vols. (New York, 1904).
21. Langer, Philosophy in a New Key, p. 287. Italics in original.
22. E. Evans-Pritchard, Witchcraft, Oracles and Magic Among the Azande (Oxford, 1937).
23. A. R. Radcliffe-Brown, Structure and Function in Primitive Society (Glencoe. Ill., 1952).
24. G. Bateson, *Naven.* 2nd ed. (Stanford. 1958). That the chronic and acute forms of this sort of cognitive concern are closely interrelated, and that response to the more unusual occasions of it are patterned on responses

established in coping with the more usual is also clear from Bateson's description, however, as he goes on to say: "On another occasion I invited one of my informants to witness the development of photographic plates. I first desensitized the plates and then developed them in an open dish in moderate light, so that my informant was able to see the gradual appearance of the images. He was much interested, and some days later made me promise never to show this process to members of other clans. Kontum-mali was one of his ancestors, and he saw in the process of photo-graphic development the actual embodiment of ripples into images, and regarded this as a demonstration of the clan's secret."

25. G. Lienhardt, *Divinity and Experience* (Oxford, 1961), p. 151ff; B. Malinowski, *Magic, Science and Religion* (Boston, 1948), p. 67.
26. S. F. Nadel, "Malinowski on Magic and Religion," in *Man and Culture*, ed. R. Firth (London, 1957), pp. 189-208.
27. Malinowski, *Magic. Science and Religion* (Boston, 1948), p. 67.
28. C. W. Smith and A. M. Dale, *The Ila-Speaking Peoples of Northern Rhodesia* (London, 1920), p. 197ff.; quoted in P. Radin, *Primitive Man as a Philosopher* (New York, 1957), pp. 100-101.
29. C. Kluckhohn and D. Leighton, *The Navaho* (Cambridge, Mass., 1946); G. Reichard, *Navaho Religion*, 2 Vols. (New York, 1950).
30. Reichard, *Navaho Religion.*
31. *Ibid.*, pp. 28-55.
32. *Ibid.*
33. This is *not*, however, to say that everyone in every society does this; for as the immortal Don Marquis once remarked, you don't have to have a soul unless you really want one. The oft-heard generalization that religion is a human universal embodies a confusion between the probably true (though on present evidence improvable) proposition that there is no human society in which cultural patterns that we can, under the present definition or one like it, call religious are totally lacking, and the surely untrue proposition that all men in all societies are, in any meaningful sense of the term, religious. But if the anthropological study of religious commitment is underdeveloped, the anthropological study of religious noncommitment is nonexistent. The anthropology of religion will have come of age when some more subtle Malinowski writes a book called "Belief and Unbelief (or even "Faith and Hypocrisy") in a Savage Society."
34. A. MacIntyre, "The Logical Status of Religious Belief," in *Metaphysical Beliefs*, ed. A MacIntyre (London, 1957), pp. 167-211.
35. The term attitude" as in "aesthetic attitude" or "natural attitude" is another, perhaps more common term for what I have here called "perspective." [For the first, see C. Bell, *Art*, London, 1914; for the second, though the phrase; is originally Husserl's, see A. Schutz, *The Problem of Social Reality*, vol. I of *Collected Papers* (The Hague, 1962).] But I have avoided it because of its strong subjectivist connotations, its tendency to

place the stress upon a supposed inner state of an actor rather than on a certain sort of relation—a symbolically mediated one—between an actor and a situation. This is not to say, of course, that a phenomenological analysis of religious experience, if cast in intersubjective, nontranscendental, genuinely scientific terms [e.g., W. Percy, "Symbol, Consciousness and Intersubjectivity," *Journal of Philosophy* 15 (1958):631-641] is not essential to a full understanding of religious belief, but merely that is not the focus of my concern here. "Outlook," "frame of reference," 'frame of mind, "orientation," "stance," "mental set," and so on, are other terms sometimes employed, depending upon whether the analyst wishes to stress the social, psycho-logical, or cultural aspects of the matter.

36. Schutz, *The Problem of Social Reality.*
37. *Ibid.*
38. S. Longer, *Feeling and Form* (New York, 1953), p. 49.
39. M. Singer, "The Cultural Pattern of Indian Civilization." *Far Eastern Quarterly 15* (1955):23-26.
40. Singer. The Great Tradition in a Metropolitan Center: Madras," in *Traditional India,* ed. M. Singer (Philadelphia, 1958), pp. 140-182.
41. R. Firth, *Elements of Social Organization* (London and New York, 1951), p. 250.
42. The Rangda-Barong complex has been extensively described and analyzed by a series of unusually giftted ethnographers and I shall make no attempt to present it here in more than schematic form. (See, for example, J. Belo, *Bali. Rangda and Barong* (New York, 1949); J. Belo, *Trance in Bali* (New York, 1960); B. DeZoete and W. Spies, *Dance and Drama in Bali* (London, 1938); G. Bateson and M. Mead, *Balinese Character* (New York, 1942); M. Covarrubias, *The Island of Bali* (New York, 1937)] Much of my interpretation of the complex rests on personal observations made in Bali during 1957-1958.
43. Belo, Trance in Bali.
44. G. Bateson and M. Mead, *Balinese Character,* p. 36.
45. Schutz, *The Problem of Social Reality,* p. 226ff.
46 Malinowski, *Magic, Science and Religion;* L. Levy-Bruhl, *How Natives Think* (New York, 1926).
47. Schutz, *The Problem of Social Reality,* p. 231.
48. W. Percy, "The Symbolic Structure of Interpersonal Process," *Psychiatry* 24 1961): 39-52.

9

Understanding God and Humanity through Process Theology

The concern for our environment has become increasingly intense as the exploitation of our natural resource has reached alarming proportions—such that they are threatening our very existence.

During the past decade, people have become aware of the dangers to the human future resulting from exploitation of the environment. This exploitation has been consistent with both the dominant economic theories and the dominant theologies of the nineteenth and twentieth centuries. Ideally these theories called for treatment of all human beings as ends rather than as means, but the power of the dominant theories has been such that their objectifying categories are readily extended to human beings. People, too, become resources, and the term human resources has become prevalent.

In practice powerless human beings and powerless societies have been treated as resources for exploitation by those who have the economic and political power to establish goals and to pursue them. In response to this situation, the task cannot be simply to improve practice in light of existing theory. It must be to change the theory. And because our theory, both in economics and theology, has both shaped and expressed our dominant perceptions and sensibility, it is necessary to change our vision of reality as well.

Process Theology

Process thought has been protesting for some time against some of

From: "Process Theology and An Ecological Model," *Pacific Theological Review* 15, no. 2 (Winter 1982): 24-27, 28; original title: "Process Theology and an Ecological Model."

the features of our dominant practice, theory, and sensibility which are now more widely recognized as damaging. In particular, process thought has offered an alternative to the dominant dualisms of soul and body, spirit and nature, mind and matter, self and other. It should be able to speak with some relevance to the contemporary situation. The theology which has appropriated these contributions of process thought is often called "process theology." The dominant thinker behind the distinctive approach of process theology is the English mathematician-philosopher Alfred North Whitehead (1861-1947)- He taught at Harvard University during his later years and has had his largest following in the United States.

Idea of Organism

In his most important book on his Gifford Lectures of 1927-28, entitled *Process and Reality,* he proposed a "philosophy of Organism." By this he meant that the actual entities of which the world is ultimately made up are better thought of as organisms than as material or mental substances. The main significance of the idea of organism here is that each entity exists only in its relation to its environment. One cannot think first of an entity and then, incidentally, of its relations to the rest of the world. On the contrary, every entity is relational in its most fundamental nature. It is constituted by its relations. Even in thought it cannot be abstracted from them.

The Ecological Model

Professor L. Charles Birch, an Australian biologist active in the World Council of Churches, and John Copp have authored a book in which they develop this point. They call theirs an ecological model of living things, and they show that this model fits the evidence of biological sciences better than the substantialist, the materialist, and mechanist models that have dominated their development. The ecological model is also more appropriate to held, relativity, and quantum theory in physics. There are a number of converging trends in the natural sciences that support a Whiteheadian, ecological understanding of nature. If process thought accepted a dualism between humanity and nature, a changed view of nature would not seem very important theologically. But those who follow Whitehead understand human beings as part of nature. The ecological model applies to us as well. Human experience, too, is constituted by its relations with the body with other people, and with nonhuman creatures. Three further clarifications of the meaning of these assertions for theology, as well as for the natural sciences, are needed.

Clarification of the Ecological Model

First, the ecological model depicts the actual entities as *events rather than as objects that exist through* time. An event occurs in its fullness and is over. Whereas our previous models have usually explained events by the motions of atoms and particles, the ecological model explains atoms and particles as well as tables and mountains, in terms of events. The explanation is finally sought at the level of the ultimate, indivisible unit events into which larger events can be analyzed. These include subatomic events but also momentary human experiences. Whitehead called these unit events "actual occasions" or "occasions of experience." The world is a vast field of actual occasions within which there emerge relatively enduring patterns of many varieties. The atom, the subatomic particle, the table, and the mountain are all societies of actual occasions with relatively enduring patterns. A human person is too.

Second, our usual ideas of such dualities as *mental and physical or subjective and objective are derived from reflection about societies* of actual occasions, such as atoms and mountains, wrongly supposed to be substances. But understood more loosely, "mental" and "physical" aspects can be found in every occasion whatsoever. These ideas cannot be applied to events or occasions. Mind and matter, as conceived according to these usual ideas, do not exist. Every occasion is a synthesis of features derived from its environing world. In this sense it is physical. Because this synthesis is not merely the mechanical product of the forces that impinge upon it, because it includes an element of selectivity and self-determination, we can also say that the occasion has a mental aspect. There are no purely mental occasions and no purely physical ones. There are only occasions in which the element of self-origination is relatively important and others in which it is negligible.

Similarly, when we think of subjects and objects in the usual way, we cannot say that an event or occasion is a subject or that it is an object. All occasions are "subjects" in the moment of their occurrence and "objects" for other occasions as soon as they are over. As it takes place it is the locus of subjectivity, that is, it receives the activity of the past, and it, in its turn, acts. It is subject to the action of other events, and it is an agent determining its response to these influences and, thereby, its effects upon the world. It actively takes account of its world. When it has taken place, it becomes part of the objective world in which other occasions occur.

Third, *every occasion in some measure transcends its world.* It transcends it, first, simply by being a new occasion. No occasion can recur. However similar an occasion may be to antecedent ones, it is a different entity. In addition, no occasion is qualitatively identical with any other. It cannot be, because no two occasions have the same spatio-temporal locus, and every locus defines a different environment or world. Since this world enters constitutively into the occasion, the occasion must be qualitatively unique. Further, as already noted, no occasion is the mere product of its world. However much the world of the occasion determines its character, the exact form of the occasion is decided only when it happens. Every occasion transcends its world by determining just how it constitutes itself out of that world. And, finally, many occasions, indeed, all living occasions, constitute themselves not only out of the world of past occasions but also out of the world of possibility or the Not Yet. They transcend their world by incorporating possibilities derived, not from it, but from God. This need not involve conscious choice, but it can, and in the human case it often does. This is the context in which we can speak meaningfully of freedom.

Those who are accustomed to contrast material or merely phenomenal nature with human existence as spiritual may be shocked by the insistence of process thought that human beings are part of an inclusive ecosystem. But it is well to recall that the dualism of the human and the natural is a modern one. For the Bible there is the one world of creatures of which human beings are a part. The welfare of humanity and the welfare of other creatures are interdependent. Process theologians rejoice that Christians are beginning to recover the sense of the unity of creation against the modern philosophical dualism of spirit and nature.

The Doctrine of God

Neither for the Bible nor for process theologians does the insistence that human beings are part of the world of creatures mean that we are not distinctive. Human experiences are the most valuable of all the events on this planet, but they are not the only loci of value. In Genesis God declares all other creatures good even before and apart from the creation of human beings, and process theologians share this biblical conviction. But human beings are created in the image of God, and process theologians agree that we share in God's power of creation in quite unique ways. As Genesis indicates, we exercise a unique power over all the other creatures. Hence we are responsible for the welfare of the whole created order on this planet as no other creature could be. That we are exercising that power so extensively for the degradation of the biosphere as well as the oppression of our powerless sisters and brothers expresses the depth of our betrayal of God's trust. The doctrine of God to which this brings us is at the center of process theology. It is above all Charles Hartshorne who has developed this aspect of process thought.

Process Theology Vs Classical Theism

Process theology has been very critical of some features of classical theism. That theism often pictures God as an immutable substance, whereas process theologians see God as the most perfect exemplification of the ecological model. Divine perfection does not consist in being totally self-contained and unaffected by creaturely joy and suffering but in being totally open, totally receptive, and perfectly responsive God, too, is constituted by relations to all things. In the case of God, these relations are complete and express the perfection of love. Through this perfection of relations, what is perpetually perishing in the world attains everlastingness in the divine life. The threat to meaning that is inherent in transience is thereby overcome. Too often, also, classical theism has spoken of God's power in a way that suggests the control of a tyrant or a dictator. It is thought that everything that happens in the world, even an earthquake or a war, must express the will of God. Many have turned against this God, and process theologians do so, too.

Process theologians do not go to the extreme of asserting that God is powerless and is to be found only in suffering. God is certainly found there, but God is found also in a child's enjoyment of play, in the joy of a happy marriage, and in the creative ecstasy of an artist. Process theology teaches that God's power is perfect and that perfect power is not coercive. Following the biblical image of parental power, we see that coercion expresses the failure of power, not its perfection. God's power lies in the gift to every occasion of some measure of transcendence or freedom and in the call to employ that freedom in love. It is this gift and call which has brought into being all that is good in our world; indeed, they have created cur world. But creatures, and especially human creatures, resist the gift of freedom and abuse it. God does not will the evil which we thereby bring about.

Process theology developed chiefly at the Divinity School of the University of Chicago. During the first three decades of this century that school was committed to socio-historical research in the service of the social gospel. During the 1930s it became more philosophical, and the influence of Alfred North Whitehead grew. The concerns for political freedom, peace, and justice did not disappear, but they ceased to control the theological program. The dominant emphasis among the theologians was an empirical, rational, and speculative approach to understanding God and God's relationship to human beings. The label "process theology" came to be used during the sixties to emphasize the rejection of static and substantial modes of thought. When the 1960s brought renewed concern for human liberation as the focus of Christian theology, most process theologians recognized that their work had become too theoretical and abstract. During the [1970s] they made efforts to display the relevance of their cosmological vision to the practical needs of the church. Thus far success has been greatest in relation to inter-faith dialogue, ecology, feminism, and pastoral work.

Much remains to be done, especially in relation to the world of politics, although a beginning has been made there as well. The language of process theology about God often leads readers to suppose that process theologians are optimistic, and it is true that they are hopeful. They hope because the giver of freedom and direction is always surprising us. The future cannot be foreseen. It is not just the unfolding of the past. It is the place where the new can be received if we will accept it. However bleak the projections of past trends into the future, we hope for a new heaven and a new earth. . . .

10

Forest in the Epics

"Only when Rāma went to the forest did he become Rāma.

Hindi saying[1]

The Narrative Ecosystem

It has often been observed that the universe of traditional Hindu narrative—to which the epics subscribe and which they, indeed, help establish—is inherently and literally "conservative": a "closed system" in which nothing is ever truly lost, but in which all things—energy, tangible substances, souls, and even stories—are endlessly recycled and transformed. That such a worldview might have tangible resonances may seem evident to anyone who has ever marvelled at the inventive reuse of objects and resources—from sandals soled with tire treads to cows contentedly grazing on yesterday's headlines—that, even today, marks much daily life in India, especially for the poor and lower middle classes. Yet, as an ever-rising flood of factory-made goods and disposable packaging feeds middle-class and elite consumerism, we would do well to invoke another prevailing epic vision which I cited earlier: that of a "crowded cosmos." In the present Chapter we discuss some characteristic features of the "narrative ecosystem" of the *Mahābhārata* and *Rāmāyaṇa, with* the eventual aim of identifying therein enduring cultural attitudes toward the natural environment as well as cultural resources that might be applied to understanding and responding to the environmental crisis of our time.

We live in an era of accelerating deforestation and proliferating scholarship. The two are not altogether unrelated, since scholarly productivity (such as the critical editing and exegesis of Sanskrit epics) consumes, like Agni, copious amounts of wood.[2] The contrast between the paradigmatic landscapes of city" and "forest" is a familiar narrative convention of the *Rāmāyaṇa* and *Mahābhārata* that has been briefly noted by scholarly translators like. A.B. van Buitenen and Sheldon Pollock.[3] It is clear enough that Indian epic heroes, destined for the eventual rule of city-states, only grow to their full stature through a period of exile and wandering in a wild" landscape that is filled both with dangers and with magical and spiritual forces—an archetypal narrative pattern that is hardly limited to South Asia but may be found in the *Märchen* and sagas of many cultures. Ourunderstanding of the city-forest dichotomy and its centrality to the classical Indian epics has developed through many years of reading, thinking about, and reading these stories, in their early Sanskrit versions (read in English translation) as well as in their later retellings through regional vernacular texts, oral performances, and iconographic representations.

Epics as Narrative of Forests

A striking feature shared by the two narratives, the *Mahābhārata* and *Rāmāyaṇa,* which are in many respects so different in character that they may even be seen as opposites, is that each contains a Book of the Forest" (the former's *Araṇyakāṇḍa;* the tatter's *Vanaparvar or Āraṇyakaparva),* which sends its heroes into the wilderness for a period which, in chronological if not narrative terms, accounts for a major portion of the central story (fourteen and twelve years lively. Moreover, the invocation of the forest as a contrasting landscape to that of the royal court and city-state is not confined to these "forest books," but is pervasive of the stories, and indeed of much of the copious narrative tradition of the Sanskrit and vernacular Purānas.[4]

Interpreting the Dialectic of Forest Environment in Epics

The two most common Sanskrit words for "forest"—*vana* and *araṇya*—appear to be nearly synonymous in usage. This is suggested by their parallel occurrence in numerous compounds in which they function identically to qualify the second member of the compound as "wild" or "of the forest" (e.g., *vana-kadali araṇya-kadalī:* "wild plantain"; *vana-cara. araṇya-cara:* "living in the forest." i.e., woodsman, wild animal). *Vana,* by far the commonest word, has the additional sense of "plenty, abundance," and can refer to a "quantity of lotuses or other plants growing in a thick cluster."[5] That the ancient forest was understood to be dense or thick is also suggested by the less common adjectival epithet *gahana* ("deep, thick, impervious, impenetrable," hence, as a noun "a thickness, a density") also sometimes applied to forest settings.[6] *Araṇya* can also mean more generically wilderness or even "desert," though its use in compounds, as already indicated, generally suggests a high density of wild vegetation; interestingly, its most archaic sense is said to be of a foreign or distant land" (cf. English "forest," derived from Latin/ofris denoting land that is "outside" human habitation and cultivation)—a derivation that may support the ecohistorical reading that land clearing for pastoralism and agriculture gradually drove the forest and many of its denizens to the peripheries of the increasingly settled Indo-Gangetic plain. Other, less common epic labels for forest settings include *vipina* ("stirring or waving in the wind"), *kānana* ("a forest, grove"; sometimes synonymously compounded with vana as in *kānanaukas = vanaukas:* "forest dweller, monkey"), and *kāntāra* ("forest, wilderness, waste")[7]

It should be noted that all these words are quite different in meaning from *jāṅgala,* which likewise carried a connotation of "wild" (as modern Hindi *jāṅgal* and its English derivative "jungle" still do), but which primarily referred to a landscape that was "arid, sparingly grown with trees and plants (though not unfertile . . .)."[8]

As Francis Zimmermann and Michael Dove have persuasively argued in recent studies the ancient *jāṅgala* was not the "dense" and relatively "distant" forest to which exiles and ascetics repaired, but rather was the preferred, encompassing ecosystem of early Indo-Aryan culture—*a* tree-studded, grass-covered savanna that was considered ideally suited to pastoralism, small settlements, occasional hunting, and limited cultivation.[9] Although this ecosystem may already have been yielding on the Indo-Gangetic plain, to more intensive agricultural and urban patterns by the period of composition of the epics, the archaic sense *of jāṅgala* survives in them; thus, in the *Mahābhārata,* the name *Kuru-jāṅgala* refers simply to the "land" or "kingdom" of the ruling Kuru dynasty, not to the denser forest tracks beyond its borders, into which the heroes are driven in exile.

The epic "forest" was often an imagined landscape—more a state of mind than a tangible environment. The research of Zimmermann and Dove suggests that *jāṅgala* remained a powerful ideological paradigm even after the landscape on which it was based had ceased to exist, or in places where it had never existed. Likewise, the deep forest *(vana, araṇya),* with its terrors and transcendent possibilities, would remain an appealing narrative even as the balance in the physical environment of South Asia shifted decisively toward urbanization and intensive cultivation, and as real forests and their wildlife were exploited almost to extinction.

The Epic Forest Scene

Huntng Forays in Epics

Enforced exile (or voluntary retirement in old age) is not the sole motive that drives kings to the forest in the epics; more commonly, indeed, almost constantly, they repair there temporarily for recreational purposes, primarily to hunt. Very often they have adventures, get separated from their companions, wander or are led from the outskirts of the wood (where they seem more comfortable and indeed more kingly) into its depths, where they lose their way and sometimes their identities, and where they meet powerful figures (demons, sages, beautiful and mysterious women) who change their lives. That kings often get into trouble through the excitement and hubris of hunting— as when Pāṇḍu slays, a mating buck who proves to be a sage, or when Daśaratha aims at the sound of an "elephant" and fatally wounds an ascetic boy—may suggest Brāhmaṇa disapproval of Kṣatriya violence. Yet the epic bards, who also recognize that the king is socially sanctioned to commit necessary and world-maintaining acts of violence (through warfare, punishment, and sacrificial ritual, as well as through hunting), do not mind, at times, reveling in it.

That this has serious consequences for the forest and its denizens seems, at such moments quite beside the point. Like the directors of a modern action film, the poets cheerfully unleash a spectacle of carnage that seems primarily intended to evoke the aesthetic mood of *vīrya* ("heroism").

Sakuntala, in the *Mahābhāratas* subsidiary narrative of Śakuntalā, King Duṣyanta sallies forth for a hunt, accompanied by a small army, and showered with flowers and amorous glances by the women of his capital. Far from the city, he enters "a wood like Indra's paradise" and proceeds to wreak havoc, slaying "many families of tigers," "thousands of deer," and "killing wild game and fowl with javelin, sword, mace bludgeon, harberd." The tone seems cheerfully celebratory, even when describing frantic herds of deer dropping unconscious as they vainly try to escape, and maddened elephants, "dropping dung and urine and streaming with blood," running amok and trampling the king's own men *(Mahābhārata* 1.7.63).[10] It just as abruptly changes to a mood of ascetic peace, and then to one of erotic abandon (for both, see below), yet in my reading at least, this does not negate the essentially positive vision of the imperial hunt: as husband of the earth (a theme that the later courtly poet Kālidasa would greatly amplify in his famed retelling of the story), King Duṣyanta is entitled and even expected to cull the big game of the forest.

Forest Exile in Ramayana

Nor is any "environmental impact statement" offered for Prince Bharata's expedition to Chitrakūta to meet with his exiled brother Rāma, accompanied by nearly the entire population of Ayodhyā. This brief excursion—the narrative purpose of which is to affirm the brothers mutual devotion and to confirm Rāma's decision to live out his term of exile—gives the *Rāmāyaṇa* poet an opportunity to describe the construction of a royal highway *(Rāmāyaṇa* 2.74), as "survey and men trained in measurement, powerful excavators who were zealous in their work; engineers, labourers, craftsmen, and men skilled in machinery; carpenters, road-levellers, woodcutters, well-drillers, pavers cane-weavers, and capable guides all set out from the city" (2.74.13). Like the builders of modern expressways, the workmen fell trees, flatten hillocks, divert streams, and, in lieu of roadside "rest areas construct multistoried mansions. Here the intended mood appears be one of admiring wonder *(adbhūta)* at the royal capacity to densively transform a natural landscape "in no time at all" (2.74.11),[11]

Destinction of Environment in Mahabharata

The *Mahābhārata's* superman Bhīma ascends Mount Gandhamādana to obtain a magical lotus for Draupadi, and proceeds Rambo-like, slaying thousands of animals and uprooting countless trees, for no apparent reason other than to show his immense strength and impatience *(Mahābhārata 3.1*46.20-60); and the *Rāmāyaṇa's* counterpart and half-brother to Bhîma, Hanūmān, destroys a forested mountain and all its denizens while leaping toward Laṅka *(Rāmāyaṇa* 5.1.10-42)—but none is perhaps more troubling to modern sensibilities than Kṛṣṇa and Arjuna's burning of the Khāṇḍava Forest at the close of Book One of the *Mahābhārata.* Ordered by the voracious Agni himself, the conflagration seems to be indirectly linked to the expansion, through forest-clearing, of the Pāṇḍavas' new kingdom of Indraprastha (though its capital city of the same name has already been built elsewhere), and it is difficult to dismiss altogether the mythohistoric explanation that the story may reflect ancient practices of deliberate burning that (according to Michael Dove) regularly transformed thick thorn-tree forest into Arya-friendly savanna.[12] But Agni doesn't simply desire wood and land; it wants "the fat of the living," and so Kṛṣṇa and his friend cheerfully use their warrior prowess to seal off the perimeters of the forest to conduct a "vast massacre" of its fleeing creatures, and hurl their bodies back into the flames. They allow virtually no living beings to escape (although, like every holocaust in the *Mahābhārata*, this one has an eventual handful of survivors.

Meanwhile, the poet indulges in a grisly and detailed description of the creatures' panic, their attempts at flight, and their cries of agony as their eyes, wings, fat, and marrow catch fire, transforming them into living torches," while "the huge flames of the happy Fire jumped to the sky and caused the greatest consternation among the gods (1.19.217)." Although modern readers may find it difficult to feel happy" while reading such descriptions (and those who, like Irawati Karva favour an ethnohistorical interpretation may recoil in horror from the supposed genocide of "naga" tribals),[14] Together with the "heroism" of Kṛṣṇa and Arjuna (which the poet shamelessly celebrates), the aesthetic sentiments intended here are seemingly those of (vicarious) fury, terror, and disgust *(raudra bhāyanaka, bībhatsa)*. The forest is utilized as a setting for the spectacle of disaster—befalling expendable others at an aesthetically safe distance—that seems to be enduringly human to enjoy.

Voluptuous Women

In the *Mahābhārata,* King Duṣyanta's recreational carnage ceases abruptly when he enters "another wood," albeit still "in search of deer. Here it is immediately apparent that a different aesthetic mood holds sway: that of *sṛṇgāra,* or eros. The scene opens with descriptions of natural beauty and abundance (trees laden with blossoms and fruits, swarms of bees and birds), but the landscape is rapidly eroticized by visions of intertwining branches, breezes that waft pollen to the trees "as though to make love to them," and of a woodland "grown in the embrace of a river" (*Mahābhārata* 1.7.64).[15] All such metaphors (and the last carries special import for the *Mahābhārata,* wherein dynasts regularly mate with river goddesses or their symoblic substitutes) suggest an erotically feminized forest, to which the epic king responds as the hypermale and world-husband he invariably is. The heady passage thus prefigures the approaching vision of the virginal beauty Sakuntala, and the king's declaration of love for her.

An equally romantic, albeit less erotically charged, vision of nature occurs in the (generally more austere and propriety-minded) *Rāmāyaṇa*. Although Rāma has earlier warned Sītā of the hardships of forest life, she has nevertheless anticipated the "pleasures I shall share with you, my mighty husband, in the honey-scented forests" *(Rāmāyaṇa* 2.24.10).[16] For a time, these expectations are indeed fulfilled, and though the couple's happy life at Citrakūṭa and Pañcavatis is only a briefly hinted at interlude in Vālmīki's version (2.50; 3.111 15; later Sītā recalls it to Hanūmān at 5.36.12-15), the descriptions of nature are lush and suggestive, and many later retellings have expanded this portion of the story into a long, erotic idyll, wherein Rāma and Sītā, tirelessly guarded by Lakṣmaṇa, sport for twelve years in an earthly paradise.[17]

Rampaging Raksasas

Rāma's admonitory refrain to Sītā in *Ayodhyākāṇḍa*— "the forest is a place of utter pain" *(Rāmāyaṇa* 2.25)—will of course prove prophetic for both of them, but his warnings of the dangers of the forest (e.g., lions, snakes, scorpions, and thorn trees), reflect a dread of the wilderness that was already present in the anomalous *Ṛgveda* hymn dedicated to the "lady of the forest" *(araṇyāni),* upon whom a frightened wayfarer, lost in the forest at twilight and imagining the terrors lurking in its shadows, calls for protection *(Ṛgveda* 10.146). The terrors of the deep woods are best represented in the epics by the horrific and cannibalistic *rākṣasas* who lurk in them, although the portrayal of these creatures is itself marked by a certain ambivalence— e.g., Vālmīki's distinction between the "wild" *rākṣasas* of the forest and their more refined, though still deadly and anthropophagous, cousins in Laṅkā; and the legions of *rākṣasas* in the *Mahābhārata* who seem, true to the apparent derivation of their name, ferocious "guardians" of remote natural beauty spots favoured by the gods (e.g., Kubera's lake on Mount Gandhamadana, in *Mahābhārata* 3.33.151-52). The entry of epic heroes into deep forest is frequently signaled by terrifying encounters with these guardian beings; a fine example is Virādha, whom Rāma and his companions encounter in the second chapter of the *Araṇyākāṇḍa*, immediately after their entry into "the wilderness of Daṇḍaka."

> Sunken-eyed, huge-mouthed, his belly deformed, he was massive, loathsome, deformed, gigantic, monstrous, a terror to behold; clad in a tiger skin dripping with grease and spattered with blood, as terrifying to all creatures as Death with jaws agape. On an iron pike he held impaled three lions, four tigers, two wolves, ten dappled antelopes, and the massive head of an elephant, complete with tusks, and smeared with gore. And he was roaring deafeningly. *(Rāmāyaṇa* 3.2.5-8)[18]

That such figures become, particularly in the *Rāmāyaṇa,* a locus for the poet's projection of the reprehensible and sociopathic traits of irreducible "otherness" has been well analyzed by Sheldon Pollock.[19] will only add that such forest scenes also provide for the evocation of moods of terror and disgust (the *rajas of bhayānaka* and *bībhatsa);* the heroes' response to such apparitions is, of course, to slay them with a characteristic display of *vīrya.*

Serene (and Scary) Sages

Although lions do not lie down with lambs in Sanskrit epics, tigers do rest beside deer in one forest setting beloved to epic bards: the *āsrama* ("place of exertion," i.e., through asceticism and Vedic study), or hermitage, of a sage. Such forests-within-the-forest appear as veritable ecopreserves, abounding in trees of many species and herds of tame animals, and also as protocampuses, full of students diligently engaged in Vedic recitation and study. These settings, evocative of the mood of tranquility *(sānta),* are frequently juxtaposed with scenes of destructive Kṣatriya exhuberance; thus, in the *Mahābhārata,* the gory excess of King Duṣyanta's hunt yields, within fifteen verses, to the tranquil groves and spotless sacrificial halls of the sage Kaṇva's hermitage—a paradise on earth "that mirrored the world of Brahmā"— and which evokes in the king "the purest joy." It evokes humility as well, for the king who just majestically supervised the slaughter of the forest's big game, now dismounts from his chariot, abandons his armour and escort, and walks alone into the protected enclosure to pay homage to its ruler *(Mahābhārata* 1.7.64).[20]

Vālmîki's *Bālakānda* offers a comparable vision of the forest hermitage of the immortal Vasiṣṭha, family preceptor to the Ikṣvāku dynasty *(Rāmāyaṇa* 1.50.22-27). Its crown jewel is the magical cow Sabalā, and when visiting King Visvāmitra attempts to seize her (since, as he puts it, "all gems belong to the king"; 1,52.9), the mood of *sānta* quickly yields to *vīrya,* as sage and king commence a deadly and protracted battle to determine who is ultimately more powerful In the process, the peaceful hermitage is trashed in an orgy of royal violence that easily equals anything wrought by *rākṣasas* (1.54.21 28).[21]

Such scenes, recapitulated, for example, in the *Mahābhārata's* Bhārgava narrative of King Kārtavīrya's destruction of the sage-Jamadagni's hermitage *(Mahābhārata* 3.33.116), bring the contrasting paradigmatic life-styles and values of king and sage into their starkest juxtaposition. It should be added that the sages' serenity and wisdom are not the sole traits they derive from their association with the forest. Often there is also a quality of wildness that verges on the nonhuman and suggests the feral, extrasocial, and even unsettling dimension of the less-settled lands. This quality is particularly evident in some of the forest-dwelling sages of the *Mahābhārata.* Thus, when Vyāsa the epic's author and the master of all sacred lore, is mentally summoned to the city of Hāstinapura by his mother Satyavatī in order to father sons on her widowed daughters-in-law, he brings not only his supernatural knowledge and fecundity, but also an all-too-natural stench and a form and visage so fearful that the princesses close their eyes or faint in his presence *(Mahābhārata* 1.7.99-100).

More feral still is Kiṃdama, "a hermit of unequaled austerities" but somewhat unusual sexual tastes—for the ill-fated Paṇḍu accidentally slays him while Kiṃdama is in the guise of a deer, engaged in mating with a doe, "because I shy away from humans, and as a deer I live with deer in the depths of the forest" *(Mahābhārata* 1.7.109). We may also recall the strange "deer-horn" sage Ṛsyasṛṅga, whose mother is indeed a doe and who grows up without human companions, save his father, Kāsyapa, who is himself described as having "the tawny eyes of a lion ... with hair as far down as his nails" *(Mahābhārata* 3.33.111). In the case of both Kiṃdama and Ṛsyasṛṅga, we may note the sages' association with the quintessential wild game animal, whose range serves as a boundary-marker for the "forest," and who repeatedly initiates epic adventure by luring royal hunters out of their settled realms and into its mysterious and protean depths.

Forest Landscape in Epics

The forest is vast and exploitable. Although kings are occasionally admonished to plant trees (especially along royal roadsides), their more characteristic concern with the forest is in clearing it or securing its abundant game. The forest is for them primarily a zone for exploitation and consumption, and there is no sense in the epics of the modern notion of the "fragility" or endangerment of the forest ecosystem. On the contrary, the destruction of huge tracts of forest or of the wildlife it contains is grist for entertaining narrative and is no more alarming to the bards and their presumed audiences than was the felling of North American forests to nineteenth-century European settlers.[22]

The forest is cherished by sages. If there is a kind of protoconservationist ethic in the epics, it is revealed in the attitudes of ashram-dwellers to their forest environment. Unlike kings who enter the forest in exile or for an occasional recreational hunt, sages choose to reside there, and they cultivate an attitude of nonviolence that transforms stretches of forest into an earthly paradise. Their behavior is set in stark contrast to that of kings, although the stories clearly celebrate both.

The forest is evocative of high emotion. As the landscape of "otherness" to the (in theory) rigidly coded realm of the sāstraically governed kingdom, the relatively more chaotic forest is the ideal locale for the evocation of intense emotional moods (terror, disgust, eroticism) that may be disruptive or incongruous in a more mundane setting.

The forest is a place of transcendence. It is generally in the forest rather than in the city-state, that transcendence of human limitations becomes possible and that communication occurs between heaven and earth; it is here that gods most often descend to communicate with human beings, and that the latter ascend to heaven, and it is here that superhuman beings and demigods are most often encountered.

The forest teems with life. The epic forest swarms with a superdensity of plant and animal species, is seldom devoid of human inhabitants (generally tribals), and not uncommonly also contains the superhuman life-forms noted earlier. It is a "crowded cosmos" that indeed suggests the complexity and abundance of the South Asian ecosystem, even as it permits epic poets to indulge in their characteristic penchant of packing their *slokas* with impressive lists.[23]

The forest is a state of mind. Although the poets display moments of keen observation and accurate description of natural phenomena, their forest landscape cannot, on the whole, be said to be naturalistic. Its particulars are always subservient to the demands of aesthetic mood, resulting at times in ecological incongruity, as when (a commonplace) the poets place peacocks, elephants, and huge fig trees on high Himalayan peaks.[24] Their forest is a stage-set, with props that can be moved around as narrative atmospherics require.

The King in the Forest

One of the implicit and overarching projects of the classical epics, especially apparent in the subsidiary and seemingly "digressive" stories incorporated into their introductory books (which form, in each case, a sort of overture or prelude to the main narrative), is the attempt to resolve the dialectical tension between the paradigmatic realms of "city/kingdom" and "forest" and their respective human life-styles through integrative characters who combine elements of both. Such attempted integration cannot escape the tension inherent in the dialectic, however, and is itself often provisional or inconclusive. It occurs relatively more harmoniously in Vālmīki's *Bālakāṇḍa,* whose principal subnarratives (largely and appropriately concerned with ancestors of Rāma) feature the "upwardly mobile" Kṣatriyas, who aspire to become sages or even gods (e.g., Bhagīratha, Visvāmitra. Triśaṅku), and sages who become royal householders or warriors (e.g., Ṛśyaśṛṅga, Paraśurāma). The comparable series of introductory narratives in the *Ādiparva* of the *Mahābhārata* are, as one might expect, more ominous, violent, and savvy of the *realpolitik* dimensions of the Brāhmaṇa-Kṣatriya relationship, and story after story depicts the unhappy outcome of the martial elite's apparently never-ending challenge to the authority of *āśrama-based* priest-scholar lineages. Here it is often the case that a tenuous balance is achieved only through the near-annihilation of the offending party—e.g., the repeated theme of the sacrificial holocaust, one of the reigning motifs of the *Mahābhārata* as a whole. Yet, together with the fundamentally Brāhmaṇa bias of both Sanskrit epics in their surviving written forms, both also reveal a theological preoccupation with Viṣṇu, displayed particularly in his literal embodiment in key personalities.

As a celestial god-king who seems to have historically absorbed many of Indra's more positive attributes, Visnu emerges in the epics as a Kṣatriya god who is adored by, and who adores, Brāhmaṇas. His favourite human incarnations, both Kṣatriya god-kings, assume a broadly mediatory role between the contending exemplars of city and forest: the priest-sage and warrior-householder. As Rāma, Viṣṇu himself becomes a sage-king who protects ascetics in the forest, yet refuses (in the city) to protect his own interests through the violent *kṣatriya dharma* advocated by his younger brother Lakṣmaṇa.

As Kṛṣṇa, Viṣṇu functions in a different (and characteristically more devious and "dark") manner, achieving his goal of world renewal indirectly through the Pāṇḍava brothers headed by Yudhiṣṭhira, and by means of a sacrificial bloodbath that lifts the earth's burden of violent, overweening Kṣatriyas. Like Rāma, Yudhiṣṭhira ultimately takes the throne as a Brāhmaṇa-friendly sage-king, whose inclinations to nonviolence (except when force is unavoidable to uphold *dharma)* have been nurtured by long years of residence in forest ashrams. In each case, achieving some kind of balance requires an extended period of residence in the forest, as if to become imbued with its characteristic values. Significantly, it is the "balanced" Kṣatriya heroes who will at times manifest a conservationist ethic: Yudhiṣṭhira is visited in a dream by weeping deer, who ask him to move the Pāṇḍavas' encampment lest their dwindled herds—"the seed of the future"—be hunted to extinction; he willingly complies *(Mahābhārata* 3.40).[25]

Epic Landscape and the Real World

In a recent article entitled "The Dialectical History of 'Jungle' in Pakistan," ecologist Michael Dove expands on and critiques the analysis of the Sanskrit term *jāṅgala* that appeared in Francis Zimmermann's groundbreaking 1987 study of Ayurveda as an intellectual system, *The Jungle and the Aroma of Meats.* Zimmermann showed that ancient *jāṅgala* was neither city nor forest, but a semiarid savanna of grasses and intermittent, low trees that was considered the ideal terrain for pastoralism and light agriculture, human settlement, ritual activity, and indeed somatic health.[26] Although Zimmermann supposed the *jāṅgala* ecosystem to have been native to much of northern South Asia, Dove's more recent fieldwork indicates that *jāṅgala* was in fact an "anthropogenic landscape" that arose from and was maintained by periodic human intervention, especially through purposely set brush-fires, to prevent it from rapidly reverting to the thornwood climax forest that he argues is naturally indigenous to the region. It was thus "an active zone of tension between society and nature ... a mediator between . . . village and forest"—ecologically speaking, a compromise between more concentrated human activity and its absence or cessation.

In late Vedic times, this "compromise" savanna ecosystem the human-engineered habitat of the black antelope, was considered the landscape most suited to the Aryan sacrificial lifeway—itself an effort at negotiating a precarious equilibrium between contending cosmic forces: Agni and Soma, order and disorder, life and death.[27] As Zimmermann shows, its characteristics, set in contrast to those of the less-favored *anupa* ("marshy" and heavily forested) lands, developed into an elaborate paradigm for ancient legalists and physicians Whereas Zimmermann is primarily interested in the rather cerebral proliferations of a Brāhrnaṇical ideology which originally grew out of the observed features of a landscape, Dove insists that ideology and other forms of human intervention actively shape the natural landscape, although ideology characteristically seeks to conceal its hand by implying that things were "always already" in the form which it has, in fact, itself gradually moulded. He argues that, as a tangible ecosystem, *the jāṅgala* was gradually eliminated through population pressure resulting in part from the preference of rulers and centralized states for intensive cultivation and settlement over pastoralism and "extensive" patterns of land use (involving light or intermittent farming). As a result, the term itself gradually changed its meaning, taking on connotations of "wilderness" and "wildness," indeed sometimes of dense vegetative cover (all alien to its archaic meaning) that it retains in its modern Romanized incarnation as "jungle."[27]

Overall the two Sanskrit epics present what may be termed a "*narrative ecosystem*" that, like the *jāṅgala* of Dove's analysis, is similarly a "zone of tension." Their complex stories—whose cyclical and fugal narrative structure nineteenth-century European scholars sometimes disapprovingly likened to a "jungle" in the latter-day sense of impenetrable tropical growth—in fact present us with a savanna-like sociocultural landscape in which the balance of power between kings and sages is maintained through periodic confrontations, and indeed, conflagrations. At the same time they offer, through some of their most cherished characters and at the deepest levels of their theology, an attempt at a more satisfying balance attained through mediation and synthesis. The heroes of these stories must fulfill their destinies as the rulers of city-states, but they are paradigmatic culture-heroes precisely because they have been to the forest, faced its terrors, and lived among (and, to a degree, as) its sages—an observation nicely encoded in the modern Hindi epigram with which the chapter I commenced. Unlike prescriptive texts, the epics achieve a less stable resolution to their fundamental tension between civilization and wildness, exploitation and conservation, king and sage. Although sage-kings like Rāma and Yudhiṣṭhira can be regarded as integrative ideals, the narrative continues periodically to challenge the stability of each, (e.g., with the disturbing yet inevitable tests and reversals of the concluding books of each epic—the *Rāmāyaṇa's Uttarakāṇḍa* and the *Mahābhārata's Svargārohaṇika parva).* Yet, this precariously balanced "narrative ecosystem" has itself been maintained with considerable stability through millennia of epic and Puranic retellings.

Relevence in Present Day Context

What resources may a modern reader or listener draw from this "narrative ecosystem" that might be applied to healing the imperiled environment of the late twentieth century? Most obviously, perhaps *the notion of balance and compromise between the competing life-styles* of kings and sages—between "consumers" and "conservers" of the environment.

Like the *jāṅgala* as described by Dove, the epic "forest" is less a pristine wilderness (such as modern conservationists; often strive to maintain) than a zone of interaction between often, competing forces. It is (to borrow the slogan of the U.S. National. Forest Service) a "land of many uses," and these do not exclude— especially in the archaic context of boundless wild lands beyond the periphery of human settlement—extensive exploitation. The presiding ideal of both epics is the sage-king who understands and governs according to *dharma,* and in each case his ultimate character is seen to blend the qualities of the Kṣatriya and the Brāhmaṇa and to have been moulded through extended experience of extraurban and indeed extrasocial realms. The resultant personality significantly tempers self-indulgence with self-control. Could one argue, in other words, that a king like Rāma would favour recycling and renewable resources over excessive waste and environmental exploitation? Although opposing attitudes may more often claim epic models: modern political parties that espouse *Rāma-rājya* and that combine a reactionary social stance with economic policies favorable to big industries and polluters.

What is most significant in our universe is not the mere fact of the abundance of life-forms which swarm through every tier of the epics' multistoried universe, but the underriding notion of balance and of the necessity for mutual survival. Epic holocausts—of deer, of Kṣatriyas, or even of venomous snakes and menacing *rakṣasas*—invariably stop short of total annihilation and reveal a kind of extrahuman perspective according to which all life-forms are seen to have a place and a right to exist. If such a world-view has a pragmatic, economic parallel, it seems that it is assuredly in the old-fashioned Indian bazaar, in which scores of tiny shops—many of which stock much the same merchandise—coexist and, yes, "compete," though without the notion of maximizing profit through destroying competitors, such as we find in the "slash-and-burn" economics of modern chain store retailing.

Mythology, too—and the classical Indian epics in particular—offers a rich terrain for imaginative journeying and introspective discovery that can proceed quite independent of circumstances in the physical environment. At the same time, the Indian epics, in their broadest tradition of interpretation, make a claim to be not simply marvellous allegorical entertainments, but also charters for an ancient and enduring ideal of good life: for the remaking of the world according to a higher order of harmony and beauty. Understanding that such a life necessarily requires the precarious balancing of the competing claims of consumption and conservation, and that it is situated within a complex web in which all organisms have a place and are entitled to survive, can help us to identify the relevance of their message for our times.[28]

Today—as developers bulldoze hillsides in Rishikesh to erect apartment blocks that will offer retirees from Delhi a little piece of Himalayan "*vanaprastha*" (the third Hindu life-phase of "withdrawal to the forest")—people in ever greater numbers are claiming the right to enjoy the best of two increasingly colliding worlds: to consume and exploit the landscape as kings and to revere and protect it as sages. But in an age in which rampaging commercial interests pose a greater menace than *rākṣasas,* the challenge to modern South Asians—and the rest of us—is to preserve and restore enough verdant and biodiverse terrain riot only to meet our pragmatic and material needs, but also to insure that future heroes (and heroines) have a place to go to "become themselves."

NOTES

1. *Jab rām ban gaye, tab hī rām ban gaye.* The saying's pun results from the fact that, since in Eastern Hindi "b" often replaces "v," the compound verb *bān jānā* ("to become, to fulfill a role or acquire a status") can also be read as *ban (van) jānā* ("to go to the forest").
2. I use the term "classical epics" to distinguish the two pan-Indian narratives from more region-bound traditions, such as the Hindi Ālhā cycle or the Rajasthani Pābhujī epic, although these have also achieved the status of local "classics."
3. See Sheldon I. Pollock, *The Rāmāyaṇa of Vālmīki,* Vol. 2, *Ayodhyākāṇḍa* (Princeton: Princeton University Press, 1986), 3-4, and *The Rāmāyaṇa of Vālmīki,* Vol. 3. *Araṇyakāṇḍa* (1991), 12-13; and J. A. B. van Buitenen, *The Mahābhārata,* book 2, *The Book of the Assembly Hall;* book 3, *The Book of the Forest* (Chicago: University of Chicago Press, 1975), 173-76.
4. For the sections that follow, include an unpublished paper by Robert Menzies on the characterization of the forest in both Sanskrit epics, written for my class on the *Mahābhārata* in spring, 1997. Noting the apparent "inconsistencies" in the epic's portrayal of the forest, Menzies identified a series of six conventional landscapes (e.g., love-bower, royal hunting ground, hermitage, demon-lair, etc.), giving examples of each.
5. Monier Monier-Williams, *A Sanskrit-English Dictionary* (Oxford: Oxford University Press. 1899; reprint, Delhi: Oriental Publishers, n.d.), 917.
6. *Ibid.,* 352.
7. *Ibid.,* 972, 270, 271.
8. *Ibid.,* 417, 408-9.
9. See Francis Zimmermann, *The Jungle and the Aroma of Meats* (Chicago: University of Chicago Press, 1987), esp. 1-19; and Michael R. Dove, "The Dialectical History of 'Jungle' in Pakistan," *Journal of Anthropological Research* 48 (1992): 231-47.1 thank geographer Paul Robbins for guiding me to the latter essay.
10. J.A.B. van Buitenen, *The Mahābhārata,* book 1, *The Book of the Beginning* : University of Chicago Press, 1973), 157-58.
11. Pollock, *The Rāmāyaṇa of Vālmīki,* 2:239-40.
12. Dove, "The Dialectical History of 'Jungle'," 236-37.
13. van Buitenen, *The Mahābhārata,* 1:417-18.
14. See Karve's essay on this passage in *Yugānta* (Delhi: Sangam Books, 1974; reprint, Hyderabad: Disha Books, 1991), esp. 114-17.
15. van Buitenen, *The Mahābhārata,* 1:158-59.
16. Pollock, *The Rāmāyaṇa of Vālmīki,* 2:135.
17. See Philip Lutgendorf. "The Secret Life of Rāmcandra of Ayodhya," in many *Rāmāyaṇas: The Diversity of a Narrative Tradition in South Asia,* ed. Paula Richman (Berkeley and Los Angeles: University of California Press, 1991), 217-34. The forest as a preferred setting for erotic play may

have its *locus classicus* in the ancient epics, but its extraordinary staying power in popular Indian art is suggested by the abrupt but obligatory (and sometimes unexplained) cut to a forest setting for the love songs of modern Hindi film musicals. The featured couple may be driving on a city street or dancing in a discotheque, but when they begin singing of their love, one can be sure that they will soon be cavorting on mountain slopes or on the wooded shores of a river, coyly peeking at each other from behind treetrunks or splashing in Water falls; the verdant forest (which Bombay crews now often go to Switzerland to film remains the preeminent landscape of *śṛṇgāra*.

18. Pollock, *The Rāmāyaṇa of Vālmīki,* 3:89. Although this vision may seem hyperbolic enough, it cannot compare with the baroque exuberance of the Tamil poet Kamban's extended retelling; see George L. Hart and Hank Heifetz, *The Forest Book of the Rāmāyaṇa of Kampaṉ* (Berkeley and Los Angeles: University of California Press. 1988), 38-45.
19. Pollock, *The Rāmāyaṇa of Vālmīki,* 3:68-84.
20. van Buitenen, *The Mahābhārata,* 1:159
21. Robert P. Goldman, *The Rāmāyaṇa of Vālmīki,* Vol. I, *Bālakāṇḍa* (Princeton: Princeton University Press, 1984). 224, 229.
22. The research of both Zimmermann and Dove suggests the essentially negative valuation of thick forest in ancient India, and helps us to understand the ominous dimensions of forest-exile; as the Pāṇḍavas manifestly know, being sent to the forest is not a good thing — it takes a paragon of positivity like Rāma to see it as such, and even he occasionally wavers.
23. E.g., even the "trackless, dreadful-looking" wilderness laid waste by the demoness Tāṭakā in Book One of the *Rāmāyaṇa* is characteristically described as abounding in life-forms (albeit ominous ones): "Echoing with swarms of crickets, it swarms with fearsome beasts of prey and harsh-voiced vultures. It is filled with all sorts of birds, screeching fearsome cries, as well as lions, tigers, boars, and elephants. It is full of *dhava, asvakarna, kakubha, bilva, tinduka, pātala,* and *badari* trees." (*Rāmāyaṇa* 1.23.12-14: Goldman, *The Rāmāyaṇa of Vālmīki.* 1:170.)
24. See, e.g., *Mahābhārata* 3.155.26-70 for an extended description of the lush, subtropical forests the Pāṇḍavas find on the highest ridges of "Mount Gandhamādana," after their ascent of the Himalayas.
25. van Buitenen, *The Mahābhārata,* 2:699.
26. Zimmermann, *The Jungle and the Aroma of Meats.* 1-19.
27. I have some difficulty with Dove's and Zimmermann's linguistic arguments, since I feel that both give too much weight to the modern English sense of "jungle" as translated back into (especially urban) Hindi-Urdu. In my own experience, although *jaṅgal* is now sometimes used as a synonym for *van* ("forest"), it is also often used by rural people to refer to grazing land on the village outskirts, or to (even temporarily) uncultivated and

overgrown tracts, a usage more consistent with the archaic sense of *jāṅgala*. Moreover, urban people use the adjective *janglī* to characterize boorish rustics, as well as "wild" animals and plants. Since I question the alleged "reversal" in meaning of the word, the two authors' conflicting explanations for it (Zimmermann's bemused observation that it is an "extraordinary misunderstanding," and Dove's insistence that it reflects "a meaningful historical process") seem of less consequence than their compelling and largely complementary arguments for the term's archaic meaning. The point on which Dove may significantly correct Zimmermann's work, however, is in the recognition that the archaic *jāṅgala* ecosystem was itself not wholly "natural," but reflected substantial human intervention in the landscape. The understanding that this was in fact land forcibly wrested from the indigenous forest actually enhances Zimmermann's analysis of the legalists' enduring dislike for the heavily forested *ānūpa* regions. It also suggests, perhaps, why the internal challenge to Vedic hyperscholasticism and its attendant ideology came initially from "forest teachings" *(āraṇyakas)* promulgated by ascetics living beyond the periphery of, or in surviving forested pockets within, the more ritually pure savannas.

28. Interestingly, the recent reincarnations of the *Rāmāyaṇa* and *Mahābhārata* as lengthy television serializations incorporated many contemporary concerns; notably the Indian government's desire to promote "national integration" and other civic and pragmatic objectives. There was also, in each, a brief bow to "reforestation." In Ramanand Sagar's *Ramayan* serial, Sage Vasiṣṭha, who is educating Rāma and his brothers in an idyllic ashram, instructs the boys to plant a mango seed, and to protect and nurture its seedling; this leads to a brief discourse on the merits of trees and the importance of protecting them *(Ramayan,* 1987, Episode 2). B. R. Chopra's *Mahabharat* contains an ecofriendly reversal of the Khāṇḍava Forest story: here the "wilderness" the Pāṇḍavas receive as a kingdom from their Kaurava cousins is not a forest but a desert. Hence no burning occurs; instead, Kṛṣṇa assists them in transforming it, through tree-planting, cultivation, and construction, into a park-like suburban landscape, bristling with rows of young saplings that look like the handiwork of the government Forestry Division *(Mahabharat,* 1990, Episode 39).

I am grateful to Christopher Key Chappie, Arvind Sharma, Mary Evelyn Tucker, the other organizers of the conference "Hinduism and Ecology," held at Harvard University's Center for the Study of World Religions, for the invitation that led to the writing of this paper. My Iowa colleagues Jael Silliman and Paul Robbins provided encouragement and valuable references. The present version has also benefited from the thoughtful comments of panel discussant Francis X. Clooney.

11

The Evolution of Eco Karma

The Message of Eco-karma

The principle of Eco-karma, a new moral principle asserts that it is our duty and responsibility to safeguard Mother Earth and all the ecological habitats as it is our duty to respect and cherish the lives of our brothers and sisters of the human family. Violation of the Earth and of any part of its web is no less a crime than doing violence to individual human beings.

Eco-karma reminds us: be aware of your interconnections with all the visible and breathing cosmos. Nature supports you in countless ways. You have the responsibility and duty to revere her-out of your respect for all creation, out of your respect for the divine, out of your respect for yourself. You have the responsibility to maintain the integrity of the divine. For all is divine.

Another message of Eco-karma is as follows. To be fully aware of yourself is to take the responsibility for all the links which connect you with this amazingly rich and mysterious world. At one point your awareness of the glory of it all becomes a moral responsibility for it all. This is a new layer added to the meaning of traditional karma.

Eco-karma emphasises that we need to be aware not only of our individual karma but of our collective karma—as a society and the human race. Eco-karma insists that we have a responsibility as a whole species to take care of the Earth and of other beings. Otherwise the consequences may be inevitable doom.

We can now see that Eco-karma represents also an enlarged principle of Christianity and of Judaism and of Islam: "As you sow, so you reap." The proper formulation of this karmic principle should include the consequences of our action toward nature and toward other beings. Bad karma are those harmful deeds, done to others, which ultimately effect us adversely. A deeper reflection immediately informs us that a wretched treatment of nature, or the elimination of other species by thousands, is bound to bring a bitter harvest to ourselves, and the consequence may be inevitable doom. The principle of Eco-karma is thus sharpening the awareness of our moral responsibility in the universe not limited to humans only.

We have enlarged the meaning of Karma in two ways The first of these ways is by seeing that between the human individual and God there are many stages which have *karmic consequence.* We have responsibilities for all these stages-in-between, including taking care of the earth, of other beings, of future generations. While taking care of these stages and attempting to accumulate positive karma, we are not forgetting about God, about our responsibility to the divine, about our inner God. But we now see this ultimate responsibility in a much broader context.

The second way of enlarging traditional meaning of karma is by seeing that we do not only have individual responsibilities but also collective responsibilities. We are thus co-responsible for collective karma of our society and of the human race. We carry on our shoulders and in our hearts collective karma for the devastation of nature, of other beings, of aboriginal people. We are not personally responsible for maltreatment of these beings. Yet we carry collective karma on our shoulders and in our consciousness.

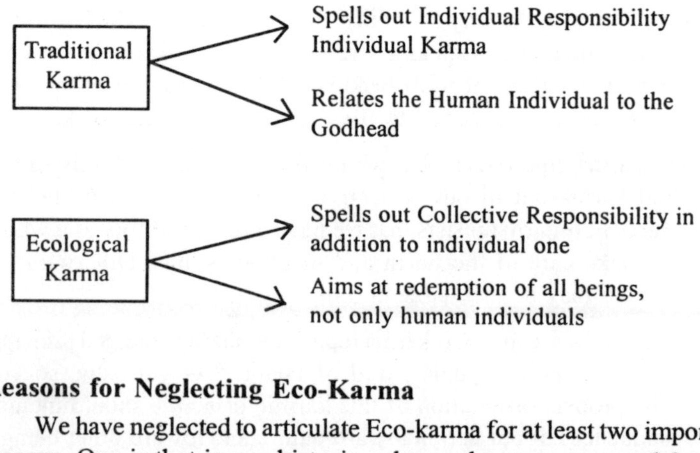

Reasons for Neglecting Eco-Karma

We have neglected to articulate Eco-karma for at least two important reasons. One is that in pre-historic cultures there was no need for this articulation. People were so woven into the web of nature that they quite naturally protected it as a part of their outer skin. The second reason is more recent. When organized religions emerged, particularly monotheistic ones, people focused their entire attention on the relationship of the human to Deity. Moral laws were then articulated along the religious lines. Eco-karma was missed as a moral principle by divine default. The deities, as it were, did not want to consider nature on the level of importance equal to them. Let us discuss these two reasons in some details.

Early man lived in the state of trance. He was so wrapped in the texture of nature, of the cosmos, of the divine forces that he was hardly conscious of where the human ends and nature begins; also hardly aware at what point natural forces assumed the divine and cosmic dimensions. What was natural, what was cosmic, what was divine was not so clearly distinguishable. For so often natural forces were endowed with divine attributes. In this primordial unity, it was quite natural and indeed inevitable, not to separate the overwhelming flow surrounding the human into people, nature and divinity but to live it all as an unbroken stream of one seamless experience. In fact, there was no choice to do it otherwise. The consciousness had not yet emerged which would allow us to separate, to chop, to atomize. In this sense early man lived in a trance. All was one. The communication with other beings of the cosmos was perfect, natural, an inherent aspects of how things were. Human consciousness did not need to sacralize nature; specifically it did not need to establish a moral law enunciating the sanctity of nature. Nature was enshrined by virtue of the prevailing cosmology. It was truly a state of naive innocence - until cultures emerged and started reflecting, articulating, establishing moral laws.

The conception of the moral law, as the edicts from God and heaven, has dominated our moral horizons for millennia, in fact until modern times. Only with Immannual Kant we witness the radical shift: "The starry heaven above you and the moral law within you." Between the time of the primordial enchantment with the natural world and the philosophy of Immannual Kant a lot has happened. Human consciousness has been articulating itself. Cultures have become more and more refined. The process of self reflection has gradually lead to self doubt: until finally it has arrived at nihilistic skepticism doubting everything: "1 doubt therefore I am." The original innocence has been lost.

Humans have acquired a distinctive sense of self-consciousness and a distinctive sense of separation from nature. The acquisition of the distinctive sense of self-consciousness and of one's uniqueness (already in Greek times: let us remember Protagoras: "Man is the measure of all things") is a triumph of human consciousness arising. But it also signifies the fall from grace, the grace of original innocence, the grace of the primordial unity of the human with the surrounding universe.

The process of articulation of self-consciousness and of the sense of human autonomy grows even further in the post-Renaissance time under the aegis of the mechanistic world view. In this period man seeks further liberation. This time from the impositions and dogmas of religious orthodoxies. We wished to abolish the tyranny of God in order to increase further our autonomy. But this also signifies a further fall from grace. Enmeshed by our scientific inventions we have lost our way in the technological jungle. In the process we have lost the sacred and alienated ourselves from nature and from ourselves.

With hindsight we can now see the immaturity of the so-called civilized man. While he was rushing from one action to another, exploring and conquering, he was not quite clearly seeing what he was doing. We can also see the immaturity of organized religions, as they pitted people against people, and as they allowed humans to savage nature and other beings. Religions have too often been exclusive, jealous, overpossessive. They established a special pact with the humans at the expense of other beings of the cosmos. The humans were kidnapped from the family of living beings and made to serve demanding and exclusive gods. This has produced bad karma - for the whole living family. We are now trying to rectify the situation. We realize that healing the Earth is part of our new Dharma, part of our new responsibility to overcome the past bad karma.

The ecological age represents a deliberate effort to establish a new unity with nature and with other beings. It is not a return to the original unity. Such returns are not possible. It is a new unity which transcends the present atomizing and manipulative consciousness in favour of ecological consciousness. It is a new way of resacralizing the world while living in a state of continuous reverence.

Eco-karma informs us that after the fall from original naive grace, we can consciously and deliberately build a new form of grace - the harmony with nature and with all creation built on the foundation of a new moral imperative. We have to establish this harmony because it is in accordance with the cosmic law, namely that all things must be in balance and harmoniously support each other. While this cosmic law was subconsciously upheld in ancient times, we can now consciously and deliberately articulate it as the prerogative of our maturity. Eco-karma celebrates the newly gained consciousness of oneness of all things in the new historic context. Eco-karma is a consequence of the ecological world view, indeed a mature daughter of it.

We have a choice of either continuing with a wrong attitude to nature which leads to inevitable doom, or of embarking on the path of Eco-karma which leads to healing and salvation. In opting out for the ecological world view we have chosen the latter. This is not only a choice of some individuals This is a choice expressing evolutionary wisdom.

The Indian Tradition

Karma is an Indian term and the Indian tradition has been most articulate about it. Yet the Indian tradition does not have a monopoly on the term. Nor should it be assumed that because the Indian culture (including Hinduism, Buddhism, and Jainism) used the term for millennia we know all that is to be known about karma and no fresh insights are warranted.

Within the Indian tradition, karma has been guided by Divine Providence. This Divine Providence is exemplified, for instance by the *Bhagavad Gita,* or by the sublime discourses of the *Upanishads,* concerning the relationships between the Brahman and the Atman.

The Hindu tradition so often articulates the relationship between the Atman and the Brahman. The true wisdom is meant to be this kind of vision which enables the individual (Atman) to unite with the absolute (Brahman). We shall agree that this is a High Road, highly commendable and lauded in all periods of history. Yet we should also remember that our world is so versatile and that between the Atman and Brahman there are many lands to travel through. That is what universal karma signifies. We must make peace in each of these lands we travel through before we reach the ultimate land of light - Brahman.

To have a clear awareness of one's relationship to Brahman (or to God) is a mark of high consciousness. Not to be fully aware that passing through the various lands on the way to Brahman involves acts and actions which have karmic consequence is a form of arrogance and hubris. "Of all you have done in the past, you eat the fruit...." At times the Indian tradition is too high minded in forgetting about everything else, save the link between the Atman and Brahman.

Stress on Man's Relationship with God Vis-a-Vis Nature

Yet one wonders after a while whether this guidance has not per chance been too divine: just like in Christianity whereby the moral sin, the closest approximation to karma, is determined solely by the religious context - of man's relationship to God - while man's other responsibilities have been obscured. The conception of sin and, by implication, of the meaning of karma in the Christian tradition is overwhelmingly determined by old commandments and too little by the new awareness of man's responsibility to nature and other beings; including other human beings outside our own religious traditions. It is frightening to think how many religious wars were fought for the sake of maintaining our image of god; how many millions of people were killed in a brutal way in these wars; and what devastation of the land occurred in the process. It is painful to think what kind of karma was the residue of this whole process.

Moreover, if it is true that all the universe is sacred, then every land we travel through is sacred. We need to pass through each accumulating good karma: and harm none. For harming any land in between, whether these be the people who are of lower status than we are. or ecological habitats, or animals, we harm ourselves, we harm Atman within: in a subtle way we also harm Brahman because we arrive at Brahman not fully clean.

We shall emphasize that we are not abandoning or diminishing the past understanding of karma. On the contrary, we are broadening and deepening it so that we can be rightly informed and guided in this difficult age fraught with torturous and unprecedented complexity. It is a joy to follow the right karma, even if it outlines a path paved with difficulties. We want to know what is right and proper for ourselves and for future generations. Sustainable life should be guided by sustainable karma. We don't want to stumble in confusion and uncertainties. For this produces bad karma. The residue of the mind's confusion is a life lived in fog. It is a joy to heal others, to heal Mother Earth - to clean, to mend, to purify. We must not be too centered on ourselves. A virtuous path of life is not a narrow lane which joins us directly with deity. It is a broad road which includes so many other beings.

Medicine men and women are highly respected in all traditional societies. They are a living symbol of healing, cleansing, repairing: bringing things to a right orbit again. We are - all of us - now called to join the ranks of the ancient 'shamans' who tirelessly worked for the benefit of all. We are called to join the ranks of Bodhisattvas. We possess the necessary powers within ourselves. We need to bring out these powers from their hiding places and make them blossom. Whether we call this new path Eco-Karma, or a labour of love, or a cosmic necessity, or a Divine Dharma, let us follow it with joy and pride, remembering with Euripides:

Who rightly with necessity
Complies in things divine
We count him skilled and wise.

Eliot's Message in Verse

T.S. Eliot is known as a poet. And mainly as a poet of the sardonic gloom and of existential malaise. On a deeper level, however, Eliot reveals himself as a precursor of the ecological epoch. His prophetic visions heralding the age of ecology are not explicit. However, when we read him aright, not by concentrating on what he denounces, but by revealing what he dearly cherishes, the message is clear.

I have often quoted these three lines:

Where is the Life we have lost in living?
Where is the wisdom we have lost in knowledge?
Where is the knowledge we have lost in information?

These lines reveal powerfully the tragic predicament of Western knowledge which is so potent and so powerful but ultimately so empty and so futile, for it has traded wisdom for information and the meaning of life for consumption. Any philosophy worthy of the 21st century must be guided by wisdom and not by merely logic or by a compendium of scientific facts and theories.

Here is another revealing vista of Eliot:

Of all you have done in the past.

You eat the fruit
Either rotten or ripe

Eliot's poetic incantations conceal deep moral insights. Yet we prefer to be enchanted by the power of poetry as we glide over its moral substratum. The 20th century has not been a moral age. It has been a nihilistic age. For this reason the proponents of the high moral road had to maintain a low profile. The prophets of high greed however have been very vocal and highly visible. Many centuries ago. Eurepides had said:

He who rightly with necessity
Complies with things divine
We count him skilled and wise.

The message is simpler than that of Eliot. Moreover, it is expressed in a positive vein: We salute those who have the courage to follow the divine road. In Eliot, the message is expressed cryptically, emphasizing the negative consequences of bad deeds.

The 20th century has not had the courage of positive visions. The best thinkers have been dancing a tortuous dance of self effacement, not daring to be positive. Instead, they tried to show how 'sophisticated' they were by deriding everything beautiful and noble and by despising higher moral values

The ecological paradigm is changing it all. It has maintained that it is right and proper to believe in things noble. It is right to comply with things divine, as Eurepides proposed. The positive vision is not a weakness of smaller minds or a prerogative of naive minds, but an expression of courage and vibrancy of one's being. The ecological paradigm challenges the pitifully barren vision of those shallow proponents of material progress who believed in knowledge without wisdom.

How relevant T.S. Eliot is for our understanding of new extensions of Karma, which we call Ecological Karma can b e seen in the following lines:

A wrong attitude to nature
Implies somewhere a wrong attitude to God
And the consequence is an inevitable doom.

This precept should have been studied by ecologists and religious people alike. But it hasn't been. Eliot is not considered to be a poet relevant to ecology. On the other hand, religious people find him an awkward companion. Let us examine more closely Eliot's precept. For the principle of Eco-karma is hiding there.

How can it be that a wrong attitude to nature can bring about an inevitable doom? Eliot does not explain rather he feels it in his bones. For this reason he says rather tentatively:

A wrong attitude to nature
Implies somewhere a wrong attitude to God.

For the religious peoples of the traditional variety, such a statement does not make sense. The ecologists missed it altogether.

However, within the ecological perspective Eliot's contention makes perfect sense. All things are connected, are parts of the same web of life. A wrong attitude to nature is a desecration of the web itself. Only when we have created a new coherent picture of the earth as a seamless web, in which all parts are interconnected, and indeed aspects of the sacred tapestry; only when we have evolved the image of Gaia as living Earth, extremely resilient but very fragile, only then can we make a full and vibrant sense of Eliot's contention.

12

Islamic Perspective of Environment Ethics

Importance of Environmental Education

In his eagreness to control nature man has ruined the environment to the extent that now his own survival is threatened. The magnitude of the situation is so appalling that now the whole worlds attention has become focussed on issues affecting environment. Environmental Education (E.E.) is gaining momentum and becoming increasingly popular as more and more countries are realising its importance and taking actions necessary for its incorporation into their educational systems (Ghaznawi, 1990). The guiding principles developed and endorsed at Tbilisi are supposed to be determiners for E.E. programmes, as the Tbilisi declaration is perhaps the most noteworthy environmental publication of its decade (UNESCO, 1978).

However, Caduto (1985) noted that the values education emphasised in the Tbilisi declaration are often neglected in most E.E. programmes. This means that such programmes do not pay enough attention to strengthening, reinforcing and fostering sound environmental values (Caduto, 1985).

The values approach to E.E. (or Environmental Values Education (E.V.E.)) is widely advocated because experience with E.E. programmes as reflections of environmental problems did not succeed in developing in people the environmental ethics necessary to guide actions in the environment (Caduto, 1985; Mostafa and Abdo, 1989; Subbarini, 1990).

Such Environmental Ethics would impose restraints on human behaviour in relation to the natural environment, because some forms of human behaviour are destructive to the environment (Yaziz, 1985).

Implications for Environmental Education

Education in the Islamic culture lays emphasis on developing in

Man the creative motive to control himself and the universe, not by confronting nature or struggling with it but by understanding its laws and governing its potential in order to develop a harmonious relationship with it (Mostafa and Abdo, 1989). This emphasis on education in Islam meets the call of E.E. to the development in people of a positive environmental ethic which favours the harmonious improvement of human wellbeing and of the quality of the environment (Caduto, 1985).

Moreover, human beings by their nature are intrinsically attracted to natural beauty, to other forms of life and to the wonders of the living world (Meadows, 1989). This idea is no more than the essence of Biocentrism, which is a sacred duty of people in the Islamic culture. Environmental Education programmes will be more effective in fostering a personal environmental ethic if oriented to people's cultural and spiritual backgrounds and implemented from a cultural perspective. The following three components of the Islamic cultural system should be considered as determiners for E.E. programmes at the formal and non-formal levels (Mekouar, 1984; Yaziz, 1985; Mostafa and Abdo, 1989):

1. Man is a distinct part of nature and has a unique position among other living and non-living components of nature, but his relation to it should be one of stewardship and not tyranny.

   Therefore, Man (God's representative on earth) "was entrusted with a particularly heavy responsibility: to live by the divine teachings on the preservation of ecological balances while assuring the proper management of the environment" (Mekouar, 1984 (p. 76)).
2. The non-materialistic environment of Man forms the moral component of the human personality which motivates Man to make sacrifices for nature.
3. The materialistic environment of Man is composed of the living and non-living components of nature which form the raw material through which Man can show his thought and creativeness in a cultural structure.

Importance of Environmental Ethics

The development of environmental ethics in people is thus *a* necessity for confronting the present disharmonious relationship between people and their environment. However, it is of paramount importance to illustrate environmental ethics in cultural contexts, as cultures have different approaches to and stances on environmental ethics (Franeka, cited in Simmons, 1988).

It is widely accepted that most environmental problems are related to the lack of an ethical basis governing the relationship between human beings and their environment (Simmons, 1988; Mostafa and Abdo, 1989). Therefore, the best outcome of E.E. is the "inculcation of environmental ethics as a precious code of behaviour in individuals and societies" (Ghaznawi, 1990) because environmental ethics are the guiding force behind the conduct of human beings towards the environment (Caduto, 1985).

Moreover, environmental ethics exert a persuasive influence on actual behaviour and a norm of reference to which actual behaviour may be evaluated (Yaziz, 1985). Environmental ethics have deep roots in the cultures of all nations. They controlled the environmental impact of pre-industrial human technologies (Yaziz, 1985). The lack of an alternative ethic for the global industrial culture which has prevailed for the last two centuries is responsible for the environmental crisis which has threatened and is still threatening quality of life at national, regional and global levels (Yaziz, 1985; Mostafa and Abdo, 1989).

There are two major approaches to environmental ethics-Biocentrism and Anthropocentrism (Yaziz, 1985).

Islam and Biocentrism

Biocentrism is the moral accountability of the effects of human actions upon the non-human level of being, irrespective of their indirect effects upon human welfare (Yaziz, 1985). The concept of biocentrism is reflected in "Faith" in Islam, which is expounded by the Holy Qur'an and Hadith (deeds and sayings of the Prophet Mohammed-*Peace Be Upon Him)*. Faith in Islam is a comprehensive concept comprising the relations between Man and his natural and human environment (Kamel, 1982). It is also a complete system for human life, showing harmony between nature and Man (Khan, 1984; Mekouar, 1984).

Biocentrism is being discussed here because it is the approach of the Islamic culture to environmental ethics, which is a determiner needed for E.E. in Arab states (Mostafa and Abdo, 1989). According to Islam, Man is a distinct part of nature and has a special position among other parts of nature-living and non-living (Ba Kader *et al.*, 1983) but his relationship to nature is not mastery but stewardship (Yaziz, 1985).

Verses from Qura'an Related to Biocentrism

He is warned indirectly of the consequences of ecological imbalances if he abuses natural resources; he is also responsible for the degradation of his own environment on land or in the sea, which may result in great ecological imbalances (Khan, 1984). These ideas are stressed in the following verses of the Holy Qur'an*:

> *And the earth we have spread out (Like a carpet): Set thereon Mountains Firm and immovable: And Produced therein all Kinds of things in due balance.*
>
> (15: 119)

> *Mischief has appeared On Land and Sea because of (the need) that the hands of men have earned That (God) may give them A taste of Some of their Deeds: in Order that they May turn back (from Evil).*
>
> (30: 41)

God has bestowed upon people the rights of enjoying his endless blessings, and all creatures are created to be used by Man, but they should not be polluted or annoyed. These ideas are stressed in the following verses of the Holy Qur'an:

> *It is He who sends down Rain from the sky: From it ye drink, And out of it (grows) the vegetation on which ye feed your cattle.*
>
> (16: 10)

> *With it He produces For you corn, olives, Date-palms, grapes, And every Kind of Fruit: Verily in this is a Sign For those who give thought.*
>
> (16: 11)

> *Do ye not see that God has subjected To Your (use) all things In the heavens and on earth. And has made His bounties Flow to you in exceeding Measure, (both) seen and unseen? Yet there are among men Those who dispute about God, without Knowledge and without Guidance, and without a Book To enlighten them.*
>
> (31: 20)

*The following and other verses in this paper are quoted from Ali (1984).

> *There is not an animal (That lives) on the earth, Nor a being that flies On its wings, but (forms Part of) communities like you. Nothing have we omitted from the Book, and they (all) shall be gathered to their Lord In the end.*
>
> (6: 38)
>
> *How many are the Creatures that carry not their own Sustenance? It is God who feeds (both) them and you: For He hears and knows (All things).*
>
> (29: 60)

The Holy Qur'an also "describes the harmonious adaptation of creation to Man's needs" (Bucaille, 1978). General remarks of that sense can be examined in the following verses of the Qur'an:

> *And cattle He has created For you (men): from them ye derive warmth, And numerous benefits, And of their (meat) ye eat.*
>
> *And ye have a sense of pride and beauty in them as ye drive them home In the evening, and as ye Lead them forth to pasture in the morning.*
>
> *And they carry your heavy loads To lands that ye could not (Otherwise) reach except with Souls distressed: for Your Lord is indeed Most Kind, Most Merciful.*
>
> *And (He has created) horses, mules, and donkeys, for you To ride and use for show, And He has Created (other) things Of which ye have no Knowledge.*
>
> (16: 5-8)

This means that the Muslim learns the appreciation of life and living things from scores of verses in the Qur'an and sayings and traditions of the Prophet Mohammed *(Peace Be Upon Him)*. The Prophet gives Muslims two examples which emphasise kindness to animals. The first one is of a woman who was doomed to Hell only because she kept a cat in captivity; she neither offered it food nor released it to seek its own food from the "vermin of the earth". The second is of a man who went down a well to get some water for a thirsty, panting dog; he had to climb up the well holding with his teeth his shoe full of water; he was rewarded by being allowed into Paradise. Again, Muslim laws rule that animals to be slaughtered should not be hungry or thirsty, should not be terrified or molested, and that the knife should be very sharp to save the sacrificed animal any unnecessary pain.

People are urged to plant trees. Very emphatically, the Prophet tells Muslims "If one of you was going to plant a palm seedling, but suddenly the Day of Judgement was announced, he should go on and plant it!" He also tells Muslims that if a man plants a tree, God will praise and reward him for any of its fruits which he eats or offers to others, or any which are stolen from him or eaten by wild animals and birds! In his talks to people, the Prophet used to refer to the palm tree as "their aunt".

On Doomsday, if anyone has a palm shoot in hand, he should plant it.

Prophet Mohammed (*Peace be Upon Him*)

REFERENCES

Ali, A.Y., 1984. *The Holy Qur'an-Text, Translation and Commentary* (That Es Salasil, Kuwait).

Ba Kader, A., Al-Sabbagh, A., Al Glenid, M. and Izzidien, M. 1983. *Islamic Principles for the Conservation of the Natural Environment* (IUCN Environmental Policy and Law Paper, IUCN).

Bucaille, M. 1978. *The Bible, The Qur'an and Science* (American Trust Publications, Indianapolis, U.S.A.).

Caduto, M. 1985. *A Guide on Environmental Values Education* (Environmental Education Series 13, UNESCO, Paris).

Ghaznawi, A.G. 1990. Environmental Education: A Measure for Fostering Compatibility of Environment, Population and Development. Proceedings of the Regional Environmental Education Seminar organised by the Arab Bureau of Education for the Gulf States, 17-20 December 1988 (Muscat, Oman), pp. 480-807.

Kamel, A.A. 1982. Faith and Cure. *Abstracts of the Second International Islamic Medicine Conference* (Ministry of Public Health, Kuwait), pp. 4-5.

Khan, K. 1984. Qur'anic Consideration of Environment (Marine and Others) and its Protection. Proceedings of the First International Conference on the Impact of Oil Spill in the Persian Gulf (University of Tehran, Iran), pp. 806-814.

Meadows, D. 1989. Harvesting One Hundredfold. *Key Concepts and Case Studies in Environmental Education* (UNEP, Nairobi).

Mekouar, M. 1984. The Islamic Ethic. *IUCN Bulletin,* Vol.15 (7-9), pp. 75-76.

Mostafa, A. and ABDO, F. 1989. Islamic determiners for environmental education and its inclusion in curricula of general education. *Dirasat Tarbawlyya,* 4(19), 206-250 *(original in Arabic).*

Simmons, D. 1988. Environmental Education and Environmental Ethics: Theory, practicc and mixed messages. *International Journal of Environmental Education and Information,* 7(2), 52-61.

Subbarini, M.S. 1990. Key issues in environmental education. *Environmental Issues,* No. 38 (Kuwait Environmental Protection Society, Kuwait).

UNESCO, 1978. Report of the Tbilisi Conference (UNESCO, Paris).

Yaziz, M. 1985. Environmental Ethics. Final Report of the Sub-regional Training Workshop in Non-Formal Environmental Education in Asia organized by University Pertanian Malaysia in co-operation with IEEP, 10-22 November 1985 (Serdang, Selandor, Malaysia).

13

Living in Harmony with Nature

Almost all the Hindu scriptures endorse the importance of having respect for all species created by God as ethes, air, fire, water, earth, plants, all creaturs, trees and plants, rivers and seas are organs of God's body as told by Lord Krishna in *Mahapurana*.

The environmental problems of today are immense because they affect the entire planet, the whole of humanity, and all life-forms. The environmental ravage looms over all countries of all continents and threatens the survival of humankind. The problems cannot be solved on a local or partial basis; they have to be tackled globally. The warming of the global climate, for example, will put the ecosystems of all countries at great risk. Only a cosmocentric, global consciousness can help. It is, therefore, useful to explore what our ancient texts say about environmental protection and the kind of relationship they recommend between humans and their natural environment. Unfortunately, for many, awareness of the ecological crisis is close to nonexistent. They do not realize that they are damaging the environment and ultimately themselves. They are cutting the very branches on which they are sitting; they do not realize their responsibility to keep these branches healthy. Human ignorance, shortsightedness, and egoism have given rise to an environmental catastrophe. A very important task, therefore, is to arouse people's public consciousness and environmental activism. This should be done on the basis of ancient and modern knowledge.

There is immense ecological vision that the Hindu scripture and traditions advocate and the Hindus can benefit from these insights and revive traditional sustainable practices, many of which they have forgotten, to their own peril. These traditional practices also have a wider relevance. We need to muster greater knowledge and available resources to prevent further damage to the life-promoting and life-sustaining characteristics of the planet.

The Concept of Dharma

One's duty to one's family, society, humanity, the natural elements, and God are all part of *dharma.* A fundamental feature of the Hindu tradition is that there is no dividing line between the sacred and secular. There is no area of life that is alien to spiritual influence. Secular and sacred concerns are inextricably interwoven. *Dharma* deals with moral as well as physical order. It espouses an integral view of life and the world by providing coherence to the diverse activities of life.

Dharma is a comprehensive term, incorporating duty, morality, law, and justice, it also refers to the structure of reality. It is a cosmic law, the law of life and development. It is *sanātoria,* eternal. It is a support of the whole universe. The purpose *of dharma* is to maintain and conserve the society and the world. *Dharma* operates in accordance with time, space, and conditions, yet maintains a balance, lest society stray from eternal principles. The moral code of conduct prescribed by the *dharmaśāstras* counteracts the individual's tendency to pursue exclusively selfish interests. *Dharma* requires from each member of society a way of life consistent with the general welfare of humankind. Lord Kṛṣṇa teaches in the *Bhagavadgītā* that only those actions are worthy and valuable that contribute to the welfare of the whole world, with all living beings in it. The prosperity and happiness of people are dependent on an ordered society, on nature, and on the cosmos as a whole. Just as the health and happiness of one person depend on all the sense organs working cooperatively, the world organism only functions smoothly when the great elements perform their work together and well. According to the *Bhagavadgītā* (3.10-13):

> The lord of all creatures, having created beings and deities declared thus: by sacrificial action you will attain prosperity; this is for you the desired milch cow, with this you cherish gods (cosmic powers) and the gods will cherish you. By mutual care and concern, there will reign general prosperity for all. The deities, being satisfied by the performance of *yajna,* supply the needs of humans. But one who enjoys these gifts without offering them in return is certainly a thief.

The concept of *dharma* provides a model of cosmic and social equilibrium; it represents the principle of preservation. *Dharma* sustains and is to be sustained in turn through human efforts; following *dharma* leads to worldly development and spiritual fulfillment *(mokṣa)*. Prosperity *(abhyudaya)* is the result of proper care and management of natural and human resources. Even divine incarnation works to restore cosmic *dharma*. Śrî Kṛṣṇa, by personal example, encourages an attitude of caring and commitment toward the earth and her creatures.

Prakrti

Prakṛti, cosmic matter, is the matrix of the entire material creation. The multiplicity and variety of things that we experience in ordinary life is traced to this single substance. According to the philosophy of Sāṃkhya in Indian thought, primordial matter is a bundle of energy. In this bundle there are positive, negative, and neutral forces, which are in a state of constant flux, each one trying to dominate the others. These are known as the three *gunus* (thread or quality) of *prakṛti* (matter), which is of great value to conscious beings. *Prakṛti* is rich and bountiful. It is powerful and fierce. It is also benevolent, tender, and delicate. It shies away from exploitation and abuse. It needs to be looked after with affection and adoration. It is compared to a delicate dancer who serves us but feels hurt if exploited. Nature serves us but reacts when abused. What nature wants is a judicious use of its resources for progress and prosperity, not indiscriminate exploitation. Initially, it cautions us to rectify our wrongs; but if we do not heed nature's warnings, it reacts vigorously.

The Doctrine of the Five Elements

The five great elements that constitute our environment are evolutes *of prakṛti;* they are distinctive elaborations of primal energy. Every element has its own life, form, and location, but all are interconnected and interdependent. They are the conditions and blessings of our individual and collective life. A sequential ordering of these elements, according to their decreasing subtlety—namely; space, air, fire, water, and earth *(ākāśa, vāyu, tejas, ap, prthvī)*—is stated in the *Nārāyaṇa Upaniṣad.* The Upaniṣads explain the doctrine of the five elements, in a holistic way, in relation to Brahman, the ultimate reality. The world cannot be understood wholly within itself. Brahman is the cause of the universe. The *Taittirīya Upaniṣad* says: "From Brahman arises *ākāśa, from akāśa* arises *vāyu,* from *vāyu* arises *tejas,* from *tejas* arises *ap,* and from *ap* arises *pṛthvi."* After creation, the transcendental Brahman enters into the universe as its life and consciousness. This is the basis of the affinity of humans with the natural world. In the *Maitrāyaṇī Upaniṣad* it is stated that the three-quartered Brahman has its roots above, and its branches below; the branches are earth, water, fire, air, and space.

The Five Elements of Nature Corresponding to Our Five Senses

The individual's body is a microcosm of the great cosmic body, which is the Supreme Being's mode of self-expression. The five subtle elements *(tanmātras)* are imperceptible; they are associated with the five senses, the gateways of human knowledge. Nose is related to earth, tongue to water, eyes to light or fire, skin to wind, and ears to space. Gross elements are the manifestation of the subtle ones. Each element has a unique attribute: space is qualified by sound; air possesses both sound and touch; fire consists of sound, touch, and color; water, in addition to the other three, has taste: and earth has odor as well as the first four attributes. Nature and the environment are not outside us; they are not alien and hostile to us. They are an inseparable part of our existence.

Divine Source of all Nature

Nature owes its significance to a transcendent principle whose mind is reflected in it; it reveals a supreme intelligence. The physical world, both animate and inanimate, is a manifestation of the ultimate reality. This world is God's world and all the things therof belong to Him. The five elements are the propelling forces of God. God is independent of the five elements, but the five elements are not independent of God. Waves belong to the ocean; the ocean does not belong to the waves. According to the *Bhāgavata Purāṇa,* the existence of God is to be realized in two stages: one is concrete and the other abstract. The abstract is the all-pervading spirit and the concrete is the physical world, visible and changing. The five elements are the ingredients of the world and also the support of life on the earth. The *Maitrī Upaniṣad* states: "The three-quarter Brahman has its roots above... its branches are *akāśa, vāyu, tejas, ap, and pṛthvi*"

The *Bhagavadgītā* (7.45) says that primordial nature is eightfold: the five elements plus mind, intelligence, and ego-sense, which constitute the lower nature of the Divine. The higher nature of the Divine relates to living beings, which uphold the world. Life has a higher value than things or property. There is not a thing in the world that is apart from the Divine, however. Kṛṣṇa says in the *Bhagavadgītā* (8.39): "Whatever is the seed of all beings, I am that, O Arjuna. There is no being either animate or inanimate which can exist without me." In the *Puruṣasūkta* of the *Ṛgveda (*10.90), the world order is compared to a cosmic being, a living organism in which each living being is related to the life of the whole. "The moon was created from his mind, the sun from his eyes, *Indra* and fire from his mouth, the wind from his breath, the atmosphere issued forth from his navel, the heaven from his head, the earth from his feet; the quarters from his ears."

Protecting the Elements of Nature

The environment has far-reaching effects on every creature. The life of our world depends upon the purity and balance of the five elements that surround us. All things are the result of the combination and permutation of these elements. Even our bodies, which at death disintegrate and dissolve into nature, are made up of these five elements. These elements are not spiritually vibrant all the time and 'in all places; but they can be made so. They have to be kept pure and in balance. If we consume polluted elements, our bodies become subject to disease and distortions. Distortions of the elements put all life-forms in danger; hence, the elements should be protected. To live in nature and in accordance with nature is to create an ideal environment free from pollution. Love of nature is the secret to protection of the environment.

Natural elements nourish life; they promote, heal, and rehabilitate life. Humans need to conserve these elements wisely, and the elements will in turn confer upon humans vitality, strength, and splendor. All forms of life are an integral part of nature. All species need to be appreciated. We should not underestimate even the termities. They eat up wood and dead trees and turn them into precious soil. All species serve creation and work for a divine purpose. There are birds, fishes, and animals of many kinds. The human species, other species, and the world of divinities are all interdependent. We are not isolated. We are participants in a large and grandly meaningful whole.

Actions Leave Both Good and Bad Effects

There is a Puranic story that the gods and demons churned the milky ocean to obtain nectar *(amṛta).* They used Mount Mandara as the churning rod and chief of the serpents Vāsuki as the rope. When they began to churn, many things other than nectar emerged, among them the deadly poison known as *hālāhala,* before which everyone fled in fright. The poison began making people giddy. Soon it became clear that it would destroy the whole world. The people sought refuge with the ever-auspicious Lord Śiva. Śiva took all the poison in his palm and swallowed it in his overflowing compassion; the poison could not harm him, but left a blue stain on his throat. Hence, he became known as *Neelakanṭha.*

Industrialization has churned the five elements excessively. In the name of development, nature has been badly mauled. Development has, no doubt, given rise to some immediate profits and material gains for some persons; but the world has become overburdened and perturbed. Development has also given rise to terrible poison in the shape of environmental pollution and long-term damage, resulting in the disequilibrium of the five elements. We need to follow the example of Siva and strive to remove the toxic components and make the five elements whole and wholesome once again.

Five Elements Role in Worship

Whenever a worship service is performed in the Hindu tradition, it is preceded by the purification of the elements, *bhūtaśuddhi,* as a necessary preliminary. The five elements are purified within the body and without. Purification comes before sanctification. It establishes harmony between macrocosm and microcosm. The offerings that are made to the deity represent the best of each of the five elements. Fragrance offered represents the essence of the earth, flowers represent the sky element, incense the wind element, water represents the water element, and light the fire element. Actions leave both their good and bad effects on the mind the subtle body. The mind, with its character, endures the death of the gross body The quality of actions performed in the present life conditions the future life. The present life itself is the result of past actions. Thus one Psychological endowment and fortunate or unfortunate circumstances are the consequences of past deeds. Hindus speak of three bodies of a person: gross, subtle, and causal. The gross body is made up of the five elements. It is also nourished by these very elements, by what we eat, drink, breathe, and so on. It is impelled by the subtle body of the soul, which is constituted by the threefold energies of *prakṛti*. Karma is stored in the subtle body. When the gross body collapses the soul, the subtle body, survives and is born again. This is reincarnation. Hindu scriptures speak not only of reincarnation but also of transmigration, that is, regression into subhuman births-which incidentally, is another argument in favor of vegetarianism.

Undermining of Nature

Humans grow in the lap of nature and receive sustenance from her. The basic needs of human beings are met by her gifts. These natural resources are not given for the selfish exploitation of one group or nation or generation by another', but are to be shared by all creation. Human life, animal life, and plant life are all interlinked. Yet humans have been abusing other forms of life; they have shown themselves to be shortsighted and selfish. The very industrial achievements of humans frequently undermine the natural environment. The crisis today is not only what humankind is doing to the environment, but also what the environment is doing to humankind. Humans are faced with air pollution, water contamination, diminished wildlife, the hazards of radiation, and polluted vegetation. Their health and prosperity are undermined. They are deprived of direct contact with nature in overgrown cities. They are led to artificial living, crime, and chaos. Rabindranath Tagore writes in *Sādhana: The Realisation of Life:*

> When by physical and mental barriers we violently detach ourselves from the inexhaustible life of nature; when we become merely man, but not man in the Universe, we create bewildering problems and, having shut off the sources of their solution, we try all kinds of artificial methods each of which brings its own crop of interminable difficulties. When man leaves his resting place in the universal nature, when he walks on the single rope of humanity, it means either a dance or fall for him; he has ceaselessly to strain every nerve and muscle to keep his balance at each step, and then in the intervals of his weariness, he fulminates against Providence and feels a secret pride and satisfaction in thinking that he has been unfairly dealt with by the whole scheme of things. (London: Macmillan, 1915, 9)

Space

Ākāṣa is the generic term for space, the subtlest and most pervasive of the five basic elements. It is practically omnipresent. It is not void or emptiness; rather, it fills any void or vacuum. It manifests itself as gravitational force. It represents openness, brightness, expansiveness. and the fullness of blooming capacity.

At Cidambaram in Tamilnadu in South India, space is worshiped as a manifestation of the Divine, It is said that God Siva lives there in the form of *ākāṣa,* or sky. The priest lifts a screen and allows the devotees to have a peep at the roof. It is said to be the most sacred spot in Cidambaram.

Manifestations of Space: *Mahākāṣa* is infinite space, *Antariksa* is the intermediary space between heaven (*svarga*) and earth *(bhū).* *Loka* is the perceptible space that fills space. *Loka* sustains people and *loka* has to be sustained by cosmic powers. Due to industrialization, space has become congested in urban areas. There is too much noise and pollution levels are dangerously high in factories and metropolitan areas. Industrialization is causing physical and psychological ailments. Overcrowding frequently leads to unrighteousness and psychological pollution.

Air

Air is an essential part of our natural environment. The atmosphere is a positive blanket of gases surrounding our planet, saving it from the hostile radiation from outer space and thus sustaining life on the earth. We all inhale and exhale; we are all connected through air.

Pollution

If any one of us pollutes the air, we harm all of us, just as the secondary smoke of smokers is dangerous to all the rest. Unwholesome air is responsible for diseases and epidemics. If we save the air from pollution, we increase our longevity. The air over many cities around the globe is becoming increasingly dirty. Asthmatics and elderly people with respiratory problems need clean air. They suffer in a polluted atmosphere. And yet, noxious gases are released into the atmosphere. We have disrupted the equilibrium of the carbon cycle by our heavy use of automobiles (400 million in the United States alone), the nitrogen cycle through repeated usage of chemical fertilizers and pesticides, and the sulfur cycle by burning crude oil and coal. We are destroying the protective ozone layer by the heavy use of chlorofluorocarbons. At the same time, we are cutting down trees that are needed to absorb the ever-increasing quantities of carbon dioxide released into the atmosphere by our industrial activities. Every minute of every day, we are losing fifty acres of our rain forests.

Nitrogen makes up 78 percent of the air we breathe, while oxygen makes up 21 percent. Nitrogen is a necessary part of the protein substance in the body-building material of humans, animals, and plants. Human bodies cannot use pure nitrogen; we acquire it when taking in proteins obtained by eating certain plants or plant-eating animals. The need for plant proteins requires that we protect the world's vegetation.

Fire

Fire is considered divine. Sun, lightning, and fire are forms of this element. The lustrous dawn (Uṣas) and the glorious orb of the sun (Sūrya) are its expressions. Sunlight is life giving and life supporting under certain conditions. For example, if the temperature is too high or too low, life cannot be sustained. The friendly aspect of the sun is personified as Mitra. He is the stimulator of life (Pūṣaṇ). He shines in every direction *(vivasvat).* Fire is a messenger to the gods. No impure thing should be thrown in the fire. Sacrificial smoke purifies sky (space) and air. The seer prays in the *Ṛgveda* (1.1): "Oh, Agni, like a father to his son, be thou easy of access to us; be with us for our welfare."

The divine sun has been worshiped in India since ancient times. There are sun temples in Kashmir (Martanda), Gujarat (Modhera), and Orissa (Konarak). The *Gāyatrī Mantra* is addressed to the sun god. It is believed that if we recite it regularly, our intellect becomes sharp. Fire possesses the power to destroy various types of poisonous elements and diseases. It can also purify the environment.

The cooperation of different elements produces benefits for living beings. While our lives are sustained by the chemical energy that we obtain from the food we eat and the oxygen we breathe, the energy actually comes from one source, sunlight. Similarly, when the sun heats air, it rises into the sky, laden with moisture. When the warm air gets to a certain height in the atmospheric space, it cools. Moisture then changes into small drops of water, which form clouds, and then it rains. And the rains help the vegetation to grow.

Water

Water is a life-sustaining, life-preserving and life-purifying element. It is one of the most common of all substances. Water constitutes about two-thirds of the earth's surface. Of this, 0.1 percent accounts for pure ground water—from all the lakes, streams, rivers, and rainfall—which is unevenly distributed throughout the world. Water not only provides an environment for life, it is a part of life itself: no water, no life. All creatures depend on water. Without water, there can be no agriculture, no fruits or vegetables. Water is sacred. Bathing and its symbolic substitute, *ācamana* (sipping water), are essential in religious rites.

Pollution: Today, water has become scarce due to the profound damage to the global water system. Vast ocean shores are littered with the debris of our industrial culture. Millions of tons of untreated sewage are released into the seas. Rivers, too, are polluted by industrial and organic waste. For example, as a byproduct of making paper and paper products, mercury and other toxic chemicals are dumped into streams and rivers, resulting in long-term, irreversible, and harmful effects. Household rubbish and human effluents are released into waters. Acid rain has damaged lakes and forests.

The importance of the purity of drinking water, the cleanliness of river water, and the protection of forests and mountains are discussed in the Ayurvedic texts. Contaminated waters are dangerous to the health of people in both villages and cities.

Puranic Story

The early life of Kṛṣṇa—the eighth incarnation of Lord Viṣṇu—who lived among the cowherds, is inspiring. He is concerned about the life-sustaining quality of the waters of the Yamuna and the life-promoting nature of Mount Govardhana. Lord Kṛṣṇa plays with the common, simple and pure cowherds and endears himself not only to his contemporaries and humanity at large, but also to cows, other animals, and the natural world. In the Puranic story, Kāliya, the serpent king, polluted the waters of the river Yamuna by emitting poison, causing harm to the people and the cattle living nearby. Kṛṣna jumped into the water and onto the serpent Kaliya attacked him with a lifted hood. Kṛṣna grew in size and danced on its hood, and the serpent could not bear the weight of the steps each of which brought blood from its mouth. Finally, the serpent prayed that it might be pardoned. Kṛṣṇa spared it and commanded it never again to pollute the Yamuna waters, to leave the river immediately, and to go to the deep of the ocean. Today, the many CEOs of chemical and fertilizer companies responsible for the pollution of rivers and lakes deserve to be so disciplined.

Importance of River-Banks

Flourishing civilizations historically developed on river-banks. It is at these centers that trade and commerce developed and connected the world with the ideas and ideals of philosophy, religion, and science. The rivers and their confluence became places of pilgrimage in ancient cultures. Ceremonies of initiation and death were and still are performed at these places. It is because of their life-giving and life-fulfilling properties that the appellation "mother" is bestowed on such rivers as Mother Gaṅgā̄. The *Gautama Dharmasūtra* says: ''One must not splash water with his feet nor enter water when one is full of dirt; one must not discharge into water blood, excreta, urine, spit, and semen."

Earth

The earth is a living organism. Hindus regard the earth as a mother deserving our reverence. She feeds us, provides us with shelter, and gives material for clothes. Earth's resources are for the entire humanity. Without her gifts, human survival is impossible. Mother Earth is called Dharaṇī, as she sustains and supports all her children. Whatever befalls Earth also befalls the children of the earth. There is a mutuality of interests between humans and Mother Earth. We cannot strip the earth and remain unaffected. If, as children, we do not take care of her, we diminish her ability to take care of us. Because of soil pollution, the earth looses its fertility and has adverse effects on agricultural production. Now, the earth is on the brink of disaster: the future health of our planet is under serious threat. How to bring redress to her? The *Atharva Veda* (12.1.64) says:

> Bearer of all things, hoard of treasures rare, sustaining Mother. Earth the golden breasted. . . . Impart to us those vitalizing forces that come O earth, from deep within your body. Whatever I dig up of you. O earth, May you of that have quick replenishment.

If we are to rejuvenate the earth', we need to reawaken our love for her.

We are part of the earth and the earth is part of us. Earth and we are part of the same whole. We are dependent on and participate in earth's life Earth is wonderful; it is beautiful. Earth shelters a vast number of species, including the humans. Hindus look upon the earth as God's body. This perception explains the Hindu morning prayer, which is said daily when the first footstep is taken on the earth: "Forgive me even for treading on you."

The green earth is suitable for the life of the animal and human worlds. Trees with wide leaves absorb moisture and give it to the earth. They prevent soil erosion. The vegetable and animal world are linked in the web of life. Organic farming is good for human health and good for the earth. The earth provides us with abundant foodstuffs. A vegetarian diet provides the required substances for a healthy life. It feeds more people and is less wasteful. *Ahiṃsā* and vegetarianism are embedded in the Hindu ideals of life. These practices may be summarized: go vegetarian; it makes you live longer and better; it is also good for the economy and the global environment.

The population explosion is causing natural resources to diminish at a terrific pace. By the year 2000, the world population will pass six billion and India's population one billion. The strain the world's population imposes on land, water, and other natural resources must be seriously considered. The rate of population growth is not in keeping with the availability of food. There is a blatant imbalance here. There is a limit to how much burden the earth can bear Hindus, hopefully well see the writing on the wall. Family planning, which they call the family welfare program," is to be vigorously pursued. There is no religious prohibition against it.

Mental pollution causes physical and environmental ravages. Disharmony, conflict, sickness, and degradation of the natural elements are the results of greed, lust, and anger. Ignorance and selfishness cause evil deed All action start in the mind. The mental environment has to be kept clean and focused. *Yajña* is the sacrificing of one's ego and the burning of impurities. When this is accomplished, one's environment and society are purified. A wiser thought, a cleaner vision, and a greater kindness appears. Honesty, love, and selfless service emerge.

Need and Greed

The bounty of nature is a source of wealth and provides for the needs of all creatures on the earth. Animals by instinct adhere to natural requirements. Humans, however have a tendency to indulge excessively and accumulate things beyond their needs; we also waste valuable resources. We squander this bounty through the multiplying of our superfluous desires and wants. This dichotomy between basic needs and excessive desires is crucial to the understanding of our ecological problem. The wealth of the world is based on the five elements: all peoples must share this gift among themselves and with other creatures. But consumerism and advertising mislead people into thinking that they need more and more. They obscure basic human needs. This leads to a "violent" society, since exploitation provides its basic motivation. By plundering and destroying nature, technology is ironically bringing humans into a position of conflict with nature. Ruthless exploitation of nature results in disaster. Exploding consumption in industrialized countries and population explosion in developing countries are ruining the resources, health, and balance of the natural elements. Unless we place limits on our extravagant consumption and throwaway mentality, we will face natural shortages and worse. Only if we stop wasting our wealth and energy can the peoples of the world be happy and contented.

The global ecological crisis is due to the quest for superfluous worldly goods. It is the result of a materialist worldview. The persistent and demonic passion for an ever-increasing standard of living is leading us to a global disaster. If technological and material development overlooks the needs of the spirit, is this really advancement? We have lost our perspective on what constitutes wealth. Our goal should be an optimally viable economic and social organization in relation to the entire planet and the good life of all humankind. Growth must be sustainable on a worldwide basis. It is unfortunate that we have traded a good life for a goods life. It is foolish to think that merely by multiplying one's wants, one is achieving happiness. The more our desires are satisfied, the greater our desires grow. The *Manusmṛti* (4.2) declares: "Happiness is rooted in contentment; its opposite is rooted in misery."

Conclusion

The earth is our common home; humanity is our family. We have to manage our household properly. Accordingly, we need to plan and work for short-term and long-term goals simultaneously. We need to adhere to environmentally friendly procedures and learn to utilize all resources efficiently. The art of balancing and accommodating the interests of the present as well as of future generations is to be practiced. Conservation relates to a care for the future. We need to promote life-styles that will improve and protect for posterity the life-sustaining characteristics of our earth, water, fire, air, and sky. Do we have any examples to follow? Look at the life of a tree, as described by an anonymous author and draw inspiration from the tree's example some ecological lessons:

> It gives its leaves to animals; it shares its flowers with bees. It gives its fruits to peoples. It provides shelter to birds and insects. It takes carbon dioxide and gives oxygen to the living world. Finally, it sacrifices itself to be used as construction material or fuel. It lives and dies for the service of others. However, it never asks anything in return. Wouldn't it be nice if we could appreciate and express our good will for it.

Let me conclude with a parable from the *Bṛhadāraṇyaka Upaniṣad* (5.2.1-3). Demons, humans, and gods, the progenies of the Creator (the Father), performed penance and pleased the Father; and they asked Him for a boon. The Father responded to their request by repeating one syllable; "da, da, da." The gods could not comprehend the meaning of the pronouncement. Father again repeated the syllable, "da" and asked. "Could you comprehend?" The gods replied, "Yes, Father 'da' means control of the senses *(damana);* we are too much involved in seeking pleasures. Lest we be carried away by sensory indulgence and forget our duties, you have given us this boon for our good. We need to exercise self-restraint." Next was the turn of the humans. The Father pronounced the syllable, "da," and asked. "What did you understand?" humans replied, "we are greedy and covetous; so you have commanded us to give gifts and make charitable donations (*dāna*) so that our greedy and grabbing nature be controlled". Lastly, when the demons asked for a boon, he repeated the same syllable, "da," and asked, "What did you comprehend?" The demons replied "We are very cruel; so 'da' signifies that we must be kind (daya)." The point of the above parable is to show, in short, that living a life of *dharma* is to live a full life, that self-control, charity, and kindness link the individual to the entire society and the universe; they lead to life affirmation and world affirmation.

The five elements were blessings for millions of years. Since the time of industrialization, they have become commodities. Sunderlal Bahuguna, a well-known follower of Mahatma Gandhi and an activist in the field of ecology, says that proponents of modern development believe in "converting nature into cash." They view nature as acommodity." Our luxuries have been gained at great cost to the environment and to other life-forms. Now that we are well into the twenty-first century, we must retrace our steps. We need to decentralize and develop small-scale industries. We need to develop beneficial, appropriate, and nonpolluting technologies, such as solar energy, nuclear fusion, wind power, wave power, and geothermal energy. The sources of these powers are the five great elements; and they are beneficial and benevolent.

To minimize consumption means to minimize harm to the environment. Even the wealthy should live a simple life and so prevent the rapid reduction of the earth's resources. Heavy industrialization inflicts violence on the environment. Bhopal, Chernobyl, and Love Canal are tragic examples To harm the environment is to harm ourselves. Our life-style should become less and less violent. The time has come to reach for an optimum standard of living, rich in spiritual qualities and values. This means a minimization of wants for society as a whole in other words, simple living high thinking.

14

The Self in Defence of the Earth

Deep Ecology proposes the woral goal of self-realization wherein the interests of another being are reacted to as our own interests. A New Paradigm is emerging in our time. Through its lens we see reality structured in such a way that all life forms affect and sustain each other in a web of radical interdependence. This organic interconnectedness is what we call our Deep Ecology.

"Deep Ecology" is a term coined by Norwegian philosopher Arne Naess, to contrast with "shallow environmentalism," a Band-Aid approach applying piecemeal technological fixes for short-term goals. Deep Ecology teaches us that we humans are neither the rulers nor the center of the universe, but are embedded in a vast living matrix and subject to its laws of reciprocity. Deep Ecology represents a basic shift in ways of seeing and valuing, a shift beyond anthropocentrism:

> Anthropocentrism means human chauvinism. Similar to sexism, but substitute *human race* for man and *all other species* for woman. [It's about the human race being oppressive to other species and the environment.
>
> When humans investigate and see through their layers of anthropocentric self-cherishing, a most profound change in consciousness begins to take place. Alienation subsides. The human is no longer an outsider, apart...
>
> What a relief then! The thousands of years of imagined separation are over and we begin to recall our true nature. That is, the change is a spiritual one . . . sometimes referred to as deep ecology (John Seed).

From: Deep Ecology Work: Toward the Healing of Self and World," Human Potential Magazine 17, no. 1 (Spring 1992): 10-13, 29-31.

There are, of course, manifold ways of evoking or provoking this change in perspective. Methods of inspiring the experience of Deep Ecology range from prayer to poetry, from wilderness vision quests to the induction of altered states of consciousness. The most reliable is direct action in defense of earth—and it is spreading today in many forms.

The Greening of the Self

The self is the hypothetical piece of turf on which we construct our strategies for survival, the notion around which we focus our instincts for self-preservation, or need for self-approval, and the boundaries for our self-interest. The latest pattern of the world is that the conventional notion of the self with which we have been raised and to which we have been conditioned by mainstream culture is being undermined. What Alan Watts called "the skin-encapsulated ego" and Gregory Bateson referred to as "the epistemological error of Occidental civilization" is being unhinged, peeled off. It is being replaced by concepts of identity and self-interest which are much wider than the conventional ego ... by what you might call the ecological self, co-extensive with other beings and the life of our planet. A desire and a capacity is being released from the prison cell of old constructs of self. This desire and capacity is arising in more and more people today as, out of deep concern for what is happening to our world, they begin to speak and act on its behalf.

Examples of activities which are currently being undertaken in defense of life on earth — actions in which people risk their comfort and even their lives to protect other speciesrange from the Chipko, or tree-hugging, movement in northern India, where, villagers fight the deforestation of their remaining woodlands, to the open seas, where Greenpeace activists are intervening to protect marine mammals from slaughter.

Among those who are shedding these old constructs of self, like old skin or a confining shell, is John Seed, director of the *Rainforest Information Centre* in Australia while fighting to save the rain forest he said "I try to remember that it's not me, John Seed, trying to protect the rain forest. Rather I'm part of the rain forest protecting myself. I am that part of the rain forest recently emerged into human thinking." This is what is meant by the greening of the self. It involves a combining of the mystical with the practical and the pragmatic, transcending separateness, alienation, and fragmentation. It is a shift that Seed himself calls "a spiritual change," generating a sense of profound interconnectedness with all life. This is hardly new to our species. In the past, poets and mystics have been speaking and writing about these ideas, but not people on the barricades agitating for social change. Now the sense of an encompassing self, the deep identity with the wider reaches of life, is a motivation for action. It is a source of courage that helps up stand up to the powers that are still, through force of inertia, destroying the fabric of life. This expanded sense of self seems to be the only basis for adequate and effective action.

Factors Nourshing Deep Ecological Consciousness

Three developments converge in our time to call forth the ecological self. They are: (1) the psychological and spiritual pressure exerted by current dangers of mass annihilation, (2) the emergence in science of the *systems* view of the world, and (3) a renaissance of nondualistic forms of spirituality.

Concern for Current Dangers of Mass Annihilation

The move to a wider ecological sense of self is in large part a function of the dangers that are threatening to overwhelm us. We are confronted by social breakdown, wars, nuclear proliferation, and the progressive destruction of our biosphere. Polls show that people today are aware that the world, as they know it, may come to an end. This loss of certainty that there will be a future is the pivotal psychological reality of our time.

While working with tens of thousands of people in North America, Europe, Asia, and Australia, helping them confront and explore what they know and feel about what is happening to their world through *"Despair and Empowerment Work."* This initiative helps them to overcome the numbing and powerlessness that result from suppression of painful responses to massively painful realities.

As their grief and fear for the world is allowed to be expressed without apology or argument and validated as a wholesome, life-preserving response, people break through their avoidance mechanisms, break through their sense of futility and isolation. Generally what they break through into is a larger sense of identity. It is as if the pressure of their acknowledged awareness of the suffering of our world stretches or collapses the culturally defined boundaries of the self.

It becomes clear, for example, that the grief and fear experienced for our world and our common future are categorically different from similar sentiments relating to one's personal welfare. This pain cannot be equated with dread of one's own individual demise. Its source lies less in concerns for personal survival than in apprehensions of collective suffering—of what looms for human life and other species and unborn generations to come. Its nature is akin to the original meaning of compassion— "suffering with." It is the distress we feel on behalf of the larger whole of which we are a part. And, when it is so defined, it serves as a trigger or getaway to a more encompassing sense of identity, inseparable from the web of life in which we are as intricately interconnected as cells in a larger body.

It is a mistake about our place in the order of things. It is the delusion that the self is so separate and fragile that we must delineate and defend its boundaries, that it is so small and needy that we must endlessly acquire and endlessly consume, that it is so aloof that we can—as individuals, corporations, nation-states, or as a species—be immune to what we do to other beings. This shift in consciousness is an appropriate, adaptive response. For the crisis that threatens our planet, be it seen in its military, ecological, or social aspects, derives from a dysfunctional and pathogenic notion of the self. This view of human nature is not new, of course. That is why this shift in the sense of self is credible to people. As the poet Theodore Roethke said, "I believe my pain." Many have felt the imperative to extend self-interest to embrace the whole. What is notable in our situation is that this extension of identity can come not through an effort to be noble or good or altruistic, but simply to be present and own our pain.

Science and the Systems View of the Self

The findings of twentieth-century science undermine the notion of a separate self, distinct from the world it observes and acts upon. As Einstein showed, the self's perceptions are shaped by its changing position in relation to other phenomena. And these phenomena are affected not only by location but, as Heisenberg demonstrated, by the very act of observation. Now contemporary systems science and systems cybernetics go yet further in challenging old assumptions about a distinct, separate, continuous self. We are open, self-organizing systems; our very breathing, acting, and thinking arise in interaction with our shared world through the currents of matter, energy, and information that flow through us. In the web of relationships that sustain these activities, there are no clear lines demarcating a separate self. As systems theorists aver, there is no categorical "I" set over and against a categorical "you" or "it."

One of the clearer expositions of this is offered by Gregory Bateson, who is earlier quoted as saying that the abstraction of a separate "I" is "the epistemological fallacy of Western civilization." He says that the process that decides and acts cannot be neatly identified with the isolated subjectivity of the individual or located within the confines of the skin. He contends that "the total self-corrective unit that processes information is a system whose boundaries do not at all coincide with the boundaries either of the body or what is popularly called 'self or 'consciousness.'" He goes on to say, "The self is ordinarily understood as only a small part of a much larger trial-and-error system which does the thinking, acting, and deciding." Bateson uses the example of a woodcutter, about to fell a tree. His hands grip the handle of the axe. Whump, he makes a cut, and then whump, another cut. What is the feedback circuit, where is the information that is guiding that cutting down of the tree? That is the self-correcting unit, that is what is doing the chopping down of the tree.

In another illustration, a blind person with a cane is walking along the sidewalk. Tap, tap, whoops, there's a fire hydrant, there's a curb. What is doing the walking? Where is the self then of the blind person? What is doing the perceiving and deciding? That self-corrective feedback circuit is the arm, the hand, the cane, the curb, the ear. At that moment that is the self that is walking. Bateson's point is that the self as we usually define it is an improperly delimited part of a much larger field of interlocking processes. And he maintains that

> this false reification of the self is basic to the planetary ecological crisis in which we find ourselves. We have imagined that we are a unit of survival and we have to see to our own survival, and we imagine that the unit of survival is the separate individual or a separate species, whereas in reality through the history of evolution, it is the individual plus the environment, the species plus the environment, for they are essentially symbiotic.

The self is a metaphor. We can decide to limit it to our skin, our person, our family, our organization, or our species. We can select its boundaries in objective reality. As the systems theorists see it, our consciousness illuminates a small area in the wider currents and loops of knowing that interconnect us. It is just as plausible to conceive of mind as coexistent with these larger circuits, the entire "pattern that connects" as Bateson said. Do not think that to broaden the construct of self this way involves an eclipse of one's distinctiveness. Do not think that you will lose your identity like a drop in the ocean merging into the oneness of Brahman. From the systems perspective, this interaction, creating larger wholes and patterns, fosters and even requires diversity. You become more yourself. Integration and differentiation go hand in hand.

Nondualistic Forms of Spirituality—Bodhisattva

A third factor that nourishes deep ecological consciousness in our world today is the *resurgence of nondualistic spirituality*. We find it in many realms—in Sufism in Islam, Creation Spirituality in Christianity, and in Buddhism's historic coming to the West. Buddhism is distinctive in its clarity and sophistication about the dynamics of self. In much the same way as systems theory does, Buddhism undermines categorical distinctions between self and other. It then goes further than systems theory in showing the pathogenic character of any reifications of the self, and in offering methods for transcending these difficulties and healing this suffering. What the Buddha woke up to under the Bodhi tree was *paticca samuppada,* the dependent co-arising of phenomena, in which you cannot isolate a separate, continuous self.

We think, "What do we do with the self, this clamorous 'I,' always wanting attention, always wanting its goodies? Do we crucify it, sacrifice it, mortify it, punish it, or do we make it noble?" Upon awaking we realize, "Its just a convention!" When you take it too seriously, when you suppose that it is something enduring which you have to defend and promote, it becomes the foundation of delusion, the motive behind our attachments and our aversions. Consider the Tibetan portrayal of the wheel of life, that mythically depicts all the realms of being. At the very center of that wheel of suffering are three figures: the pig, the rooster, and the snake—they represent: delusion, greed, and hatred—and they just chase one another around and around. The linchpin of all the pain is the notion of our self the notion that we have to protect that self or conquer on its behalf—or do something with it.

The point of Buddhism, and, for that matter of Deep Ecology too, is that we do not need to be doomed to the perpetual rat-race. The vicious circle can be broken. It can be broken by wisdom, meditation, and morality—that is, when we pay attention to our experience and our actions and discover that they do not have to be in bondage to a separate self. The sense of interconnectedness that can arise is imaged—one of the most beautiful images coming out of the Mahayana—as the jewelled net of Indra. It is a vision of reality structured very much like the holographic view of the universe, so that each being is a jewel at each node of the net, and each jewel reflects all the other, reflecting back and catching the reflection, just as systems theory sees that the part contains the whole.

The Bodhisattva Experience

The awakening to our true self is the awakening to that entirety, breaking out of the prison-self of separate ego. The one who perceives this is the bodhisattva—and we are all bodhisattvas because we are all capable of experiencing that—it is our true nature. We are profoundly interconnected and therefore we are all able to recognize and act upon our deep, intricate, and intimate inter-existence with one another and all beings. That true nature of ours is already present in our pain for the world. When we turn our eyes away from that homeless figure, are we indifferent, or is the pain of seeing him or her too great? Do not be easily duped by the apparent indifference of those around you. What looks like apathy is really the fear of suffering. But the bodhisattva knows that to experience the pain of all beings it is necessary to experience their joy. It says in the Lotus Sutra that the bodhisattva hears the music of the spheres, and understands the language of the birds, while hearing the cries in the deepest levels of hell.

Ineffective Nature of Moral Sermous

One of the things I like best about the ecological self that is arising in our time is that it is making moral exhortation irrelevant. Sermonizing is both boring and ineffective. As Arne Naess says, "The extensive moralizing within the ecological movement has given the public the false impression that they are being asked to make a sacrifice to show more responsibility, more concern, and a nicer moral standard. But all of that would flow naturally and easily if the self were widened and deepened so that the protection of nature was felt and perceived as protection of our very selves."

Please note this important point: virtue is not required for the greening of the self or the emergence of the ecological self. The shift in identification at this point in our history is required precisely because moral exhortation doesn't work, and because sermons seldom hinder us from following our self-interest as we conceive it.

The obvious choice, then, is to extend our notions of self-interest. For example, it would not occur to me to plead with you, "Oh, don't saw off your leg. That would be an act of violence." It wouldn't occur to me, or you, because your leg is part of your body. Well, so are the trees in the Amazon rain basin. They are our external lungs. And we are beginning to realize that the world is our body. This ecological self, like any notion of selfhood, is a metaphoric construct and a dynamic one. It involves choice: choices can be made to identify at different moments with different dimensions or aspects of our systemically interrelated existence, be they hunted whales or homeless humans or the planet itself. In doing this, the extended self brings into play wider resources—courage, endurance, ingenuity—like a nerve cell in a neural net opening to the charge of the other neurons.

There is the sense of being acted through and sustained by those very beings on whose behalf one acts. This is very close to the religious concept of grace. In systems language we can talk about it as a synergy. But with this extension, this greening of the self, we can find a sense of buoyancy and resilience that comes from letting flow through us strengths and resources that come to us with continuous surprise and sense of blessing.

15

Hindu Strategy for Dharmic Ecology

Since the late 1980s, there has been a steadily growing awareness among the people of India about the ecological challenges facing their society. There has also been an impressive growth of regulatory and administrative institutions to deal with the problems of pollution and environmental conservation, at both national and state levels. At the same time, the mounting pressures of population, expanding urbanization, and growing poverty have led to the ecologically unsustainable exploitation of natural resources that is threatening the fragile balance in India.

The many environmental problems India faces may be summarized as follows: (1) continuous degradation, in varying degrees, of productive land (due to increased salinity and alkalinity, desertification, waterlogging, and deforestation); (2) shortage of wood fuel and fodder for rural needs, which jeopardizes existing forests; (3) depletion of the forest cover, which in turn threatens the survival of indigenous biodiversity and affects wildlife habitat; (4) excessive and unwise use of pesticides and fertilizers and ill-advised agricultural practices (including monoculture), which further stresses the fragile environment; and (5) poorly monitored and inadequately enforced environmental regulations for various natural resource extraction activities (such as mining, metallurgy, aggregate production, and other manufacturing industries).

A cursory glance at the extent of some of these major environmental problems reveals that all India's environmental issues are interconnected and together constitute an increasingly deteriorating environment and rapid depletion of natural resources—whether the issue in question is health hazards caused by water and air pollution, such as the use of fuel wood or dung for cooking purposes; population pressure and urbanization straining the resources of local governments that have to provide various civic amenities, the dearth of which imperils the quality of life of people living in urban areas; myopic land management policies that are severely straining the ecosystem in order to meet people's requirements of food and other agricultural products; long-term degradation of land and increasing desertification which is jeopardizing people's futures; the use of hazardous chemicals to meet today's short-term needs without an eye to future costs; or the rapid shrinkage of natural resources such as grazing land and the lack of fodder, firewood, and timber due to deforestation. India faces yet another major challenge to its environmental well-being: continuing poverty coupled with growing population and the attendant side effects of enhanced industrial activities (including human settlement patterns and movements). The existence of poverty affects the meager natural resources that India wishes to protect and conserve: people are so desperate to improve their families' living conditions that they do not hesitate to damage the environment if the short-term gains ensure fulfillment of their family's daily basic needs.[1]

India's population has crossed the one billion mark is increasing at the rate of 2.11 percent annually, which means about 17 million people are added each year. Furthermore, India has probably the largest cattle population on the earth—about 500 million domesticated animals—with only 13 million hectares of grazing land. The multiplying population of both human beings and animals is putting tremendous pressure on India's environment. In the race for survival, both animals and human beings suffer. In addition, over 250 million children, women, and men suffer from malnutrition. The prospects for the future are alarming indeed. Needless to say, India faces a double jeopardy in attempting to industrialize quickly while confronting poverty and a growing population. India's environmental problems are complex and the choices available are difficult. Vision and "environmentally sound" foresight based on a holistic approach to problem-solving are required and entail bringing the secular, socioeconomic, cultural, religious, and traditional domains together.

This chapter examines India's ecospirituality against the context of dharmic ecology from four interrelated perspectives. These are: (1) *Vāsudeva sarvam,* the Supreme Being resides in all beings; (2) *Vāsudhaiva kuṭumbakam,* the family of Mother Earth; (3) *Sarva-*

bhūa-hitā, the welfare of all beings; and 4) Dharmic ecology as a strategy toward putting into practice the Hindu concept of ecocare.

VĀSUDEVA SARVAM, THE SUPREME BEING RESIDES IN ALL THINGS

Bhagavadgita Presence of God in Nature

One of the main postulations of the *Bhagavadgītā* is that the Supreme Being resides in all. Chapter 7, verse 19, states:

> Only after taking many births is a wise person able to comprehend the basic philosophy of the creation; which is: whatever is, is Vāsudeva. If anyone understands this fundamental, such a person is indeed a Mahatma.[2]

Later, in chapter 13, verse 13, the Lord Krsna says: "He resides in everywhere" *(sarvam āvṛtya tiṣṭhati).* As explained in the *Srīmad Bhāgavata Mahāpurāna* (book 2, discourse 2, verse 41), "ether, air, fire, water, earth, planets, all creatures, directions, trees and plants, rivers, and seas, they all are organs of God's body; remembering this, a devotee respects all species." Further, the definition of a pundit is one who treats a cow, an elephant, a dog, and an outcaste with the same respect shown to the Brahman endowed with great learning and yet humble *(Gītā* 5.18). Thus, the basic concept is: seeing the presence of God in all, and treating the creation with respect without harming and exploiting others *(vāsudevaḥ sarvam iti).* The *Srīmad Bhāgavata Mahāpurāṇa* (2.2.45) confirms this fundamental principle: a good devotee is the one who sees in all creation the presence of God *(sarva bhūteṣu yaḥ pasyed bhagvadbhāvāmātmanaḥ).*

Mahābhārata: Such veneration, respect, and acceptance of the presence of God in nature is required of Hindus in order to maintain and protect the natural harmonious relationship between human beings and nature.[3] In the *Mahābhārata,* it is claimed that all living beings have soul, and God resides as their inner soul: *Sarvabhūtātmbhūtastho* (Moksadharma Parva, chapter 182, verse 20). It also means that all this universe and every object in it has been created as an abode of the Supreme God; it is meant for the benefit of all; individual species must therefore learn to enjoy its benefits by existing as part of the system, in close relationship with other species and without permitting any one species to encroach upon the others' rights. This stipulation is later endorsed in the *Mahabharata,* where it is stated:

> The Father of all creatures, Lord God, made the sky. From sky he made water, and from water made fire *(agni)* and air *(vāyu)*. From fire and air, the earth *(pṛthivī)* came into existence. Actually, mountains are his bones, earth is the flesh, sea is the blood, and sky is his abdomen. The sun and moon are his eyes. The upper part of the sky is his head, the earth is his feet, and directions are his hands. *(Mahābhārata,* Moksadharma Parva, 182.14-19)

Thus, at least for the Hindus of the ancient period, God and nature were one and the same. While Prajapati (the "Lord of Creatures" of the Rgveda) is the creator of the sky, the earth, the oceans, and all the species, he is also their protector and eventual destroyer. He is the only Lord of Creation. Human beings have no special privilege or authority over other creatures; on the other hand, they do have more obligations and duties.[4]

Gītā: Creation and Annihilation upto Supreme will Hindu scriptures attest to the belief that the creation, maintenance, and annihilation of the cosmos is completely up to the Supreme Will. In the *Gītā,* Lord Krsna says to Arjuna: "Of all that is material and all that is spiritual in this world, know for certain that I am both its origin and dissolution" *(Gītā* 10.8). "By my will it is manifested again and again and by my will it is annihilated at the end" *(Gītā* 9.8). Furthermore, the Lord says: "I am the origin, the end, existence, and the maintainer (of all)" *(Gītā* 10.32). Thus, for Hindus, God and *prakṛti* (nature) are interrelated.

Reverence to all Species: Furthermore, the Hindu belief in the *cycle of birth and rebirth,* wherein a person may come back as an animal or a bird, means that Hindus are called to give other species not only respect, but reverence. This reverence finds expression in the doctrine of *ahimsā,* nonviolence (or non-injury) against other species and human beings alike. It should be noted that the doctrine of *ahiṃsā* presupposes the doctrines of *karma* and rebirth *(punarjanma).* The soul continues to take birth in different life-forms, such as birds, fish, animals, and humans. Based on this belief, there is a profound opposition in the Hindu religion (and in Buddhist and Jaina religions) to the institutionalized breeding and killing of animals, birds, and fish for human consumption. From the perspective of Hindu religion, the abuse and exploitation of nature for selfish gain is considered unjust and sacrilegious.

God Reincarnates in the Form of Animals and Humans: One of the central tenets of Hinduism is the doctrine of reincarnation, when the Supreme Being was himself incarnated in the forms of various species. The Lord says: 'This form is the source and indestructible seed of multifarious incarnations within the universe, and from the particle and portion of this form, different living entities, like demigods, animals, human beings and others, are created" *(Srīmad Bhāgavata Mahāpurāṇa* 1.3.5). Among the various incarnations of God are a fish, a tortoise, a boar, and a dwarf. His fifth incarnation was as a man-lion. As Rama, God was closely associated with monkeys, and, as Krsna, he was surrounded by cattle. These are some examples where different species are accorded reverence.

Almost all the Hindu scriptures place a strong emphasis on the notion that God's grace cannot be received by killing animals or harming other creatures. That is why not eating meat is considered both appropriate conduct and one's *dharma.* For example, as mentioned in the *Viṣnu Purāṇa:* "God, Kesava, is pleased with a person who does not harm or destroy other nonspeaking creatures or animals" *(Viṣnu Purāṇa* 3.8.15). Further, the pain a human being causes other living beings to suffer will eventually be suffered by that same person, either in this life or in a later rebirth.

Consequences of Killing Animals: It is through the transmigration of the soul that a link has been provided between the lowliest forms of life and human beings. In the *Manusmṛti,* the laws of Manu, a warning is given: 'A person who kills an animal for meat will die of a violent death as many times as there are hairs of that killed animal" *(Manusmṛti* 5.38). The *Yājñavalkyasmṛti* warns those who kill domesticated and protected animals of hellfire *(ghora naraka):* "The wicked person who kills animals which are protected has to live in hellfire for the days equal to the number of hairs on the body of that animal" *(Yājnavalkyasmṛti,* Acaradhyayah, verse 180). And, the *Narasiṃha Purāṇa* states that a person who roasts a bird for eating will surely be a sinner:

> O Wicked person! what is the use of you taking a bath in sacred rivers, doing pilgrimage, worshiping, and performing *yajnas* if you roast a bird for your meals.[5]

Yhe Grain Sacrifice: The *Mahābhārata* describes an event in which the *ṛṣis* and gods debated the merits of offering grain or the lamb (goat) as the sacrifice, *yajna*. The *ṛṣis* insisted that, according to the Vedas, the sacrificial material ought to be the grain only, and thus no animal should be killed for the purpose of *yajña:*

> The *ṛṣis* told the Gods that according to the Vedas and *srutis,* the sacrificial offering should be of grain. The term "Aj" does not mean animal or goat as you denote, the term means only grain or seed. Thus, an animal must not be sacrificed. Further, that which sanctions the killing of any animal cannot be a true Dharma of a moral people.[6]

Thus, it would seem that the practice of grain sacrifice may have started from that time.

Lord Siva's Habitat and Biodiversity

How to protect and conserve the biological diversity is exemplified by the family and habitat of the god Siva, his consort Pārvatî, and his two sons Kārttikeya and Ganesa. His habitat is Mount Kailāsa, with snowy peaks representing the cosmic heavens. The nascent moon on his forehead denotes tranquillity; the constant stream of Gangā's water from the interplaited lock of hair on his head indicates the purity and preeminence of water; Nandi, the bull, as his mount, represents livestock; serpents signify the presence of toxicity in nature; the lion used by his consort Pārvatî represents wildlife; the peacock, the mount of Kārttikeya, one of the most colorful birds, represents the avian species; and the mouse, the mount of Ganesa, represents pests. Thus, various forms of animate and inanimate life are represented in the household and habitat of Lord Siva. However, another important significance of the family of Lord Siva is the harmonious relationship between natural enemies. In Lord Siva's household, various natural enemies live in harmony with each other. The carnivorous lion's food is the vegetarian bull, the peacock is the enemy of the serpent, and the mouse is the serpent's food; nevertheless, all live together. Thus, when a devotee worships the family of Lord Siva, he or she observes this coexistence and is influenced by what in contemporary times might be seen as analogous to the concept of ecological harmony and respect for biological diversity.

All Activity has its Side Effects: Like the Churuing of the Nectar with its Side Effect of Poison

A story from Hindu scriptures illustrates this coexistence between good and evil. Cursed by the *mahārṣi* Durbhasa, the *devas* (demigods) were deprived of their divine vigour and strength. Soon, they were defeated by the *asuras* (demons) and dislodged from their heavenly abode. They then prayed to Lord Viṣṇu to seek his intervention. Lord Viṣṇu suggested that the only course open to them lay in securing the Nectar of Immortality, which would make them invincible. In order to obtain this nectar, they had to put every herb in the cosmic sea of milk and churn the sea by using the mountain of Mandarachal as a pestle and the snake king, Vāsuki, as the noose. To churn the sea, they needed the assistance of the demons to hold one end of the rope. The demons agreed to assist on the condition that the nectar received from the churning would be shared equally. From their churning, the most sought after nectar was obtained, along with many precious stones, wealth, and worldly riches. But, along with these priceless and rare items, a most venomous poison was produced. If that poison was not immediately disposed of, *sarvanāsa* (total annihilation) of the entire universe could result; however, no one. god or demon, was willing to touch this most fatal toxic waste. Finally, all went to Lord Siva for help in stopping the obliteration of the universe. Siva agreed to take care of the toxic waste by drinking it, and thus the impending disaster was averted.

Later, with the assistance of Lord Viṣṇu, the demigods were able to trick the demons out of their share of the nectar, so that only the gods became immortal. This story instructs us that the consequences of an activity can be both beneficial and disastrous. Both nectar and poison result from the same activity, and one cannot be acquired without the other. In contemporary terms, an ecological balance has to be maintained between the nectar of riches and the side effects (poisons) of technology and industrialization. As we live on the same planet, we suffer or benefit together.

Thus, we see that every entity and living organism is part of one large extended family system *(kutumba)* presided over by the eternal Mother Earth, Devî Vasundharā. The development of humanity from creation until now has taken place nowhere else but on Earth. Our relationship with Earth, from birth to death, is like that of children and their mother. The mother, in this case Earth, not only bears her children but also is the main source of fulfillment of their unending desires. It is Earth which provides energy for the sustenance of all species. And, just as one ought not insult, exploit, or violate one's mother, but be kind and respectful to her, so should one behave toward Mother Earth. We are enjoined to take care of God's creation by engaging in ecostewardship.

VASUDHAIVA KUṬUMBAKAM, THE FAMILY OF MOTHER EARTH

Atharva Veda in Praise of Mother Earth

In the *Atharva Veda,* an entire hymn, the Pṛthivi Sūkta, has been devoted to praise of Mother Earth. The hymn's sixty-three verses integrate many of the thoughts of Hindu seers concerning the concept of nature, the dependence of human beings on Earth, and the resultant respect required.[7] These verses are addressed to Devî Vasundharā, Mother Earth. Earth is seen as the abode of a family of all beings (humans and others alike). *Vasudhā* means "this earth," while *kuṭumba* means "extended family"—including human beings, animals, and all living beings. Every entity and organism is a part of one large extended family system presided over by the eternal Mother Earth. It is she who supports us with her abundant endowments and riches; it is she who nourishes us; it is she who provides us with a sustainable environment; and it is she who, when angered by the misdeeds of her children, punishes them with disasters:

> O Mother Earth! Sacred are thy hills, snowy mountains, and deep forests. Be kind to us and bestow upon us happiness. May you be fertile, arable, and nourisher of all. May you continue supporting people of all races and nations. May you protect us from your anger (natural disasters). And may no one exploit and subjugate your children."

The hymn's composer, the Atharva *ṛṣi,* envisions Mother Earth in her pristine nature, not denuded of her natural cover. The Pṛthivî Sūkta also exemplifies the relevance of environmental sustenance, agriculture, and biodiversity to human beings.[9] The three main segments of our physical environment—water, air, and soil—are highlighted and their usefulness detailed. The various water resources, such as seas, rivers, and waterfalls, flow on Earth *(Atharva Veda* 12.3).

All Elements of Nature are Equal

Verse 2 of this hymn depicts the majesty of mountains and rivers, the beauty of small springs, and the invaluable tiny medicinal plants which save the lives of humans. But all these elements are treated equally by Mother Earth, who does not discriminate between the high and mighty *(uddhataḥ)*, such as mountains and oceans, and the low *(prayataḥ)*. For Mother Earth, all species are of equal value; she has not accorded any one species special authority over other species. Thus, humans do not have the authority to destroy the environment at the expense of others, including their own species, in nature.

All Attributes of the Earth Belong to Everyone

The Pṛthivī Sūkta maintains that attributes of the earth (such as its firmness, purity, and fertility) are for everyone, and that no one group or nation has special authority over it. That is why the welfare of all and hatred toward none constitute the core values for which people on this planet ought to strive (verse 18). For example, there is a prayer for the preservation of the original fragrance of the earth (verses 23 and 25) so that its natural legacy is sustained for future generations. There is also a prayer which says that even when people dig the earth, either for agricultural purposes or for extracting minerals, they should do so in such a way that her vitals are not hurt and that no serious damage is done to her body and appearance (verse 35).

Unity of All Races

The Pṛthivī Sūkta enunciates the unity of all races and among all beliefs; further religious, linguistic, and cultural harmony is urged, with a prayer that Mother Earth bestow upon all the people living in any part of the world the same prosperity for which the *ṛṣi* Atharva of India has pleaded:

> Mother Earth, where people belong to different races, follow separate faiths and religions and speak numerous languages, cares for them in many ways. May that Mother Earth, like a Cosmic Cow, give us the thousandfold prosperity without any hesitation, without being outraged by our destructive actions.[10]

In verse 63 of this hymn, a prayer is offered to Mother Earth and her blessings are sought for all:

> O, our Mother Earth! May we possess the intellect and wisdom which enable us to speak in concord with heavenly beings, may we continue to enjoy your blessing of hidden riches, glory, and realization of material and spiritual well-beings.[11]

In summary, it can be said that the Pṛthivī Sūkta, whose sixty-three verses have been dedicated to Mother Earth, is the foremost ancient spiritual text from India, enjoining all human beings to protect, preserve, and care for the environment. This is beautifully illustrated in verse 16, which says that it is up to us, the progeny of Mother Earth, to live in peace and harmony with all others:

> O Mother Earth! You are the world for us and we are your children; let us speak in one accord, let us come together so that we live in peace and harmony, and let us be cordial and gracious in our relationship with other human beings.[12]

These sentiments denote the deep bond between the earth and human beings and exemplify the true relationship between the earth and all living beings, as well as between humans and other forms of life. The Sūkta guides us to behave in an appropriate manner toward nature and defines our duty toward the environment.

Sarva Bhūta Hitā, the Common Good of All Beings

How is the welfare of all beings related to the Hindu view of life? As mentioned earlier, the prerequisite for understanding this concept in Hindu thinking is to accept the view that Brahman (the Supreme Being) is the ultimate source-and cause of the universal common good, not only of humans but of all beings in creation. That common good, for Hindus, is the concept of *sarva-bhūta-hitā,* the highest ethical standard that Hindus ought to apply, according to their *dharma.* Further, the Hindu tradition requires that a common good (such as protection of the environment, welfare of the poor and needy, or the well-being of other living beings) takes precedence over a private good (including individual material and personal well-being).

Under such a system, a dharmic citizen should act for *sarva-hitā:* enhancing the common good of all together. In other words, the term "common good" can be related to the concept of *sarva-kalyāṇkarī-karma,* which denotes a deed resulting in the common good of all. This also relates to the concept of "caring for others," meaning a deed *(karma),* which results in universal welfare based on mutual cooperation and respect. To reiterate, the question of *sarva-bhūta-hitā* care and taking care of the others or serving others, is entirely intertwined with the concept of dharmic ecology. It is an obligation that human beings owe, not only to each other, but also to all of nature and the entire cosmos. The requisite duties and mode of conduct to perform *sarva-bhūtahitā,* and to protect and sustain the common good, has been provided in Hindu scriptures. For example, this advice is given by Lord Kṛṣṇa in the *Gītā:*

> One ought to understand what is duty, and what is forbidden in the commands laid down by the scriptures *[sāstras].* Knowing such rules and regulations, one should behave as ordained by scriptures.[13]

Lord Krsna later says:

> O Partha! that understanding by which one knows what ought to be done and what ought not to be done; what is to be feared and what is not, what is obligatory and what is permitted, leads to the righteous path *[Sattvika Pṛavrtti].*[14]

That righteous path in the Hindu religion is called *dharma.*

Dharma

Dharma is one of the most intractable and unyielding terms in Hindu, Buddhist, and Jaina religions and philosophies. Instead of discussing the root and theological or philosophical definitions of the term, the author of the *Mahābhārata* goes directly to the common usage of the term:

> Dharma exists for the general welfare *(abhyudaya)* of all living beings; hence, that by which the *welfare* of all living creatures IS sustained, that for sure is *Dharma."*[15]

As a set of duties: Thus, *dharma* can be considered an ethos, a set of duties, that holds the social and moral fabric together by maintaining order in society, building individual and group character, and giving rise to harmony and understanding in our relationships with all of God's creation. Duty toward humanity and God's creation is an integral part of Hindu ecology and *dharma.* While all other species conduct themselves according to the *dharma* of their kind, only human beings, because of free will, think that they are very powerful and act in an adharmic manner. Such acts are to be avoided, as *ṛṣi* Markandeya says in the *Mahābhārata* during a conversation with the Pandavas:

> O king, all creatures act according to the laws of their specific species as laid down by the Creator. Therefore, none should act unrighteously *(adharma),* thinking, "It is I who is powerful."[16]

Universe as Extended Family: Dharma requires that one consider the entire universe an extended family, with all living beings in this universe members of the same household. This is also known as the concept of *vasudhaiv kuṭumbakam,* discussed above. Only by considering the entire universe as a part of one's extended family can one develop the necessary maturity and respect for all other living beings. The welfare and caring of all *(sarva-kalyānkarī-hitā)* is realized through the golden thread of spiritual understanding and cooperation.

Helps to master our Bases instincts's: Dharma can help us master our baser characteristics, such as our greed and our exploitation, abuse, mistreatment, and defilement of nature. Before we can hope to change the exploitative tendencies of society, it is absolutely essential that we discipline our own inner thoughts. This is where the role of *dharma* comes into play. It is important to appreciate that the concept of *dharma* can be used in any culture (although the term has·become synonymous with the practices and rituals of Hinduism, Buddhism, and Jainism). *Dharma* in its pure form can be the mechanism that creates respect for nature, since it transcends institutional structures, bureaucratic impediments, and rituals associated with organized religions; it enables people to center their values upon the notion that there is a cosmic ordinance and a natural or divine law that must be maintained.

Dharma thereby provides a code of conduct as well as a vision. It serves both as a model and an operative strategy for the transformation of human character. And, if the goal of transformation is to achieve an environmentally conscious and sustainable world, then *dharma's* precept that reward after death can be attained through actions in this world may provide the incentive for humanity to seek peace with nature.[17] The manifestation of *dharma* necessitates, however, the acceptance of the concept of *karma.*

Karma and the Environment

Action-Reaction Chain: The term *karma* comes from the root *kr,* meaning "to do," and thus has a general connotation of "action," but in its broadest sense it applies also to the effects of such actions. People often confuse the law of *karma* with the law of destiny. This misunderstanding needs to be rectified because an appropriate understanding is essential to appreciate the use of this precept in Hindu and Buddhist ways of life. A brief definition of the law of *karma* is that each act, wilfully performed, leaves a consequence in its wake. These consequences, also called *karma-phala* (fruits, or effects, of action), will always be with us, although their impact may not be felt immediately.

Thus, the law related to *karma* tells us that every action performed creates its own chain of reactions and events, some of which are immediately visible, while others take time to surface.

Environmental pollution is but one example of the *karma* of those people who thought that they could continue polluting the environment without realizing the consequences of their actions for future generations. For example, those who buried the toxic waste in Love Canal (near Niagara Falls, in New York State) thought that by concealing their actions, the problem would go away; instead it surfaced a few years later. Every action creates its own reaction. What is important to know is that a right action, that is a dharmic action, generates beneficial results, while an adharmic action results in harmful effects.

It is not always easy to foresee the consequences of one's actions, but one should be ready either to overcome obstacles that arise or suffer the repercussions of one's actions. Once *karma* has started, it continues without a break; even though a person may be dead, his or her *karma* survives in the form of a memory and carries over into the next life. This is stated in the *Mahābhārata:*

> An action, which has been committed by a human-being in this life, follows him again and again (whether he wishes it or not).[18]

Facing the Consequences of Actions: Furthermore, it is stated in the *Brahmavaivarta Purāṇa* that whatever action, good or bad, is knowingly performed by a person, he or she must face its consequences.[19] Sometimes karmic justice is indecipherable to individuals, when an individual's family and later descendants are forced to pay for the past crimes and mistakes of that person. Bhisma acknowledges this to King Yudhisthira in the *Mahābhārata:*

> O king, although a particular person may not be seen suffering the results of his evil actions, yet his children and grandchildren as well as great-grandchildren will have to suffer them.[20]

Such suffering may continue to visit humanity unless we realize that the destruction we are inflicting on our natural surroundings will result in dire consequences for current and future generations. Only if we recognize and act on this philosophy of life will people start paying due respect to nature and taking active responsibility for the care of the environment. Understanding this is the key to the point being made here, and it draws on the concept that people living in any part of the world are our brothers and sisters. All of our actions are interrelated with and interconnected to what eventually happens in this world. Although we may not face the consequences individually, someone is going to be burdened by or benefit from our actions.

Dharma an Karma: It is in this context that the concepts of *dharma* and *karma* become meaningful. Once our *dharma* and *karma* to the environment are appropriately understood, their precepts recognized, and their relevance to environmental protection and conservation accepted, then a common strategy for ecospirituality and stewardship can be developed. Such a strategy will depend much upon how different people together

1. perceive a common future for society;
2. act both individually and 'as a group toward that end; and
3. realize that each individual has a moral obligation to support his society's goal, since his acts will have repercussions on the future of society and on his own destiny.

Dharmic Ecology in Action

The effectiveness of any religion in protecting the environment depends upon how much faith its believers have in its precepts and injunctions. Its value also depends upon how those precepts are transmitted and adapted in everyday social interactions. In the case of the Hindu religion, some of its precepts became ingrained in the daily life and social institutions of a certain segment of the population. Two such examples illustrate this point. The nation would do well in cultivating its traditional conservation practices such as there preserved by the Bishnois.

The Bishnois, Defenders of the Environment

The Bishnois, a small community in the state of Rajasthan, practice environmental conservation as a part of their daily religious duty. They believe that cutting a tree or killing an animal or bird is sacrilege. Their religion, an offshoot of Hinduism, was founded by Guru Maharaj Jambaji, who was born in 1451 C.E. in the Marwar area. When he was young, he witnessed how, during a severe drought, people cut down trees to feed animals; when the drought continued, nothing was left to feed the animals, which resulted in their deaths. Jambaji thought that if trees were protected, animal life would be sustained, and his community would survive. So he formulated twenty-nine injunctions. Principal among them was a ban on the cutting of any green tree and killing of any animal or bird. His community accepted these injunctions. Over time, their geographic area developed into a lush dense forest with substantial trees.

About three hundred years later, when the king of Jodhpur wanted to build a new palace, he sent his soldiers to the Bishnoi area to secure timber for it. Villagers protested, and when soldiers would not pay any attention to the protest, the Bishnois, led by a woman, encircled the trees in order to protect them with their bodies. The soldiers had orders to bring timber, so they began killing the villagers. As the soldiers continued, more and more of the Bishnois came forward to honor the religious injunction of their guru. Finally, when the king heard about this human sacrifice, he ordered his soldiers back to Jodhpur and gave the Bishnois state protection for their beliefs. Even today, the Bishnoi community continues to protect trees and animals in their area with the same zeal. Their dedication became the inspiration for the Chipko movement of 1973.

The Chipko Movement

In March 1973, in the town of Gopeshwar in Chamoli district, Uttar Pradesh, villagers formed a human chain and encircled earmarked trees to keep them from being felled for a nearby factory producing sports equipment. The same situation later occurred in another village, when forest contractors wanted to cut trees under license from the Government Department of Forests. Again, in 1974, women from the village of Reni, near Joshimath in the Himalayas, protested logging by hugging trees and forced the contractors to leave. Since then, the Chipko Andolan (movement) has continued to grow from a grassroots ecodevelopment movement.[21] The genesis of the Chipko movement has its background not only in religious belief, but also in ecological or economic concerns. Villagers have noted how industrial and commercial demands have denuded their forests, how they cannot sustain their livelihood in a deforested area, and how floods continually play havoc with their small agricultural communities.

Women, specifically, have seen how men tend not to mind destroying nature in order to get money, while they themselves have to walk miles in search of firewood and fodder or other suitable grazing. In a sense, the Chipko movement is a feminist movement to protect nature from the greed of men. In the Himalayan areas, the pivot of the family is the woman. It is the woman who worries most about nature and its conservation in order that its resources are available for her family's sustenance. On the other hand, men often go away to distant places in search of jobs, leaving the women, children, and elders behind.

These two examples are illustrative of the practical impact of Hinduism on environmental conservation, or dharmic ecology in action. The Bishnoi and Chipko experiences demonstrate that when appeals to secular norms fail, one can draw on cultural and religious sources for environmental conservation.

Contribution of Hindu Religion in Environmental Preservation

There is no doubt that Hindu religion and culture, in ancient and medieval times, has provided a system of moral guidelines for environmental preservation and conservation. Environmental ethics, as propounded by the ancient Hindu scriptures and seers, was practiced not only by common persons, but by rulers and kings. They observed these fundamentals, sometimes as religious duties, often as rules of administration or obligations for law and order, but always as principles properly entwined with the Hindu way of life. That way of life did enable Hindus as well as other religious groups residing in India to use natural resources but to have no divine powers of control and dominion over nature and its elements. The Hindu belief that so long as Mother Earth is able to sustain magnificent mountains, lush forests, streams and rivers, and related endowments, she will be able to nourish all, particularly the human race and its progeny. This is expressed in the following prayer to the goddess Durga:

> So long as the earth is able to maintain mountains, forests, trees, etc., until then the human race and its progeny will be able to survive.[22]

If such has been the tradition, philosophy, and ideology of Hinduism, what then are the reasons behind the present environmental crisis facing India? As we have seen, Hindu ethical beliefs and religious values do influence people's behaviour toward others, including our relationship with all creatures and plant life.

Influence of Destructive Forces: If, for some reason, those noble values become displaced by other beliefs that are either thrust upon the society or transplanted from another culture through invasion, then the faith of the masses in the earlier cultural tradition is shaken. As appropriate answers and leadership are not provided by the religious leaders and priests, the masses become ritualistic, caste-ridden, and inward-looking. However, besides the influence of alien cultures and values, what has really damaged India's environment are the forces of materialism, consumerism, individualism, and corporate greed, the blind race to industrialize the nation immediately after achieving independence, and the capriciousness and corruption among forest contractors and ineffective enforcement by forest officials.[23] All these acted against the maintenance, or resurgence, of respect for nature in India. Under such circumstances, religious values that had acted as sanctions against environmental destruction were sidelined as insidious forces worked to inhibit the transmission of ancient values that encouraged respect and due regard for God's creation.

Putting Dharmic Ecology into Practice

How can those ancient values and wisdom be transmitted into practice? Can there be a practical dharmic ecology? It is not sufficient to examine and extol the ancient wisdom of Hindu seers, to dwell on the Vedic heritage, and then simply hope that a self-correcting process for environmental problems will set in. What is more important is how to put into practice that ecocare vision and make it relevant to modern times. I would propose the following strategy. The Hindu religion and its followers should become effective advocates and practitioners of the concept of ecocare and dharmic ecology, rather than staying on the sidelines.

Suggestions: Hindu religious leaders should:

1. take the initiative and help secular institutions by providing timely and appropriate advice to encourage greater integration of ecocare heritage into educational curriculam;
2. strengthen the capability of secular institutions to meet their goals of sustainable development and environmental conservation;
3. promote the concept of *sarva-bhūta-hite ratāh* (to serve all beings equally);
4. take the lead in promoting the concept of *vasudhaiv*

kuṭumbakam, the family of Mother Earth, and the obligation of humanity to accept a world of material limits;

5. protect and restore places of ecological, cultural, aesthetic, and spiritual significance; and
6. build partnerships across social, economic, political, and environmental sectors, including dialogue with other religions and spiritual traditions.[24]

The choice before the Hindu religion (as well as before all other religions) is either to care for the environment or be a silent participant in the destruction of planetary resources. Partnership with secular institutions must be forged and cooperation fostered at local, regional, national, and international levels. An environmental and sustainable development strategy, based on the lines suggested above, could offer a way of bridging the gap and making the essential link between secular, scientific, and spiritual forces.

An environmental stewardship that draws upon the Hindu concept of *dharma* and *karma* to the environment can provide new ways of valuing and acting. It can promote policies for sustainable development and introduce environmental protection initiatives. *Dharma,* if globally manifested, will provide the values necessary for an environmentally caring world and will not advance economic growth at the cost of greed, poverty, inequality, and environmental degradation. There is an urgent need to instill in all people a respect for nature and to strengthen decision-making processes in favor of environmental protection. This must be the focal point for a new global consciousness in an environmentally caring world. Can the Hindu religion take up this challenge and act upon it as an integral part of its conscious strategy and vision for a sustainable future?

Therefore, a new universal consciousness must be developed that believes in at least two dictums: "what we sow is what we reap" and "everything is connected to everything else"; and our inherent *dharma,* or obligation, is toward the environment. These two concepts are intertwined with a third: *sarva-bhūta-hite ratāh,* serve all beings equally. The Hindu religion, like other religions and spiritual traditions, has the capacity to move the individual toward the divine because of its belief in divinity in nature; thus, it is imperative that such an inherent capacity is strengthened to its ultimate end. To achieve this, we need a new paradigm of thought, a dharmic ecology, perhaps. By developing such a paradigm, drawing upon the concept of *dharma* and *karma,* and based on the notions of *vasudeva sarvam, vasudhaiv kuṭumbakam,* and *sarva-bhūta-hitā,* we may be able not only to sustain the present generation, but also to leave a healthy legacy for future generations.

NOTES

1. O.P. Dwivedi, *India's Environmental Policies, Programmes and Stewardship* (London: Macmillan, 1997), 21.
2. Bahūnāṃ janmanām ante jñanvān māṃ prapadyate,
   Vāsudevaḥ sarvam iti sa mahātmā sudurlabhaḥ.
   (Bhagavadgītā 7.19) All translations are my own.
3. O.P. Dwivedi, "Vedic Heritage for Environmental Stewardship," *Worldviews: Environment. Culture, and Religion* 1, no. 1 (April 1997): 25-36.
4. O.P. Dwivedi, B.N. Tiwari, and R.N. Tripathi, "Hindu Concept of Ecology and the Environmental Crisis," *Indian Journal of Public Administration* 30, no. 4 (January-March 1984): 33-67. We first presented this paper at the annual conference of the Canadian Asian Studies Association, University of British Columbia, Vancouver, 4 June 1983. When it appeared in the *Indian Journal of Public Administration,* it may have been the first such research paper to be published.
5. *Pakṣi dagdhaḥ sudurbudhhe pāpātman sāmprataṃ vṛthā.*
   Vṛthā snānam vṛthā tirthaṃ vṛthā japtaṃ vṛthā hutaṃ.
   (Narasiṃha Purāṇa, 13.44)
6. *Bijaiyarjñesu yaṣtvyamiti vai vadikī sruti*
   Aj sanjñani bijani cchāgan no hantumarhatha
   Naiṣa dharmaḥ satām devā yatra vadhyeta vai pasuḥ
   Idam krtayugaṃ sreṣthaṃ kathaṃ vadhyeta vai pasuḥ.
   (Mahābhārata. Santiparva, Moksadharma, 337.4-5)
7. O.P. Dwivedi. *Vasudhaiv Kutumbakam: A Commentary on Atharvediya Prithivi Sukta,* 2d ed. (Jaipur: Institute for Research and Advanced Studies. 1998).
8. *Giryaste parvatā hima vanto raṇyaṃ te prthivī syȯnamastu̥*
   Babhrum kṛuṣhnaṃ rohīṇīm vishvarūpāṃ dhruvaṃ bhūmiṃ pṛithivi mindraguptāṃ
   Ajītohato akṣhatoadhyatḥaṃ prithivīmaham.
   (Atharva Veda, Kanda 12, hymn 1. verse 11)
9. Dwivedi, *Vasudhaiv Kutumbakam.*
10. *Janaṃ bibhratī bahudhā vivācasam nāndharmāṇaṃ pṛithivi yathaukasam Sahastraṃ dhārāḥ dravinasya me duhāṃ dhruveva dhenurana pasphurantī. (Atharva Veda,* Kanda 12, hymn 1, verse 45)

11. *Bhūme mātarni dhehi bhadrayā supratisthitam*
    Samvidana divā kave shriyā mā dhehi bhūtyām.
    (Atharva Veda, Kanda 12, hymn 1, verse 63)
12. *Tā naḥ prajāḥ saṃ duhatāṃ samagrā vacho madhu pṛithivi dhehi mahyam. (Atharva Veda,* Kanda 12, hymn 1, verse 16)
13. *Tasmāc chāstram pramāṇaṃ te kāryākāryavyavasthitau*
    Jñatvā shāstra vidhānoktaṃ karma kartum ihārhasi.
    (Gītā 16.24)
14. *Pravṛttiṃ ca nivṛttim ca kāryākārye bhayābhaye*
    Bandhaṃ mokṣaṃ ca yā vetti buddhiḥ sā Pārtha sāttvikī.
    (Gītā 18.30)
15. *Prabhāvarthaya bhūtānām dharma pravacanaṃ kṛtam*
    Yah syāt prabhav saṁyuktam sa dharma iti niścayaḥ.
    (Mahābhārata, Shanti Parva, chapter 109, verse 10)
16. *Sarvāni bhūtāni Narendra paśya tathā yathāvad vihitaṃ vidhātra*
    Svayonitaḥ karmā sadā caranti neśe balasyeti cared dharmaṃ.
    (Mahābhārata, Vanaparva, chapter 25, verse 16)
17. O.P. Dwivedi, "Our Karma and Dharma to the Environment," in *Environmental Stewardship: History, Theory, and Practice,* ed. Mary Ann Beavis, 59-74 (Winnipeg: Institute of Urban Studies, University of Winnipeg, 1994).
18. *Yesām ye yāni karmāṇi prak sṛiṣtyam pratipedire*
    Tāny eva pratipādyante srigyamānāḥ punaḥ punaḥ.
    (Mahābhārata, Shanti Parva, chapter 232, verse 16)
19. *Na Bhuktam Kṣīyate Karma Kalpa koṭiṣtairapi*
    Avaśyamaiva bhoktavyam krtam karma śubha ā subhaṃ.
    (Brahmavaivarta Parāṇa, Prakṛti. 37.16)
20. *Pāpaṃ karma kṛtam kiṃcid yadi tasmin na dṛśyate*
    Nṛpate tasya putreṣu pautreṣu api ca naptriṣu.
    (Mahābhārata, Shanti Parva, chapter 139, verse 22)
21. Chandi Prasad Bhatt, "Chipko Movement: The Hug That Saves," in *The Hindu Survey of the Environment. 1991* (Madras: The Hindu, National Press, 1991), 17.
22. *Yāvadbhūmaṇḍalaṃ dhatte sāsailvavana kānanam,*
    Tāvat tiṣṭhati mediriyaṃ śāntātiḥ putra-pautrikī.
    (Durgā Saptaśati. Devi kavacham, verse 54)
23. Ashish Kothari, "Forest Bill: Old Wine in a New Bottle," in *The Hindu Survey of the Environment, 1995* (Madras: The Hindu. National Press, 1995). 51-54.
24. Dwivedi, *India's Environmental Policies, Programmes and Stewardship.*

16

Honouring Our Planet

The planet, our mother, grandmother earth, is physical and therefore a spiritual, mental, and emotional being. Planets are alive, as are all their byproducts or expressions, such as animals, vegetables, minerals, and climatic and meteorological phenomena. Our physicality—which always and everywhere includes our spirituality, mentality, emotionality, social institutions, and processes—is a microform of all physicality. Each of us reflect, in our attitudes toward our body and the bodies of other planetary creatures and plants, our inner attitude toward the planet. And, as we believe, so we act. A society that believes that the body is somehow diseased, painful, sinful, or wrong, a people that spends its time trying to deny the body's needs, aims, goals, and processes—whether these be called health or disease—is going to misunderstand the nature of its existence and of the planet's and is going to create social institutions out of those body-denying attitudes that wreak destruction not only on human, plant, and other creaturely bodies but on the body of the earth herself.

Believing that our mother, the beloved earth, is inert matter is destructive to yourself. (There's little you can do to her, believe it or not.) Such beliefs point to a dangerously diseased physicality.

Disturbing the Balance of Our Planet

Being good, holy, and/or politically responsible means being able to accept whatever life brings—and that includes just about everything you usually think of as unacceptable, like disease, death, and violence. Walking in balance, in harmony, and in a sacred manner requires staying in your body, accepting its discomforts, decayings, witherings, and blossomings and respecting them. Your body is also a planet, replete with creatures that live in and on it. Walking in balance requires knowing that living and dying do not mean cheating her of your flesh, your pain, your joy, your sensuality, your desires, your frustrations, your unmet and met needs, your emotions, your life. In the end you can't cheat her successfully, but in the attempt to do so, you can do great harm to the delicate and subtle balance of the vital processes of planetary being.

A society based on body hate destroys itself and causes harm to all of grandmother's grandchildren.

In the United States, where milk and honey cost little enough, where private serenity is prized above all things by the wealthy, privileged, and well washed, where tension, intensity, passion, and the concomitant loss of self-possession are detested, the idea that your attitudes and behaviors vis-a-vis your body are your politics and your spirituality may seem strange. Moreover, on suggesting that passion—whether it be emotional, muscular, sexual, or intellectual—is spirituality, it may seem even stranger. In the United States of the privileged, going to ashrams and centers to meditate on how to be in one's immediate experience, on how to be successful at serenity when the entire planet is overwrought, tense, far indeed from serene, the idea that connected spirituality consists in accepting overwroughtness, tension, and violence, may seem not only strange but downright dangerous.

The patriarchs have long taught the Western peoples that violence is sin, that tension is the opposite of spiritual life, that the overwrought are denied enlightenment. But we must remember that those who preached and taught serenity and peacefulness were teaching the oppressed how to act—docile slaves who deeply accept their place and do not recognize that in their anguish lies also their redemption, their liberation, are not likely to disturb the tranquillity of the ruling class.

Tranquility: Members of the ruling class are, of course, utterly tranquil. Why not.' As long as those upon whose labor and pain their serenity rests don't upset the apple cart, as long as they can make the rules for human behavior—in its inner as well as its outer dimensions—they can be tranquil indeed and can focus their attention on reaching nirvanic bliss, transcendence, or divine peace and love. And yet, the time for tranquillity, if there ever was time for it, is not now. Now we have only to look, to listen, to our beloved planet to see that tranquillity is not the best word to describe her condition. Her volcanic passions, her hurricane storms of temper, her tremblings and shakings, her thrashings and lashings indicate that something other than serenity is going on. And after careful consideration, it must occur to the sensitive observer that congruence with self, which must be congruence with spirit, which must therefore be congruence with the planet, requires something more active than serenity, tranquillity, or inner peace.

Emergence as Sacred Planet

Our planet, my beloved, is in crisis; this, of course, we all know. We, many of us, think that her crisis is caused by men, or white people, or capitalism, or industrialism, or loss of spiritual vision, or social turmoil, or war, or psychic disease. For the most part, we do nor recognize that the reason for her stare is that she is entering upon a great initiation—she is becoming someone else.

Our planet, is gone coyote, *heyoka,* and it is our great honor to attend her passage rites. She is giving birth to her new consciousness of herself and her relationship to the other vast intelligences, other holy beings in her universe. Her travail is not easy, and it occasions her intensity, her conflict, her turmoil—the turmoil, conflict, and intensity that human and other creaturely life mirror. And as she moves, growing and learning ever closer to the sacred moment of her realization, her turmoil, intensity, agony, and conflict increase. We are each and all a part of her, an expression of her essential being. We are each a small fragment that is nor the whole but that, perforce, reflects in our inner self, our outer behavior, our expressions and relationships and institutions, her self, her behaviors, her expressions and relationships, her forms and structures.

We humans and our relatives the other creatures are integral expressions of her thought and being We are not her, but we take our being from her, and in her being we have being, as in her life we have life. As she is, so are we. In this time of her emergence as one of the sacred planets in the grandmother galaxy, we necessarily experience, each of us in our own specific way, our share or form of her experience, her form. As the initiation nears completion we are caught in the throes of her wailings and contractions, her muscular, circulatory, and neurologic destabilization. We should recognize that her longing for the culmination of the initiatory process is at present nearly as intense as her longing to remain as she was before the initiation ceremony began, and our longing for a new world that the completion of the great ceremony will bring, almost as great as our longing to remain in the systems familiar to us for a very long time, correspond.

Her longing for completion is great, as is ours; our longing to remain as we have been, our fear that we will not survive the transition, that we will fail to enter the new age, our terror at ourselves becoming transformed, mutated, unrecognizable to ourselves and all we have known correspond to her longing to remain as she has been, her fear that she will fail the tests as they arise for her, her terror at becoming new, unrecognizable to herself and to all she has known.

Members of Our Planet

What can we do in times such as these? We can rejoice that she will soon be counted among the blessed. That we, her feathers, talons, beak, eyes, have come crying and singing, lamenting and laughing, to this vast climacteric.

This includes all womankind, all mankind. And more. It also includes all our relatives, the four-leggeds, the wingeds, the crawlers; of the plants and seasons, the winds, thunders, and rains, the rivers, lakes, and streams, the pebbles, rocks, and mountains, the spirits, the holy people, and the gods and goddesses—of all the intelligences, all the beings. Including even the tiniest, those no one can see; and of the vastest, the planets and stars. Together you and I and they and she are moving with increasing rapidity and under ever increasing pressure toward *transformation*.

Now, now is the time when mother becomes grandmother, when daughter becomes mother, when the living dead are released from entombment, when the dead live again and walk once again in her ways. Together we all can rejoice, take up the tasks of attending, take up the joy of giving birth and of being born, of transforming in recognition of the awfulness of what is entailed, in recognition of what it is we together can and must and will do. Thus, now this is the time of her initiation, of her new birth. It could also be the time of mutation, for transformation means to change form; This could also be the climacteric, when the beloved planet goes through menopause and takes her place among the wise women planets that dance among the stars.

Celebration Time for Our Planet

At a time such as this, what indeed can we do.' We can sing *Heya-*

hey in honoring all that has come to pass, all that is passing. Sing, honoring, *Heya-hey* to all the beings gathering on all the planes to witness this great event. From every quadrant of the universe they are coming. They are standing gathered around, waiting for the emergence, the piercing moment when she is counted among those who are counted among the wise. We can sing *Heya-hey* to the familiar and the estranged, to the recognized and the disowned, to each shrub and tree, to each flower and vine, to each pebble and stone, to each mountain and hill. We can sing *Heya-hey* honoring the stars and the clouds, the winds and the rains, the seasons and the temperature. We can think with our hearts, as the old ones do, and put our brains and muscles in the service of the heart, our mother and grandmother earth, who is coming into being in another way. We can sing *Heya-hey,* honoring.

What can we do, rejoicing and honoring, to show our respect? We can heal. We can cherish our bodies and honor them, sing *Heya-hey* to our flesh. We can cherish our being—our petulances and rages, our anguishes and griefs, our disabilities and strengths, our desires and passions, our pleasures and delights. We can, willingly and recognizing the fullness of her abundance, which includes scarcity and muchness, enter inside ourselves to seek and find her, who is our own dear body, our own dear flesh. For the body is not the dwelling place of the spirit—it is the spirit. It is not a tomb, it is life itself. And even as it withers and dies, it is born; even as it is renewed and reborn, it dies.

Frequency of Refusal of Life Forces in and Around Us

Think: How many times each day do you habitually deny and deprive her in your flesh, in your physicality? How often do you willfully prevent her from moving or resting, from eating or drinking what she requests, from eliminating wastes or taking breath? How many times do you order your body to produce enzymes and hormones to further your social image, your "identity," your emotional comfort, regardless of your actual situation and hers? How many of her gifts do you spurn, how much of her abundance do you deny? How often do you interpret disease as wrong, suffering as abnormal, physical imperatives as troublesome, cravings as failures, deprivation and denial of appetite as the right thing to do? In how many ways do you refuse to experience your vulnerability, your frailty, your mortality? How often do you refuse these expressions of the life force of the mother in your lovers, your friends, your society? How often do you find yourself interpreting sickness, weakness, aging, fatness, physical differences as pitiful, contemptible, avoidable, a violation of social norm and spiritual accomplishment? How much of your life is devoted to avoiding any/or all of these? How much of her life is devoted to avoiding any and all of these?

Healing the Self

The mortal body is a tree; it is holy in whatever condition; it is truth and myth because it has so many potential conditions; because of its possibilities, it is sacred and profane; most of all, it is your most precious talisman, your own connection to her. Healing the self means honoring and recognizing the body, accepting rather than denying all the turmoil its existence brings, welcoming the woes and anguish flesh is subject to, cherishing its multitudinous forms and seasons, its unfailing ability to know and be, to grow and wither, to live and die, to mutate, to change. Healing the self means commiting ourselves to a wholehearted willingness to be what and how we are—beings frail and fragile, strong and passionate, neurotic and balanced, diseased and whole, partial and complete, stingy and generous, safe and dangerous, twisted and straight, storm-tossed and quiescent, bound and free.

What can we do to be politically useful, spiritually mature attendants in this great transformation we are privileged to participate in? Find out by asking as many trees as you meet how to be a tree. Our mother, in her form known as Sophia, was long ago said to be a tree, the great tree of life: Listen to what they wrote down from the song she gave them:

> I have grown tall as a cedar on Lebanon,
> as a cypress on Mount Hermon;
> I have grown tall as a palm in Engedi,
> as the rose bushes of Jericho;
> as a fine olive on the plain,
> as a plane tree I have grown tall.
> I have exhaled perfume like cinnamon and acacia;
> I have breathed out a scent like choice myrrh,
> like galbanum, onzcha and stacte,
> like the smoke of incense in the tabernacle.
> I have spread my branches like a terebinth,
> and my branches are glorious and graceful.

I am like a vine putting out graceful shoots,
my blossoms bear the fruit of glory and wealth.
Approach me, you who desire me,
and take your fill of my fruits.[1]

NOTE

1. Quoted by Susan Cady, Marian Ronan, and Hal Taussig, SOPHIA: *The Future of Feminist Spirituality* (San Francisco: Harper & Row, 1986), 29.

17

The Dharma of Ecological Philosophy

Philosophy and its Ideals

The light of understanding is such a peculiar thing. It does not come with the cramming of more and more bookish knowledge into your head. Yes, the light is there to be seen. But it is now more obscured than in previous times. We therefore require a special insight and special energy to penetrate the clouds of this obscurity—in order to see our purpose and our destiny. We also need new insights to see our new responsibilities, new realms of our Philosophy and its ideals of Dharma. Those who are most sensitive and seeing, now perceive that the most important aspects of our present Dharma is saving the Earth. Philosophy has travelled through many roads. At times it attempted to scale the most demanding high altitude paths leading to heaven. It then became theology—the search for God. At other times it explored the chambers and galleries of the palace of human wisdom.

This is the most classic road of philosophy, epitomized by its very name 'philo-sophia', a love of wisdom. Sometimes it was satisfied with being the synthesis of knowledge. Unmindful of wisdom, it then wanted to be the queen of the sciences—distilling what it thought was most essential in human knowledge. Sometimes, particularly in the 20th century, it had the ambition of being a science, as precise as physics and mathematics; hence it couched itself in the language of mathematical logic. Philosophy, particularly as envisaged by Socrates and Plato, was also the quest for a meaningful life, for a worthwhile life. This quest has been gradually eliminated from the course of Western philosophy. But this quest has never been abandoned within the Indian tradition, within which philosophy has often been pursued as a path of 'Moksha' (liberation), as a guide to human destiny. This has been the strength of the Indian tradition and its philosophy. This ideal of philosophy—as Moksha—is quite close to the meaning of the term Dharma. Dharma is this wonderful invention of the human mind which can inspire simple people to a philosophical life. A system of thought which can make simple people to embrace a philosophy is certainly a wonderful achievement of human creativity. The Indian tradition is to be congratulated on this score.

Dharma and Philosophy

Although Dharma has many shades of meaning its conception as a guide on the path of right duty is quite essential. Equally essential is the meaning of Dharma as spelling out our obligation to become liberated. These forms of Dharma which illumine for us the path of our destiny and make us aware that it is our duty to pursue them, are essentially forms of philosophy. Thus Dharma is a form of philosophy. For what else can it be? It is usually regarded as something apart from philosophy, as something deeper, as a voice of heaven. But how can you understand this voice, how can you understand its depth, if not through your philosophical faculties? Philosophy does not need to be shallow. And Dharma is not necessarily always *deep.*

Understanding Dharma

Some forms of Dharma are shallow The understanding of the shallowness or the depth of philosophy or of Dharma, for that manner is essentially philosophical understanding. Thus there is a philosophical imprint on all forms of Dharma. Understanding Dharma is not a mindless process. It requires a deep philosophical sensitivity, but not necessarily a wealth of philosophical knowledge. It requires an awareness of the wonderful intricacies of human destiny and of the sense of belonging to the larger cosmos -even if this awareness is not explicitly articulated in the individual's mind.

Why would you follow any path of Dharma if deep down you did not understand that—in spite of its thorns—it is a beautiful path. A path of duty is a path of beauty. It is a philosophical path, a path of wisdom—whether one is clearly aware of this or not. Yet this is not how Dharma *is* usually conceived. It is often received as something immediate, as commands from Heaven, as a voice of our destiny or an inner declaration of who we are and what is our mission. Even if it were so, we need to notice that: if Dharma is *a voice* of Heaven, then the heavens are very philosophical; if Dharma is a voice of deities, these deities are very philosophical; if Dharma is a voice of our inner conscience, this conscience is very philosophical.

It clearly follows that Dharma is a result of and a companion of understanding. But not any kind of understanding. As you understand so you act. The higher your understanding the higher your Dharma. The lower your understanding the lower your Dharma. Creatures with no understanding have no Dharma. They follow their instincts and their animal urges. When you explain the relationship of physical facts to each other, this understanding does not lead to any Dharma.

The higher a being you arè, the more luminous is your understanding of the subtle intricacies of Dharma—even if it is not a verbal understanding. Dharma is a daughter of understanding in the world which has purpose and meaning. Dharma is a meaning. Dharma is purpose. Without meaning and purpose, without understanding and wisdom. Dharma would be some kind of blind groping, meaningless gestures of an actor who frantically frets his hour upon the stage and then is seen no more.

Lord Shiva was continuously vigilant, constantly ready to be of help in maintaining the order of things which might have crumbled without him. Also, Lord Krishna, as is explained in the Gita, must be constantly vigilant, cannot rest even for one minute; for if he does, the whole world might turn to chaos. We are the messengers of Shiva and Krishna. Nay, we are their embodiments and their energy. The more clearly we grasp it the more we become like them—in magnanimity, power, insight, love and understanding. But we need to have courage-to grasp it and to live it. This courage is a form of understanding. Thus, the circle closes : we need courage to increase understanding. As our understanding increases, so our courage does. Then we are capable of performing our higher Dharmas.

There is a direct correlation between deeper understanding and being called to perform higher dharmas. And yet, in our times, we do not expect learned scholars to understand the realms of higher Dharma. Although their knowledge is so vast, their understanding is so small. The forms of bookish understanding are not the ones that lead to understanding the purpose and meaning of the universe and of our own life. The roads of bookish understanding are not the roads to the energy of Krishna and Shiva.

Ecology

The idea of Ecology has been around us for a quarter of a century. We have become used to it. We consider its ramifications good, namely, to have clean air, clean water, clean soil. But ecology is much deeper and much more far reaching than cleaning the polluted physical environment. Though important it is only a small part of the task; yes, a *small* part. For what is ultimately responsible for the polluted planet is not dirty technologies but polluted minds - careless, unseeing and alienated. Contaminated minds produce, almost of necessity, contaminated environments. The contaminated mechanistic mind has weakened (and sometimes contaminated) the sources of our spiritual life. This mind has separated us from the sacred. Hence, our spiritual life has been weakened—both on the individual level and on the level of whole cultures. By allowing to contaminate your mind, you dim your intelligence and blunt your sensitivities, and thus make your life less radiant and more obtuse; ultimately, you diminish yourself as a person. This point is of great importance but usually unappreciated.

The present condition of humanity is forlorn as we dwell in polluted physical environment, in polluted mental environments, in polluted spiritual environments. We need to purify ourselves in so many ways. Traditional poojas are insufficient. Our minds so often resemble a garbage container rather than a beautiful shining shrine of God. The ecology of mind is still in its infancy. Let us be aware that we need to purify our mind not through some old fashion rituals, but through something much more drastic but also more lasting. We need to change the whole structure of our consciousness which is programmed to manipulation, to mechanistic thinking, to an instrumental treatment of people and nature. In effect, we need to create the reverential mind.

We rarely realize that the contaminated physical environment leaves behind its shadow which is contaminated mental and spiritual environments. A true work of ecology is healing all the three environments simultaneously; physical, mental and spiritual. Thus, our Dharma must be extended and deepened to include new realms.

Ecological Dharma

Hence the importance of Ecological Dharma—not only for the preservation of the earth as such, but for the preservation of the conditions which enable us to become human, thus enable us to follow the path of the Buddha or the path of Shiva or the path of Krishna; or whatever spiritual path we have chosen to follow. Seen in this light, ecological Dharma is of importance second to none! If you are a spiritual person, you must care about ecology for its is your spiritual cradle. In our times the ecological and the spiritual become one.

To revere the Buddha or Krishna is to work for the salvation and healing of the planet. True prayer and true meditation in our time becomes ecological prayer—such a form of meditation and action which helps to heal the planet, which helps to heal other human beings, which helps to heal all other beings—including the forests, soil and polluted rivers. This new form of redemption—ecological redemption is truly universal in nature. It is based on universal compassion towards all beings—threatened by man's excessive technological activities. To see what is most important for the well being of all sentient beings (and semi-sentient beings such as the soil and forests), to see what is most important for our inner peace and our ascent towards the Buddha, we need a new perspective

- the Ecological Perspective, and a new form of Dharma
- Ecological Dharma.

In our times the most important task is to clean the earth, to cleanse ourselves from mental pollution. Our minds are as polluted as our bodies, as is our air. our rivers, our soil. Preserving the continuity of the earth and the integrity of our souls are very important aspects of our present Dharma. Thus Dharma acquires a distinctly green or ecological dimension. Whatever divides us (our cultures, our tongues, our religions, our economic systems) one thing that unites us is ecology—the care for the earth, the care for future generations, the care for the well being of all sentient beings. It is not sufficient nowadays to care for yourself, for your spiritual well being, for your religious community. You must extend this care to the entire earth—for this is your dwelling, your temple, your sangha, your vessel in which spiritual attainments can be perfected on your way to Bodhisattva and then to the Buddha.

If we lose the environment, if we destroy the earth, we lose God, we then destroy the grounds for all other possibilities, for becoming spiritual beings and ultimately enlightened beings. Previous Buddhas, including Gautama, were not so aware of the frailty of the planet earth as the ground for cultivating our humanity and our spirituality. For to say it once more, if this ground is denied, our spiritual journey comes to an end.

Much of the present teaching of both Hinduism and Buddhism is steeped in the past. And much of it is a repetition of old dogmas. Non-attachment is (by and large) a noble and liberating principle. But we need to re-examine its meaning in view of the importance of Ecological Dharma. We cannot be too detached from the earth. We need to cling to the earth -though the phrase may alarm some orthodox Hindus or Buddhists. To care for the earth, to work for its healing and salvation means to be attached to the earth, though we may say that it is not a selfish attachment.

The meaning of ecological Dharma calls for a new reflection on, and indeed a significant revision of some ancient spiritual traditions, including Buddhism, Hinduism and Christianity. Ecological Dharma informs us that the ecological reconstruction, working close to nature, bringing back labour intensive occupations, in general, working for the ecological catharsis, is the road which leads us to the fold of right livelihood. Thus , Ecological Dharma appears to be an essential vehicle to bring us back to right livelihood which is so essential to our spiritual wellbeing. Unless we find the road reconnecting us with right livelihood—not only for a select few but for countless millions—we cannot claim that our spiritual message is relevant to our times. Wrong livelihood is destroying people's souls and is undermining the sustainability of the planet.

What is the specific Dharma of Ecological Philosophy? It is to reassure us that philosophy is not dead; that in fact, it has a most important role to play, at this particular time, when wisdom has been replaced by information. Another aspect of the Dharma of Eco-Philosophy is moral guidance. Modernism and Post-modernism have disintegrated in the quick sand of nihilism and moral confusion. Traditional philosophy has not been able to help us in combating this moral decay. Ecological philosophy proposes new imperatives for moral actions and for the moral regeneration of the individual. The moral regeneration is a most important part of our spiritual regeneration. Yet another and perhaps the most important aspect of the Dharma of Eco-Philosophy, is to make us understand that the ecology of mind, the ecology of the spirit, and the ecology of physical environment are aspects of each other; and that the pollution of physical environment inevitably leads to the pollution of the mind and the spirit. This understanding also informs us that the degradation of physical environment is a consequence of the polluted minds and sullied souls.

Ecological Philosophy is itself a form of Dharma. Once you understand things in their true connections, once you see them in their true light, you must act accordingly—in order to bring them back to a right alignment. To understand aright is to act aright. The Dharma of Ecological Philosophy tells you that you must put your own house in order. It also instructs us that we must be teachers—all of us. We must spread the necessary light, in spite of all the obstacles and the crippling influence of the structures of darkness. Right education is the foundation of right awareness, which in turn is the foundation of all our thinking and of our action. Right education is the right implementation of the right values. An ancient Chinese expression says : if you are preparing for one year, plant rice; if you are preparing for 25 years, plant the trees; if you are preparing for 100 years, plant right education.

Summary

The Dharma of ecological philosophy, in a nutshell, is singing the right song with the unfolding universe which is so beautiful but also fraught with so many dangers and pitfalls. May we have enough *courage to bear the light which is required of us to make the universe luminous and kind.*

The practice of universal compassion in our times requires the work of the ecological reconstruction and ecological healing unprecedented in history. As the ecological crisis has brought about an enormous sea of new suffering, the ecological cleansing is the vehicle of the cessation of suffering. *Ecology is the noble truth of our times. Eco-philosophy is the Dharma of our times.*

Our times call for new resources of imagination, for new resources of inner power to meet the unprecedented peril to the life of the planet and to our own spiritual lives. The two are aspects of each other. A new ecological Dharma is called for. This Dharma required of us to be passionately attached to the earth, which of course does not mean the childish clinging to material possessions and to consumption.

REFERENCES

Henryk Skolimowski, *Dancing Shiva in the Ecological Age,* Clarion Press, New Delhi, 1991; Indian Institute of Ecology and Environment, New Delhi, 1995.

- *Living Philosophy,* Eco-philosophy as a Tree of Life, Penguin, London, 1992.
- *A Sacred Place to Dwell,* Element Books, U.K. 1993.
- *The Participatory Mind, A New Theory of Knowledge and of the Universe, Penguin,* London, 1994.
- *Eco-Yoga, Practice and Meditations for Walking in Beauty on The Earth,* Gaia Books, London, 1994.

Index

M

N

S

T

U

V

W